The Coherence of the Collections
in the Book of Proverbs

The Coherence of the Collections in the Book of Proverbs

Seenam Kim

PICKWICK PUBLICATIONS

An imprint of *Wipf and Stock Publishers*
199 West 8th Avenue • Eugene OR 97401

THE COHERENCE OF THE COLLECTIONS IN THE BOOK
OF PROVERBS

ISBN 10: 1-55635-518-1
ISBN 13: 978-1-55635-518-9

Cataloging-in-Publication data:

Kim, Seenam.
    The coherence of the collections in the book of Proverbs / Seenam
    Kim.

    xvi, 292 p.; 23 cm.

    ISBN 10: 1-55635-518-1
    ISBN 13: 978-1-55635-518-9

    Includes bibliographical references.

    1. Bible. O.T. Proverbs—Criticism, interpretation, etc. 2. Bible. O.T.
    Proverbs—Criticism, redaction. 3. Bible. O.T. Proverbs—Language,
    style. 4. Wisdom literature—Comparative studies. I. Title.

BS1465.2 .K45 2007

Manufactured in the U.S.A.

Contents

List of Tables

List of Abbreviations

AB	Anchor Bible
ANETS	Ancient Near Eastern Texts and Studies
BASOR	*Bulletin of the American Schools of Oriental Research*
BASORSup	Bulletin of the American Schools of Oriental Research: Supplement Series
BDB	Brown, F., S. R. Driver, and C. A. Briggs. *A Hebrew and English Lexicon of the Old Testament*
BETL	Bibliotheca ephemeridum theologicarum lovaniensium
BKAT	Biblischer Kommentar, Altes Testament. Edited by M. Noth and H. W. Wolff
BLS	Bible and Literature Series
BZAW	Beihefte zur Zeitschrift für die alttestamentliche Wissenschaft
CahRB	Cahiers de la Revue biblique
CBQ	*Catholic Biblical Quarterly*
CBQMS	Catholic Biblical Quarterly Monograph Series
CC	Continental Commentaries
ConBOT	Coniectanea biblica: Old Testament Series
HALOT	*The Hebrew and Aramaic Lexicon of the Old Testament.* Koehler, L., W. Baumgartner, and J. J. Stamm.
HAT	Handbuch zum Alten Testament
HSM	Harvard Semitic Monographs
HUCA	*Hebrew Union College Annual*
ICC	International Critical Commentary
Int	*Interpretation*
JAOS	*Journal of the American Oriental Society*
JBL	*Journal of Biblical Literature*
JNES	*Journal of Near Eastern Studies*
JNSL	*Journal of Northwest Semitic Languages*
JSOT	*Journal for the Study of the Old Testament*
JSOTSup	Journal for the Study of the Old Testament: Supplement Series
K	Kethib
LBH	Late Biblical Hebrew
MH	Mishnaic Hebrew
NCBC	New Century Bible Commentary
NIB	*New Interpreter's Bible*
NICOT	New International Biblical Commentary on the Old Testament
NIDOTTE	*New International Dictionary of Old Testament Theology and Exegesis.* Edited by W. A. Van Gemeren. 5 vols. Grand Rapids, 1997

OBO	Orbis biblicus et orientalis
OTL	Old Testament Library
OtSt	*Oudtestamentische Studiën*
PWM	*Prophets and Wise Men*
Q	Qere
RB	*Revue biblique*
SBLDS	Society of Biblical Literature Dissertation Series
SBT	Studies in Biblical Theology
SJT	*Scottish Journal of Theology*
s. v.	under the word
TDOT	*Theological Dictionary of the Old Testament.* Edited by G. J. Botterweck and H. Ringgren. Translated by J. T. Willis, G. W. Bromiley, and D. E. Green. 14 vols. Grand Rapids, 1974–2004
TLOT	*Theological Lexicon of the Old Testament.* Edited by E. Jenni, with assistance from C. Westermann. Translated by M. E. Biddle. 3 vols. Peabody, Mass., 1997
TWOT	*Theological Wordbook of the Old Testament.* Edited by R. L. Harris, G. L. Archer Jr. 2 vols. Chicago, 1980
VOT	*The Vocabulary of the Old Testament*
VT	*Vetus Testamentum*
VTSup	Supplements to Vetus Testamentum
WBC	Word Biblical Commentary
ZAW	*Zeitschrift für die alttestamentliche Wissenschaft*
ZBK	Zürcher Bibelkommentare

Preface

The division of the book of Proverbs into seven collections is legitimate because of the presence of the internal titles in the book. The legitimacy of the division is further substantiated by the fact that the collections are dissimilar to one another in regard to the style and the subject matter of sayings. In addition to this, the foreign and anonymous authors indicated in the titles, and the so-called "Egyptian connection" of collection III (22:17—24:22), make the book appear as a collection of collections containing Israelite and non-Israelite wisdom sayings. When the book is viewed in this way, the collections are understood as having been formed in different wisdom circles and in different periods.

Such an understanding of Proverbs was the motivation for me to undertake this study to see how the language of the book would fare with the seemingly separated nature of the collections. Would it reveal distinctive features of each collection? And at the same time would it indicate the coherence of certain collections which share common wisdom elements? To find the answers to these questions, the occurrence of words in the collections has been investigated, and the investigation, in turn, has produced the lists of the exclusive words in the seven collections, which are intended to be exhaustive. Based on the lists, it is reasonably possible to argue that the exclusive words in a given collection represent the distinctive wisdom features of the collection which are not found in other collections, and that the collections which share common wisdom terms are coherent. In the second case, the argument for coherence has been made not solely on the ground of the occurrence of a word but on the coherent usage of the term in the collections.

As far as the writer is concerned, this study is the most thorough attempt to investigate the relationship between the seven collections on the basis of the wisdom vocabulary. This volume also contains the tables of categorized terms according to the meaning or the root. The writer hopes the lists of the exclusive words to be helpful to others whose interest is in the book of Proverbs.

The main part of this book was written during my sabbatical year that I spent in Grand Rapids, Michigan, in 2004–2005. It is my great joy now to acknowledge the helps that have enabled me to complete this study. My special thanks go to the International Theological Seminary and its faculty for the uncommon institutional support in granting me an extended sabbatical leave. I am also thankful to Lugene Schemper and Paul W. Fields, the librarians of Calvin Theological Seminary, for their kind, professional assistance. During the entire period of my stay in Grand Rapids, Carl Kromminga and his wife Joan constantly paid warm attention to me, treating me as if I was their guest from California. I wish them the best in many more years to come. There are also friends and colleagues to whom I am grateful for their encouragement although there names are not mention here. My wife Christina deserves my heartfelt thanks. During my absence from home, she did all the house chores alone, including mowing the lawn! This book is dedicated to her as a token of my gratitude and affection.

Seenam Kim
International Theological Seminary
El Monte, California
May 2007

Introduction

Wisdom is commonly characterized as international, and sometimes secular as well. When the sage of Proverbs says that piety to God is the beginning of wisdom (Prov 9:10; cf. 1:7) or that the Lord is the giver of wisdom (Prov 2:5), he may be viewed as attempting to "localize" or "nationalize" international wisdom by associating it with the Israelite deity. However, considering the fact that the "tree of life" is mentioned only in Genesis (ʿēṣ haḥayyîm in 2:9; 3:22, 24) and Proverbs (ʿēṣ ḥayyîm in 3:18; 11:30; 13:12; 15:4) in the Old Testament, it is probable that he is not the first person who has tried such an attempt, unless he is the author of the creation story. As far as the Old Testament is concerned, numerous examples point to the possibility that the association of wisdom with the Lord is not a product of a later period but a pervasive idea throughout the history of Israel. If the inseparable relationship between wisdom and religion is granted, the emphasis that wisdom is the main, necessary principle in the daily life of human beings is misleading because it gives an impression that wisdom can operate in human life apart from religion. As indicated in Deut 6:4–9, the daily human life is the very area in which God wants to be remembered and honored. Various definitions of wisdom formulated by some leading scholars, however, place an emphasis on the practical aspect of wisdom, giving, more or less, the impression of wisdom that is independent of religion. For example, the definition of wisdom as "experiential knowledge of life" (von Rad), "natural or acquired intellectual ability" (Whybray), "taḥbulôt, steering skills" (Zimmerli), or "to know and do the right thing" (Crenshaw) is a practical definition of wisdom, with no notion of religion, that can be applied internationally.[1]

As for the definition of wisdom, it is difficult to find a ready-made definition of wisdom in the OT itself. The difficulty may be due to the fact that the usage of the root ḥkm in the OT is complex. Although the frequency of the noun ḥokmâ "wisdom" in the OT is significant (153 times), it is only in Job 28:28 where the meaning of the word is clearly defined: "the fear of the Lord is wisdom."

Another example which comes close to Job 28:28 would be Deut 4:6 in which obedience to God's command is called wisdom of Israel: "You shall keep and practice because it is your wisdom and discernment to the eyes of the nations . . . ," (or it can be understood that God's law is Israel's wisdom). In the two texts the meaning of wisdom is virtually the same: wisdom is the piety to God expressed as the fear of the Lord or obedience to his law.

In this study, the meaning of wisdom will be understood in its relationship to God and within the framework of Israelite religion. As a result, the international aspect of wisdom that has been indicated by the similarities between the book of Proverbs and Mesopotamian and Egyptian wisdom literatures will not be included in the scope of this study. The main reason for the position taken here is the understanding that proverbial resemblance can exist between nations simply because of similar socio-economic lifestyles, not because of any direct contact between them. Numerous superficial similarities in proverbial forms and contents can be cited between two nations with no relationship. The following is a presentation of proverbs to illustrate the point that unintended but remarkably similar wisdom material can exist between two unrelated cultures. Some sayings have been taken from the book of Proverbs and a Chinese wisdom book for the purpose, and have been paired according to their types and themes (the Chinese sayings are from *The Wisdom of the Orient*).[2]

a. Numerical Sayings

"There are four things which do not allow people to rest:
    long life, reputation, rank, and riches" (p. 141).

"Three things are never satisfied, four never say, 'Enough':
    Sheol, barren womb, the earth that is never satisfied with
        water, and fire that never says, 'Enough'" (Prov 30:15–16).

b. Better-sayings

"Better be upright with poverty
    than depraved abundance" (p. 186).

"Better a little with righteousness
    than abundant income with no justice" (Prov 16:8).

c. Sayings about a Wife

"A virtuous woman is a source of honor to her husband;
    a vicious one causes him disgrace" (p. 198).

"A virtuous woman is the crown of her husband,
    but a shameful one is like rot in his bones" (Prov 12:4).

d. Sayings about Scales

"Just scales and full measure injure no man" (p. 174).

"A just balance and scales belong to the Lord,
    all the weights in a pouch are his work" (Prov 16:11).

e. Sayings about Riches and Poverty

"It is harder to be poor without murmuring
    than to be rich without arrogance" (p. 32).

"Lest I become satisfied and deny, saying, 'Who is the Lord?'
    or lest I become poor and steal,
        blaspheming the name of my God" (Prov 30:9).

f. Sayings about Servants

"Girls and servants are the most difficult people to handle.
    If you treat them familiarly, they become disrespectful;
        if you keep them at a distance, they resent it" (p. 34).

"He who pampers his servant from childhood,
    he will be rebellious later on" (Prov 29:21).

g. Sayings about Child Education

"If you love your son, give him plenty of cudgel;
    if you hate your son, cram him with dainties" (p. 189).

"He who spares his rod hates his son,
    but he who loves him disciplines him early" (Prov 13:24).

h. Sayings about Rebuke and Flattery

"He who tells me of my faults is my teacher;
    he who tells me of my virtues does me harm" (p. 192).

"The wounds from a friend are trustworthy,
    but the kisses of an enemy are excessive" (Prov 27:6).

i. Sayings about God

"The Master (Confucius) said: 'Would that
    I could do without speaking!'
Tzŭ Kung said: 'If our Master never spoke, how could we,
    his disciples, transmit his doctrines?'

The Master replied: 'Does God speak?
    The four seasons hold on their course,
        and all things continue to live and grow.
    Yet, tell me, does God speak?'" (p. 34).

"He who knows what God is,
    and who knows what man is, has attained" (p. 124).

The last two Chinese sayings without counterparts from Proverbs are added to the comparison to point out that ancient Chinese wisdom is not secular, although the God in the sayings refers to an undefined deity or reverence to the heaven. All the similarities in the comparison must be attributed to pure coincidence even if they appear significant. However, when such proverbial resemblance is found between Israel and one of its neighboring nations, influence from one to the other is often suggested, sometimes legitimately, sometimes unwarrantedly.

With regard to the secular aspect of wisdom, it is the position of this study that the sage did not intend to present wisdom as secular in Proverbs. On the contrary, it is clear that the sage of Proverbs made great efforts from the beginning to the end of the book to define the place of wisdom in Israelite religion. Such a defining effort is evidently shown in the fact that the divine name in Proverbs is almost always YHWH (87 times). This fact becomes significant when one considers the phenomenon that the same divine name is never used in Ecclesiastes and Job chapters 3–37 with two exceptions (Job 12:9; 28:28; for the divine names used in the three Wisdom books, see Table 1.15). Because the obvious purpose of Proverbs is to present wisdom in its relationship to the Lord, a secular interpretation of the sayings in the book would be against the intention of the sage and the final form of the book.[3] As we shall see later, both the Lord and wisdom play the governing role in human life without competition or tension between the two: the purpose of wisdom teaching is to lead one to the fear of the Lord (15:33). This harmonious relationship between God and wisdom in Proverbs makes von Rad say that Israel had only one world of experience in which rational perceptions and religious perceptions were not differentiated.[4]

Before the investigation of the relationship between the seven collections in Proverbs, it is necessary to explain the governing principles which are operative in this study. One of the principles is to take the characters, identified or unidentified, who appear in Proverbs as Israelites as long as the context permits. I have tested the principle in the reading of the book, and the outcome shows that this position is tenable in almost all cases. For example, the parents, the son, Lady Wisdom, and the adulterous woman are certainly Israelites whose God is the Lord. Despite the fact that the kings in Proverbs show no nationality except in 1:1 and 25:1, they also are taken as Israelite kings, because the language of God's promise to David in 2 Samuel 7 and the description of God's throne in Psalms are similar to the language used to describe the stability of the royal throne in Proverbs. I will apply the principle of religious reading even to the sayings ascribed to the non-Israelite figures in chapters 30 and 31. A careful reading of the text will indicate that the first halves of both chapters have been subjected to an editorial procedure to transform the sayings to be coherent in the religious context of Proverbs. It seems that it is the same editorial procedure which lies behind the stories of the pious foreigners in the OT such as Balaam, Job, and his friends. In connection with Agur's sayings, some have tried to locate the origin of the question in 30:4—"Who has gone up to heaven and come down?"—in Mesopotamia.[5] However, the fact that the speaker is a foreigner does not warrant that one must find the origin of the question in a foreign nation. Rather, the fact that the sayings of Agur at 30:2–3 are loaded with words and phrases which occur elsewhere in the OT points to the possibility that the question must be interpreted in the context of the OT. For example, the wisdom terms, *bînâ*, *ḥokmâ*, and *da'at*, in 30:2–3 are stock words in Proverbs, and the use of *ba'ar* in 30:2–3 in connection with wisdom terms is consistent with its use elsewhere in the OT (Pss 73:22; 92:7; cf. Prov 12:1). Another important factor that the question in 30:4 should not be singled out to locate its origin in Mesopotamia is the presence of the peculiar phrase *da'at qĕdōšîm* in 30:3. This phrase occurs in 9:10 to refer to the Lord by means of parallelism. Although Agur is a foreigner, the background of the question in 30:4 must be interpreted in the context of the OT because (a) Agur has been transformed to appear as a believer of the Lord, (b) the theme of going up to heaven is not infrequent in the OT (e.g., Genesis 28; Moses in Exodus 19 and 24; Deuteronomy 30; Psalm 139; Amos 9), and (c) the words and expressions around the question are reminiscent of the passages in the OT. Another significant reason not to seek a Mesopotamian connection in regard to 30:4 is the possibility that Prov 30:2–4 may not be a Hebrew translation of an Aramaic text but originally a Hebrew composition, although it is not certain how much foreign thought is reflected in the text which was supposedly written by a foreign author (Agur). When one considers 31:1–9 which is also ascribed to a foreign author, the possibility of this statement increases considerably. Although the two Aramaic words (*bar* "son" and *mĕlākîn* "kings") in 31:1–9 may give an impression that the text is a Hebrew translation of an Aramaic text, E.Y. Kutscher explains convincingly that it is not the case. Due to the fact that the two Aramaic words are very common words, Kutscher does not think that they are the surviving words from the original text. Nor is it likely, according to him, that Hebrew should have borrowed such simple words from Aramaic. He rather thinks that the presence of the Aramaic words is intentional to add a foreign flavor (or Aramaic coloring) to the text which is supposed to have been spoken by a foreigner.[6] Kutscher's explanation of 31:1–9 and the language of 30:2–4 which is repeated elsewhere in the OT support the view that 30:2–4 may be a Hebrew text ascribed to a foreign author.

Another governing principle of this study is to prefer a religious reading of a text when both secular and religious readings are permissible. I will argue later that the traditional OT religious terms still retain their religious aspects in Proverbs (see Table 1.4 for the words related to Israelite religion).

In terms of methodology, this study is an attempt to understand the characteristics of each collection and the relationship between collections through the examination of exclusive words. In this study exclusive words refer to the verbs or adjectives/nouns that occur only in one or some of the collections (e.g., exclusive words in collection I or exclusive words in collection I, II, and III). According to my count, the number of verbs, adjectives, and nouns that occur in Proverbs is 1,264 (467 verbs and 797 adjectives/nouns). The collections have been grouped together according to the occurrence of exclusive words, resulting in 72 groups of collections (see Appendix A for the groups and the number of exclusive words in each group). In the tables and appendixes, the frequency of a word in the OT and Proverbs is indicated side by side with a forward slash sign (/). For example, in the case of " ʾōraḥ 59/19," the first number "59" indicates the frequency of ʾōraḥ in the OT and "19" indicates the frequency of the word in Proverbs. For the division of Proverbs, I follow the common practice which divides the book into seven parts. The term "collection" is used in a loose sense to designate each part of the book. The following is the division of Proverbs with the size of each collection indicated by percentage:

Collection I	1:1–9:18	256 verses	(28%)
Collection II	10:1–22:16	375 verses	(41%)
Collection III	22:17–24:22	70 verses	(7.7%)
Collection IV	24:23–34	12 verses	(1.2%)
Collection V	25:1–29:27	138 verses	(15.1%)
Collection VI	30:1–33	33 verses	(3.6%)
Collection VII	31:1–31	31 verses	(3.4%)

1. The Relationship between Collection I and Other Collections

The purpose of this section is twofold. First, the features of collection I will be discussed by examining selected words of exclusive words, which are more relevant to wisdom. And second, the literary relationship between collection I and other collections will be sought using the same approach, that is, the examination of the use of exclusive words in those collections. The examination of exclusive words will be conducted in the order of the groups of the collections tabulated in Table 1.1. The collections have been grouped together in the ascending order (e.g., I, I-II, I-II-III, I-II-III-IV, and so on) according to the occurrence of 571 exclusive words (212 verbs and 359 adjectives/nouns) in collection I and other collections.

Table 1.1
The Groups of the Collections and the Number of Exclusive Words

I	168	I-II-IV	3	I-III-V-VI	1
I-II	87	I-II-IV-V	8	I-III-V-VII	1
I-II-III	26	I-II-IV-V-VI	1	I-III-VI	2
I-II-III-IV	2	I-II-IV-V-VI-VII	2	I-III-VII	2
I-II-III-IV-V	4	I-II-V	49	I-IV	5
I-II-III-IV-V-VI	7	I-II-V-VI	11	I-V-VI	1
I-II-III-IV-V-VI-VII	2	I-II-V-VI-VII	2	I-V	38
I-II-III-IV-V-VII	5	I-II-V-VII	11	I-V-VI	2
I-II-III-V	35	I-II-VI	8	I-V-VII	4
I-II-III-V-VI	9	I-II-VII	5	I-VI	8
I-II-III-V-VI-VII	13	I-III	13	I-VI-VII	2
I-II-III-V-VII	7	I-III-IV	1	I-VII	7
I-II-III-VI	6	I-III-IV-V	1		
I-II-III-VII	5	I-III-V	5		

Table 1.1 shows the distribution of the 571 exclusive words in 40 different combinations of the collections. Although certain factors, such as the size of a

collection, frequency of a word in the OT, and the significance of a word in the wisdom context, must be taken into consideration in an attempt to establish literary relationship between collections, the significance of Table 1.1 is that the numbers of the exclusive words can serve as indicators for the possibility of close relationship between given collections. For example, the higher numbers of the exclusive words in several groups of the collections (I-II [87], I-V [38], I-II-III-V [35], and I-II-III [26]) imply higher possibility of literary links between the collections. The use of Table 1.1 in connection with Appendix C will facilitate one's finding of words which are more commonly used in Proverbs. For example, it is indicated in the table that only two words occur in all the seven collections (I-II-III-IV-V-VI-VII), and Appendix C will show that the two words are *dābār* "word" (36 times) and *lēb* "heart" (99 times). The investigation of the frequency will then show an important aspect of the use of *lēb* in Proverbs: as a word, it not only occurs in all the seven collections, but has the highest frequency among the verbs, adjectives, and nouns that appear in Proverbs. The highest frequency of the word naturally implies the important role of the heart in the wisdom context of Proverbs. Table 1.1 and Appendix C will also help one find out that, although far less frequent than *lēb*, each of the two main wisdom terms, *ḥākām* "wise" (47 times) and *ḥokmā* "wisdom" (42 times) occurs in six collections (*ḥākām* in I-II-III-IV-V-VI and *ḥokmā* in I-II-III-V-VI-VII), confirming their importance in wisdom material. In passing, it could be point out that although certain words, such as *lēb* (99 times) and *derek* "way" (75 times), occur quite frequently in Proverbs, their significance in the wisdom context has been overlooked because of the emphasis on the wisdom (*ḥkm*) words.

(1) Exclusive Words in Collection I

a. Verbs (56)

אבה	54/4	to consent	אתה	21/1	to come
בקע	51/1	to cleave	דרך	62/1	to tread
הרג	167/2	to kill	חבק	13/2	to clasp
חמל	41/1	to spare	חמס	8/1	to wrong
חצב	25/1	to hew	טבח	11/1	to slaughter
טבע	10/1	to sink	יסד	42/1	to establish
יקש	10/1	to lure	ישן	25/1	to sleep
יתר	105/1	to remain over	כוה	2/1	to burn
מגן	3/1	to deliver	מהר	64/3	to hasten
מלל	7/1	to rub	מסך	5/2	to mix
מתק	6/1	to be sweet	נבט	69/1	to look
נגע	150/1	to touch, strike	נגף	49/1	to strike, smite

נָדַח	55/1	to banish	נוּע	40/1	to waver
נוּף	37/1	to besprinkle	נָזַל	18/1	to flow, trickle
נָטַף	18/1	to drop, drip	נָסַך	26/1	to set, install
נָשַׂג	50/1	to overtake	סָרַר	17/1	to be stubborn
עָלַס	3/1	to rejoice	עָנַד	2/1	to bind
עָרַך	75/1	to arrange	פּוּץ	1/1	to flow
פָּלַח	5/1	to cleave	פָּלַס	6/3	to weigh
פָּתַל	5/1	to twist	צוּד	17/1	to hunt
צָעַד	8/1	to step, march	קוּץ	9/1	to abhor, dread
קָרַב	291/1	to be near	רָבַד	1/1	to deck
רָהַב	4/1	to act proudly	רָעַף	5/1	to trickle, drip
שָׂטָה	6/2	to turn aside	שִׂיח	20/1	to complain
שָׂרַף	117/1	to burn	שָׂרַר	7/1	to act as prince
שָׁאַן	5/1	to be at ease	שׁוּח	5/1	to sink down
שָׁעַן	22/1	to lean over	שָׁפַך	115/2	to pour
שָׁקַד	18/1	to watch	שָׁקַף	22/1	to look out

b. Adjectives/Nouns (112)

אַהַב	2/1	love	אֹהַב	2/1	love
אָהָל	4/1	perfume	אָחוֹת	114/1	sister
אֵטוּן	1/1	thread, yarn	אַיָּלָה	11/1	doe
אֵל	5/1	strength, power	אָמוֹן	2/1	artificer
אָסָם	2/1	storehouse	אֲפֵלָה	10/2	darkness
אֶצְבַּע	31/2	finger	אֶשְׁנָב	2/1	window-lattice
בַּד	158/2	separation	בְּרִית	283/1	covenant
גַּאָה	1/1	pride	גְּבוּרָה	61/1	strength
גִּבְעָה	59/1	hill	גַּף	4/1	body, self
גַּרְגְּרוֹת	4/4	neck	דַּד	4/1	breast
דּוֹד	61/1	beloved, uncle	הוֹד	24/1	splendor, vigor
חֶבֶל	50/1	cord	חַד	4/1	sharp
חוּג	3/1	vault (heaven)	חֲמֻטָה	1/1	dark-hued stuff
חִידָה	17/1	riddle	חַי	239/1	living
חַלּוֹן	31/1	window	חָלָל	91/1	pierced one
חֵלֶק	1/1	smoothness	חֶלְקָה	6/1	smoothness
חָסִיד	32/1	kind, pious	טֶבַח	12/2	slaughter

יָחִיד	9/1	only (one)	יַעֲלָה	1/1	goat
יֶקֶב	15/1	wine-vet	יָקוֹשׁ	4/1	fowler
כָּבֵד	14/1	liver	כִּכָּר	55/1	loaf of bread
כֶּסֶא	2/1	full moon	כְּסִילוּת	1/1	stupidity
כֶּסֶל	6/1	confidence	לֵבָב	252/2	heart
לוּחַ	43/2	tablet	לִוְיָה	2/2	wreath
לְזוּת	1/1	crookedness	לֶכֶד	1/1	capture
לַעֲנָה	8/1	wormwood	מַאֲכָל	30/1	food
מָבוֹא	25/1	entrance	מוֹדָע	2/1	kinsman
מוּם	19/1	blemish	מוֹסָד	13/1	foundation
מוֹר	12/1	myrrh	מוֹרֶה	7/1	teacher
מְזוּזָה	19/1	door-post	מַטְמוֹן	5/1	hidden treasure
מְלִיצָה	2/1	satire	מַעְגָּל	16/7	track, way
מִפְעָל	1/1	work	מִפְתָּח	1/1	opening
מָרוֹם	54/3	height	מְשׁוּבָה	12/1	turning back
מִשְׁמָר	22/1	guard, watch	נֹגַהּ	20/1	brightness
נֶגַע	78/1	stroke	נֹכַח	25/2	front
נְעוּרִים	46/2	youth	נָקִי	43/2	clean, innocent
נָקָם	17/1	vengeance	נֶשֶׁף	12/1	twilight
עֵדָה	149/1	congregation	עַיִן	28/1	spring
עֶכֶס	2/1	anklet	עַמּוּד	111/1	pillar
עֲנָק	3/1	necklace	עָפָר	110/1	dust
עִקְּשׁוּת	2/2	crookedness	עֶרֶב	135/1	evening
עָרְמָה	6/3	craftiness	עֶרֶשׂ	10/1	couch
עָתֵק	1/1	valuable	פָּז	9/1	gold
פַּחַד	49/4	dread	פְּתַיוּת	1/1	simplicity
צְבִי	12/1	gazelle	צוּקָה	3/1	distress
צְרוֹר	10/1	bundle, pouch	קֶדֶם	87/2	front, east
קִנְיָן	10/1	acquisition	קִנָּמוֹן	3/1	cinnamon
רְפֻאוֹת	1/1	healing	שָׂבָע	8/1	plenty
שְׂמֹאול	54/2	left hand	שְׁאָוָה	1/1	storm
שׁוֹאָה	13/1	devastation	שׁוּק	4/1	street
שַׁחַק	21/2	dust, cloud	שֹׁטֵר	25/1	official
שִׁית	2/1	garment	שֻׁלְחָן	71/1	table
שֶׁלֶם	87/1	peace offering	שַׁעֲשֻׁעִים	9/2	delight
שִׁקּוּי	3/1	drink	שֹׁר	3/1	navel-string

שֵׁשׁ	135/1	six	תֵּבֵל	36/2	world
תְּהוֹם	36/4	abyss, ocean	תּוֹצָאָה	23/1	outgoing
תְּחִלָּה	22/1	beginning	תִּירוֹשׁ	38/1	new wine

The number of words which are found only in collection I is 168 (56 verbs and 112 adjectives/nouns). Since the examination of the use of every exclusive word is realistically impossible and not all the 168 words are of equal significance in the wisdom context, selection of more relevant words becomes inevitable for the purpose of this study. A survey of the 168 exclusive words indicates that some of the unique aspects of collection I can be represented by certain words which convey similar or the same connotations. The exclusive words which are considered significant to connote similar ideas have been collected and divided into the following four categories to examine their usage in collection I:

     a. Words for "Way"

     b. Words for the parts of the body

     c. Words related to Israelite religion

     d. Feminine abstract nouns with the ending -ût

A. Words for "Way": *ma'gāl, šûq*

In collection I, the words that refer to "way" call for attention because no less than five different words are employed to denote a way in the collection. The five words are *'ōraḥ, derek, nĕtîbâ, ma'gāl,* and *šûq,* and the last two words, *ma'gāl* and *šûq,* are exclusive to collection I. It is noted in the list of the exclusive words in collection I that the frequency of all the words but five falls in the range from one to three. Only five of the 168 words have the frequency ranging from four to seven. It thus becomes significant to note that *ma'gāl* is one of the most frequent exclusive words in collection I, occurring seven times. The use of various terms to denote a way and the high frequency of *ma'gāl* indicate that the way is one of important themes in collection I.

An interesting phenomenon is observed in synonymous parallelism in which *ma'gāl* stands with its synonyms. Of the five words for a way (*'ōraḥ, derek, ma'gāl, nĕtîbâ,* and *šûq) šûq* does not occur with *ma'gāl* in synonymous parallelism. However, *ma'gāl* occurs in synonymous parallelism with two main words for a way, *derek* (4:11, 26; 5:21) and *'ōraḥ* (2:15; 5:6). It is also noted that the same synonymous relationship exists between *nĕtîbâ* and the two words (*derek* and *'ōraḥ*): *nĕtîbâ//derek* in 1:15; 3:17; 7:25; 8:2 and *nĕtîbâ//'ōraḥ* in 8:20. *Derek* and *'ōraḥ* also occur together in synonymous parallelism (e.g., 2:8, 13). However, it is remarkable that the two synonyms, *ma'gāl* and *nĕtîbâ,* never occur together in synonymous parallelism.[1] More remarkable is the fact that they never occur together in the same chapter in collection I: *ma'gāl* occurs in chapters 2, 4, and 5 while *nĕtîbâ* is found in chapters 1, 3, 7, and 8. The interwoven pattern of the occurrence of *ma ʿgāl* and *nĕtîbâ* and no concurrence of the two in synonymous parallelism in collection I indicate that, although they are synonymous in meaning, the two words were intentionally differentiated in the collection. In order to explain the phenomenon that the two words do not occur in the same chapter, a further study may be necessary.

i. *Ma ʿgāl* "way" (seven times)[2]

The word occurs 16 times in the OT, 7 of which are in collection I of Proverbs. In collection I *ma ʿgāl* occurs in synonymous parallelism with *derek* (3 times) and *ʾōraḥ* (twice). The usage of *ma ʿgāl* in the OT indicates that the word has two basic meanings. Its first meaning is a ring or circle formed by a circular military encampment (1 Sam 17:20; 26:5, 7). In the texts of First Samuel the word is understood as an equivalent to *maḥănê* "camp." Similarly, *ma ʿgāl* in Mishnaic Hebrew means the ring of wagons set up for protection.[3] The second meaning of *ma ʿgāl* is "path." Commentators generally agree that in all its seven instances in collection I *ma ʿgāl* means a wagon track or a branch way off the main road.[4] A. Meinhold explains it as a road created by a heavy cart pulled by an ox or a mule.[5] Like its synonyms, *ma ʿgāl* is a morally neutral term to denote a way that belongs to both good and bad persons. Since the word usually occurs in synonymous parallelism with other words for the way, its notion as a branch way is understood in a hierarchical sense in relation to the parallel words. In the five instances (2:15, 18; 4:11; 5:6, 21) *ma ʿgāl* occurs in the second colon, indicating that its semantic role is dependent on the synonymous word in the first colon. For example, in 5:21 *derek* is used in the first colon and *ma ʿgāl* in the second: "The ways (*derek*) of a man are before the eyes of the Lord, and he observes all his paths (*ma ʿgāl*)." Here the meaning of the second colon would be that even a man's small branch ways (minor conducts) cannot escape the examination of the Lord.

In connection with the occurrence of *ma ʿgāl* in collection I, it may be reasonable to suggest that the understanding of the collection entails a certain degree of rural setting. Besides *ma ʿgāl*, there are in fact other terms in the collection, which are related to agriculture and hunting: "the firstfruits of all your produce" (3:9), "new wine" (3:10), "wine-vet" (3:10), "bird-trap" (7:23), and "fowler" (6:5). *Ma ʿgāl* and these words indicate that the setting of Proverbs 1–9 is not entirely urban as some have recently suggested but complex reflecting both rural and urban elements.[6]

ii. *Šûq* "lane, street" (7:8)

Although *šûq* is not a regular road to travel but a street or a market-street for business transactions,[7] it is included here because it occurs once in synonymous parallelism with *derek* (7:8). The noun is a rare word occurring only four times in the OT. Interestingly, it occurs only in the books traditionally attributed to Solomon: once each in Proverbs (7:8) and Song of Songs (3:2) and twice in Ecclesiastes (12:4, 5). According to *HALOT*, the origin of *šûq* is explained in two ways: it has been borrowed directly from Akkadian *sūqu(m)*, or indirectly borrowed from Akkadian through Aramaic. In 7:8 *šûq* is a place which an aimless young man walks by at a night time to meet an adulterous woman.

iii. The Metaphor of the Way in Collection I

Due to the fact that in collection I the way is frequently denoted by five different words, a brief discussion about the significance of those words in the collection would be appropriate.

Table 1.2
Words for the Way

Word	Freq.	Meaning	I	II	III	IV	V	VI	VII
ʾōraḥ	59/19	way	12	6	1				
derek	706/75	way	29	33	2		5	5	1
měsillâ	27/1	highway		1					
maʿgāl	16/7	path	7						
nětîbâ	21/6	path	5	1					
šûq	4/1	street	1						

NOTE: "Freq." means frequency. In all the tables in this book, the roman numerals from I to VII stand for the seven collections (e.g., I stands for collection I and II collection II so on). The first number in the frequency indicates the frequency of the word in the OT and the second number its frequency in Proverbs (e.g., 59/19 means that ʾōraḥ "way" occurs 59 times in the OT and 19 times in Proverbs.

Two things are immediately observed in the table. First, the frequency of *derek* (75 times) and its occurrence in six collections indicate that *derek* is the most frequent and common term for the way in Proverbs. Second, collection I is distinguished from other collections for its employment of a variety of terms for a way: five different words occur a total of 54 times in collection I. In view that collection II, as the largest collection in Proverbs, has only two words (*derek* and ʾōraḥ) which occur more than once, the rich occurrence of the words for the way in collection I must be considered significant.

Then, what is the significance of the theme of the way in collection I? When one considers the well-known fact that in the OT the use of the term "way" is mostly figurative to denote the conducts of persons and nations,[8] it is implied by the frequency and variety of the words for the way in collection I that one of the main concerns of the collection is to instruct one about the way of life, especially the right way of life. Some have already noted this feature of collection I, and have advanced the understanding of the way as an important metaphor in collection I. For example, N. C. Habel calls the way (*derek*) in chapters 1–9 a nuclear symbol which has a system of satellite symbols, such as the two ways, two hearts, two companions, and two houses of Wisdom and Folly. He examines those contrasting concepts in three wisdom contexts ("old" international wisdom, wisdom in Yahwistic religion, and the wisdom of cosmological reflection), and confirms that the way is a key symbol in Proverbs 1–9.[9] Although R. C. Van Leeuwen disagrees with Habel, proposing that all the metaphors including the way are part of the larger metaphoric system with underlying notion of limits and boundaries established by God, he acknowledges that Habel's study of the way has uncovered the fundamental aspects of the metaphoric system of Proverbs 1–9.[10] M. V. Fox does not accept Van Leeuwen's liminality theory, but agrees with Habel's view, saying that the polarity of the two ways is the most fundamental metaphor in Proverbs 1–9. As his own conclusion, Fox offers a slightly modified view of the way, "Many Paths and Two Paths," which is clearly built upon Habel's "Two Way" theory.[11] Although the three views are not in complete agreement, the importance of the way as one of the fundamental metaphors in Proverbs 1–9 is commonly emphasized by them.

On the basis of the diversity and frequency of the terms shown in the table, we may conclude that in Proverbs the metaphor of the way belongs predominantly to collection I, and that it is a powerful and persuasive vehicle which the father has used to teach his son about life and death, good and evil, and godliness and ungodliness to the Lord.

B. Words for the Parts of the Body:
lēbāb, gargĕrôt, dad, šōr, ʾeṣbaʿ, kābēd, śĕmōʾwl

Our discussion will be focused on the seven exclusive words under this heading, which designate the elements of the human body. For two reasons it is anticipated that the terms for the parts of the body would be used frequently in Proverbs. First, in a normal sense learning and practicing wisdom involve various human organs. Learning wisdom is usually accomplished through the faculties of cognition such as the ears for hearing, the eyes for seeing, and the heart for remembering. Likewise, practicing wisdom requires agents of action such as the hands, feet, and speaking organs. Second, many sayings in Proverbs deal with various human characters, tendencies, and emotions, giving them moral values of good or bad. As indicated before, a person is often classified in the wisdom context as morally good or bad by means of the moral value of a part of his body (e.g., a lying tongue, lying lips, a pure heart, or being wise in one's own eyes). This way of evaluation of a person in Proverbs also requires frequent use of the terms for the parts of the human body. As we shall see below, 45 different terms are used in Proverbs to designate the invisible and visible elements of a person. In the absence of comparable lists from other biblical books, it would be difficult to know whether the number of the terms in Proverbs is relatively large or small. However, when one considers that ten of the 45 terms are rare words, occurring ten times or less in the OT, the use of the terms in Proverbs is considered a significant phenomenon.

Recently the importance of the body parts in the process of learning has been carefully studied by Nili Shupak. In her comparative study of Egyptian and Israelite wisdom terms, Shupak points out that some organs of the body are essential in the world of education and wisdom. She mentions five organs (the ear, tongue, mouth, belly, and heart) as necessary in acquiring (the ear), expressing (the tongue and mouth), and storing knowledge (the belly and heart).[12] However, Shupak's explanation is considered partial because she limits her explanation to the relationship between the five terms and education. The reason that Proverbs frequently mentions various parts of the body is not only because they function as channels to acquire knowledge and wisdom, but, more importantly, because they often represent the moral value of a person. It is frequently noted in Proverbs that an element or a part of the body is praised or condemned as if it were solely responsible for a particular conduct. For example, in Proverbs 6:17–18 five parts of the body are described as morally bad: haughty *eyes*, a lying *tongue*, *hands* that shed innocent blood, a *heart* that devises evil thoughts, and *feet* that are quick to run to evil. On the other hand, the same organs receive good remarks in other sayings: "A joyful *heart* makes the face look good" (15:13), "the gentleness of the *tongue* is a tree of life" (15:4), "one who is good of the *eye* (the generous one) will be blessed" (22:9), and "a gold ring or an ornament of fine gold is a wise man who reproves a listening *ear*" (25:12). In these examples, it is not the whole person but a part of the body that is either praised or condemned.

The 45 terms for the parts of the body are listed in Table 1.3 in the order from inside (or invisible) to outside and from top to bottom of the body.

Table 1.3
Words for the Elements of a Human Being

Word	Freq.	Meaning	I	II	III	IV	V	VI	VII
rûaḥ	378/21	spirit	1	13			6	1	
nepeš	753/56	soul	10	29	6		10		1
lēb	599/97	heart	19	51	13	2	10	1	1
lēbāb	252/2	heart	2						
qereb	227/3	inner part		2			1		
raḥam	32/1	womb						1	
kābēd	14/1	liver	1						
kilyâ	31/1	kidney			1				
gerem	5/2	bone		1			1		
ʿeṣem	126/5	bone	1	4					

Term	Ref	Gloss	1	2	3	4	5	6	7
bāśār	270/4	flesh	2	1	1				
šě'ēr	16/2	flesh	1	1					
dām	360/8	blood	4	1			2	1	
śēbâ	19/2	gray hair		2					
rō'š	600/10	head	6	2	1		1		
pānîm	2040/18	face	3	6		2	7		
'ōzen	187/14	ear	4	4	3		3		
'ayin	868/48	eye	11	17	8		9	3	
'ap'ap	10/4	eyelid	3				1		
'išôn	5/3	pupil	2	1					
'ap	277/16	nose		8	2		4	2	
pê	502/55	mouth	13	30	1		6	2	3
śāpâ	176/46	lip	6	32	3	2	3		
šēn	55/3	tooth		1			1	1	
mětall'ôt	3/1	jawbone					1		
hēk	18/3	palate	2		1				
lāšôn	109/19	tongue	2	12			4		1
lōa'	1/1	throat			1				
gargārôt	4/4	neck	4						
'ōrēp	33/1	neck					1		
hêq	38/5	bosom	2	3					
dad	4/1	breast	1						
gēw	6/3	back		2			1		
beten	72/8	belly		5	1		1		1
šōr	3/1	navel	1						
motnayim	47/2	loins						1	1
yāmîn	139/3	right hand	2				1		
śěmō'wl	54/2	left hand	2						
zěrōa'	91/1	arm							1
yād	1617/31	had	8	14		1	3	2	3
kap	193/9	palm	2	2	1				4
hōpen	6/1	palm						1	
'eṣba'	31/2	finger	2						
šôq	19/1	leg					1		
regel	243/15	foot	11	1			3		

The table shows two features of collection I in regard to the terms for the components of the body. First, collection I contains more terms of the body parts (29 terms) than other collections.[13] Second, the peculiarity of collection I is indicated by the fact that seven of the 29 terms (24%) occur exclusively in the collection (no collection has more than three exclusive terms). This means that the vocabulary of the terms of the body in collections I is not only larger but also more peculiar. For example, *gargārôt* "neck" occurs four times only in collection

I in the entire OT. It is also interesting to note that, while *lēb* occurs in all collections, *lēbāb*, a favorite word for "heart" in Deuteronomy, is found twice only in collection I. Another interesting phenomenon in collection I is that the word *'ap* "nose, anger" is completely absent in it although the noun occurs in the two other major collections II (eight times) and V (four times). The usage of *'ap* in its 16 instances in Proverbs shows that the word is used only twice to refer to the actual nose of the body, once of a human (30:33) and the other of an animal (11:22), but in all other instances *'ap* always means "anger." The absence of *'ap* in collection I thus indicates that the theme of anger or patience (expressed by the association of *'rk* and *'ap*) is not present in chapters 1–9. There is only one instance of anger in collection I, represented by *ḥēmâ* to describe the anger of an offended husband (6:34). No verbs or nouns related to anger are used in collection I except this instance.[14]

The terms for the parts of the body appear mainly in three types of sayings in collection I. The three are the introduction of the parents' instructions, the description of Wisdom, and the sayings about the strange woman. For example, in the introduction of the parents' instructions, the father asks his son to pay attention to his words through the *ear* and *heart* (2:2) and entreats him to keep his teaching like the *apple* of his *eye*, to bind them on his *fingers*, and to write them on the tablet of his *heart* (7:2–3). As motivation, he promises his son that the reward will be the wreath for his *head* and necklaces for his *neck* (1:9). The father warns his son against the dangerous strange woman because her *lips* drip honey and her *palate* and *tongue* are smoother than oil (5:3; 7:24). On the other hand, the *palate* of Wisdom proclaims truth, her *lips* abhor the wicked, and the words of her *mouth* are righteous (8:7–8). She holds long life in her *right hand* and wealth and honor in her *left hand* (3:16).

i. *Lēbāb* "heart" (4:21; 6:25)

In Proverbs *lēbāb* occurs only twice in collection I (4:21; 6:25). Although *lēbāb* is interpreted in late rabbinical homiletics as "double heart" or "the seat of two opposite inclinations,"[15] no such a semantic distinction is possible between *lēb* and *lēbāb* in the OT. Nonetheless, one conspicuous phenomenon in the use of *lēbāb* is that it is heavily preferred in Deuteronomy to *lēb* by a ratio of 12:1 (*lēbāb* 47 times and *lēb* 4 times).[16] Interestingly, this situation is reversed in Proverbs where *lēb* is used 97 times and *lēbāb* only twice (Ecclesiastes shows the same tendency, *lēb* 41 times and *lēbāb* once). The two rare instances of *lēbāb* in collection I may be considered a stylistic variation to the dominant use of *lēb* (21 times), but the phraseology and theme involving *lēbāb* are reminiscent of the use of the noun in Deuteronomy. In Prov 4:20–21 the son is admonished to keep the father's words (*dābār*) in his heart (*lēbāb*). It is in Deuteronomy where *lēbāb* is often mentioned in connection with God's words (*dābār*) as a place to store the words (e.g., Deut 6:6; 11:18; 32:46). In Prov 6:25 the son is admonished by the father not to desire the strange woman, "Do not covet ('al taḥmōḏ her beauty in your heart (lēbāb)." The verb ḥmd "to desire" occurs in the OT 18 times, but the object of the verb is a woman only in three instances: twice in the Tenth Commandment of the Decalogue (Ex 20:17; Deut 5:21) and Prov 6:25. Although the prohibition of coveting a neighbor's wife is identical in Ex 20:17 and Deut 5:21, Prov 5:26 is considered closer to the text in Deuteronomy than the text in Exodus, because in Deuteronomy coveting another man's wife is differentiated from coveting his properties by the use of ḥmd for a wife and 'wh for properties. The use of ḥmd in connection with a woman indicates that the father warns his son against the strange woman (the wife of another man),[17] using the language of the Decalogue. The possibility of the link between Prov 6:25 and the Decalogue is heightened by the occurrence of the theme of adultery in 6:32, "One who commits adultery with a woman is senseless." This similarity supports Moshe Weinfeld's view that Deuteronomy is closely connected to Proverbs, although his argument that Deuteronomy is dependent upon wisdom literature is questionable.[18]

ii. *Gargārôt* "neck" (four times)[19]

Although *gargārôt* occurs four times in collection I, the noun could be treated as a *hapax legomenon* because it is not found elsewhere in the OT. In its four instances in collection I, the neck (*gargārôt*) signifies a place to display the status of honor (1:9; 3:22) and to bind the teachings of the parents (3:3; 6:21). In 1:9 ʿănāq "necklace" occurs in connection with *gargārôt*, and other texts in which ʿănāq occurs indicate that ṣawwā'r is the usual term for the neck to wear a necklace (Judg 8:26; Song 4:9; cf. Song 1:10; Judg 5:30). Although outside the OT *gargārôt* is found in Mishnaic Hebrew and Ben Sira (31:16; 36:11),[20] it does not necessarily indicate a very late date of collection I, because the theme "writing on the tablet of the heart," which occurs with "binding around the neck (*gargārôt*)" in Prov 3:3, is also found in Jer 17:1. *Gargārôt* may have been used in wisdom circles during the period of Middle Hebrew.

iii. *Dad* "breast" (5:19)

Dad occurs four times in the OT: three times in Ezekiel and once in Proverbs. In the three instances in Ezekiel (23:3, 8, 21) *dad* is mentioned in the figurative description of Israel as a prostitute. Although some consider *daddêha* "her breasts" in Prov 5:19 tenable in the context, others prefer to read it as *dōdêhā* "her love," in view of 'ăhābâ "love" in the second colon and *nirwê dōdîm* "let us take our fill of love" in Prov 7:18.[21] Fox mentions a case in which *dd* appears as a Semiticism in an Egyptian text with the meaning "love making."[22] However, considering that the author's intent in Prov 5:15-20 is to make the meaning symbolic or allegorical, *dad* fits better in the context than *dōd* which makes the meaning too explicit.

iv. *Šōr* "navel-string" (3:8)

Šōr occurs three times in the OT (Ezek 16:4; Prov 3:8; Song 7:3). The meaning of *šōr* is "navel" or "navel-string," and it occurs with the meaning in Song 7:3 and Ezk 16:4. However, the same meaning in Prov 3:8 ("it will be healing for your *šōr* ") is disputed, prompting three different interpretations of the word in the context. The first view keeps the word as it is, arguing that changes are unnecessary. Interpreters who support this view take the navel as a figure of speech to represent the whole body or as the "center of the body" which reminds us of the vitally essential binding between the embryo and mother.[23] The second view is to read the word as *bāśār* or *šĕʾēr* (both "flesh") on the grounds of the translation of the LXX and the expression "flesh/bones" as a standard word pair attested in Gen 29:14; 2 Sam 5:1; Job 2:5; Prov 14:30.[24] The third view which is proposed by Driver takes the meaning of the word as "health," but this view is called questionable by others.[25] We keep the word intact in the text in favor of the first opinion, because as the center of the body it represents a channel through which the whole body is nourished.

v. *ʾeṣbaʿ* "finger" (6:13; 7:3)

ʾeṣbaʿ occurs 31 times in the OT. The noun occurs 15 times in Leviticus, Exodus, and Numbers mainly in the context where the priest is instructed to use his *ʾeṣbaʿ* "finger" to sprinkle animal blood in sacrifice. In Proverbs the word occurs twice, once in reference to the sign language made by an evil man using his fingers (6:13), and in other instance to refer to the finger as a place to tie the father's words (7:3). These two verses show resemblance to Isa 58:9, Deut 6:8, and 11:18. In Isa 58:9 the verb *šlḥ* "to send" is associated with *ʾeṣbaʿ* to form an idiom *šĕlaḥ ʾeṣbaʿ* "sending a finger." Both this expression and "directing with his fingers" (*mōrê bĕʾeṣbĕʿōtāyw*) in Prov 6:13 are understood as an act of "finger pointing" in derision or accusation.[26] Proverbs 6:13 actually contains three body movements made with the eyes, feet, and fingers, and these three movements make R. E. Murphy suggest that the OT sages have paid close attention to body signs.[27]

The act of binding the father's words to fingers in Prov 7:3 resembles the teaching in Deut 6:8 and 11:18, "Tie them as symbols on your hands." In his comment on Prov 7:3, Fox explains the command as a figurative act, never practiced in Jewish society.[28] At this point one may ask why the sage in collection I used "fingers" instead of "hand" which is the more practical part of the body to tie things to. Although it is not certain, Weinfeld's explanation appears plausible: he points out that a "reminder" is the common function of the binding in the two texts (Prof 7:3; Deut 6:8; 11:18), and continues to explain that the parents' words tied to fingers emphasize the ornamental aspect, while God's words tied to the hand function as sign.[29]

vi. *Kābēd* "liver" (7:23)

The term occurs 14 times to refer to the liver in the OT: nine times in Leviticus, twice in Exodus, and once each in Ezekiel, Lamentations, and Proverbs. In all but two instances (Prov 7:23; Lam 2:11) it always refers to the liver of an animal. It denotes the human liver only in Prov 7:23 and Lam 2:11. However, the use of the word in Prov 7:23 and Lam 2:11 differs from each other. In Prov 7:23 it refers to the organ in its literal sense ("till an arrow pierces his liver"), while it denotes the seat of sorrow in Lam 2:11 ("my liver is poured out on the ground"). The *kābēd* as the seat of emotions, such as anger and melancholy, is found frequently in later periods: in Aramaic and Syriac *kabdâ* means "the seat of anger" and its denominative verb *kbd* means "to be angry."[30]

C. Words Related to Israelite Religion
bĕrît, 'ēdâ, šelem, ḥāsîd

The third group of words for discussion consists of exclusive terms which are deemed relevant to Israelite religion. Unlike in other biblical books, speaking about religious features of Proverbs would be considered inconsequential because of the characterization of the book chiefly as international, secular, and non-historical.[31] With the understanding of Proverbs as international and secular in nature, it is inevitable to explain the presence of the religious expressions in the book as a phenomenon developed in late Israel's wisdom tradition.[32] As a result, this understanding of Proverbs makes interpreters prefer the secular or neutral meaning of a given word to its religious meaning in order to put the interpretation in line with international wisdom. This is precisely the difficulty that we face in our discussion of religious terms in Proverbs. For example, *tôrâ* is predominantly associated with God in the OT, but the noun never occurs with the Lord in Proverbs: in its 13 instances, it occurs seven times independently, five times in connection with the parents, and once with wisdom. Due to the association of *tôrâ* with the parents and wisdom, the noun is interpreted as human or wisdom instruction, but not as divine instruction.[33] However, a closer look at its instances reveals that the religious meaning of the noun is as equally possible as a secular meaning at least in collection V (28:4, 4, 7, 9; 29:18) and in collection I (6:23). W. Zimmerli emphasizes the international aspect of wisdom in such a way that it (or "the structure of wisdom") cannot be altered even after being put in Israelite thinking.[34] He further emphasizes that the people mentioned in Proverbs are never the people elected by Yahweh, and that the king in the book is never the anointed king of God's people Israel and the son of David.[35] For him, even the familiar biblical expressions, like "inherit the land" and "redeemer," are not clear references to the history of Israel. Consequently, when he defines the theological structure of wisdom as "man's going out into

God's created world to apprehend, establish ,and order it through knowledge,"[36] it is not certain whether there is any distinction in his creation theology between the god who is behind *ma'at* and the Lord who appears in Proverbs. M. V. Fox rather maintains an unambiguous position on this issue. In one of his earlier studies of wisdom he explains the three gradually developing stages of the religion in Proverbs, and points out that, in spite of being called Yahweh, the God in the proverbs of stage I (the "Egyptian" stage), is "different from the Yahweh of the rest of the Bible."[37]

Before discussing the religious terms in Proverbs, it is necessary to address several governing principles in this study. First, although Proverbs is undoubtedly an end product of a centuries-long process, the religious sayings in the book are not necessarily secondary additions to theologize older, secular sayings. It is not difficult to imagine that God-sayings were already in circulation in Israelite society even before the time of Solomon. If the stories in First Samuel reflect at least the historical situation of Israel in the 11th century B. C., 1 Sam 16:7 can be taken as an example to suggest the existence of God-sayings in Israel's earlier period.[38] The purpose of the proverb in 1 Sam 16:7 is to stress the difference between divine knowledge and human knowledge: "Man sees with the eyes, but the Lord sees the heart." As a God-saying, 1 Sam 16:7 shows resemblance to Prov 21:2 in regard to the contrast between a human way and God's way: "Every way of a man is straight in his eyes, but the Lord tests hearts." The second halves of the two proverbs commonly point out that God alone knows true human motives in the heart. R. N. Whybray has conducted a thorough examination of God-sayings in Proverbs, but his explanation about the function of those sayings seems inconclusive by his own accounts.[39] His view with regard to the function of God-sayings in Proverbs is that some of God-sayings are intended to reinterpret adjacent secular sayings.[40] Even if his suggestion is acceptable, God-sayings as a whole should not be viewed as late compositions to counter or correct older secular sayings.

The second governing principle is that the OT itself does not distinguish between secular and religious sayings. In Israel certain popular sayings with no reference to God were used among individuals and sometimes between God and people: for example, "Out of the wicked comes forth wickedness" (1 Sam 24:14, between David and Saul), "Let not him who girds on his armor boast as he who puts it off" (1 Kgs 20:11, between Ahab and Ben-Hadad), "Like mother, like daughter" (Ezek 16:44, between God and Israel), and "The fathers have eaten sour grapes and the children's teeth are set on edge" (Jer 31;29; Ezek 18:2, between God and Israel).[41] These sayings are considered secular because they do not bear any religious marks, but it is certain that they are at ease in the religious context without any tension. Regarding the issue of secular and religious sayings, we fully agree with L. Boström who says, "While the book of Proverbs demonstrates that many issues could be considered without explicit appeal to divine ordinances, this is far from proof of a secular mindset. Appeal to reason, tradition, and common sense do not need to be understood as standing in opposition to theological thinking."[42] On the other hand, there are proverbial sayings which contain religious terms: "Like Nimrod, a mighty hunter before the Lord" (Gen 10:9) and "Is Saul also among the prophets?" (1 Sam 10:11; 19:24).[43] It is noted in the examples that Israelite kings and prophets quoted secular sayings when they were deemed necessary in a given situation. The use of secular sayings in the religious context is well described by von Rad who says that Israel had only one world of experience in which "rational perceptions and religious perceptions were not differentiated."[44]

Finally, it is the position taken in this study that, except the foreigners who are explicitly identified so, as in Proverbs 30:1 and 31:1, the intent of the editor is to present all the characters who appear in Proverbs, such as the parents, the strange woman, Wisdom, the righteous, and the wicked, as Israelites whose religion is Yahwism. As we shall see later, even some of the sayings in chapters 30 and 31, which are supposed to be of foreign origins are colored with Israelite religion and presented in a coherent way with the material which follows. The parents (or teachers) in Proverbs are not secular parents who might appear in international wisdom material but the believers of the Lord, because they state clearly that the purpose of their teaching and wisdom is to make the son understand the fear of the Lord (2:1–5). They also warn the son that understanding (*bînâ*) apart from faith in the Lord is not a thing to rely on (3:5). Most of all, the first parental instruction in 1:8 that immediately follows the motto of the book in 1:7 sets the tone that the parents must be understood as believers of the Lord in the rest of the book. Based on the understanding that Proverbs was intended to be read by Israelites, and that the editor's position was not neutral in respect to nationality and religion, we suggest that the society and people described in Proverbs also be understood in light of Israelite culture and religion, as far as such a reading is possible, instead of suppressing it in favor of a secular reading. The universal and secular aspects of wisdom cannot be denied, but at the same time no one would deny that one of the distinctive features of Proverbs is to establish a place for wisdom within the framework of Israelite religion, using minimal religious terminology.[45] This feature is seen best in the description of God as the giver of wisdom (e.g., 2:6) and in the relationship between the fear of the Lord and wisdom (e.g., 1:7; 9:10). Although there is no way of knowing the extent of editorial reworking on the sayings in collections III, IV, VI, and VII, the collections known for their foreign connections, a good example for editorial efforts to integrate foreign wisdom material into Israelite world view would be the queen mother's instruction in 31:1–9. Proverbs 31 consists of two distinct literary units, the words for Lemuel (vv. 1–9) and the acrostic poem of an ideal wife (vv. 10–31). Although the first unit is a non-Israelite wisdom instruction written in a different style, M. Lichtenstein and V. A. Hurowitz point out that the two units share common terms, expressions, and themes, thus indicating that they were carefully molded into one composition by an author or editor.[46] R. E. Murphy, agreeing with Lichtenstein, also suggests that 31:1–9 is a Hebrew composition despite the mention of the foreign king, Lemuel.[47] This type of editorial reworking is not new in the OT, because there are other prominent non-Israelite characters who were taken up into the Old Testament and presented within the context of Israelite religion (e.g., Job and his friends, Daniel [from Ugarit], and Balaam).[48] It is therefore out of question that the editor of Proverbs has reshaped the foreign wisdom material in the process of incorporation to make it fit in the context of Israel religion. At this point, one may think of the presence of the two Aramaic words, *bar* "son" and *mĕlākîn* "kings," in 31:2–3, and consider them as surviving foreign words that had escaped the eyes of the editor. However, considering the fact that the two Aramaic words are extremely common words, it is likely that a Hebrew composer intentionally used the Aramaic words to add an Aramaic flavor to the speech which is supposed to be ascribed to a foreigner.[49]

On the basis of the governing principles and the traditional religious terms in the OT, the following words have been tabulated in the table as religious terms in Proverbs:

Table 1.4
Words Related to Israelite Religion

Word	Freq.	Meaning	I	II	III	IV	V	VI	VII
YHWH	6828/87	YHWH	19	55	5		6	1	1
ʾĕlōhîm	2603/5	God	3				1	1	
ʾĕlôah	57/1	God					1		
ḥāsîd	32/1	godly	1						
qōdeš	477/1	holiness		1					
qādôš	116/2	holy	1					1	
tĕpillâ	77/3	prayer		2			1		
zebaḥ	162/5	sacrifice	1	4					
šelem	87/1	peace offering	1						
ṭāhôr	95/3	clean		2				1	
brk	256/6	to kneel	2	2			1	1	
ʾešer	45/8	blessedness	3	3			2		
mĕʾērâ	5/2	curse	1				1		
ʾšm	36/1	to be guilty						1	
ʾāšām	46/1	guilt		1					
ḥaṭṭāʾt	221/7	sin	1	5	1				
ḥaṭṭāʾ	19/3	sinful	1	1	1				
ʿāwôn	229/2	iniquity	1	1					
tôrâ	220/13	instruction	6	1			5		1
ʿēdâ	149/1	assembly	1						
qāhāl	122/3	congregation	1	1			1		
gʾl	60/1	to redeem			1				
ḥesed	246/10	faithfulness		1	8				1
yirʾâ	44/14	fear	5	8	1				
miṣwâ	181/10	command	7	3					

běrît	283/1	covenant	1		
neder	60/3	vow	1	1	1

i. *Běrît* "covenant" (2:17)

Běrît is one of the four exclusive religious terms in collection I. The noun appears in 2:17 in reference to a strange woman who "abandons the companion of her youth and forgets the covenant (*běrît*) of her God." Regarding the meaning of *běrît*, Fox reviews the interpretations of ancient and modern commentators, and summarizes the meaning of *běrît* in three ways: (1) the covenant refers to a marriage agreement but her God is a pagan god, (2) it refers to the covenant at Sinai, and (3) it is the marriage agreement between the woman and her husband, with God as the witness of the marriage.[50] Following Hugenberger's explanation that the ideal of marriage is sometimes expressed as a covenant, Fox suggests that the third view is the best interpretation. The passages which are often cited to support that *běrît* can denote a marriage agreement are Mal 2:14; Hos 2:18–22; Ezek 16:8, 59, 60, 62.

Under the governing principles, the strange woman and her husband in 2:17 are viewed as Israelites who practice Israelite religion, and, more importantly, the context of Proverbs 2 indicates that this is the only possibility.[51] Having identified the characters as Israelites, we want to argue for the second view that *běrît* in 2:17 refers to the covenant at Sinai, not a marriage contract. Fox does not choose the second view as a correct interpretation because (1) the Sinai covenant would not be called "the covenant of *her* God" and (2) Proverbs is not a place to expect the Sinai covenant. With regard to his first reason, the comparison of the Prov 2:17 and the following three examples indicate that it is possible to take the phrase "the covenant of her God" as a reference to the Sinai covenant:

Prov 2:17b	*ʾet běrît ʾělōhêhā šākēhâ*
	she forgot the covenant of her God
Lev 2:13	*melaḥ běrît ʾělōhêka*
	Salt of the covenant of your God
Deut 29:11	*lěʿobrěkā biběrit YHWH ʾělōhêka*
	Your entering into the covenant of the Lord your God
Deut 4:23	*pen tiškěḥû ʾēt běrît YHWH ʾělōhêkem*
	Lest you forget the covenant of the Lord your God

Since the covenant in the three examples clearly denotes the Sinai covenant and the phrases ("covenant of your God") show the same structure like "covenant of her God" in Prov 2:17, there is no reason to reject the understanding that the covenant in Prov 2:17 refers to the Sinai covenant. Moreover, if the covenant in Prov 2:17 refers to the marriage agreement between the woman and her husband, "*her* covenant" would be more natural for the sense than "the covenant of her God."

Next, a brief examination of the passages that are often cited to support the third view (covenant as marriage agreement) would be necessary in order to establish the meaning of *bĕrît* in Prov 2:17. The first place to examine is Ezekiel 16, but before examination we are reminded that the purpose of Ezekiel 16 is to condemn Israel, employing the metaphor of an unfaithful wife, for her breaking of the covenant relationship with God. By God's opening speech to Ezekiel (16:2), "Let Jerusalem know of her abominable practices" (16:2), the reader is prepared to be aware of the point of the story to be told later on. In 16:8, God, seeing that her time for love had come, "entered into a covenant (*bĕrît*)" with her. Undoubtedly, *bĕrît* in this context refers to a marriage contract. Nonetheless, it would be impossible for anyone at this point not to think that the Sinai covenant is the real reference of *bĕrît* in the text. The same can be said of *bĕrît ʿōlām* "an everlasting covenant" in Ezek 16:60, because in its 16 instances in the OT the phrase *bĕrît ʿōlām* is never used for a covenant between humans. Similarly, another instance of *bĕrît* in Ezek 16:62 ("I will establish my *covenant* with you") clearly refers to the Sinai covenant because the next sentence ("and you will know that I am the Lord") indicates that the context is no longer a marriage metaphor.

We now turn to the instances of *bĕrît* in Malachi. First of all, Meinhold points out, on the basis of his interpretation of Mal 2:14, that *bĕrît* in Prov 2:17 does not mean a marriage contract. According to him, the phrase "the wife of your covenant" (*ʾēšet bĕrîtekā*) in Mal 2:14 means that, like the husband, the wife also belongs in the same covenant relationship with God.[52] His argument becomes more convincing if we follow his explanation of Mal 2:10 in which one man's unfaithfulness to his fellow man is equated with profaning the "covenant of our father" (*bĕrît ʾăbōtēnû*). Therefore, when the strange woman abandons the life-companion of her youth (Prov 2:17), her act is seen as tantamount to ignoring the covenant of God, specifically, the Seventh Commandment.

The phrase *ʾĕlōhêhā* "her God" in Prov 2:17 still needs more explanation because of the fact that *YHWH* is used predominantly in Proverbs while the occurrence of *ʾĕlōhîm* is rare (87 times to 5 times, for the divine names in Proverbs, see Table 1.20). On the use of *ʾĕlōhîm* in 2:17, we agree with Fox who points out that in 2:17 "her God must be Yahweh."[53] Then, the reason for not using *YHWH* in 2:17 could be explained as the editor's reluctance to use the divine name in association with the immoral woman, which is a similar phenomenon found in the conversation between the serpent and Eve in Gen 3:1–5 where "God" is used instead of the expected "the Lord God."

ii. ʿēdâ "assembly" (5:14)

In Prov 5:14, the son is warned by his father (or teacher) that, if he commits adultery, he would stand in the middle of the congregation (*qāhāl*) and assembly (ʿēdâ) with regret for not listening to his instruction. Commentators take the juxtaposition of *qāhāl* and ʿēdâ in 5:14 as hendiadys to strengthen the meaning "assembly." Murphy in fact comments that translating the two terms as "congregation and assembly" is a pointless distinction.[54] Although commentators acknowledge the political or judicial function of ʿēdâ in the Israelite tradition in the Old Testament, the term in 5:14 is understood as a general public which will humiliate the son in an open place.[55]

Since the position of this study is, as long as the text permits, to view the people and society described in Proverbs in the Israelite setting, we want to consider the meaning of ʿēdâ in 5:14 under this guiding principle. Our examination begins with the use of ʿēdâ in the OT. ʿēdâ occurs 149 times in the OT, 125 of which are in the four books (Exodus, Leviticus, Numbers, and Joshua) which describe Israel from the time of Exodus to the settlement in Canaan. It is noted that ʿēdâ occurs heavily in Numbers (83 times). On the other hand, the occurrence of ʿēdâ is very rare in Prophets and the late books (only three times in the 15 Prophetic books and only once in the late books). Although it is true that the term is also used for the gathering of animals, that is, a herd (ʿēdâ) of bulls (Ps 68:31) and a swarm (ʿēdâ) of bees (Judg 14:8), and for the gathering of bad people, such rare usage of the term is not to be emphasized to interpret ʿēdâ in 5:14 as a secular term. The main use of the term is to refer to the community of Israel as in the phrase "the assembly of (the sons of) Israel" (about 40 times). In his linguistic investigation of the parallel passages between Numbers and Ezekiel, Avi Hurvitz notes that ʿēdâ is completely absent in Ezekiel. In addition to this, the word is not employed at all in Ezra, Nehemiah, and Chronicles. This phenomenon makes him draw the conclusion that the absence is "a clear indication of the term's gradual falling into disuse" in later biblical books.[56] Also, he notes that *qāhāl* occurs in the place of ʿēdâ in those books as the designation of the assembly of Israel. His findings about ʿēdâ can be summarized as follows: (1) ʿēdâ is an ancient term attested in Ugaritic; (2) it almost completely disappeared in the late books; (3) its synonym *qāhāl* survived throughout the late period; and (4) the surprising occurrence of ēdâ in the Dead Sea Scrolls and Ben Sira is to be explained as an artificial revival to adopt antiquarian biblical expressions.[57] In his findings, the last one is particularly important for our discussion of ʿēdâ. It would be difficult to tell precisely when the artificial revival of ʿēdâ began in Israelite writings. However, because ʿēdâ occurs ten times in Psalms, twice in Job, and once in Proverbs, it may be probable that the disappearance of the term observed by Hurvitz (and Milgrom) is confined to the late prosaic books (Ezekiel, Ezra, Nehemiah, and Chronicles), while ʿēdâ has continued to survive in poetic books (Psalms and Wisdom books except Ecclesiastes).

With regard to Prov 5:14, it can be suggested, on the basis of two grounds, that the public mentioned in the verse is not a general throng but an assembly of Israelite town people to investigate the hypothetical adultery. First, it appears that *ʿēdâ* preserved in the poetic books is understood in its traditional sense. In the following instances of *ʿēdâ* in Psalms, the term connotes a juridical assembly (1:5; 82:1) or the community of Israel (74:2; 111:1):

Ps 1:5   Therefore the wicked will not stand in the judgment (*mišpāṭ*),
             sinners in the assembly (*ʿēdâ*) of the righteous.

Ps 82:1   God stands in the great assembly (*ʿēdâ*),
             he judges (*yišpōṭ*) among gods.

Ps 74:2   Remember your people (*ʿēdâ*) you purchased of old.

Ps 111:1   I will praise the Lord with all my heart,
             in the council of the upright and in the assembly (*ʿēdâ*).

Several centuries after Proverbs, *ʿēdâ* still functions as a judicial assembly in Sira 7:7, "Be guilty of no evil before the assembly at the gate (*ʿdt š'r*)." Second, we are reminded that in Prov 5:7–14 the son is warned not to commit adultery with the strange woman.[58] In a normal society, a case of adultery for a trial would be brought first not to a general public gathered because of curiosity but to an assembly of the elders or leaders of a town. Examples for such a trial abound in the Bible, Apocrypha, and secular historical writings. After the open trial, the guilty party is often punished by death or suffers public humiliation in various ways. For these two reasons, we suggest that *ʿēdâ* in 5:14 refers to a judicial assembly. Even if *qāhāl* and *ʿēdâ* in 5:14 are a hendiadys, the juxtaposition of the two words is to emphasize the notion of the judicial assembly, not of a general public. The father reminds the son that, if he commits adultery, he will stand before the Israelite community for humiliation and punishment. R. N. Whybray appears to acknowledge the traditional aspect of the two terms when he says, "the mention of the congregation and assembly (v. 14) strikes a specifically Israelite note altogether foreign to the character of these instructions."[59]

iii. *Šelem* "peace offering" (7:14)

Šelem occurs 87 times in the OT, and the fact that the majority of its occurrences are in Leviticus and Numbers (49 times) affirms that it is a cultic term. The occurrence of the noun outside the Pentateuch and Historical books is extremely rare, occurring only in Ezekiel (six times), Amos (once), and Proverbs (once). It is remarkable to note that the strange woman's first sentence to a young man (Prov 7:14) is loaded with words that convey religious notions ("sacrifices," "peace offerings," "to pay," and "vows"). Although some say that the implication of the strange woman's invitation to the young man in Prov 7:14 involves pagan cultic prostitution,[60] there is no question that those words are to be understood only in connection with the Israelite sacrificial ordinances. A survey of the instances of *šelem* reveals that the noun occurs about 50 times in the phrase, "the sacrifices of peace offering" (*zibḥê šelāmîm*), mostly in Leviticus and Numbers. This confirms that the term belongs to the priestly vocabulary. Besides *šelem*, the expression "to pay a vow" (*šillam nedeṛ*) in Prov 7:14 (cf. Job 22:27) is another indicator that the strange woman speaks the language of Israelite sacrifice. M. Weinfeld notes that in the Pentateuch the verb *šlm* occurs with the noun *neder* only in Deut 23:22, and strongly suggests links between Deuteronomy and Wisdom books.[61] His view also supports our position that the strange woman is an Israelite who uses the vocabulary that belongs to the Israelite cult.

iv. *Ḥāsîd* "pious" (2:8)

Ḥāsîd refers to a person who practices *hesed* "loyalty, faithfulness."[62] The distribution of *ḥāsîd* in the OT shows several peculiar features of the word: (1) *ḥāsîd* never occurs in prose but only in poetic texts (32 times); (2) most of its instances are in Psalms (25 times); and (3) the word never occurs more than once in other books. Its distribution in the OT indicates that *ḥāsîd* is a cultic term, belonging to middle biblical Hebrew (MBH). The predominant occurrence of *ḥāsîd* in Psalms affirms that it is a religious term, and its occurrence in Prov 2:8 in association with the Lord ("he [*YHWH*] protects the way of his faithful ones [*ḥăsîdāyw*]")[63] proves that the religious aspect of the term is not lost in the wisdom context.

The theological aspects of collection I represented by the four terms (*bĕrît*, *'ēdâ*, *šelem*, and *ḥāsîd*) can be summarized in the following way: (1) one of the father's main concerns for his son is adultery because the sin will put his son to stand before the Israelite assembly for punishment (*'ēdâ*); (2) the father also teaches the son the necessity of faithfulness to the Lord in order to enjoy the divine protection in life (*ḥāsîd*); (3) the strange woman is portrayed as an Israelite woman who practices the ordinances of Israelite sacrifice (*šelem*); and (4) the strange woman's unfaithfulness to her husband is tantamount to breaking the Israelite covenant with God (*bĕrît*).

In addition to this, the fact that collection I contains 20 of the 28 religious terms in Table 1.4 confirms the commonly held view that collection I is the most theologized collection among the three Solomonic collections (I, II, and V). This observation is at odds with Whybray's view on the religious aspect of collection I. He points out that the paucity of references to Yahweh in collection I is remarkable, and that, apart from 3:1–12, the Lord does not play a major role in the collection.[64] His comment would give an incorrect impression that collection I is less theological or religious than other collections. In contrast to his view, it should be pointed out that, besides the divine name, religious ideas are expressed in collection I by means of the terms that are related to Israelite religion. That is why many view collection I as the most theologized collection despite the fewer instances of the divine name in it.

D. Feminine Abstract Nouns with the Ending -ût :
rip'ût, 'iqqšût, lāzût, kĕsîlût, pĕtayyût

The fourth group of exclusive words in collection I consists of words which have a peculiar linguistic element. They are feminine abstract nouns with the termination -ût. With regard to various noun patterns in Hebrew, the ending -ût seems to have a clearer historical picture of development than other forms. In his important linguistic study of the books in the OT, S. R. Driver points out that the occurrence of malkût is prevalent in the later books (Chronicles, Ezra, Nehemiah, Esther, and Daniel), while the earlier books prefer mamlākâ or mĕlûkâ.[65] The fact that the author of Chronicles replaced mamlākâ with malkût in three parallel texts (2 Sam 5:12=1 Chr 14:2; 2 Sam 7:12=1 Chr 17:11; 2 Sam 7:16=1 Chr 17:14) is often cited as evidence for the popularity of the feminine abstract noun with -ût ending in late biblical Hebrew (LBH). Also, the numerous instances of the same feminine noun form in Mishnaic Hebrew (MH) confirms that the linguistic phenomenon was wide spread in LBH, possibly through Aramaic influence.[66] However, this should not give an impression that the feminine abstract noun pattern is to be found mainly in late biblical books. The same form is also found in earlier books: for example, mamlākût "kingdom" (Josh 13:12, 21, 27, 30, 31; Hos 1:4; 2 Sam 16:3; Isa 15:18), zĕnût "fornication" (Num 14:33; Hos 4:11; 6:10), gēʾût "majesty" (Isa 9:17; 12:5; 26:10; 28:1, 3), gālût "exile" (Amos 1:6, 9; Isa 20:4), ḥāzût "vision" (Isa 21:2; 28:18; 29:11), and kĕsût "covering" (Gen 20:6; Ex 21:10; 22:26).[67] These examples imply that, if the linguistic phenomenon has to be ascribed to Aramaic influence, the influence must be differentiated as the early or late stage of Aramaic influence, because the books in which the instances of the ending -ût are found do not allow the same date. With regard to Aramaic influence, R. Polzin cautiously points out that at least eight elements must be considered in establishing chronological judgments of texts which involve Aramaisms.[68] His suggestion is considered relevant particularly to Proverbs, because some have attempted to date collection I and other parts of Proverbs as late, without paying proper attention to the complex aspects of Aramaic influence. He says, "Aramaisms can be useful as evidence for a possible late date of a text but can say nothing for early dating of chronologically problematical text."[69] He also points out that using Aramaisms for dating Job, Proverbs, and Song of Songs is particularly difficult.[70] Since the sayings in Proverbs are complex in nature with regard to the setting and the time of composition, a more cautious approach must be taken in dating collections in Proverbs.

Before the examination of the feminine abstract nouns with the ending -ût in Proverbs, we present a table which shows the occurrences of those nouns in Proverbs.

Table 1.5
Feminine Abstract Nouns with the Ending -ût

Word	Freq.	Meaning	I	II	III	IV	V	VI	VII
rip'ût	1/1	healing	1						
ʿiqqĕšût	2/2	perversity	2						
lāzût	1/1	perversity	1						
kĕsîlût	1/1	stupidity	1						
pĕtayyut	1/1	naivety	1						
ḥaklîlût	1/1	dullness			1				
'akzĕriyyût	1/1	cruelty						1	
ʿaṣlût	1/1	laziness							1

In his attempt to date the book of Proverbs, H. C. Washington lists six feminine abstract nouns, and says that "frequent in Proverbs is the feminine abstract substantive with the termination -ût."[71] His statement is somewhat misleading because it gives an impression that, besides the six words, one can expect to find more such nouns in Proverbs. Table 1.5 shows that there are actually only eight feminine abstract nouns with the ending -ût in Proverbs. Several things are observed in the table. First, all of the feminine abstract nouns are not only exclusive to Proverbs, but are *hapax legomena* except ʿiqqĕšût (this word also could be treated as a *hapax legomenon* because it occurs twice only in collection I in the entire OT). The second peculiar phenomenon observed in Table 1.5 is that none of the eight words is found in collections II, the largest collection, but collection I contains five of them. Collection I is clearly distinguished from other collections in this regard.

As far as the patterns of the abstract nouns are concerned, it is striking to note that the formations of the eight abstract nouns differ from one another. No two words share the same pattern. Despite the different patterns, most of the abstract nouns seem to have been formed through the same linguistic development. The detected common development is as follows: root > adjectival form > addition of the -ût ending:

ʿqš	ʿiqqēš	ʿiqqĕšût	qittĕlût pattern
ksl	kĕsîl	kĕsîlût	qĕtîlût pattern
pty	petî	pĕtayyût	qĕtallût pattern
ḥkl[72]	ḥaklîl	ḥaklîlût	qatlîlût pattern
(*kzr)	'akzārî	'akzĕriyyût	'aqtĕliyyût pattern
ʿṣl	'āṣēl	ʿaṣlût	qatlût pattern
rp'	(*rip'ā)	rip'ût	qitlût pattern
lwz	(*lāz)	lāzût	

Although the date of the linguistic development cannot be known, if the words were coined in wisdom circles, it would be probable that wise men formed the feminine abstract nouns not directly from the roots but by adding the ending -ût to the already existing adjectives. Since adjectival forms are diverse, this lin-

guistic development could explain why the abstract nouns display no same patterns among themselves.

What then is the significance of the feminine abstract nouns concentrated in
collection I? Since we have pointed out that the feminine abstract nouns had
been built on their cognate adjectives, we will first consider the significance of
the relationship between the nouns and adjectives. A survey of the instances of
the three adjectives which stand behind the abstract nouns in collection I reveals
an interesting phenomenon (the supposed adjectives of *rip'ût* and *lāzût* are not
found in Proverbs). As shown below, the three adjectives occur in all the three
major collections (I, II, and V), and, in case of *kĕsîl*, it occurs once in collection
III also.

'iqqēš	(7 times)	I–2	II–4		V–1
kĕsîl	(49 times)	I–4	II–30	III–1	V–14
petî	(15 times)	I–9	II–5		V–1

What is remarkable is that all the three adjectives are known as belonging
to the wisdom vocabulary.[73] It is thus reasonable to say that the coherence of the
three major collections is indicated at least by the three wisdom terms. However,
considering the fact that, while the three adjectives are common to collections I,
II, and V, the feminine abstract nouns formed from them are found only in collection I, one may ask why the linguistic phenomenon is restricted to collection
I. A relatively simple answer would be to ascribe the heavy presence of the
feminine abstract nouns in collection I to the influence of Aramaic and consequently to say that collection I was composed later than other collections.[74]
However, this answer would have difficulty to explain why collection I alone
was subjected to such heavy Aramaic influence among the seven collections. If
the five feminine abstract nouns are the sign of Aramaic influence, how could
the other collections escape the influence? For those who support the theory of
Aramaic influence, the last question is particularly difficult to answer because
the coherent relationship of collection I to the two other major collections (II
and V) is evident. For example, the expressions, *lĕšôn šeqer* "lying tongue" and
'ēd šeqer "false witness," and words like *tôkaḥat* "rebuke," *yāšār* "upright," *'ēṣâ*
"counsel," and *māšāl* "proverb," which are considered significant in the wisdom
context, occur only in the three collections. The coherence of the three collections indicates that the heavy occurrence of the feminine abstract nouns in collection I must be explained from a different angle, not as a sign of Aramaic influence or late composition. As we shall see later, the diverse linguistic features
that are common to collections I, II, and V point to the possibility that the phenomenon of the feminine abstract nouns cannot be used to separate collection I
from the two major collections in order to characterize it as a late collection or a
collection subjugated to Aramaic influence. Rather, the strong links that exist
between the three collections suggest that the phenomenon of the feminine abstract noun is to be ascribed to the author's tendency or literary style. Another
significant factor to support this view is that, as we pointed out earlier, virtually
all of the eight feminine abstract nouns are *hapax legomena* in the OT. Although

Aramaisms are found in almost all layers of Hebrew in the OT,[75] none of the eight nouns occurs elsewhere in the OT. This peculiarity of the eight nouns also implies that the first five words in the table have been coined by the author of collection I.

In sum, we suggest, on the basis of the four groups of exclusive words in collection I, that the following subjects are important features of the collection: (1) the metaphor of the way, (2) the use of various terms for the elements of a human being, (3) the terms related to Israelite faith and tradition, (4) and the feminine abstract nouns with the -ût ending. In addition to this, we have emphasized that the religious meanings of běrît, ʿēdâ, šelem, and ḥāsîd are still acceptable in the wisdom context. Also, the context permits all the characters and society described in collection I to be understood within the Israelite religion and tradition. Finally, the distinctive literary aspect represented by the feminine abstract nouns indicates the distinctive literary tendency of the author of collection I.

(2) The Relationship between Collections 1 and II

a. Verbs (36)

אגר	3/2	to gather	I-1	II-1
בחר	172/8	to choose	I-4	II-4
בלע	49/3	to swallow	I-1	II-2
בצע	16/2	to gain by evil	I-1	II-1
המה	34/4	to murmur	I-3	II-1
זרה	39/4	to scatter	I-1	II-3
חטא	238/6	to miss, sin	I-1	II-5
חיה	283/4	to live	I-3	II-1
חמד	18/4	to desire	I-2	II-2
חרש	27/7	to devise evil	I-3	II-4
ישר	25/5	to be straight	I-3	II-2
כלה	206/3	to complete	I-1	II-2
לוז	6/5	to turn aside	I-4	II-1
לכד	121/4	to capture	I-2	II-2
מאן	41/3	to refuse	I-1	II-2
מאס	76/2	to reject	I-1	II-1
נאץ	31/3	to contemn	I-2	II-1
נבע	11/4	to pour out	I-1	II-3
נחה	39/3	to lead, guide	I-1	II-2
נטש	40/3	to forsake	I-2	II-1
נסח	4/2	to pull away	I-1	II-1

נצב	116/2	to stand	I-1	II-1
סלל	11/2	to lift up	I-1	II-1
עזז	11/3	to be strong	I-2	II-1
ערב	8/2	to be sweet	I-1	II-1
פוק	7/4	to bring out	I-2	II-2
קנה	84/13	to acquire	I-6	II-7
קרץ	5/3	to nip, pinch	I-2	II-1
קשׁר	44/4	to bind	I-3	II-1
רוה	15/4	to drench	I-2	II-2
רוץ	80/4	to run	I-3	II-1
רעב	12/3	to be hungry	I-1	II-2
שׂכל	61/13	to be prudent	I-1	II-12
שׁחר	13/5	to look early	I-3	II-2
שׁכן	129/5	to abide	I-4	II-1
תעה	50/5	to wander	I-1	II-4

b. Adjectives/Nouns (51)

אוֹר	122/4	light	I-2	II-2
אוֹצָר	79/4	storehouse	I-1	II-3
אִישׁוֹן	5/3	pupil (eye)	I-2	II-1
אַכְזָרִי	8/4	cruel	I-1	II-3
אַלּוּף	69/3	friend	I-1	II-2
בֶּטַח	42/4	security, trust	I-3	II-1
בְּלִיַּעַל	27/3	worthlessness	I-2	II-1
גָּאוֹן	49/2	pride	I-1	II-1
גּוֹרָל	78/4	lots	I-1	II-3
זֶבַח	162/5	sacrifice	I-1	II-4
חֵיק	38/5	bosom	I-2	II-3
חָרוּץ	6/4	gold	I-3	II-1
חֶרְפָּה	73/2	reproach	I-1	II-1
חֹשֶׁךְ	80/2	darkness	I-1	II-1
טַל	31/2	dew	I-1	II-1
יֹשֶׁר	14/5	uprightness	I-2	II-3
כִּיס	5/2	bag, purse	I-1	II-1
כֹּפֶר	13/3	ransom	I-1	II-2
לֶקַח	9/6	learning	I-4	II-2
מַחֲשָׁבָה	50/8	thought	I-1	II-7

מִצְוָה	181/10	command	I-7	II-3
נֶגֶד	151/4	in front of	I-1	II-3
נֹעַם	7/3	pleasantness	I-1	II-2
נְתִיבָה	21/6	path	I-5	II-1
סוּפָה	15/2	storm-wind	I-1	II-1
עָוֹן	229/2	iniquity	I-1	II-1
עֲטָרָה	23/5	crown	I-1	II-4
עָנָו	21/3	the afflicted	I-2	II-1
עֶצֶב	6/4	pain, toil	I-1	II-3
עֶצֶם	126/5	bone	I-1	II-4
עֵת	294/5	time	I-3	II-2
פַּח	25/2	bird-trap	I-1	II-1
פֶּלֶג	10/2	channel	I-1	II-1
פֶּתַח	164/6	entrance	I-5	II-1
צְדָקָה	157/18	righteousness	I-2	II-16
קָלוֹן	17/8	dishonor	I-3	II-5
קֶרֶת	5/4	town, city	I-3	II-1
רֵאשִׁית	51/5	beginning	I-4	II-1
רְפָאִים	8/3	shades, grave	I-2	II-1
רָצוֹן	56/14	goodwill	I-1	II-13
רֶשַׁע	30/5	wickedness	I-2	II-3
שָׂמֵחַ	21/4	glad, joyful	I-1	II-3
שְׁאֵר	16/2	flesh	I-1	II-1
שׁוֹר	79/3	bull	I-1	II-2
שֹׁחַד	23/4	bribe	I-1	II-3
שַׁלְוָה	8/2	quietness	I-1	II-1
שָׁלוֹם	237/3	peace	I-2	II-1
שָׁנָה	874/5	year	I-4	II-1
תְּבוּאָה	41/8	income	I-3	II-5
תָּוֶךְ	418/8	midst	I-5	II-3
תּוּשִׁיָּה	12/4	wisdom	I-3	II-1

Collections I and II are the two largest collections which together account for 69% of the text of Proverbs. There are 87 words (36 verbs and 51 adjectives/nouns) that occur exclusively in the two collections, and 13 of them have been selected, on the grounds of frequency and significance in relation to wisdom, to be examined for the relationship between the two collections.

A. *Tûšiyyâ* "sound wisdom" (four times)[76]

Tûšiyyâ is one of the synonyms of wisdom (*ḥokmâ*), and is considered a technical term in Wisdom books, or if we borrow Whybray's expression, the word belongs to the intellectual tradition in the OT.[77] *Tûšiyyâ* occurs 12 times in the OT: six times in Job, four times in Proverbs, and once each in Isaiah and Micah. Its ten occurrences in Job and Proverbs affirm that the noun belongs to the wisdom vocabulary. However, *tûšiyyâ* takes on various shades of meaning in the context where in occurs, largely because the meaning of the noun's root is uncertain.[78] For example, in Isa 28:29 it occurs in synonymous parallelism with *ʿēṣâ* "counsel," and its meaning is understood similarly: "he (the Lord) makes counsel (*ʿēṣâ*) wondrous, he makes *tûšiyyâ* great." Seven different words occur in synonymous parallelism with *tûšiyyâ* in its 12 instances: *ḥokmâ* (Job 11:6; 26:3), *ʿēṣâ* (Isa 28:29; Prov 8:14), *maḥšābâ* (Job 5:12), *ʿezrâ* (Job 6:13), *ʿōz* (Job 12:16), *māgēn* (Prov 2:7), and *mĕzimmâ* (Prov 3:21). Its association with "wisdom (*ḥokmâ*)," "counsel (*ʿēṣâ*)," "help (*ʿezrâ*)," "thought (*maḥšābâ*)," and "protection (*māgēn*)," indicates that *tûšiyyâ* is practical wisdom to deal with problems. It sometimes refers to "success," the outcome of exercising such wisdom.[79]

Tûšiyyâ occurs three times in collection I in reference to God, Wisdom, and the son. That the Lord stores up *tûšiyyâ* for the upright (2:7) means that it is a divine gift for good people. In 8:14, the personified Wisdom declares that *tûšiyyâ* and *ʿēṣâ* belong to her, indicating that one who finds her can find *tûšiyyâ* as a blessed consequence of finding wisdom. In 3:21 the son is commanded by the father to keep *tûšiyyâ* and *mĕzimmâ* "discretion," because they will be his life and honor. M. Fox explains that *tûšiyyâ* is an intellectually neutral faculty which anyone can possess. So deceitful people can cheat and harm honest people by using *tûšiyyâ*.[80] However, his view of *tûšiyyâ* is difficult to accept because of the fact that in its 12 instances in the OT the noun is never used in association with foolish or morally negative people to denote an intellectual ability to deceive others. The only instance in which *tûšiyyâ* is mentioned in a negative context is Job 26:3, in which Job sarcastically replies to his friend Bildad by saying, "you have taught *tûšiyyâ* greatly." This indicates that Bildad is in possession of *tûšiyyâ*, but, in the theological debate of the wise men in Job, he cannot be considered a morally negative character. He is only a theological opponent against Job, with a different understanding of human suffering. In the remaining instances of *tûšiyyâ*, the noun conveys positive connotations through its association with God and Wisdom: *tûšiyyâ* belongs to God and Wisdom (Job 12:16; Prov 8:14), God makes it great (Isa 28:29), and he stores it up for the upright (Prov 2:7). *Tûšiyyâ* rather appears to be a noble quality that negative people cannot possess. It is said in Job 5:12 that crafty people cannot achieve *tûšiyyâ* ("success"), and, regardless what the meaning of *niprād* (literally "an isolated man") may be in Prov 18:1, an abnormal person in society cannot accept *tûšiyyâ*.

The four instances of *tûšiyyâ* in collections I (three times) and II (once) do not show any literary resemblance between the two collections, and are considered insufficient to establish a link between them.

B. *Nĕtîbâ* "path" (six times)[81]

Nĕtîbâ occurs 21 times in the OT, always in poetic texts: six times in Proverbs, four times each in Job and Isaiah, twice each in Psalms and Jeremiah, and once each in Judges, Hosea, and Lamentations. One peculiar aspect of the usage of *nĕtîbâ* in Proverbs is that, it always occurs in the second colon in synonymous parallelism with *ʾōraḥ* (8:20; 12:28) and *derek* (1:15; 3:17; 7:25; 8:2). This phenomenon implies that the semantic role of *nĕtîbâ* in those instances is dependent on the parallel word in the first colon. Delitzsch attempts to define the relationship of the three synonymous words, *derek*, *ʾōraḥ*, and *nĕtîbâ*, according to their occurrences in Job 6:18, Jer 18:15, and Isa 43:16. The hierarchical order established by him is that *derek* always means the way in general and smaller ways are denoted by *ʾŏrḥôt* or *nĕtîbôt*.[82] As we have pointed out in earlier discussion, *maʿgāl* is another term in Proverbs to denote a branch way off the main road. Then, we can put the four terms in the following order: *derek*, *ʾōraḥ*, and *nĕtîbâ/maʿgāl*.

Like its other synonyms, *nĕtîbâ* is used in a neutral sense to refer to a path of both negative and positive characters. However, when it is used in a positive context, *nĕtîbâ* is associated with best qualities of life: "all her (wisdom's) ways (*nĕtîbôtêhā*) are peace" (3:17), "I (wisdom) walk in the way of righteousness, in the middle of the paths (*nĕtîbôt*) of justice" (8:20), and "In the way of righteousness is life, and immortality (in) a way, a path (*nĕtîbâ*)" (12:28).[83]

The only instance of *nĕtîbâ* in collection II (12:28) is insufficient to establish a link between collections I and II.

C. *Qālôn* "shame" (eight times)[84]

Qālôn is found 17 times in the OT, all in poetic texts. In Wisdom books it occurs nine times: eight times in Proverbs and once in Job. The noun also occurs seven times in Prophets (twice in Hosea, twice in Jeremiah, and once each in Isaiah, Habakkuk, and Nahum), mainly in reference to the Israelite exile as a shameful event to come in near future. The use of *qālôn* in Proverbs is to denote a painful emotion caused by a sense of guilt or embarrassment, and in this sense it is inevitably associated with negative conducts or persons, such as fools (3:35), adultery (6:33), a scornful man (9:7; 22:10), pride (11:2), and one who rejects instruction (13:18).

A link between collections I and II is indicated by the use of *qālôn* in 6:33 and 18:3. In the first text the father warns the son that an adulterer will never escape shame (*qālôn*) and disgrace (*ḥerpâ*). The two words occur again in the same order in 18:3 in reference to a wicked man. Considering the fact that *ḥerpâ* appears only twice in Proverbs, the occurrences of *qālôn* and *ḥerpâ* as pair words in 6:33 and 18:3 are viewed as the same wisdom diction. Similarly, the association of the *lēṣ* with *qālôn* in 9:7 and 22:10 reflect the same wisdom expression in collections I and II.

D. *Šĕ'ēr* "flesh" (twice)[85]

Šĕ'ēr occurs 16 times in the OT: six times in Leviticus, three times in Psalms, twice each in Proverbs and Micah, and once each in Exodus, Numbers, and Jeremiah. Regarding the use of the word in Semitic languages, Avi Hurvitz points out that both in Akkadian and Ugaritic *šĕ'ēr* is paired with "blood" in synonymous parallelism as "flesh//blood."[86] The pairing of flesh and blood (*šĕ'ēr* and *dām*) is also found in Jer 51:35. In the OT one significant phenomenon observed in the distribution of *šĕ'ēr* is that the noun does not occur at all in late biblical books. Hurvitz, following Ben Iehuda who explains that *šĕ'ēr* was replaced by *bāśār* in late Hebrew and by *biśrâ* in late Aramaic, points out that *šĕ'ēr* disappears not only in late Hebrew but also in late Aramaic.[87] The disappearance of *šĕ'ēr* in late biblical books indicates that the two instances of the noun in Proverbs (5:11; 11:17) are the reflection of old Hebrew tradition. Although no literary affinity is found between 5:11 and 11:17, the exclusive occurrence of *šĕ'ēr* in the two places in Proverbs may be a sign for the close relationship between collections I and II.

E. *Miṣwâ* "commandment" (ten times)[88]

Miṣwâ occurs 181 times in the OT, and its distribution shows that it occurs frequently in Deuteronomy (43 times) but it is rarely used by prophets (only ten times in the 15 Prophetic books). Another aspect of the noun in its use in the OT is that *miṣwâ* is used mainly to denote God's command. Its use for a human command is much less (e.g., a king's command in 2 Kgs 18:36 and a father's instruction in Jer 35:14). Rarely, the noun also denotes binding conditions imposed by a legal transaction as in Jeremiah's purchase of his cousin Hanamel's field (Jer 32:11).

In Proverbs *miṣwâ* occurs seven times in collection I and three times in collection II. The main difference in the usage of *miṣwâ* in the two collections is that, while it refers to the instruction of the parents in collection I (except in 6:23), it occurs independently in collection II. The unattached form of *miṣwâ* in collection II is thus possible to be understood in two ways: *miṣwâ* as God's commandment or as the instruction of wise men. For example, in "He who fears *miṣwâ* will be rewarded" (13:13), *miṣwâ* could be understood either in the secular wisdom context or in the context of Israelite religion. For two reasons, however, it can be argued that *miṣwâ* in 13:13 refers to God's commandment. First, in 13:13 *miṣwâ* is connected to *yārē'*, the participle of *yr'* "to fear," and functions as the object of the participle. The reason that *miṣwâ* must be understood as God's commandment is due to the peculiar usage of *yr'* in Proverbs. The root *yr'* occurs 22 times in Proverbs: 14 times in the phrase "fear of the Lord" and eight times as a finite verb or participle. What is striking with regard to the usage of the root *yr'* is that God is predominantly the object of the act "to fear" in those 22 instances (18 times). In two instances (3:25; 31:21), the objects of *yr'* are "terror" and "snow," and in 14:16 the object is unspecified. Apart from 13:13, at least one thing is clear: the instruction of wise men is never the object "to fear" in Proverbs. Considering the fact that the use of the root *yr'* in reference to God is overwhelming, and that the sage or his instruction is never the object to fear, it seems that *miṣwâ* in 13:13 refers to a divine command, not the instruction of wise men. Second, the possibility of a religious reading of 13:13 is reinforced by *yěšullam* "he will be rewarded." Although a secular understanding of the verb is possible if one chooses to understand the implication of the verb as the benefits of moral living, a religious understanding is equally possible in the sense that God will bless one who obeys him, like in the following example: "the Lord will reward (*yešallem*) you" (25:22d).

We now turn to the occurrence of *miṣwâ* in 6:23 which is the only instance of the word appearing unattached to the parents in collection I. A religious reading is also possible for *miṣwâ* and *tôrâ* in 6:23, despite the association of the two terms with the parents in 6:20, "father's command (*miṣwâ*)" and "mother's instruction (*tôrâ*)." In 6:23 (the parents') *miṣwâ* and *tôrâ* are compared to *nēr* "lamp" and *'ôr* "light." This comparison clearly echoes the description of God's word in Ps 119:105, "Your word is a lamp (*nēr*) to my feet and a light (*'ôr*) for my path." It is thus possible to say that the functional aspect of the parental teaching is the same as that of God's word to guide one in his/her life. The resemblance between Prov 6:23 and Ps 119:105 indicates that the parental instruction is to the son what God's instruction is to Israelites. That the parents' instruction plays the role of God's word to their son is proper because they are God-fearing parents and because their desire is to make the son fear God (cf. 2:5; 3:5). At any rate, our point is that a religious tone is inherent in 6:23 because the father uses the language related to God's instruction (*miṣwâ* and *tôrâ* in comparison to *nēr* "lamp" and *'ôr* "light"). Understanding *miṣwâ* as a mere human instruction ignores the religious setting involving the Israelite parents and Israelite home education.

The same can be said of *miṣwâ* in 19:16, "He who keeps a *command* keeps his life, he who despises his ways will die." It is possible that the noun refers to the sage's command, but it is equally possible in this case that it refers to God's Torah.[89]

These examples illustrate that the secular interpretation of the sayings in

Proverbs is sometimes by choice not by necessity. Since our position under the governing principles is that almost all the characters appearing in Proverbs are Israelites, we emphasize that religious interpretation must be heard whenever it is possible. James L. Crenshaw also emphasizes the inherent religious aspect of Proverbs in the following way: ". . . wisdom contained a religious element from the beginning."[90]

Finally, in order to understand other aspects of *miṣwâ*, we want to examine the verbs which are used in association with the noun. It is noted that, when *miṣwâ* is given to a person, the recipient is commanded with the following verbs: *ṣpn* "to store" (2:1; 7:1), *nṣr* "to keep" (3:1; 6:20), and *šmr* "to keep" (4:4; 7:2; 19:16). The verbs reveal an important aspect of *miṣwâ* that the instruction represented by the noun is not a short-term but enduring instruction that requires constant obedience. Another aspect of *miṣwâ* is that it requires a respectful response from a person. It is said in 13:13 that one who *fears* a command (*miṣwâ*) will be rewarded.

The difference between collections I and II in using *miṣwâ* is that the noun almost always refers to the instruction of the parents in collection I while it occurs independently in collection II.

F. Ṣĕdāqâ "righteousness" (18 times)[91]

Table 1.6
The Derivatives of the Root Ṣdq

Word	Freq.	Meaning	I	II	III	IV	V	VI	VII
ṣdq	41/1	to be just	1						
ṣĕdāqâ	158/18	righteousness	2	16					
ṣedeq	119/9	righteousness	5	2			1		1
ṣaddiq	206/66	righteous	4	49	3	1	9		

Table 1.6 shows that the root *ṣdq* occurs predominantly in collection II (68 times in collection II and 26 times in all other collections). The high frequency of *ṣdq*-words in collection II is largely because the collection contains the sayings which describe the contrasting lifestyles of the righteous and the wicked.

Ṣĕdāqâ occurs 158 times in the OT. The term occurs rarely in the Pentateuch (9 times) and Historical books (11 times), while its occurrence is far more frequent in Prophets (74 times) and Psalms (34 times). This distribution implies the double semantic realms of the term: the ethical realm based on God's word preached by prophets and the cultic realm practiced in the temple.

Ṣĕdāqâ occurs 18 times in Proverbs, and the number is the fourth highest in the OT after Isaiah (36 times), Psalms (34 times), and Ezekiel (20 times). The use of *ṣĕdāqâ* in collection I is unique in the sense that it is associated with the personified Wisdom: wealth, glory, and *righteousness* are with Wisdom (8:18), and she walks in the path of *righteousness* (8:20). It is interesting to note in 8:18 that *ṣĕdāqâ* is listed, along with wealth (*ʿōšer*), glory (*kābôd*), and riches (*hôn*), as a reward of Wisdom for those who find her. The juxtaposed relationship of the four words indicates that *ṣĕdāqâ* is a valuable and honorable quality which is comparable to wealth and glory. In 8:20, *ṣĕdāqâ* is paired with *mišpāṭ*, and the pairing of the two terms is clearly in line with their usage in the OT. In view of the fact that the two words comprise the central part of the Lord's requirement to Israel, Wisdom, walking in the path of *ṣĕdāqâ* and *mišpāṭ*, must be understood as an exemplary figure who fulfills God's requirement. In this sense, it can be said that the association of Wisdom with *ṣĕdāqâ* and *mišpāṭ* places her in the center of the Israelite religion.

If one wonders what benefits righteousness can bring in life, the instances of *ṣĕāqâ* in collection II will provide a good understanding of the importance of the term. The four important functions of *ṣĕdāqâ* are to save from death, to give life, to provide protection, and to give honor:

Ṣĕdāqâ to save from death:	10:2; 11:4, 6
Ṣddāqâ and life:	11:19; 12:28; 21:21
Ṣĕdāqâ and protection/security	11:5, 18; 13:6; 14:34; 16:12
Ṣĕdāqâ to give honor:	16:31; 21:21

Several sayings in which *ṣĕdāqâ* occurs will be discussed bellow to point out that righteousness in those sayings is understood better in the context of Israelite religion than in the secular context. First of all, the occurrence of *ṣĕdāqâ* in two God-sayings makes it obvious that the term belongs to Israelite religion: "He (the Lord) loves one who follows righteousness" (15:9b), and "Doing righteousness and justice (*mišpāṭ*) is more preferable to the Lord than sacrifice" (21:3). It is said in the three instances in collection II (10:2; 11:4, 6) that *ṣĕdāqâ* is able to rescue people from death. It is however not immediately clear what kind of death is meant in those texts. A secular reading of the three texts (10:2; 11:4, 6) would understand the death as premature death resulting from one's own unwise lifestyle. However, 11:4a can provide a clue for the nature of the death in 11:4b and possibly in 10:2b as well. The two sayings, 10:2 and 11:4, are parallels, but 11:4 contains a phrase which is not found in 10:2: "Wealth does not profit *on the day of wrath*, but righteousness saves from death." In 11:4a the phrase that can provide a clue for the nature of death in 11:4b is *yôm ʿebrâ* "the day of wrath." As far as 11:4 is concerned, it is natural to say that the nature of the death hinges on the meaning of the *day of wrath*. The interpretation of the day of wrath is divided into two: some interpret the expression as referring to a life-threatening disaster in general,[92] and others suggest that its underlying meaning is God's judgment day or at least the same idea adapted in a wisdom setting.[93] The comparison of the following texts shows three common elements: the ineffective power of wealth, the verb "to save" (*nṣl*), and "the day of wrath."

Ezek 7:19   "Neither their silver nor their gold can save (*nṣl*) them on
                    the day of the Lord's wrath (*yôm ʿebrat YHWH*)"
Zeph 1:17   "Neither their silver nor their gold can save (*nṣl*) them on
                    the day of the Lord's wrath (*yôm ʿebrat YHWH*)"

Prov 11:4   "Wealth does not profit on the day of wrath (*yôm ʿebrat*),
                   but righteousness saves (*nṣl*) from death"

The same theme and the literary similarities in the three texts lead to the inevitable conclusion that the day of wrath in Prov 11:4 is a short form of "the day of the Lord's wrath." Moreover, in view that "the day of wrath" (*yôm ʿebrâ*) in Zeph 1:15 refers to "the great day of the Lord" in Zeph 1:14, it is possible that the same phrase in Prov 11:4 also conveys the notion of the day of the Lord. Consequently, the death in Prov 11:4 is to be interpreted in the context of God's judgment.

Besides "the day of death," the religious aspect of the three sayings (10:2; 11:4, 6) can be explained from another angle. The context of the three sayings indicates that death or salvation takes place on the day of the wrath in relation to two morally opposing groups, one group represented by *ṣĕdāqâ* or *yĕšārîm* and the other by *rešaʿ* or *bōgĕdîm*. According to R. B. Y. Scott, classifying people as the righteous or the wicked is basically a religious act. He points out that the sayings about the righteous and wicked in Proverbs mainly refer to "religious belief and non-belief and corresponding character and behavior" because "the criterion for the division is acceptance or rejection of obedience to Yahweh's commandments, both cultic and ethical."[94] Since the two opposing classifications (the righteous and the wicked) are based on one's obedience or disobedience to the law of the Lord, understanding the righteous and the wicked who occur in Proverbs only as morally positive or negative persons without religious connotations is not sufficient.

The usage of *ṣĕdāqâ* in collections I and II shows that, while collection I focuses on Wisdom's relation to righteousness, the functional aspects of righteousness are emphasized in collection II.

G. Ḥārûṣ "gold" (four times)[95]

Table 1.7
Words for Gold

Word VII	Freq.	Meaning	I	II	III	IV	V	VI
ḥārûṣ	6/4	gold	3	1				
ketem	9/1	gold					1	
paz	9/1	pure gold	1					
zāhāb	387/7	gold		4			3	

Table 1.7 reveals several phenomena in regard to the use of the terms for gold in Proverbs. First, four different terms for gold are used in Proverbs, and their occurrence is confined to the three major collections (I, II, and V).[96] The absence

of "gold" and "silver" in the smaller collections may be ascribed to the subject matter. Secondly, it seems that each of the three major collections has a favorite term for gold: *ḥārûṣ* is used mainly in collection I and *zāhāb* is used in collections II and V.

Collection I	*ḥārûṣ* (three times)
Collection II	*zāhāb* (four times)
Collection V	*zāhāb* (three times)

Thirdly, collection I is separated from the other two main collections by the fact that *zāhāb*, the most general term for gold in the OT, is completely absent in the collection. Considering the 387 occurrences of *zāhāb* in the OT, the lack of the term in collection I is considered peculiar. Another table is presented below to show the peculiar distribution of the three rare terms for gold in the OT (*ḥārûṣ*, *ketem*, and *paz*).

Table 1.8
Distribution of the Three Terms for Gold in the OT

	ḥārûṣ	*ketem*	*paz*
Isaiah		13:12	13:12
Psalms	68:14	45:10	19:11; 21:4; 119:127
Job		28:16, 19; 31:24	28:17
Proverbs	3:14; 8:10, 19; 16:16	25:12	8:19
Song		5:11	5:11, 15
Lam.		4:1	4:2
Daniel		10:5	
Zech.	9:3		

It is observed in the table that all the instances of the three terms are in poetic texts except *ketem* in Dan 10:5, and that two of the terms tend to occur together in the same place. For example, both *ketem* and *paz* occur together in Isa 13, Job 28, Song 5, and Lam 4. A further examination of the instances reveals that the gold represented by the three terms seems not to be real but to refer to legendary or imaginary gold to convey the notion of glory, opulence, or rarity. It is striking that they are never used to refer to any actual golden products in narrative texts.[97] For example, Isaiah prophesies a disaster against Babylon, using two terms for gold: "I (the Lord) will make man rarer than pure gold (*paz*) and human rarer than the gold (*ketem*) of Ophir" (Isa 13:12). On the basis of Isa 13:12 and the passages cited in the table, it is possible to conclude that the three types of gold serve as a symbol for rarity and preciousness, and that therefore in the OT they exist only in the unrealistic world of poetry and wisdom.

Ḥārûṣ is exclusive to collections I and II. Unlike *zāhāb* which is not found in some Semitic languages, *ḥārûṣ* is an ancient word attested in Akkadian, Ugaritic, and Phoenician.[98] The instances of *ḥārûṣ* in Zechariah, Psalms, Proverbs, and Ben Sira imply that the word has survived mainly in a poetic or wisdom text. The use of *ḥārûṣ* in collections I and II is consistent. It always occurs in the same structure and in the same context: it occurs in synonymous parallelism with *kesep* "silver" in a comparative sentence in order to emphasize the superior value of wisdom to *ḥārûṣ* and *kesep*.

H. *Rāṣôn* "favor" (14 times)[99]

Rāṣôn occurs 56 times in the OT. In Proverbs four different words occur in antithetic parallelism with *rāṣôn*: *tahpûkâ* "perversity" (10:32), *tôʿēbâ* "abhorrence" (11:1, 20; 12:22; 15:8), *ʿebrâ* "anger" (14:35), and *zaʿap* "rage" (19:12). These antonyms indicate that the central semantic aspect of *rāṣôn* is acceptance or a favorable feeling. Of the 14 instances of *rāṣôn* in Proverbs, seven times it refers to the favor of the Lord (8:35; 11:1, 20; 12:2, 22; 15:8; 18:22), four times the favor of a king (14:35; 16:13, 15; 19:12), and three times the favor for morally good people (10:32; 11:27; 14:9). Although *rāṣôn* is sometimes used in a neutral sense in the OT as in Esth 1:8, "to do according to the pleasure (*rāṣôn*) of each man," in Proverbs the term is used mainly in connection with religious or morally good persons, except in 16:15 and 19:12. Since *rāṣôn* occurs in two identical verses (8:35b=18:22b, "and he obtains favor from the Lord"), a link between the two collections is certain.

I. *Leqaḥ* "learning, persuasiveness" (six times)[100]

Leqaḥ occurs nine times in the OT: six times in Proverbs and once each in Isaiah, Deuteronomy, and Job. The nine instances of *leqaḥ* show that the narrow meaning of the noun is difficult to identify with exactness. Outside Proverbs the noun occurs in synonymous parallelism with *bînâ* "understanding" (Isa 29:24) and *ʾimrâ* "saying" (Deut 32:2), and in Proverbs the strange woman tries to seduce a young man with much of her *leqaḥ* (7:21), a father can give good *leqaḥ* to a son (4:2), and *leqaḥ* can be increased by hearing wisdom or teaching (1:5; 9:9; 16:21, 23). The literary milieus in which *leqaḥ* occurs reveal several aspects of the noun. First, *leqaḥ* occurs four times as the object of the verb *ysp* "to add, increase" (1:5; 9:9; 16:21, 23), with a wise man or a righteous man as the subject (1:5; 9:9; 16:21, 23). However, this should not be interpreted in such a way that only morally good people can possess *leqaḥ*. Contrary to this, the adulterous woman in 7:21 also possesses much of *leqaḥ*. Second, *śāpâ* "lip" occurs three times in association with *leqaḥ* (7:21; 16:21, 23), clearly indicating that the nature of *leqaḥ* is to be verbalized in speech, and that, in order to make *leqaḥ* effective, it must be heard or taught (1:5; 4:1–2; 9:9). Third, it appears that the father (4:2), adulterous woman (7:21), the wise man (1:5; 16:23), and the righteous man (9:9) are already in possession of *leqaḥ*.

On the basis of the instances of *leqaḥ* in Proverbs, we suggest that the noun denotes to a body of knowledge which can be effective only through speech to others. The occurrences of *leqaḥ* in Prov 7:21 and Isa 29:24 indicate that the purpose of the verbalized *leqaḥ* is to make the other agree to the speaker. Also, the close association of *leqaḥ* with the verb *ysp* is understood that the noun does not denote an innate talent but knowledge that can be expanded through learning (hearing).

The association of *leqaḥ* with the verb *ysp* in 1:5; 9:9; 16:21, 23 shows that its use in collections I and II is consistent.

J. *Lwz* "to turn aside" (five times)[101]

Lwz is a rare verb, occurring only six times in the entire OT, mainly in Proverbs (five times). Its synonymous relation to the verb *ʿqš* "to twist" (2:15) and antithetic relation to the verbs *nṣr* "to keep" (3:21), *yšr* "to be straight" (3:32; 14:2), and *šmr* "to keep" (4:21) indicate that *lwz* denotes a failure to be in a right place or a failure to be straight.

The two facts that *lwz* as a rare verb is exclusive to collections I and II, and that the three words, the Lord, *nālôz*, and *yšr*, are commonly found in the two God-sayings (3:34; 14:2) indicates the coherent use of the verb in the two collections.

K. *Qrṣ* "to nip, pinch" (three times)[102]

Qrṣ is another rare verb which occurs only five times in the OT (three times in Proverbs and once each in Psalms and Job). The use of the verb in connection with eyes or lips as the objects to nip or pinch is consistent in the OT, except in Job. In Ps 35:19; Prov 6:13; 10:10; 16:30, the acts denoted by *qrṣ* are understood as a kind of body language (e.g., winking the eye or compressing the lips) to express mockery to others.

A link between collections I and II is indicated by the use of *qrṣ* in association with the eye in 6:13 and 10:10.

L. *Nsḥ* "to pull, tear" (twice)[103]

The verb *nsḥ* occurs only four times in the OT: twice in Proverbs and once each in Deuteronomy and Psalms. Although the subject of the verb is not mentioned in Deut 28:63, God is clearly understood as the subject of the action "pulling." In Prov 2:22b *nsḥ* in the *qal* poses difficulty for translation. The context and its synonymous relationship with *yikkārētû* "they will be cut off" in 2:22a demand the *qal* form to be vocalized as a passive form. In that case God is understood as the subject of "pulling" as in Deut 28:63, because *ʾĕlōhîm* is already mentioned a few lines earlier in Prov 22:17. Moshe Weinfeld, who holds a strong view that Deuteronomy has been influenced by Wisdom books, points out that the verb, a Hebrew counterpart of Akkadian *nasāḫu* "to exile," connotes the idea of "ejection from the land" in Deuteronomy and Proverbs.[104] Although a secular understanding of *nsḥ* is not impossible in Prov 2:22, the Deuteronomic tradition of the land is undoubtedly echoed in Prov 2:21–22: "The upright will dwell in the land, and the blameless will remain in it. But the wicked will be cut off from the land, and the unfaithful will be uprooted from it." A religious reading of Prov 2:21–22 is supported by R. N. Whybray who explains that the land in 2:21–22 must refer to the land which was promised and then given to Israel by the Lord.[105] In 15:24 the Lord is described as tearing down (*nsḥ*) the house of the proud, while preserving the widow's landmark.

Although the two instances of *nsḥ* in collections I and II are insufficient to establish a link between the two collections, the use of the rare verb in connection with God in 2:22 and 15:25 does not appear accidental.

M. *Ḥrš* "to plow, devise" (seven times)[106]

Proverbs is distinguished from other books in the OT in regard to the frequency and meaning of *ḥrš*. As to the frequency, the verb occurs 27 times in 13 books of the OT, but it never occurs more than twice in any book except Proverbs (seven times). The meaning of *ḥrš* is basically "to engrave," "to plow," or "to devise." One notable phenomenon about the meaning of the verb is that, while *ḥrš* denotes the first two meanings in other books ("to engrave" or "to plow"), the last meaning "to devise" in connection with evil or good is found only in Proverbs, except 1 Sam 23:9. This phenomenon suggests that the third meaning ("to devise, plan") is a metaphorical meaning which may have been developed in wisdom circles. In six of its seven instances in Proverbs, *ḥrš* denotes an act of planning an evil or a good thought. For negative use, the verb occurs in connection with *ra ʿ* "evil," *rā ʿâ* "evil" (3:29; 6:14; 12:20; 14:22) or *maḥšĕbôt ʾāwen* "sinful thoughts" (6:18). Once it is used positively in 14:22b ("Kindness and faithfulness are for those who *plan* good"). In Proverbs the only instance in which it denotes an agricultural meaning "to plow" is in 20:4 ("a sluggard does not plow [*ḥrš*] in early winter").

The consistent use of *ḥrš* in collections I and II is evidently indicated by the association of the verb with *ra ʿ* or *rā ʿâ* in 3:29; 6:14; 12:20; 14:22 and by the formulaic phrasing, *lēb* + participle of *ḥrš* + *ra ʿ*, in 6:14 and 12:20.

The use of 13 exclusive words in collections I and II have been examined above. Many of those words are words of low frequency in the OT, but occur mainly in the two collections. The examination shows no significant difference between the two collections in regard to the usage of the words. On the other hand, coherence of the two collections is indicated by the consistent use of the words in the same phraseologies and contexts. Although collection I is distinguished from other collections because of its characteristic essay-type sayings, the exclusive occurrence of the rare words and the same usage of some of the words in collections I and II indicate the coherent aspects of the wisdom vocabulary in the two collections.

(3) The Relationship
between Collections I, II, and III

a. Verbs (11)

אָרַב	26/6	to ambush	I-3	II-1	III-2
הָגָה	25/3	to moan	I-1	II-1	III-1
כָּרַת	285/4	to cut off	I-1	II-1	III-2
לִיץ	28/18	to mock	I-6	II-11	III-1
מָלֵא	250/7	to be full	I-4	II-2	III-1
נָטָה	185/12	to stretch	I-8	II-3	III-1
נָצַל	213/12	to rescue	I-4	II-6	III-2
רָעַע	93/6	to be evil	I-1	II-3	III-2
רָפָה	46/3	to relax	I-1	II-1	III-1
רָצָה	56/3	to be pleased	I-1	II-1	III-1
תָּקַע	68/4	to clap	I-1	II-2	III-1

b. Adjectives/Nouns (15)

אֹמֶר	55/22	word	I-14	II-5	III-3
אֹרַח	59/19	way	I-12	II-6	III-1
בָּשָׂר	270/4	flesh	I-2	II-1	III-1
חַטָּא	19/3	sinful	I-1	II-1	III-1
חַטָּאת	221/7	sin	I-1	II-5	III-1
יָקָר	36/5	precious	I-3	II-1	III-1
יִרְאָה	44/14	fear	I-5	II-8	III-1
יֵשׁ	138/13	existence	I-2	II-9	III-2
כֹּחַ	125/5	strength	I-1	II-2	III-2
מְזִמָּה	19/8	plan	I-5	II-2	III-1
נָוֶה	32/3	abode	I-1	II-1	III-1
רֹב	151/12	abundance	I-2	II-9	III-1
שֵׂכֶל	16/6	prudence	I-1	II-4	III-1
תַּהְפֻּכָה	10/9	perversity	I-4	II-4	III-1
תַּחְבֻּלָה	6/5	counsel	I-1	II-3	III-1

An examination of the exclusive words to find links between the three collections would be an interesting and challenging task, because the first two collections are ascribed to the Israelite king Solomon while collection III is ascribed to unknown wise men. The commonly accepted view that there is a strong connection between collection III and Egyptian wisdom material could create an anticipation that the wisdom climate of collection III would not be similar to that of the two collections.[107] Such an anticipation will make the investigation of the exclusive words in the three collections interesting to see how collection III will fare with the two Solomonic collections. The number of words that are exclusive to the three collections is 26 (11 verbs and 15 adjectives and nouns), and the use of eight exclusive words in the three collections will be examined below.

A. *Tahpûkâ* "perversity" (nine times)[108]

Tahpûkâ occurs ten times in the OT, and nine of them are in Proverbs. The only instance of the word outside Proverbs is in the Song of Moses (Deut 32:20), a poem known for its numerous linguistic affinities to Wisdom books, especially, to Proverbs.[109] In Proverbs the perverse quality denoted by *tahpûkâ* is used in connection with speech (2:12; 8:13; 10:31, 32; 23:33) and a person's disposition or mind (2:14; 6:14; 16:28, 30). A distinctive aspect of the word is that it always occurs in the plural form.[110] The association of *tahpûkâ* with the mouth (8:13; 10:32), tongue (10:31), and the verb *dbr* "to speak" (2:12) indicates that the sage's concern is not only a perverse character but also a perverse speech, such as a false testimony or a lie intended to harm others. It is interesting to note that *tahpûkâ* is also used in connection with the speech of a drunkard whose mind is impaired by alcoholic influence. In this case, the noun highlights the incoherent aspect of a drunken man's speech.

The fact that *tahpûkâ* is almost exclusive to collections I, II, and III in the entire OT is sufficient to suggest coherency between the three collections. The consistent use of the noun in the three collections is indicated by the association of *tahpûkâ* with the speaking organs, the mouth and tongue, in 8:13; 10:31, 32 (I and II) and the same expression, "speaking (*dbr*) *tahpukôt*," in 2:12; 23:33 (I and III).

B. *Tahbûlâ* "steering, guidance" (five times)[111]

Tahbûlâ is another word that occurs only in the plural in poetic books. It occurs six times in the OT: only in the two Wisdom books (five times in Proverbs and once in Job 37:12). The three occurrences of *tahbûlâ* in Ben Sira (6:25; 35:16; 37:17) greatly enhance the possibility that the noun belongs to the wisdom vocabulary. In light of the root *hbl* "to bind" and the nouns *hebel* "rope" and *hōbēl* "sailor," the basic meaning of *taḥbûlâ* is understood as linked to a sailor's skill to steer a boat through troubled waters.[112] Applying the notion of steering a boat to wisdom, W. Zimmerli explains that the sapiential use of *taḥbulôt* conveys the steering skill of a boat to master the reality which one encounters in life.[113]

Of the five instances of *taḥbulôt* in Proverbs, it occurs once in collection I (1:5): "a discerning person will gain guidance (*taḥbulôt*)." This instance of the noun in the introduction of Proverbs implies that, although it is not found in the OT except in Job 37:12, the editor of collection I was aware of the presence of the rare term in the following sections of the book. Twice *taḥbulôt* occurs in the context of warfare, referring to plans for war: "Wage war with *taḥbulôt*!" (20:18b) and "For you are to wage war with *taḥbulôt*" (24:6a). In 11:14 *taḥbulôt* denotes a national policy: "Without *taḥbulôt* a people falls." However, in 12:5 *taḥbulôt* is used in association with the wicked to make a contrast to the righteous: "The thought (*maḥšěbôt*) of the righteous is justice, the *taḥbulôt* of the wicked are deceit." The negative use of *taḥbulôt* in 12:5 has caught the attention of W. McKane who holds the view that the old wisdom material had been reinterpreted by Yahwistic piety in Proverbs. Of the instance of the noun in 12:5, he explains that in old wisdom *taḥbulôt* and *maḥăšābôt* are akin but in 12:5 a pejorative meaning is given to *taḥbulôt* to make it stand against *maḥăšābôt*. According to him, the shift from a positive to a negative meaning is due to the Yahwistic reinterpretation of the old wisdom.[114] McKane, however, appears to have overlooked the fact that the connotation of *maḥăšābôt* also shifts from positive to negative in 15:26, "The plans (*maḥšěbôt*) of an evil person are an abomination to the Lord." F. M. Wilson notes the failure of McKane, and points out that, since *taḥbûlôt* and *maḥšěbôt* in wisdom literature are ethically neutral with no inherent moral value, McKane's reinterpretation theory is not valid.[115] The instance of *taḥbulôt* in 12:5 is a clear example to show that the noun is a neutral term that can be used in reference to both good and bad people.

We now return to the use of *taḥbulôt* in collections I, II and III. The following three sayings taken from collections II and III show a remarkable relationship between them:

20:18b	*ûbětaḥbulôt ʿăśê milḥāmâ*
	"and wage war with strategies!"
11:14b	*ûtěšûʿâ běrōb yôʿēṣ*
	"but victory is in a multitude of counselors"
24:6ab	*kî bětaḥbulôt taʿăśê lěka milḥāmâ*
	ûtěšûʿâ běrōb yôʿēṣ
	"for you are to wage war with strategies,
	and victory is in a multitude of counselors"

The comparison indicates the relationship between the three texts in the following way, 20:18b + 11:14b = 24:6. There is no way of knowing whether the two sayings from collection II (20:18b; 11:14b) are the results of partial borrowing from the saying from collection III (24:6), or conversely two originally self-contained lines (20:18b; 11:14b) were taken up by an editor to form a single saying in 24:6. Regardless of the direction of influence between the three texts, it is clear that there is a connection between collections II (20:18b; 11:14b) and III (24:6).

In addition to this, it is probable that the editor of collection I (or the author of the introduction in 1:1–6) who used *taḥbulôt* in the introduction of the book (1:5) had known the instances of the term in collections II and III. In this sense it could be suggest that the instances of *taḥbulôt* in the three collections are linked.

C. *Mĕzimmâ* "discretion, scheme" (eight times)[116]

Mĕzimmâ occurs 19 times in the OT: eight times in Proverbs, five times in Psalms, four times in Jeremiah, and twice in Job. The meaning of *mĕzimmâ* "plan" is understood as neutral, and its moral value as good or bad is dependent upon the context in which it occurs. Of the 19 instances of *mĕzimmâ* in the OT, nine times the word refers to prudence in the wisdom context or the plan of God (Prov 1:4; 2:11; 3:21; 5:2; 8:12; Jer 23:20; 30:24; 51:11; Job 42:2) and ten times it refers to a wicked plan of people in general or morally negative people (Prov 12:2; 14:17; 24:8; Pss 10:2, 4; 21:12; 37:7; 139:20; Job 21:27; Jer 11:15).

In Proverbs *mĕzimmâ* denotes both a positive and a negative meaning. It occurs in collection I with a positive a meaning in synonymous parallelism with *ʿormâ* (1:4; 8:12), *tĕbûnâ* (2:11), *tûšiyyâ* (3:21), and *daʿat* (5:2; 8:12). On the other hand, its use in collections II and III is negative (12:2; 14:17; 24:8). For example, the phrase *ʾîš mĕzimmôt* is paired with *qĕṣar ʾappayim* "a quick-tempered person" in 14:17. *Mĕzimmâ* is another term which McKane uses to explain his Yahwistic reinterpretation theory. According to him, *mĕzimmâ* belongs to the vocabulary of old wisdom and the pejorative meaning is due to a reinterpretation.[117] If we follow his view, then, the usage of *mĕzimmâ* in collection I represents the tradition of old wisdom and the three instances of the term in collections II and III (12:2; 14:17; 24:8) must be understood as the consequences of the reinterpretation. However, because of the fact that in Job and Jeremiah *mĕzimmâ* denotes both a positive and a negative meaning (e.g., a positive meaning in Job 42:2; Jer 23:20 and a negative meaning in Job 21:27; Jer 11:15), his explanation for the same phenomenon in Proverbs is questionable.

The usage of *mĕzimmâ* in collections II and III is consistent in two ways: it occurs in the three instances always in the plural, and it occurs in association with *ʾîš* (12:2; 14:17) or *baʿal* (24:8), both of which denote the same meaning "man of wicked schemes." Although the singular form of *mĕzimmâ* seems to be preferred in collection I, the plural form also occurs in 5:2 and 8:12, implying that the difference in the number is not significant.

D. *Yir'â* "fear" (14 times)[118]

Opinion differs as to how often *yir'â* is a noun or an infinitive in the OT.[119] Our examination of *yir'â* is based on Even-Shoshan's concordance where the form is taken as a noun occurring 44 times in the OT.

J. Becker, whose work is still considered one of the most thorough studies on the fear of God, points out that the phrase *yir'at YHWH* "fear of the Lord" in collection I of Proverbs occurs in close relationship with *da'at* "knowledge" (1:7, 29; 2:5; 9:10; cf. Isa 11:2; 33:6).[120] However, the reader of Proverbs should be reminded that the connotation of *da'at* in those instances is not always the same. For example, in the phrase *rē'šît da'at* "beginning of knowledge" in 1:7, the noun is undoubtedly synonymous with *ḥokmâ* "wisdom," but in the phrase *da'at qĕdōšîm* "knowledge of the Holy One" in 9:10 the noun connotes a pious attitude or aptitude.[121] According to Becker who classifies the fear of the Lord into three categories (cultic, moral, and nomistic), the expression *yir'at YHWH* in Proverbs denotes a moral idea toward God. Although his study has the merit of presenting the fear of God in an integrated way, certain passages involving *yir'at YHWH* do not fit well in his categories. For example, in his explanation of the relationship between the fear of God and the idea of retribution in collection II, he interprets that "little" in "little with the fear of the Lord" in 15:16 refers to the property that causes no trouble because it was gained through the fear of God. He thus concludes that the meaning of 15:16 is retributive and moral.[122] In this case, however, McKane's explanation seems to be more natural and reasonable than that of Becker. McKane understands "little with the fear of the Lord" as the state of being poor with the fear of the Lord, and explains that the intention of 15:16 is to give a positive religious value to poverty, that is, poverty is not always negative.[123] He finds support for his interpretation from Mark 10:25 where wealth is considered adverse to the fear of God. According to McKane's understanding which is considered better than that of Becker, the context of 15:16 in which *yir'at YHWH* occurs is religious, not moral.

A survey of the instances of the phrase *yir'at YHWH* in Proverbs shows one peculiar aspect of the use of the phrase, the emphasis of the functional aspect of *yir'at YHWH*. The intention of the sayings in which the phrase occurs is to educate the reader about the benefits that are rewarded by the fear of the Lord. One of the most important benefits of the fear of the Lord is stated in the motto of the book (1:7): "The fear of the Lord is the beginning (*rē'šît*) of knowledge." Of the several meanings of *re'šît* in the verse ("first in time," "chief part," and "the best part"), Fox considers that the temporal meaning, "first in time," is the best.[124] He also explains that the concern of 1:7 is to locate "the place of the fear of God in the learning process."[125] When understood in this way, the fear of God is the first requirement in learning, and only after one has acquired the fear of God, the person can go on to learn everything else, including wisdom (cf. 9:10;

15:33; 2:5).

Another benefit of the fear of the Lord is seen in the use of the phrase in reference to evil in two sayings: "The fear of the Lord is to hate evil" (8:13) and "Turning from evil is by the fear of the Lord" (16:6). These two sayings indicate that the function of the fear of the Lord is to provide one with motivation and ability to avoid evil. Three instances of *yir'at YHWH* testify that the fear of the Lord is the cause or source of (long) life (10:27; 14:27; 19:23). It is also said in another three sayings that the blessings of the fear of the Lord are "strong safety," "wealth, honor, and life," and "fulfillment of hope" (14:26; 22:4; 23:17). The functional aspects of the fear of the Lord in Proverbs may be summarized as follows:

The fear of the Lord to gain Wisdom	1:7; 2:5; 9:10; 15:33
The fear of the Lord to lengthen life	10:27; 14:27; 19:23
The fear of the Lord to avoid evil	8:13; 16:6
The fear of the Lord to gain blessings	14:26; 22:4; 23:17

Apart from the phrase *yir'at YHWH,* the same theme is also expressed in Proverbs by the use of the verb *yr'* with *YHWH* as its object (3:7; 14:2; 24:21). What is remarkable is the fact that the theme of fearing the Lord expressed by the noun and verb is exclusive to collections I, II, and III, implying that the presence of the theme in the three collections is not accidental. The coherence of the three collections is that they share the same religious aspect, specifically represented by the theme, "fear of the Lord." The only exception to this phenomenon is the occurrence of the same theme in 31:30, "she who fears the Lord will be praised." As commonly known, it is likely that the occurrence of "fear of the Lord" in 31:30 is due to an intentional insertion to form a literary inclusio in connection with 1:7.

One may ascribe the exclusive occurrence of the theme, the fear of the Lord, in collections I, II, and III to the redactor in a later period, but at any rate the final form of the book shows that the three collections are linked by the important theme.

E. *'rb* "to ambush" (six times)[126]

'rb occurs 41 times in the OT. It occurs with the meaning "to ambush" mainly in reference to military maneuvers (e.g., 7 times in Joshua, 14 times in Judges, and 3 times in 1 Samuel). In Proverbs the verb is used in two ways. First, *'rb* describes the ambush of the wicked to kill the innocent (1:11, 18; 12:6; 24:15).[127] In these four instances, *dām* "blood" occurs three times as the object of the verb (1:11, 18; 12:6). Second, the verb is also used to describe the lurking of the strange woman in wait of a victim (7:12; 23:28). The association of the verb with blood in collections I and II (1:11, 18; 12:6) indicates that the use of *'rb* in

the two collections is consistent, and the use of the verb in collections I and III (7:12; 23:28) to describe the adulterous woman as lying in wait for a young man clearly links the two collections.

F. *Lyṣ* "to speak boastfully" (18 times)[128]

As listed in BDB, *lēṣ* "mocker" is taken in this study as the participle of *lyṣ*, but *mēliṣ* "interpreter" is not included here because its derivation from *lyṣ* is not certain. The verb is found 23 times in the OT: 18 times in Proverbs, twice each in Isaiah and Psalms, and once in Hosea. Since the verb also occurs in Ben Sira (eight times) and Psalm 1 (a wisdom psalm), Shupak says that it belongs to the biblical wisdom vocabulary.[129] In Proverbs the root is predominantly used as substantive *lēṣ* (14 times) while occurring only four times as a finite verb. *Lēṣ* occurs in synonymous parallelism with *petî* "a naive fool" (1:22), *rāšāʿ* "a wicked person" (9:7), and *kĕsîl* "a fool" (1:22; 19:29) and in antithetic parallelism with *ḥākām* "a wise person" (9:8, 12; 13:1; 21:11) and *nābôn* "a discerning person" (14:6; 19:25).

Although the *lēṣ* "mocker" is known as the worst type of fool in Proverbs, M. V. Fox points out an interesting phenomenon that is overlooked by many. He notes that "the *lēṣ* may be apt to deride and mock others, but nowhere is he clearly shown doing so."[130] It is thus possible that one is called *lēṣ* not because of his mocking attitude to others in general but because of his scornful attitude toward his teacher (cf. 9:7, 8). Because of the mocker's close-mindedness to reproof, Shupak considers him incorrigible, and classifies the *lēṣ* as "worse than the *pĕtî* and the *kĕsîl*."[131]

Then, one may ask who this *lēṣ* is. In its first instance in 1:22, the *lēṣîm* are mentioned along with two other types of fool, *pĕtayim* "naive ones" and *kĕsîlîm* "fools," all of them as fools not responding positively to the invitation of Wisdom. If one assesses the *lēṣ* solely on the basis of 1:22–27, the mocker is not different from the other two types of fool in the sense that all of them have failed to recognize Wisdom's call. What makes the *lēṣ* unique among other fools is his defiant attitude shown in learning process. First of all, the *lēṣ* demonstrates hatred toward reproof. One who tries to instruct the mocker will experience shame (9:7). For this reason, one is advised in 9:8 not to try to reprove him: "Do not reprove a mocker, or he will hate you." It is his nature not to listen to a rebuke (13:1), and he does not like anyone who tries to correct him (15:12). A retributive idea is expressed in the punishment of the *lēṣ*: it is said in 3:34 that the Lord will mock (*yalîṣ*) the mockers (*lēṣîm*), and the mocker alone will bear the consequences of his conduct (9:12). Other negative aspects of the *lēṣ* are: he is an arrogant person (21:24) and a cause for strife (22:10). However, the *lēṣ* can be useful for the purpose of correcting other fools: when the *lēṣ* is punished, the *petî* will learn from the punishment and become wise (19:25; 21:11). In other words, the only usefulness of the *lēṣ* is to be a negative example for other fools not to follow. The description of the *lēṣ* in 24:9 seems to be perfect to summarize all the references of the mocker in Proverbs: "a mocker is an abomination to the humanity (*ʾādām*)."

Considering the fact that the participial form *lēṣ* occurs predominantly in Proverbs in the OT (14 out of 16 times), the occurrence of the participial form in collections I, II, and III is an indicator for the coherent aspect of the three collections.

G. *Tq* ᶜ "to strike the hands together" (four times)[132]

The verb *tq* ᶜ occurs 68 times in the OT. The significance of the verb in connection with wisdom is that in only five of the 68 instances *tq* ᶜ has the meaning "to clap the hands" in order to become a guarantor for others and the five instances are only in Wisdom books (four times in Proverbs and once in Job). This peculiar use of the verb in Proverbs and Job suggests that it is only in the wisdom circles that the verb is understood as a technical term for surety.

The four instances of the verb in Proverbs show the following peculiarities: it is used in association with *kap* "hand" (6:1; 17:18; 22:26), and it always occurs in synonymous parallelism with ᶜ*rb* "to pledge" (6:1; 11:15; 17:18; 22:26). These two peculiarities and its meaning found only in the wisdom context indicate the coherent aspect of collections I, II, and III that the three collections share the common wisdom language of surety.

H. *ʾōraḥ* "path" (19 times)[133]

ʾōraḥ occurs 59 times in the OT, 30 of which are in two Wisdom books (19 times in Proverbs and 11 times in Job). A survey of the instances of *ʾōraḥ* in the OT reveals that the noun belongs to poetic language. The only exception is the instance in Gen 18:11, but there also it is used not literally but figuratively: "for Sarah the way (*ʾōraḥ*) as a woman has ceased."

It is noted that *ʾōraḥ* is used in Proverbs in two distinctive ways. First, the path denoted by *ʾōraḥ* is rarely used for morally negative people (1:19; 2:15; 4:14; 22:25), but is used more frequently in association with words that denote rectitude or life:

ʾōraḥ + *mišpāṭ*	2:8; 17:23
ʾōraḥ + *yōšer, yāšār*	2:13; 15:19
ʾōraḥ + *ḥayyîm*	2:19; 5:6; 10:17; 12:28; 15:24
ʾōraḥ + *ṣaddîq, ṣĕdāqâ*	2:20; 4:18; 8:20; 12:28

Second, among its synonyms, *ʾōraḥ* is closer to *derek* than to two other synonyms, *maᶜgāl* and *nĕtîbâ*: the noun (*ʾōraḥ*) occurs eight times in synonymous parallelism with *derek* but only twice with each of the two synonyms.[134]

Also, the closer relationship of *ʾōraḥ* with *derek* than with *maʿgāl* and *nětîbâ* is implied in the order of the words in parallelism: while *maʿgāl* and *nětîbâ* always occur in the B colon in synonymous parallelism with *ʾōraḥ*, the position of *derek* with *ʾōraḥ* is equally divided between the A colon (2:20; 3:6; 9:15; 15:19) and B colon (2:8, 13; 4:14; 12:26).

In its 19 instances, *ʾōraḥ* occurs ten times in the plural and nine times in the singular. A survey of those instances indicates that the use of the plural or the singular may reflect the tendency of a collection rather than the actual significance of the number. For example, the plural form of *ʾōraḥ* seems to be more favored than the singular in collection I (eight times to four times) while the reversed phenomenon is observed in collection II (five times in the singular but only once in the plural). The use of *ʾōraḥ* in association with *ḥayyîm* indicates that the number of the noun is not to be taken strictly in exegesis. We find *ʾorḥôt ḥayyîm* in 2:19 but *ʾōraḥ ḥayyîm* in 5:6 and 15:24 (cf. 10:17), and it is doubtful whether the first phrase means "many paths of life," while the second means only one path of life.[135]

The use of *ʾōraḥ* in positive contexts is as follows: the Lord protects and makes straight the path of the just (2:8; 3:6), life and wisdom can be found in the path of righteousness (12:28; 8:20), and the path of life is for the wise and those who keep discipline (15:24; 10:17). In negative contexts, the evil paths are crooked (2:15), and they are the cause to lose life (1:19). Therefore, the son is commanded not to enter the path of the wicked (4:14). In 22:25 the son is also told not to associate with hot-tempered people because friendship with them will lead to learning their lifestyles (*ʾorḥôt*). Morally negative people tend to turn away from the path of life (2:13; 5:6), or to distort the path of justice (17:23). Considering that in the expression "path of life" the path itself is equally important as the final destination, ignoring the "path" of life means death (5:6). An important aspect of the path is well described by M. V. Fox: ". . . once a person enters onto this path, he is likely to follow it to the end. It becomes his natural course and, in spite of its difficulties, is easier to stay on than to leave."[136]

The consistent use of *ʾōraḥ* in collections I and II is clearly indicated by the following four expressions: *ʾōraḥ*+ *mišpāṭ* (2:8; 17:23), *ʾōraḥ* + *yōšer/yāšār* (2:13; 15:19), *ʾōraḥ* + *ḥayyîm* (2:19; 5:6; 10:17; 12:28; 15:24), and *ʾōraḥ* + *ṣaddîq/ṣědāqâ* (2:20; 4:18; 8:20; 12:28). Also, despite the only one instance of *ʾōraḥ* in collection III (22:25), the exclusive occurrence of *ʾōraḥ* in collections I, II, and III indicates the coherent wisdom aspect of the three collections.

(4) The Relationship
between Collections I, II, III, and IV

בָּנָה	373/4	to build	I-1	II-1	III-1	IV-1
מוּסָר	50/30	discipline	I-13	II-13	III-3	IV-1

Mûsār "discipline" (30 times)[137]

Only two words occur exclusively in the four collections (*bnh* and *mûsār*), and since *bnh* is a common verb in the OT (373 times), only the use of *mûsār* in the four collections will be discussed below.

Mûsār occurs 51 times in the OT: 30 times in Proverbs, eight times in Jeremiah, five times in Job, twice each in Isaiah and Zephaniah, and once each in Deuteronomy, Ezekiel, Hosea, and Psalms. The peculiar aspect of the occurrence of *mûsār* in the OT is that it occurs only once in the Pentateuch (Deut 11:2) and is not found in the historical books and late books. The large number of occurrence of *mûsār* in Proverbs (30 times) is a sufficient indication that the word belongs to the wisdom vocabulary although it occurs only five times in Job and none in Ecclesiastes. On the basis of her study of Egyptian and Hebrew wisdom terms, Shupak points out a significant aspect of *mûsār*. According to her, *mûsār*, like its Egyptian counterpart, has a double meaning, reproof on the one hand and physical punishment on the other.[138]

The punishing aspect of *mûsār* is frequently found in the OT, including Proverbs. A survey of the instances of *mûsār* in the OT shows that it is a didactic method which takes various forms of punishment, such as beating with a rod (Prov 13:24; 22:15; 23:13), suffering (Isa 53:5; Job 5:17), and disasters from God (Jer 2:30; 5:30; Ezk 5:15).

Several features of *mûsār* are noted in its 30 instances in Proverbs. First, about a half dozen terms occur in parallelism with *mûsār*, and among these *tôkaḥat* appears to be the most prominent synonym of *mûsār*.

mûsār and *tôkaḥat*	3:11; 5:12; 10:17; 12:1; 13:18; 15:5, 10, 32
mûsār and *daʿat*	8:10; 12:1
mûsār and *ʾimrê daʿat*	19:27; 23:12
mûsār and *daʿat bînâ*	4:1
mûsār and *tôrâ*	1:8
mûsār and *gěʿārâ*	13:1

It is further noted in the eight instances of *tôkaḥat* that it always occurs in the same poetic structure in relation to *mûsār*, that is, *mûsār* always in the first colon and *tôkaḥat* in the second colon. This relationship between *mûsār* and *tôkaḥat* implies the supporting role of the second word to the first (e.g., "My son, do not reject the discipline [*mûsār*] of the Lord, and do not abhor his reproof [*tôkaḥat*]" in 3:11). In addition to this, *mûsār* never occurs in the second colon as far as parallelism is concerned.[139] The frontal position of *mûsār* in parallelism may prove that it is one of the main words in education.

Although several sayings in Proverbs support Shupak's view that physical punishment is part of *mûsār*, the association of the term with the verbs *šmʿ* "to hear" (1:8; 4:1; 8:33; 19:27), *ʾhb* "to love" (12:1), and *prʿ* "to neglect" (13:18;

15:32) points to the possibility that the persuasive and non-threatening aspect of *mûsār* is stronger than the punishing aspect. For an intellectually mature person (or a wise man), acquiring *mûsār* is possible only through observation, as shown in 24:32, "I saw and took a lesson (*mûsār*)."

With regard to the use of *mûsār* in collections I, II, III, and IV, the following usages of *mûsār* indicate coherence between the collections: *mûsār* with *lqh* "to take" (1:3; 8:10; 24:32), the juxtaposition of *mûsār* and *hokmâ* (1:2; 1:7; 15:33; 23:23), *mûsār* and *'āb* (1:8; 4:1; 13:1; 15:5), and *mûsār* and *'ěwîl* "fool" (7:22; 16:22).

(5) The Relationship
between Collections I, II, III, IV, and V

צַדִּיק	206/66	righteous	I-4	II-49	III-3	IV-1	V-9
רָאה	1299/13	to see	I-2	II-2	III-3	IV-1	V-5
רָשָׁע	263/78	wicked	I-7	II-54	III-4	IV-1	V-12
שָׂפָה	176/46	lip	I-6	II-32	III-3	IV-2	V-3

Ṣaddîq "righteous" (66 times)[140]
and Rāšāʿ "wicked" (78 times)[141]

Four words are exclusive to collections I, II, III, IV, and V, and of the four words, the use of *ṣaddîq* and *rāšaʿ* will be discussed in a combined way. The reason for examining the two words together is because they often appear together as pair words in a saying to classify humanity into two contrasting categories, the *righteous and wicked*.[142] Table 1.9 confirms below the close relationship between *ṣaddîq* and *rāšāʿ*, in terms of the patterns of their frequency and distribution in Proverbs.

Table 1.9
The Derivatives of the Roots Ṣdq and Ršʿ

Word	Freq.	Meaning	I	II	III	IV	V	VI	VII
ṣdq	41/1	to be just		1					
ṣedeq	119/9	righteousness	5	2			1		1
ṣĕdāqâ	157/18	righteousness	2	16					
ṣaddiq	206/66	righteous	4	49	3	1	9		
rāšāʿ	263/78	wicked	7	54	4	1	12		
ršʿ	35/2	to be wicked		2					
rešaʿ	30/5	wickedness	2	3					
rišʿâ	14/2	wickedness		2					

On the one hand, the table shows that in Proverbs the most widely used words to convey the notions of righteousness and wickedness are *ṣaddîq* and *rāšā ʿ*, but, on the other hand, the table also shows that the occurrence of other words derived from the two roots, *ṣdq* and *ršʿ*, are almost exclusively confined to collections I and II.

The contrasting human characters represented by *ṣaddîq* and *rāšā ʿ* is particularly prominent in chapters 10–15 (II) and 28–29 (V), in which antithetic parallelism is often employed as a vehicle to make the contrast. For example, within collection II, *ṣaddîq* and *rāšā ʿ* occur together only four times in 17:1–22:16, while the same two words occur together 30 times in Chapters 10–15.[143] In collection V, *ṣaddîq* and *rāšā ʿ* occur in the same sentence only once in chapters 25–27 but seven times in chapters 28–29.[144] The two words rarely occur in antithetic parallelism in other collections.

One of our main concerns in dealing with *ṣaddîq* and *rāšā ʿ* is to understand the two terms in the religious context rather than the secular context. Of the religious aspect of the two terms, McKane and Scott point out that *ṣaddîq* and *rāšā ʿ* convey religious connotations because the two terms refer to the character and behavior classified by Israelite religion.[145] For this reason, McKane classifies the short sayings which contain the two terms as "Class C" sayings (religious). The strong religious aspect of *ṣaddîq* is proved by the close relationship of the word with the Lord. In five instances of *ṣaddîq* the Lord is directly involved in the various areas of the life of the righteous:

House	The curse of the Lord is on the house of the wicked,	
	but he blesses the dwelling of *the righteous*.	(3:33)
Food	The Lord does not allow *the righteous* to hunger,	
	but he rejects the desire of the wicked.	(10:3)
Prayer	The Lord is far from the wicked,	
	but he hears the prayer of *the righteous*.	(15:29)
Security	The name of the Lord is a strong tower,	
	the righteous run to it and are set on high.	(18:10)
Court	He who justifies the wicked and he who condemns	
	the righteous, both of them are an abomination	
	to the Lord	(17:15)

The five sayings commonly emphasize that it is the Lord who exercises his sovereign authority to protect the righteous who appear in the wisdom context.

One significant observation made in connection with the righteous and wicked is that religious notions are still conveyed by the two terms even when the name of the Lord is not mentioned. A religious reading is especially possible in a text where a passive verb is used in connection with *ṣaddîq* or *rāšā ʿ*. For example, 11:31 reads: "If the righteous are rewarded (*yĕšullam*) on earth, how much more the wicked and the sinner." Here, the passive verb *yĕšullam* paired with the adverbial phrase "on earth" conveys a strong implication that there will be a judgment on earth for the conducts of the righteous and the wicked. For those who prefer a secular reading in the wisdom context, the implied judgment in this context could mean the retribution according to the deed-consequence theory. However, the usage of *šlm* in Proverbs indicates that the verb consistently means "to repay" or "to make restitution" by a specific agent.[146] For example, a thief has to *repay* for stealing (6:31), the strange woman has to *fulfill* her vow (7:14), an offended person should not say, "I will *repay* evil" (20:22), a guarantor must *pay back* the debt (22:27), and the Lord will *reward* a compassionate person (19:17; 25:22). In light of these examples, we suggest that the repayment in 11:31 is by the judgment that comes from the Lord (cf. 13:13).[147] If the Lord is the one who rewards the righteous, the syntax of 11:31 emphasizes that he is the one who also judges the wicked and the sinner. The syntax in view is "*hēn* A . . . , *ʾap kî* B . . . ." ("if A [the righteous] . . . , how much more B [the wicked and the sinner] . . . ."). The conditional notion conveyed by this syntax is that the future state of B hinges on the future state of A. In other words, the certainty of the restitution for the righteous guarantees the same future event for the wicked and the sinner but in a more emphatically punitive sense. Therefore, the meaning of 11:31 is that one who vindicates the righteous on earth will also punish the wicked and the sinner.

In connection with the use of *ṣaddîq* and *rāšāʿ*, Proverbs chapter 10 shows a distinctive feature. The two terms occur there frequently in association with the parts of the body to form phrases like "the mouth of the righteous" or "the lips of the righteous": with the mouth (10:6, 11 [twice], 31, 32), with the head (10:6), with the tongue (10:20), with the heart (10:20), and with the lips (10:21, 32). But elsewhere in Proverbs the two terms occur only once in connection with the parts of the body (the righteous heart and the mouth of the wicked in 15:28). In this sense, chapter 10 is distinguished from other chapters. Since the mouth, tongue, and lips are speech organs, the purpose of the sayings which involve those terms in chapter 10 is to describe the power of positive and negative words spoken by the righteous and wicked. The words of the righteous are understood as life-giving and extremely beneficial to others: the mouth of the righteous is the fountain of life (10:11) and a tree bearing the fruit of wisdom (10:31), the tongue of a righteous man is precious like the choice silver (10:20), and his lips speak favorable things (10:32), nourishing many (10:21). In contrast to this, the speech of the wicked is characterized as destructive. The mouth of the wicked pours out evil and perverse things (10:32; cf. 15:28), and conceals violence (10:6, 11). In addition to this, the heart of the righteous ponders how to answer to others (15:28), but the heart of the wicked is of little value (10:20). The most prominent theme associated with the righteous is that they are good in nature and do profitable things to others (10:7, 16; 11:28, 30; 13:9, 25; 15:6; 23:24; 12:5, 10, 26; 13:5; 21:15, 26; 28:1; 29:7).

The description of the righteous as enduring and well-protected is another frequently mentioned theme in Proverbs: they stand firm forever, even after seven falls (10:25, 30; 12:3, 7, 12; 24:16), and they are delivered from various adverse situations (11:8, 31; 12:13, 21; 13:21; 14:32; 29:6). The righteous sometimes gain benefits even from the wicked: the wicked store up wealth only to give to the righteous (13:22), or the wicked themselves become a ransom for the righteous (21:18). The righteous prevail over the wicked at the end (14:19; 21:12). That the descendants of the righteous also enjoy protection (11:21; 20:7) reminds us of the divine promise in the Decalogue (Ex 20:6).

Apart from the effects of the righteous and wicked to other individuals, some sayings in collections II and V show that the ṣaddîq and rāšaʿ have significant contrasting effects on their community. The city rejoices when the righteous are blessed and when the wicked perish (11:10). When the community is under the control of the wicked, people groan and go into hiding (28:12, 28; 29:2). Also, between the righteous and the wicked, one group has a direct effect on the other in such a way that, when one group declines in the community, the other prospers: "when they (the wicked) perish, the righteous become many" (28:28; cf. 29:16). The intention of the sayings about the relationship between the community and the two contrasting types of people is to point out that the wicked make living conditions of the community unbearable.

Although the righteous are emphasized in Proverbs as protected and blessed, the book, on the other hand, acknowledges that in reality they face various difficulties in life: the righteous are treated unjustly in the court (17:15; 18:5; 24:24), they are punished (17:26), and they are humiliated before the wicked (25:26). Then, what is the sage's attitude about the dire situations in which the righteous unjustly suffer? Does he merely describe the suffering of the righteous as a matter of fact, or does he offer remedies to correct the situations of unjust suffering? In order to find an answer to the question, we limit ourselves to one social issue, injustice in the court of law, because the sayings related to the subject are more frequent than other subjects. It is striking to note in the following examples that the sage uses three different approaches to deal with the problem of injustice. First, the sage employs *God's displeasure* as the ultimate condemnation of the judicial injustice: "He who acquits the wicked and he who convicts the righteous, both are an *abomination* to the Lord" (17:15). The sage, however, deals with the same judicial problem in a different way in 18:5. This time the sage seems to appeal directly to the human conscience: "Lifting up the face of the wicked in order to oppress the righteous in the court is *not good*" (18:5; cf. 17:26). In this saying the sage does not resort to any threats or punitive measures for the crime, but simply gives the moral value "not good" to the inverse justice. The giving of the moral value is considered one of the solutions to stop the wrongful practice in the law court. Finally, we see that the same judicial problem is still handled in another way in 24:24: "One who says to the wicked, 'You are innocent', peoples will curse him, nations will denounce him." It is clear that this time the sage uses the public (or international) opinion to correct the judicial injustice. He threatens a corrupt judge that the public will condemn him for his unjust practice in the court.

Because of the high frequency of ṣaddîq and rāšaʿ in Proverbs (66 times and 78 times) and the OT (206 times and 263 times), it may not be significant to establish links between the collections I, II, III, IV, and V, on the basis of the use of the two words. However, the themes which have been discussed above (e.g., the community and the righteous/wicked and the judicial injustice) indicate that some of the collections share the same wisdom material and language.

(6) The Relationship
between Collections I, II, III, IV, V, and VI

אָדָם	561/45	man	I-8	II-21	III-3	IV-1	V-10	VI-2
אִישׁ	2179/90	man	I-10	II-45	III-4	IV-3	V-27	VI-1
אָמַר	5298/24	to say	I-9	II-4	III-2	IV-2	V-4	VI-3
הָלַךְ	1549/39	to go	I-21	II-12	III-1	IV-1	V-3	VI-1
חָכָם	138/47	wise	I-6	II-28	III-3	IV-1	V-8	VI-1
כּוּן	217/20	to be firm	I-5	II-9	III-2	IV-1	V-2	VI-1
שׁוּב	1059/23	to return	I-3	II-6	III-3	IV-2	V-8	VI-1

Seven words are exclusive to the six collections: *ʾādām, ʾîš, ʾmr, hlk, ḥakām, kwn,* and *šwb*. And among these only the use of *ḥakām* will be discussed below because other words are of less significance in the wisdom context.

Ḥākām "wise" (47 times)[148]

Table 1.10
Words for Wisdom

Word	Freq.	Meaning	I	II	III	IV	V	VI	VII
ḥokmâ	153/42	wisdom	19	14	4		3	1	1
ḥākām	138/47	wise	6	28	3	1	8	1	
daʿat	91/40	knowledge	13	20	5		1	1	
tĕbûnâ	42/19	understanding	8	9	1		1		
ʿēṣâ	88/10	counsel	3	6			1		
mûsār	50/30	instruction	13	13	3	1			
bînâ	37/14	understanding	10	1	2			1	
mĕzimmâ	19/8	plan, scheme	5	2	1				

śēkel	16/6	prudence	1	4	1	
taḥbûlâ	6/5	counsel	1	3	1	
leqaḥ	19/6	instruction	4	2		
tûšiyyâ	12/4	wisdom	3	1		
mô'ēṣâ	7/2	counsel	1		1	
zimmâ	29/3	plan		2	1	
'ārûm	11/8	shrewd		7		1
'ormâ	6/3	shrewdness	3			

It is well-known that wisdom is expressed through a variety of synonyms in Proverbs. Although the three major collections in Proverbs are collections I (28%), II (41%), and V (15%), as long as wisdom terms are concerned, it can be said that collection III (7.7%) takes the place of collection V as the third major collection. Table 1.10 shows that each of collections I and II contains 14 wisdom terms and collection III has 11 terms while collection V has only six. The table also reveals several more interesting phenomena with regard to the distribution of the wisdom terms. First of all, seven of the wisdom terms which commonly occur in collections I and II are not found at all in collection V. It is significant to note that each of da'at, tĕbûnâ, and 'ēṣâ occurs only once in collection V, and that mûsār and bînâ are completely absent in it. On the other hand, collections I, II, and III share nine wisdom terms, and four of them are exclusive to the three collections (bînâ, mĕzimmâ, śēkel, and taḥbûlâ). This phenomenon suggests that the wisdom climate of collection V considerably differs from that of collections I, II, and III, or that, as long as wisdom terms are concerned, collections I and II are more homogeneous with collection III than with collection V. It is remarkable that, although collection III is about a half of collection V in size (7.7% to 15.1%), the situation is reversed between the two when it comes to the wisdom vocabulary (11 words to six words). It is safe to say, based on the table, that the significant wisdom terms in collection V are only ḥokmâ and ḥākām. However, it may not be correct to say that the presence of the fewer wisdom terms in collection V means less wisdom elements in it, because it appears that wisdom themes are expressed in collection V in different ways. For example, mûsār is considered an important term for child education because of its high frequency (30 times) in Proverbs. But the absence of mûsār in collection V should not be interpreted as lack of the subject (child education) in it. The same subject is expressed in different ways in collection V (e.g., 29:15, "A rod and reproof give wisdom, but an unrestrained child makes his mother ashamed"; cf. 27:11; 29:17).[149] The seemingly dissimilar character of collection V to collections I, II, and III in regard to wisdom terms may be explained as the emphasis of collection V on different subjects. For example, according to R. C. Van Leeuwen, the sayings and admonitions in chapters 25–27 deal with various social situations, and they are primarily directed to the young men of the royal court.[150] Of the content of chapters 28–29, Whybray points out that the *tōrâ*, the contrast between the righteous and wicked, and the educational material for children and kings are the main concerns of these chapters.[151] Therefore, the presence of fewer wisdom terms in collection V may be due to the emphases on social concerns and royal elements.

We now turn to the use of *ḥākām*, the only significant wisdom term that occurs in collections I, II, III, IV, V, and IV. Various words occur with *ḥākām* either in antithetic or synonymous parallelism. *Ḥākām* occurs in synonymous parallelism with *nābôn* (three times), *ṣaddîq* (three times), and *ʾîš daʿat* (once). More significant is the occurrence of *ḥākām* in antithetic parallelism. Four terms occur in antithetic parallelism with *ḥākām* as contrasting moral characters to a wise man: *kĕsîl* (12 times), *ʾĕwîl* (seven times), *lēṣ* (four times), and *ʾîš lāšôn* (once). The four terms may denote four different types of fool. As pointed out before, some say that the *kĕsîl* and *ʾĕwîl* are morally perverted fools but with possibility of correction,[152] and that the *lēṣ* is worse than other types of fool because of his scornful and rejecting attitude to instruction.[153]

In contrast to fools, how is a wise man (*ḥākām*) described in Proverbs, or what are the characteristics of a wise man? A survey of the instances of *ḥākām* in Proverbs shows that a wise man is frequently characterized as one who has the ability to improve. Also, a wise man is often described as one who possesses an unquenchable desire to learn more. This ever learning and improving character of a wise man is well represented in 9:9, "Give (instruction) to a wise man and he will become wiser." Also, the effectiveness of a wise man's ability to learn is emphasized by the fact that the sentence, *yôsip leqaḥ* "he will increase learning," occurs four times in reference to the *ḥākām* (1:5; 9:9; 16:21, 23). Since a wise man always desires to improve himself, he loves knowledge and the person who corrects him (9:8). This attitude toward instruction sharply contrasts the wise and the mocker (*lēṣ*). A wise man is closely associated with *daʿat* "knowledge" (10:14; 15:2, 7; 18:15; 21:11), and, as a result, his speech has life-giving power (12:18; 13:14). This does not mean that a wise man likes to speak. On the contrary, silence is an important feature of a wise man. That is why even a fool is mistakenly considered wise when he is silent (17:28).

However, Proverbs does not describe a wise man as perfect. A wise man has his own weakness which is difficult to overcome. The weakness may be called "wisdom without humility." In the world of wisdom the most dangerous or foolish person seems to be a self-styled wise man ("wise in one's own eyes"). The phrase, *ḥākām bĕʿênāyw* "wise in his eyes," occurs five times in Proverbs, once in collection I and four times in collection V (3:7; 26:5, 12, 16; 28:11). The dangerous pitfall for a wise man is well illustrated in 26:12, "Have you seen a man wise in his own eyes? A fool (*kĕsîl*) has more hope than he does." Van Leeuwen points out that this saying may be a warning to all not to look down upon a fool, because when one does it, he himself is "wise in his own eyes." However, it may be more reasonable to understand that the saying is particularly aimed at a wise man to warn that wisdom without humility is worse than foolishness. When wisdom serves the purpose of self-exaltation, it is no longer wisdom. Murphy perfectly reveals the ironical aspect of wisdom in his own question and answer: "When does wisdom cease to be wisdom? When you think you are wise." Although the danger of becoming a self-styled wise man concerns all, Proverbs specifically mentions three classes of people as having more potential to easily fall into the danger. They are the *kĕsîl* "the fool" (26:5), *ʿāṣēl* "the sluggard" (26:16), and *ʾîš ʿāšîr* "a rich man" (28:11). Although Proverbs does not conclude that it is impossible for those people to attain wisdom, they have to take the right procedure of learning in order to be wise (cf. 6:6; 13:20; 19:20; 21:11).

If wisdom without humility is worse than foolishness, how can one avoid the pitfall of wisdom? According to 3:7, religious piety is the necessary remedy to perfect wisdom: "Do not be wise in your own eyes, but fear the Lord and turn from evil."

The 47 instances of *ḥākām* in the six collections (I, II, III, IV, V, and VI) are considered consistent. Some frequently found expressions, such as "he will increase learning" and "wise in his own eyes," indicate that closer relationship exists between some collections.

(7) Words Occurring in All the Collections

דָּבָר	1442/36	word	I-4	II-16	III-2	IV-1	V-9	VI-3	VII-1
לֵב	601/97	heart	I-19	II- 51	III-13	IV-2	V-10	VI-1	VII-1

Of the 1,264 words (verbs and adjectives/nouns) that are found in Proverbs, only two words, *dābār* and *lēb*, occur in all the collections. They are not typical wisdom terms (such as wisdom, wise, knowledge, and others) but common nouns, one representing speech and the other the inmost element of a human being. One of the implications of their occurrence in all the seven collections is that speech and the human heart are indispensable elements in every aspect of human life, including the wisdom context.

A. *Lēb* "heart" (97 times)[156]

Lēb occurs 601 times in the OT. A significant phenomenon in regard to the distribution of the word in the OT is that it occurs far more frequently in Psalms (102 times) and Proverbs (97 times) than any other books. The 199 occurrences of *lēb* in Psalms and Proverbs account for about one third (33%) of the total occurrence of the word in the OT (601 times). The heavy occurrence of the word in the two books implies that the heart is the essential element in worshiping God (Psalms) and in living with other human beings (Proverbs). In other words, the heart is the common ground for religion and wisdom, and for this reason the two cannot be separated from each other.[157]

Lēb must be regarded important in Proverbs not only because it occurs in all the collections but also because it has the highest frequency among the 1,264 words that occur in the book (its frequency becomes 99 times if two occurrences of *lēbāb* are included).

A conspicuous phenomenon involving *lēb* is the frequent association of the noun with the Lord. The key idea of the Lord's relationship to the heart is that he alone knows the true motivation of every human heart: all human hearts are before the Lord (15:11) and he alone can examine and weigh the heart (17:3; 21:2). Even in the sayings in which the Lord is not mentioned he is still implied as the one who has the total knowledge of the human heart (e.g., "Does he who examines the hearts not understand?" in 24:12). The Lord not only knows the true motivation of the human heart, but overrules its plans to direct the course of human life according to his will. It is thus natural that the idea of determinism by the Lord is inherent in some God-sayings, as shown in the following example: "The heart of a man plans his way, but *the Lord* determines his steps" (16:9). Both the heart of a king (21:1) and the hearts of ordinary people (16:1; 19:21) are ruled by the Lord's sovereignty. Abominable to the Lord is a crooked or proud heart (11:20; 16:5; cf. 21:4). Since the Lord knows what is in the heart, no one can say, "I have cleansed my heart, I am pure from my sin" (20:9).[158]

In Proverbs a profound anthropological understanding of a human being may be found in the sayings which deal with the joy and sorrow of the heart.[159] Some of the sayings which involve the heart describe how *lēb* affects the body and soul as a whole person. On one hand, the joyful heart has an effect of a good medicine, facilitating healing (17:22) and making the face look good (15:13), but, on the other hand, the negative state of the heart has a psychosomatic effect on a whole person: the anxious heart weighs a man down (12:25). The most profound effect of the heart on a person is seen in 15:13b in its relationship to the spirit: "When the heart is in pain, the spirit is crushed." The heart appears susceptible to unfulfilled hope: "Delayed hope makes the heart sick" (13:12).[160] The brief saying in 14:13 keenly points out that a hollow laughter cannot hide the deep sorrow felt by the heart: "Even in laughter the heart aches." The unique role of the heart in perceiving the deepest sorrow and joy is also indicated in 14:10: "Only the heart knows its own bitterness, and no one else can share its joy."

The heart is the seat not only of the deepest sorrow and joy but also of the highest degree of trust. Total trust in God and a person is accomplished only through the heart. Therefore, a son is instructed by his father to trust the Lord with all his *heart* (3:5), and a husband trusts his wife in his *heart* (31:11). The instructions of Wisdom and parents become effective when they are received by the *heart* of a person (2:2; 3:1, 3; 4:4, 25; 6:21; 7:3; 10:13; 15:32; 23:12, 26). Negatively, the heart is also the place where evil schemes are deliberated for execution (6:14, 18; 10:20; 12:20; 15:7; 24:2; 26:23, 25).

The peculiar use of *lēb* in Proverbs is that the noun forms a unique phrase in combination with *ḥāsēr* "lacking" to denote a type of fool ("senseless one"). It is significant to note that the phrase *ḥăsar lēb* is found 11 times only in Proverbs in the entire OT.[161] This phenomenon suggests that *ḥăsar lēb* is an expression to refer to a specific type of fool known only in the wisdom circles reflected in Proverbs. Therefore, the occurrence of this peculiar wisdom phrase (*ḥăsar lēb*) in collections I, II, and IV clearly indicates the coherent wisdom aspect of the three collections.[162] Interestingly, Shupak classifies the *ḥăsar lēb* and the *petî* as positive fools in her attempt to make a gradation of foolishness in Proverbs, as she has done for the Egyptian terms.[163] A survey of the instances of *ḥăsar lēb* shows that a person designated by the phrase is often unable to see the immediate, serious consequences of his conduct. Because of this mental inability to perceive what lies ahead, the *ḥăsar lēb* commits adultery (6:32), pursues vain things (12:11), despises his friends (11:12), regards foolishness as joy (15:21), and puts up security for his neighbor (17:18). *Ḥăsar lēb* occurs in connection with *petî* (7:7; 9:4=9:16), *'ĕwîl* (10:21), and *'āṣēl* "sluggard" (24:30). It is noted in 10:13 that physical punishment is necessary in teaching the *ḥăsar lēb*.

B. *Dābār* "word" (36 times)[164]

Table 1.11
Words for Speech

Word	Freq.	Meaning	I	II	III	IV	V	VI	VII
'mr	5298/25	to say	9	4	2	2	4	4	
'ēmer	55/22	word	14	5	3				
'imrâ	37/1	word						1	
dbr	1151/9	to speak	2	2	4		1		
dābār	1442/36	word	4	16	2	1	9	3	1
millâ	38/1	word			1				
nĕ'um	373/1	utterance						1	
ngd	369/2	to announce	1				1		
l''	3/1	to talk wildly	1						
bṭh	4/1	to talk rashly	1						

The table shows that *dābār* and *'ēmer* (including *'ōmer*) are the two main nouns to denote *word* in Proverbs.[165] However, the two nouns differ in their distribution in Proverbs. While *dābār* occurs in all collections, *'ēmer* is found only in collections I, II, and III, an indication of the coherent aspect of the three collections. We will first examine the instances of *dābār* and *'ēmer* and then compare the usage of the two words in Proverbs.

It is often pointed out that, while the sayings attributed to Solomon are called *mĕšālîm* (1:1, 10:1; 25:1), the sayings of other individuals are called *dĕbārîm*. (22:17; 30:1; 31:1). The differentiation may be mainly due to the historical statement in 1 Kgs 5:12 (E 4:32), "he spoke three thousand *māšāl* 'proverbs'." B. K. Waltke suggests that *māšal* may convey a honorific notion because of its association with Solomon, and that the association may be due to the three common letters (*m*, *š*, and *l*) in the name Solomon and the word *māšāl*.[166] If it is the case, the use of *māšāl* in connection with Solomon and *dābār* in connection with other authors seems intentional.

The usage of *dābār* in Proverbs shows that *word* has power to build up and to destroy. A good word can revive the heart of a man pressed down by anxieties (12:25; cf. 15:30), and the efficacy of a timely and appropriate speech is incomparable (15:23; 25:11). In contrast to this, *dābār* spoken by a morally negative person is destructive. The words of the wicked are likened to a bloody ambush (12:6), and a hurting word stirs up anger (15:1). Reiterating a (damaging) word separates close friends (17:9). In the ancient world where a successful communication between two parties was entirely reliant upon a messenger's integrity and intelligence, employing a fool to send *words* is like "cutting off the feet" (26:6). Since *dābār* can play a powerful role in life, the sage advises to speak with caution: "Do you see a hasty man with words? A fool has more hope than he does" (29:20; cf. 18:13; 16:20).

We have observed in Table 1.11 that *word* is denoted mainly by the two nouns *dābār* and *ʾēmer* in Proverbs (36 times and 22 times). However, in the OT *dābār* is much more frequent than *ʾēmer* (1442 times to 55 times). The distribution of *ʾēmer* in the OT shows that it occurs more frequently in Wisdom books (22 times in Proverbs and 12 times in Job) than other books. It is also noted in the distribution that *ʾēmer* is completely absent in the late biblical books. Ecclesiastes shows difference from the two other Wisdom books in regard to the use of *ʾēmer*. While both *dābār* and *ʾēmer* are frequently used in Job and Proverbs, *ʾēmer* is completely absent in Ecclesiastes. *ʾēmer* is used in Proverbs in reference to the speeches of the father (7 times), Wisdom (twice), and the strange woman (twice). In 16:24 *ʾēmer* appears to have life-giving power like *dābār*. "Pleasant words (*ʾimrê*) are like a honeycomb, sweet to the soul and healing for bones."

(8) The Relationship
between Collections I, II, III, and V

a. Verbs (16)

בגד	49/9	to be unfaithful	I-1	II-6	III-1	V-1
בין	171/33	to understand	I-9	II-14	III-3	V-7
בקש	225/14	to seek	I-1	II-9	III-1	V-3
דבר	1151/9	to speak	I-2	II-2	III-4	V-1
זור	78/15	to be a stranger	I-7	II-5	III-1	V-2
משל	81/11	to rule	I-1	II-5	III-1	V-4

נָפַל	434/15	to fall	I-2	II-7	III-2	V-4
נָצַר	61/18	to keep	I-10	II-5	III-1	V-2
עָרַב	22/9	to give in pledge	I-1	II-5	III-2	V-1
פָּתָה	28/5	to be simple	I-1	II-2	III-1	V-1
קָרָא	738/19	to call	I-12	II-5	III-1	V-1
שָׂמַח	154/16	to be glad	I-1	II-6	III-4	V-5
שָׁחַת	187/5	to be ruin	I-1	II-1	III-1	V-2
שָׁלֵם	117/10	to be sound	I-2	II-6	III-1	V-1
שָׁמַע	1159/30	to hear	I-12	II-11	III-3	V-4
שָׁמַר	411/31	to keep	I-15	II-12	III-1	V-3

b. Adjectives/Nouns (20)

אֱוִיל	26/19	foolish	I-2	II-13	III-1	V-3
אִוֶּלֶת	25/23	folly	I-1	II-17	III-1	V-4
אֹזֶן	187/14	ear	I-4	II-4	III-3	V-3
אַחֲרִית	61/13	end	I-2	II-5	III-4	V-2
אֵיד	24/6	distress	I-3	II-1	III-1	V-1
אֱמֶת	127/12	faithfulness	I-2	II-6	III-3	V-1
חֶדֶר	38/6	chamber	I-1	II-3	III-1	V-1
חֵמָה	125/8	heat, rage	I-1	II-5	III-1	V-1
כְּסִיל	70/49	fool	I-4	II-30	III-1	V-14
מָדוֹן	23/19	contention	I-2	II-10	III-1	V-6
מָוֶת	161/19	death	I-4	II-13	III-1	V-1
נָכְרִי	45/9	foreign, alien	I-5	II-1	III-1	V-2
נַעַר	240/7	lad	I-2	II-3	III-1	V-1
עוֹלָם	437/6	long duration	I-1	II-2	III-2	V-1
צָרָה	72/8	distress	I-1	II-4	III-2	V-1
רֹאשׁ	600/10	head	I-6	II-2	III-1	V-1
רַע	142/21	evil	I-6	II-10	III-2	V-3
רָעָה	319/21	evil	I-4	II-12	III-2	V-3
תְּבוּנָה	42/19	understanding	I-8	II-9	III-1	V-1
תּוֹעֵבָה	117/21	abomination	I-3	II-13	III-1	V-4

Thirty-six words occur exclusively in the four collections (16 verbs and 20 adjectives/nouns). Among these, the use of four nouns, ʾiwwelet, mādôn, kĕsîl, and tôʿēbâ, which are considered more relevant to wisdom, will be discussed below.

A. *’iwwelet* "folly" (23 times)[167]

’iwwelet is one of the wisdom terms which predominantly occur in Proverbs. The word occurs 25 times in the OT: 23 times in Proverbs and twice in Psalms. Although the *’ĕwîl* "fool" is expected to possess the foolish quality *’iwwelet* because of the cognate relationship between the two words,[168] a survey of the instances of *’iwwelet* reveals that the foolish quality is more closely related to the *kĕsîl* than any other types of fool. The two cognate terms, *’ĕwîl* and *’iwwelet*, occur together only in two places (16:22; 27:22), while *’iwwelet* occurs 11 times in reference to *kĕsîl* (12:23; 13:16; 14:8, 24 [2x]; 15:2, 14; 17:12; 26:4, 5, 11). The most frequently represented idea by the *kĕsîl* in connection with *’iwwelet* is that the mouth (or heart) of the *kĕsîl* brings out nothing but *’iwwelet* (12:23; 13:16; 14:24; 15:2, 14): for example, it is said in 12:23, "The heart of fools (*kĕsîlîm*) announces folly (*’iwwelet*)," and in 13:16, "A fool (*kĕsîl*) spreads folly (*’iwwelet*)." The two instances of *kĕsîl* in 26:4 and 26:5 are well known because of the juxtaposition of the two sayings in a contrasting way ("Do not answer a fool . . . ." and "Answer a fool . . . ."). No matter how the two sayings are interpreted, the key reason that one has to decide to answer or not to answer the *kĕsîl* is because of the folly (*’iwwelet*) of the *kĕsîl*.[169] The sage advises that folly should not be handled lightly because the effect of folly in the hand of a fool is deadly. The dangerous aspect of *’iwwelet* is poignantly illustrated in 17:12 with some exaggeration: "Encounter a bear robbed of a cub, but not a fool (*kĕsîl*) in his folly (*’iwwelet*)." It appears in 26:11 that folly has an effect to make a fool forgetful of unpleasant experiences in the past: "Like a dog that returns to its vomit, a fool (*kĕsîl*) repeats with his folly (*’iwwelet*)."

According to 22:15, the sage's view of *’iwwelet* is that folly is inherent in young people, and that it is removable if a right teaching method is applied to a person at his young age: "a rod of discipline makes it (*’iwwelet*) far from him (a youth)." The necessity of the early discipline in 22:15 is understandable if one considers the extreme difficulty in removing folly from a fool: "Even if you pound a fool (*’ĕwîl*) in a mortar . . . his folly will not depart from him" (27:22). On the basis of 22:15 and 27:22, we may summarize the sage's view of *iiwwelet* as follows: (1) folly is common to young people, (2) but discipline in childhood normally removes it from a youth, and (3) folly which remains in a person from his childhood is difficult to eradicate by any means.

Although *’iwwelet* occurs only once in collections I (5:23) and III (24:9), the predominant occurrence of the noun in Proverbs (23 out of 25 times in the OT) is a sufficient ground to say that collections I, II, III, and V share a common wisdom feature in regard to folly.

B. *Mādôn* "strife" (19 times)[170]

Although it is insignificant for our purpose, the discussion of *mādôn* involves the issue of Kethib-Qere (K-Q), because seven of the 19 instances of *mādôn* are marked with Q in the MT. James Barr, building upon R. Gordis' study of K and Q, points out that in most cases the difference between K and Q involves only one element in the consonantal text.[171] Barr also points out that the letters most frequently involved in the K-Q problem are *yôd* and *wāw*.[172] The following table confirms that the differences in the K-Q forms of *mādôn* in Proverbs also involve the two letters.

Table 1.12
Kethib-Qere Forms of *Mādôn*

6:14	K *mdnym*	Q *midyānîm*	21:19	K *mdwnym*	Q *midyānîm*
6:19	*mĕdānîm*		22:10	*mādôn*	
10:1	*mĕdānîm*		23:29	K *mdwnym*	Q *midyānîm*
15:1	*mādôn*		25:24	K *mdwnym*	Q *midyānîm*
16:2	*mādôn*		26:20	*mādôn*	
17:1	*mādôn*		26:21	K *mdwnym*	Q *midyānîm*
18:1	*midyānîm*		27:15	K *mdwnym*	Q *midyānîm*
18:1	K *mdwnym*	Q *midyānîm*	28:25	*mādôn*	
19:1	*midyānîm*		29:22	*mādôn*	
21:9	*midyānîm*				

It is observed in the table that, in the seven cases of the K-Q of *mādôn*, the nature of the difference between the two groups is phonetic, not semantic. However, there are several elements that require explanation. First of all, the singular *mādôn* occurs seven times and none of the instances is involved in the K-Q controversy. In other words, the K-Q problem is restricted to the plural. It is noted, however, that not all the 12 plural forms are subject to the K-Q problem. The reason is because the plurals appear in three different forms: *mdnym* (6:14), *mdwnym* (18:19; 21:19; 23:29; 25:24; 26:21; 27:15), and *midyānîm* (18:18; 19:13; 21:9). It is observed that the first two plural forms are Ks, and that they are uniformly replaced with the Q form *midyānîm* in the margin of the MT. One significant observation here is that all the seven Ks appear to be correct grammatically. The first plural form *mdnym* in 6:14 should be vocalized as *mĕdānîm* because the form occurs in that way in 6:19 and 10:12. Then, *mdnym* is understood as the plural of *mĕdān* (or *mādān* which is not attested in the OT). Also, morphologically, the second plural form *mdwnym* is certainly to be vocalized as *mĕdônîm*, the plural of *mādôn*. However, both *mdnym* and *mdwnym* are corrected by the scribe to be read as *midyānîm* (Q). The third plural form *midyānîm* is left untouched because it is identical with the Q, and it is considered to be the plural of the unattested singular *midyān*. The observations can be summarized as follows:

1. The singular *mādôn* occurs seven times
2. *Mdnym* (*mĕdānîm*) is supposed to be the plural of *mĕdān*
   (or *mādān*)

3. *Mdwnym* (*mĕdonîm*) is supposed to be the plural of *mādôn*
4. *Midyānîm* is supposed to be the plural of **midyān*

Considering that the Ks (*mdnym* and *mdwnym*) are grammatically legitimate thus requiring no corrections, it becomes obvious that the main purpose of
the K-Q system in Proverbs is not always to correct erroneous forms.[173] Also,
the notion that Q is preferred to K is questionable here because the Ks and Qs in
the texts are equally satisfactory. If we limit ourselves to the discussion of Qs of
mādôn, the intention of the K-Q system must be explained from a different angle. In view that the reader is advised by the scribe to read *mdnym* and *mdwnym*
as *midyānîm*, the Q is understood as a scribal attempt to unify the phonetically
different but semantically identical forms with a third form (*midyānîm*) which
appears to have been the scribe's choice for the unification purpose. On the basis
of this explanation, we may explain the K-Q problem of *mādôn* in the following
way: having noted that the sages in Proverbs had employed the three different
plural nouns with the same meaning "strife," all being derived from the same
root *dyn*, the scribe decided to unify them by imposing his choice of reading
midyānîm on the two different forms (*mĕdānîm* and *mĕdônîm*). One thing
which is difficult to explain is why the scribe did not mark *mĕdānîm* in 6:19 and
10:12 with a Q, as he did on the same word in 6:14. The untouched form in 6:19
and 10:12 may not be ascribed to the scribe's inconsistency or lapse, because the
marginal notes on the word in both places indicate that the scribe was aware of
the existence of the two instances. It is equally difficult to explain why
midyānîm became the scribe's choice among the three different forms. Based on
the root *dyn*, C. H. Toy explains that the scribal correction is a late attempt to
bring out the *yôd* of the root by using *midyānîm*.[174] His explanation may be
grammatically reasonable, but the question still remains, "Why is such a scribal
effort necessary when the root is discernible from the meaning without the help
of the Q?" Delitzsch offers a different explanation. He implies that there may
exist a connection between the three nouns in our discussion and Abraham's two
sons, *mĕdān* and *midyān*, through Ketura (Gen 25:2).[175] Although the implications by the connection are not clear, Delitzsch's suggestion is attractive because
the two names coincide with the two singular forms which can be deduced from
mdnym, and *midyānîm*.

We now return to the examination of the use of *mādôn* in Proverbs. What
does the book say about the cause of strife (*mādôn*) among people? Three different types of morally negative people are described as *sending* (*šlḥ*) strife
among others: a worthless man (*'ādām bĕliyya'al*) in 6:12–14, a false witness
(*'ēd šeqer*) in 6:19, and a perverse man (*'îš tahpukôt*) in 16:28. Strife is also
stirred up (*grh*) by an angry or a greedy man (15:18; 29:22; 28:25). The association of *mādôn* with the verbs, *grh* "to stir up" and *'wr* "to awake" imply that
strife is an inherent human tendency that can be roused by provoking factors.
That is why angry or greedy men *stir up* strife among others (15:18; 29:22;
28:25), and hatred *awakes* strife in people (10:12). It is surprising that a wife is

mentioned no less than five times as the cause of domestic strife (19:13; 21:9, 19; 25:24; 27:15). Three sayings offer remedies for strife: strife will end if a mocker or a gossiper are removed from the community (22:10; 26:20), and the lot can settle strife among powerful rivals (18:18).

The coherent use of *mādôn* in collections I, II, III, and V can be summarized in the following way: the verb *šlḥ* is used in connection with *mādôn* in collections I and II (6:14, 19; 16:28), the Kethib form *mdwnym* is found in collections II, III, and V (18:19; 21:19; 23:29; 25:24; 26:21; 27:15), *mĕdānîm* that is not marked as a Q occurs in collections I and II (6:19; 10:12), and the singular form *mādôn* is found seven times in collections II and V (15:28; 16:28; 17:14; 22:10; 26:20; 28:25; 29:22).

C. *Kĕsîl* "fool" (49 times)[176]

Table 1.13
Words for Folly

Word	Freq.	Meaning	I	II	III	IV	V	VI	VII
'ĕwîl	26/19	fool	2	13	1		3		
'iwwelet	25/23	foolishness	1	17	1		4		
ba'ar	5/2	stupid		1				1	
ḥăsar lēb	11/11	senseless	4	6		1			
kĕsîl	70/49	fool	4	30	1		14		
kĕsîlût	1/1	foolishness	1						
lēṣ	16/14	mocker	4	9	1				
nābāl	17/3	fool		2				1	
petî	19/15	naive fool	9	5			1		
pĕtayyût	1/1	foolishness	1						

It is observed in the table that in Proverbs the three most frequent terms for a fool or folly are *kĕsîl* (49 times), *'iwwelet* (23 times), and *'ĕwîl* (19 times), in the order of frequency, and that these three terms are found in all the three Solomonic collections (I, II, and V) and collection III. This common vocabulary of folly confirms the coherent wisdom aspect of the four collections. However, the absence of the two important terms for a fool, *ḥăsar lēb* (11 times) and *lēṣ* (14 times), in collection V suggests that there is some distance between collection V and the two other major collections (I and II), at least the words for fools are concerned.

Another feature shown in the table is that, as we have pointed out earlier, the abstract notion of folly represented by the feminine ending -*ût* (*kĕsîlût* and *pĕtayyût*) is found only in collection I.

Kĕsîl, the word under discussion, occurs considerably in the OT (70 times). However, the distribution of the word in the OT reveals a peculiar pattern. All

the instances of *kĕsîl* are confined only to three books: 49 times in Proverbs
(70%), 18 times in Ecclesiastes, and 3 times in Psalms. Based on this distribution, it is safe to say that *kĕsîl* almost exclusively belongs to the wisdom domain. Another feature of *kĕsîl* revealed in Table 1.13 is that, among the seven
types of fool, the *kĕsîl* is the most frequently mentioned fool in Proverbs. The
relatively high frequency of the word in collections II, V, and Ecclesiastes implies a link between them.[177]

Although the gradation of Hebrew fools suggested by Shupak may be a
useful guideline to understand the degree of foolishness between different types
of fool, some sayings indicate that such a gradation must be used only as a
guideline, not in a strict sense. According to her gradation, the *kĕsîl* is understood as the second most positive fool after the *hăsar lēb/petî*. The reason for the
positive evaluation of the *kĕsîl* is mainly because he is mentioned in synonymous parallelism more often with the positive fool the *petî* than with the negative one the *lēṣ*.[178] However, in some cases the *kĕsîl* gives an impression that he
too is an incorrigible fool like the *lēṣ*. For example, the brutal comparison of the
kĕsîl to some of domestic animals, such as a horse (26:3), donkey (26:3), and
dog (26:11), signifies his stubbornness and stupidity that defy any attempt to
change him. Moreover, he has no intention of acquiring wisdom (17:16), and
displays the same scornful attitude which the incorrigible fool the *lēṣ* possesses:
"Do not speak to the ears of a fool (*kĕsîl*), for he will despise your prudent
words" (23:9, cf. 9:8). In addition to this, the frequent mention of the *kĕsîl* to
make a contrast against various wise men indicates that he represents a typical
fool standing on the opposite side of wise men. *Kĕsîl* occurs in antithetic parallelism with a half dozen different words related to wisdom: with *hākām* (3:35;
10:1; 13:20; 14:16; 15:2, 7, 20; 21:20; 29:11), with *ʿārûm* (12:23; 13:16; 14:8),
with *nābôn* (14:33; 15:14), with *mēbîn* (17:10), with *ʾîš tĕbûnâ* (10:23), and
with *hokmâ* (17:24).

We have pointed out before that the foolish quality *ʾiwwelet* "folly" is
more frequently associated with the *kĕsîl* (11 times) than any other types of fool.
A survey of the instances of the *kĕsîl* shows that some of his conducts are characterized not only by folly (*ʾiwwelet*) but also by a lack of moral discernment.
For example, he exalts disgrace (3:35), brings out evil and folly from himself
(10:18; 15:2; 18:6; 29:11), enjoys planning evil (10:23), and hates to turn away
from evil (13:19). In addition to this, the *kĕsîl* often brings grief to his parents
and do not show appropriate respect to them (10:1; 17:21, 25; 19:13; 15:20).
One is warned not to have association with the *kĕsîl* (13:20; 14:7; 23:9; 26:6,
10). He actively rejects knowledge or wisdom (1:22; 18:2; 17:16; 26:7=26:9),
and is confident of himself (14:16; 28:26). It appears that physical punishment is
the main method for his education (19:29; 26:3; cf. 17:10). Ironically, however,
the bright side of the *kĕsîl* is that he has more hope than a self-styled wise man
(26:12) or a man who is hasty in speech (29:20). The *kĕsîl* is evidently the main
theme of chapter 26. The word occurs in every verse in 26:1–12, except in verse
2.

The discussion of the instances of *kĕsîl* shows that the use of the word in collections I, II, III, and V is consistent with no discernible difference that can separate one collection from the others. Besides this, the predominant occurrence of the word in Proverbs (70%) indicates that the *kĕsîl* is a common concern in the collections.

D. *Tô'ēbâ* "abomination" (21 times)[179]

In Proverbs and elsewhere in the OT, *tô'ēbâ* conveys the repulsive and abhorrent feelings of God and men. Although the word occurs in association with God in various ways, the exact phrase *tô'ăbat YHWH* is found only in two books in the OT, Proverbs (11 times) and Deuteronomy (8 times). This exclusive occurrence of the phrase "the abomination of the Lord" in Proverbs and Deuteronomy increases the probability of a connection between the two books. M. Weinfeld, noting that the expression "an abomination of God" is found in the Teaching of Amenemope and some Babylonian sources, suggests that the formula is sapiential in character. As for the relationship between Deuteronomy and Proverbs with regard to the phrase "the abomination of the Lord," he concludes that, because of the antiquity of wisdom literature in ancient Near East, the direction of influence is from Proverbs to Deuteronomy rather than the contrary.[180] Whether the exclusive occurrence of the phrase in the two books is due to the influence from one to the other or due to drawing from the common source by the authors, it is clear that the phenomenon is significant.

Of the usage of *tô'ēbâ* in Proverbs, it is significant to note that the word sometimes occurs in the context of worship (e.g., sacrifice and prayer). For example, the sacrifice of the wicked is an abomination to the Lord (15:8; cf. 21:27), and the prayer of one who does not obey the law is an abomination (28:9). In passing, we point out that, although *tôrâ* in collection I often refers to the instruction of the parents, the law in 28:9 must be understood as referring to God's Law, not human instruction, because of its association with prayer.[181]

Apart from its religious use, the phrase ("abomination to the Lord") is often used in connection with general evil conducts. It is said in 6:16–19 that the Lord abhors evil inclinations for pride, falsehood, violence, and quarrel. Similarly, in other instances *tô'ăbat YHWH* is used in connection with the attitudes of the wicked in general: crooked or proud heart (11:20; 16:5), false lips (12:22), the thoughts or ways of the wicked (15:26; 15:9), and one who goes in a wrong way (3:32). Nevertheless, it is significant to note that, among various unethical practices in Israelite society, two types of perversion are more specifically mentioned as an abomination to the Lord than other crimes. They are the use of dishonest scales (11:1; 20:10, 23; cf. 16:11) and the inverse justice in the court of law (17:15; cf. 18:5; 24:23–25; 28:21). The specific and frequent mention of these two crimes implies that dishonesty in business and corruption in the judicial system were widespread in Israelite society in the time of the wise men.

Under the circumstances, the usual victims of the crimes would be the poor and the righteous as shown in the messages of the eighth century prophets in Israel and Judah. The frequent mention of the two crimes (dishonest scales and judicial injustice) in Proverbs indicates that the society described in the book does not differ from that described in the books of the eighth century prophets.

Tôʿēbâ is also used among humans. An illuminating example to understand its appropriate use for humans would be its instance in 29:27 (cf. 24:9): "An evildoer is an *abomination* to the righteous, and an upright man is an *abomination* to the wicked." It is clear in this example that *tôʿēbâ* denotes a strong dislike or a repulsive feeling that exists mutually between two contrasting characters. In a similar sense, fools (*kĕsîl*) are so entirely at home in evil that it is an *abomination* to them to turn from it (13:19). On the other hand, it is said in 16:12 that the abomination of kings is doing wickedness. This saying serves as warning to kings so that they may uphold righteousness by abhorring wickedness.

For the theological significance of the expression *tôʿăbat YHWH*, we may draw two observations from R. E. Clements' study of the abomination in Proverbs.[182] First, in the summary of his study Clements concludes that the purpose of connecting abomination to the Lord is to "lend a more urgent and extreme form of condemnation to the reproof."[183] It appears that his understanding of the phrase as an extreme form of condemnation is based on D. Winton Thomas' explanation of the phrase *lēʾlōhîm* "to God." According to Thomas, the expression "to God" in certain contexts conveys a superlative sense.[184] Being understood in a superlative sense, "abomination to the Lord" is the sage's most powerful condemnation of crimes in society, and his use of the expression in the wisdom context suggests that in Proverbs wisdom is integrated into Israelite religion mainly by the two important formulas, "fear of the Lord" and "abomination to the Lord." The first formula establishes the position of wisdom in Israelite religion: the fear of the Lord is the beginning of wisdom (9:10; cf. 1:7). The sage's use of the second formula declares the ultimate authority of the Lord to condemn and correct morally negative characters and behaviors. In some sense, it could be said that, as prophets relied on the divine authority by using the formula "Thus says the Lord," so the Israelite wise men relied on the divine authority by using the formula "abomination to the Lord."

Second, Clements' study of "abomination to the Lord" exposes the weakness of the act-consequence theory. If the consequence inevitably follows the act all the time, there is no need for the sage to threaten bad people with the expression ("abomination to the Lord"). By this expression, the sage implies that some evil doers go unpunished in this world against the act-consequence theory, as Job complains. In that case, the Lord's displeasure takes the place of the consequence as the ultimate punishment or condemnation. This does not necessarily invalidate the legitimacy of the act-consequence theory. It affirms that "these act-consequence arguments could only be upheld as true in a broad sense."[185] In his study of God in Proverbs, L. Boström also points out the inadequate aspect of the act-consequence theory. He explains that in general Proverbs has little interest in showing exact consequences of actions, and suggests that the term "character-consequence" is more appropriate than act-consequence because the consequences mentioned in Proverbs are related to the total lifestyle and disposition of the person.[186]

With regard to the use of *tô ʿēbâ* in collections I, II, III, and V, it is noted that the expression "an abomination to the Lord" is found in collections I and II, and that "abomination" and "prayer" occur together in 15:8 and 28:9, showing similarity between collections II and V. Collections III and V are linked by a common theme of abomination between two contrasting types of people (24:9; 29:27):

24:9   "A foolish plan is sin,
           and a mocker is an abomination to a man."
29:27   "An evildoer is an abomination to the righteous,
           and an upright man is an abomination to the wicked."

(9) The Relationship
between Collections I, II, III, V, and VI

אָב	1225/26	father	I-5	II-11	III-4	V-4	VI-2
אַיִן	789/38	not	I-9	II-13	III-2	V-13	VI-1
גֶּבֶר	66/9	man	I-1	II-1	III-1	V-3	VI-3
דַּעַת	91/41	knowledge	I-14	II-20	III-5	V-1	VI-1
הוֹן	26/18	wealth	I-4	II-8	III-1	V-3	VI-2
חכם	27/13	to be wise	I-5	II-4	III-2	V-1	VI-1
עַיִן	868/46	eye	I-11	II-16	III-7	V-9	VI-3
שְׁאוֹל	65/9	Sheol	I-4	II-2	III-1	V-1	VI-1

Of the eight words which occur exclusively in the five collections, the use of the four words (*hôn, daʿat, ḥkm,* and *ʾāb*) will be examined below.

A. *Hôn* "wealth" (18 times)[187]

Table 1.14
Words for Wealth

Word	Freq.	Meaning	I	II	III	IV	V	VI	VII
ʾôṣār	79/5	treasure	1	4					
hôn	26/18	wealth	4	8	1		3	2	
ḥayil	244/5	wealth		2					3
ḥōsen	5/2	wealth		1			1		
ʿšr	17/6	to be rich		4	1		1		
ʿāšîr	23/9	rich		7			2		
ʿōšer	37/9	riches	2	6				1	

It is observed in the table that *hôn* has the highest frequency, and that it is the only term that occurs in all the four larger collections in Proverbs. Although *hôn* is not found in two other Wisdom books (Job and Ecclesiastes), its occurrence in the four collections indicates that it is a favorite term for wealth in Proverbs. *Hôn* occurs 26 times in the OT: 18 times in Proverbs, four times in Ezekiel, three times in Psalms, and once in Song of Songs. A survey of the instances of the term in Ezekiel, Psalms, and Song of Songs supports M. V. Fox's view that *hôn* is movable wealth distinct from other types of properties, such as real estate or crops.[188] Outside Proverbs *hôn* occurs in the context of commercial activities. The four instances of *hôn* in Ezekiel are in chapter 27 which is a lament for Tyre, a city once famous for its being the center of trade of the region. In Song 8:7 the word again occurs in a commercial context in which an attempt to buy love with *hôn* is ridiculed. In Ps 44:13 God sells off his people, not receiving any *hôn* as price. Although *hôn* is a morally neutral term, it conveys a negative, materialistic notion in Ezekiel and Song.

The negative aspect of *hôn* is more frequently mentioned in Proverbs. For example, wealth (*hôn*) is described as useless on the day of wrath, that is, on the day of Lord's judgment (11:4), and one is advised that wealth gained through unjust methods does not last long (13:11; 28:8, 22). In 19:14 the Lord is put in contrast with the parents to teach the son that wealth may be inherited from parents but true blessings are only from the Lord: "House and wealth (*hôn*) are an inheritance of parents, but a prudent wife is from the Lord." However, wealth is not always viewed as negative in Proverbs. The positive side of wealth is that one can use it to honor the Lord (3:9), and that wealth is one of the benefits which Wisdom gives to humans (8:18; 24:4). The sage also describes the practical effects of having wealth: it provides a sense of security (10:15; 18:11), and makes many friends (19:4).

The use of *hôn* is considered consistent in collections I, II, III, and V, but its use in collection VI is distinctive because the word is used there not as a common noun but as an interjection "Enough!" (30:15, 16).

B. *Da ʿat* "knowledge" (40 times)[189]

Da ʿat occurs 91 times in the OT, 58 of which are in Wisdom books (40 times in Proverbs, 10 times in Job, and 8 times in Ecclesiastes). Whybray acknowledges that the majority of the instances of *da ʿat* are found in Wisdom books, but refuses to take it as a significant word in wisdom tradition because of its numerous occurrences in other books.[190] Unlike him, however, others consider the noun to be significant in Wisdom books. For example, Shupak says that *da ʿat* is "characteristic of the wisdom vocabulary."[191] M. V. Fox points out that, while *da ʿat* can denote any cognition ranging from common knowledge to elevated wisdom, it is as significant as *ḥokmâ* because both terms have their origin in God, have a similar semantic range, and occur about 40 times each in Proverbs.[192] The significance of *da ʿat* in the wisdom context is that it is often indistinguishable from *ḥokmâ*.

In Proverbs *da ʿat* stands in synonymous parallelism with various terms: *yirʾat YHWH*(1:29; 2:5; 9:10), *ḥokmâ* (2:6, 10; 14:6), *mûsār* (8:10; 12:1), *ʿormâ* (8:12), and *tĕbûnâ* (17:27). In antithetic parallelism, however, *ʾiwwelet* "folly" occurs frequently with *da ʿat*, (12:23; 13:16; 14:18; 15:2, 14).

The most important aspect of *da ʿat* in Proverbs is its theological notion that it is associated with God and piety ("the fear of the Lord"). God is related to knowledge as its source and protector. As source, three important intellectual gifts, wisdom, *knowledge*, and understanding, come from the Lord (2:6). As protector, God not only gives knowledge, wisdom, and other things, but preserves and safeguards them by subverting deceptive words: "The eyes of the Lord protect knowledge, but he destroys the words of the unfaithful" (22:12). Knowledge sometimes denotes not only cognition but also a pious attitude, especially, when it is associated with God, as shown in 2:5: "Then, you will understand the fear of the Lord, and you will find the knowledge of God." In this context, the synonymous relationship between "the fear of the Lord" and "the knowledge of God" demands "knowledge" to be understood as a pious attitude not as mere intellectual cognition. Therefore, when one rejects one of the two, he is expected to reject the other as well: "Because they hated knowledge, and did not choose the fear of the Lord" (1:29). About the relationship between the fear of the Lord and the knowledge of God, Fox, on one hand, points out that the two have much the same qualities and functions, but, on the other hand, he says that there is difference between the two in a temporal sense. According him, fear comes before knowledge, because one can fear God before having knowledge of him.[193] Such differentiation between the fear of God and knowledge of God is possible only if one understands the first as an instinctive emotional phenomenon and the second as an outcome of learning process. However, the Bible indicates that putting the fear of the Lord and the knowledge of God in a temporal sequence may not be so simple as Fox suggests. The instances of the verbs *lmd* "to learn, teach" and *yr*ʾ "to fear" in Deuteronomy show that the temporal sequence of fear and knowledge is rather the other way around. For example, in Deut 6:1–2 Moses says that God has commanded him to teach (*lmd*) Israelites so that they and their children may fear (*yr*ʾ) the Lord. It becomes clear from this example that the fear of the Lord follows the knowledge of God on one's relationship with God. This sequence confirms the commonly held view that the fear of the Lord is the totality of human response, including obedience (loyalty), reverence (worship), and morality (holiness).

In Proverbs people can be divided into two groups in terms of their relationship to knowledge. One group consists of those who already possess knowledge, or those who seek and readily acquire knowledge. They are the *nābôn* "the intelligent" (14:6; 15:14; 18:15; 19:25), the *ḥākām* "the wise" (10:14; 15:2, 7; 14:15; 21:11), and the *ʿārûm* "the prudent" (12:23; 13:16; 14:18). In contrast with these, we find four types of people who inherently possess negative attitudes toward knowledge. They are characterized as fools or morally negative people: the *kěsîl* "the fool" (1:22; 14:7; 15:7), the *petî* "the simple" (14:18), the *lēṣ* "the mocker" (1:22, 29), and the *rāšāʿ* "the wicked" (29:7). They hate knowledge or do not understand it. In general, one who loves instruction loves knowledge (12:1).

The peculiar expression *daʿat qědôšîm* "knowledge of the Holy One" is found only in collections I and VI (9:10; 30:3), implying that there is a link between the two collections.[194] Knowledge refers to the father's instruction in collections I and III (2:10; 5:2; 22:17, 20; 23:12). In view that collections I, II, and V are ascribed to Solomon, collection V shows an incongruous aspect with the two other collections in the fact that *daʿat* occurs only once in the collection while it appears 13 times in collection I and 20 times in collection II (cf. Table 1.10).

C. Ḥkm "to be wise" (13 times)[195]

Although a close relationship between the verb *ḥkm* and Wisdom books is anticipated, it is still somewhat surprising to note that it occurs only eight times outside the three Wisdom books in the OT. True to its meaning, *ḥkm* occurs more frequently in Wisdom books: 13 times in Proverbs, four times in Ecclesiastes, and twice in Job. In order to facilitate the understanding of the use of *ḥkm* in Proverbs, we will ask hypothetical questions related to the verb, and will attempt to answer to the questions. The first question one may want to ask with regard to *ḥkm* would be, "Who needs to be wise?" If a wise man is described as still having need to be wiser (9:9; cf. 1:5), the answer is everyone without exception. In Proverbs, however, one of those who have to be wise is undoubtedly the son (or pupil). The son is repeatedly commanded by the parents and Wisdom to hear their instruction to become wise (e.g., 8:33; 23:15, 19; 27:11). The sage's command to be wise in 6:6 indicates that a lazy person needs to be wise: "Go to the ant, Sluggard [*ʿāṣēl*], look at its ways, and be wise!" The last example (6:6) implies that laziness is a sign of lack of wisdom, and that wisdom is the remedy to correct laziness.

Another fundamental question that one may ask in connection with the verb *ḥkm* is "How can one become wise?" It is generally understood in Proverbs that learning from a teacher or parents is to become wise, and that such learning requires an obedient attitude from a son (or a student). With regard to the methods of ancient education, Shupak explains that the ancient Egyptian learning demanded blind obedience, incessant rebukes, and beatings.[196] However, such harsh aspects of learning pointed out by her are not so conspicuous in Proverbs, although obedience, rebuke, and beating are mentioned in the book. The frequent association of *ḥkm* with the verb *šmʿ* rather indicates that *hearing* is the main method to learn or acquire wisdom in a normal situation (8:33; 19:20; 23:19). On the other hand, however, the process of visual learning appears to be an effective method for the fool. For example, the *ʿāṣēl* is told to go to ants for a visual scrutiny to learn from their industrious activity (6:6). The effectiveness of visual learning is also implied in 21:11 where it is said that, while beating has no effect on the more stubborn fool (the mocker), the *petî* can learn a lesson by watching the punishment of the first: "When the mocker is punished, the naive one becomes wise."

The use of the verb *ḥkm* in collections I, II, III, V, and VI appear to be consistent: the son is commanded to be wise in collections I, III, and V (8:23; 23:15, 19; 27:11), the association of the act of hearing with becoming wise in collections I, II, and III (8:33; 19:20; 23:19), and the ant as a symbol of wisdom in collections I and VI (6:6; 30:24).

D. *ʾāb* "father" (26 times)[197]

ʾāb occurs 26 times in Proverbs: five times in collection I, 11 times in collection II, four times each in collections III and V, and twice in collection VI. In view that collection I contains ten lengthy instructions of a father to his son,[198] it is surprising that *ʾāb* occurs only five times in those ten instructions (actually three times because *ʾāb* in 3:12 and 4:3 does not refer to the father of the son). Although the discussion of the father's identity is not within the scope of our discussion, it is certain that the identity of the father in collection I is not always unequivocal but complex allowing a second probability.[199] Although the instructions in collection I are clearly intended for the son, it is difficult to understand that the father in the collections is an actual father because not many actual fathers in ancient Israel would have been capable of teaching their sons with the same piety, divine authority, and knowledge described in collection I. At any rate, it is certain that the father in the collection is a figure who has two functional images, a father and a teacher.[200] The rare occurrence of ʾāb in collection I is undoubtedly due to the frequent use of the first person pronominal suffix to refer to the father (e.g., "my instruction," "my words," or "my command"). However, an important factor that makes the ten instructions appear parental is the frequent occurrence of "son!" (bēn occurs 26 times in collection I).

It is noted in collections I, II, III, V, and VI that the father is often associated with two instructional terms, mûsār (1:8; 4:1; 13:1; 15:5) and miṣwâ (2:1; 3:1; 4:4; 6:20; 7:1, 2). Also, the verbs śmḥ "to be glad" and gyl "to rejoice" occur frequently in connection with the father (10:1; 15:20; 17:21; 23:24, 25; 29:3). These two phenomena imply that joy is the reward which the father desires to experience in his son's wisdom education. Such desire of the father is emphasized in a negative way by his fear of son's failure in education. It is significant to note that the most frequently found theme in reference to the father is the unhappiness caused by his son's failure to be wise or to obey the parents' instruction (15:5; 17:21, 25; 19:13, 26; 20:20; 28:7, 24; 30:11, 17). The equal responsibility of the father and mother in child education is evinced by the collocation of the two parents in 12 instances (1:8; 4:3; 6:20; 10:1; 15:20; 19:26; 20:20; 23:22, 25; 28:24; 30:11, 17).

Several common themes are found in the use of ʾāb in collections I, II, III, V, and VI: the son bringing joy to the parents in collections II, III, and V (10:1; 15:20; 23:24, 25; 29:3), the son showing a disrespectful attitude to the parents in collections II, V, and VI (15:5; 17:21, 25; 19:13, 26; 20:20; 28:7, 24; 30:11, 17), and the father's admonition to pay attention to his teaching in collections I and III (1:8; 4:1; 6:20; 13:1; 23:22).

(10) The Relationship
between Collections I, II, III, V, VI, and VII

a. Verbs (4)

אכל	807/14	to eat	I-1	II-3	III-3	V-4	VI-2	VII-1
ידע	940/35	to know	I-10	II-8	III-7	V-6	VI-3	VII-1
נתן	2011/33	to give	I-12	II-8	III-2	V-5	VI-1	VII-5
קום	629/10	to rise	I-1	II-2	III-2	V-2	VI-1	VII-2

b. Adjectives/Nouns (9)

אֵם	220/14	mother	I-3	II-4	III-2	V-2	VI-2	VII-1
בַּיִת	2036/37	house	I-15	II-12	III-2	V-3	VI-1	VII-4
בֵּן	4891/59	son	I-26	II-21	III-4	V-3	VI-2	VII-3
דֶּרֶךְ	706/75	way	I-29	II-33	III-2	V-5	VI-5	VII-1
חָכְמָה	153/42	wisdom	I-19	II-14	III-4	V-3	VI-1	VII-1
יהוה	6828/87	Lord	I-19	II-55	III-5	V-6	VI-1	VII-1
לֶחֶם	297/23	bread	I-5	II-5	III-2	V-6	VI-3	VII-2
מֶלֶךְ	2518/32	king	I-2	II-14	III-2	V-7	VI-3	VII-4
פֶּה	502/55	mouth	I-13	II-30	III-1	V-6	VI-2	VII-3

Thirteen words (4 verbs, 8 adjectives/nouns, and the divine name *YHWH*) occur in the six collections, and the use of the three words, *YHWH*, *ḥokmâ*, and *melek*, in the collections will be examined below.

A. *YHWH* (87 times)[201]

Table 1.15
Divine Names in Three Wisdom Books

	YHWH	*ʾĕlōhîm*	*ʾĕlôah*	*ʾēl*	*Šadday*	*Qādôš*	*ʾădōnāy*
Job	32	17	41	55	31	1	1
Proverbs	87	5	1	(4)		2	
Qoheleth		40					

NOTE: In Proverbs, *ʾēl* occurs in two personal names, Ithiel (30:1) and Lemuel (31:1, 4).

Although Job, Proverbs, and Ecclesiastes commonly deal with wisdom, Table 1.15 shows that each of the three books has a distinctive character in using the divine names. The most conspicuous phenomenon observed in the table is that Ecclesiastes uses only one divine name (*ʾĕlōhîm*) while diverse divine names are employed in Job and Proverbs. This phenomenon becomes even more conspicuous by the fact that *ʾĕlōhîm* occurs in Ecclesiastes predominantly with the definite article (*hāʾĕlōhîm* 32 out of 40 times). In the case of Job, the book is characterized by its heavy use of two uncommon divine names in the OT, *ʾĕlôah* and *Šadday*. Another peculiar aspect of Job is the unbalanced occurrence of *YHWH* in the book. Although *YHWH* occurs 32 times in Job, the divine name does not occur in chapters 3–37 (except 12:9 and 28:28) which consist of the dialogues between Job, the three friends, and Elihu. In view of the complete absence of the divine name *YHWH* in Ecclesiastes and its limited occurrence in the seven chapters of Job (chs. 1–2 and 38–42), it is remarkable that the deity of Proverbs is almost exclusively identified as *YHWH* (87 times). Because the use of the divine name *YHWH* in Proverbs is too consistent to be harmonized with the composite nature of the book, some ascribe the consistency to the hand of the late redactor or collector. This understanding naturally leads to the assumption that God-sayings in Proverbs were composed later than other sayings. However, the existence of God-sayings elsewhere in the OT indicates that at least some of the God-sayings in Proverbs could be old. The following two examples prove that religious proverbs containing the divine name are associated with old traditions: "Like Nimrod, a mighty hunter before *the Lord*" (Gen 10:9) and "Man looks at the outward appearance, but *the Lord* looks at the heart" (1 Sam 16:7). Especially, the last example (1 Sam 16:7) indicates that, even though the redactor may ultimately be responsible for the almost unvarying use of the divine name in Proverbs, all the God-sayings cannot be dated to a late period. Regardless of the date of the God-sayings, the sage's intent in using the divine name in Proverbs is clearly to emphasize the Lord's sovereignty in the realm of wisdom. This understanding brings us into agreement with von Rad, who explains that the presence of Yahwism in Proverbs is to answer the question regarding the place of wisdom in Israelite faith rather than the place of the Lord.[202] Another significant phenomenon in regard to the divine name in Proverbs is the frequency. The investigation of the frequency of the verbs, adjectives, and nouns in Proverbs shows that the divine name *YHWH* has the third highest frequency (87 times) after *lēb* "heart" (97 times) and *ʾîš* "man" (90 times). More significant than the frequency is the fact that God-sayings appear in almost all collections (no God-sayings in collection IV) and, especially, in all the literary styles of the sayings in Proverbs, such as essay-type sayings, sayings in antithetic or synonymous parallelism, and sayings in an acrostic poem. It is particularly difficult to explain the existence of God-sayings in various styles as "Yahwistic" reworking. Those who support such a view have to say that the redactor has composed different types of God-sayings to place them according to the types of the sayings in the collections. This position is inconceivable. It is rather more natural to think that various types of God-sayings existed long before the activities of collection and redaction.

In addition, because of the great degree of disagreement with the MT, the three main ancient versions, the LXX, Peshitta, and Targum, cannot be used to suggest that the divine name *YHWH* replaced *ʾĕlōhîm* in Proverbs in a later period.[203] For example, even though the LXX represents the deity in Hebrew Proverbs either with θεός (20 times) or κύριος (more than 60 times),[204] there are sufficient reasons to doubt that the 20 instances of θεός are the faithful renderings of Hebrew *ʾĕlōhîm*. The following examples taken from 3:33–34 prove the point:

MT 3:33a	*mĕᵓērat YHWH bĕbēt rāšā ᶜ*
	"The curse of the *Lord* is in the house of the wicked"
LXX 3:33a	κατάρα θεοῦ ἐν οἴκοις ἀσεβῶν
	"The curse of *God* is in the houses of the ungodly"

The LXX shows "God" in the place of "Lord," causing some interpreters to think that *ᵓĕlōhîm* was the original word in the Hebrew text. However, in the next line we see the following unexpected translation:

MT 3:34a	*ᵓim lallēṣîm hûᵓ yālîṣ*
	"if he (*YHWH*) mocks the mockers"
LXX 3:34a	κύριος ὑπερηφάνοις ἀντιτάσσεται
	"the Lord stands against arrogant people."

Surprisingly, the translator, after using θεός in 3:33a, now uses κύριος in the place where the third person pronoun supposedly refers to θεός. One may say that the translator mistakenly took *hûᵓ* as the divine name, but the possibility is excluded because it involves too much conjecture. If the divine name were *ᵓĕlōhîm* in 3:33a, the translator should have used θεός in 3:34a, not κύριος. The examples testify that the translator of the LXX was not consistent in translating the divine name, making uncertain how may of the 20 instances of θεός are actual renderings of *ᵓĕlōhîm*. It seems possible that the translator exercised a certain degree of freedom even in dealing with the divine name.

Now, the contents of the God-sayings in Proverbs will be examined below in order to understand the image of the Lord presented in wisdom material. A survey of the 87 instances of the divine name shows that the Lord is frequently associated with the following themes: the fear of the Lord, the abomination to the Lord, the divine retribution, the human way and the divine way, the Lord as Creator, the Lord's knowledge, trusting the Lord, and, finally, the Lord and wisdom.

i. The Fear of the Lord

One of the more frequently found expressions involving the divine name is the fear of the Lord: the noun *yirᵓâ* occurs 14 times in association with the Lord and the verb *yrᵓ* occurs four times with the Lord as its object to fear.[205] Since we have already examined the use of the expression "fear of the Lord," our discussion will be brief this time. First of all, the theme is found in four collections (I, II, III, and VII) in connections with the following terms: wisdom or knowledge (1:7; 2:5; 9:10; 15:33), evil (3:7; 8:13; 16:6), life (14:27; 19:23), and reward (10:27; 14:26; 22:4; 31:30). In the first four instances (1:7; 2:5; 9:10; 15:33) the relationship between the fear of the Lord and wisdom can be summarized as follows:

Wisdom/knowledge begins with "fear of the Lord" (1:7; 9:10)
Wisdom leads to the understanding of "fear of the Lord" (2:5)
Wisdom's instruction is "fear of the Lord" (15:33)

Based on these sayings, we can conclude that the fear of the Lord is the starting point, goal, and substance of wisdom teaching.

The fear of the Lord is mentioned in three instances (3:7; 8:13; 16:6) in connection with the problem of evil. According to 3:7 ("Fear the Lord and shun evil!"), it is understood that the fear of the Lord and an evil lifestyle cannot co-exist. The first does not tolerate the second. In 8:13 strong emotional dislike of evil is equated with the fear of the Lord: "The fear of the Lord is to hate evil." It is clearly stated in 16:6 that the piety is the motivation for one to shun evil: "Turning from evil is by the fear of the Lord." Not only does the fear of the Lord forbid doing evil, but it provides the motivation and strength to turn away from evil.[206] The vitally important function of the fear of the Lord is seen in the association of the phrase with human life: "The fear of the Lord is the fountain of life" (14:27) and "The fear of the Lord is for life" (19:23). Finally, the fear of the Lord is the basis of reward for the pious: fearing the Lord will bring the reward of a long life (10:27; 22:4), wealth, honor (22:4), and praise from others (31:30).

ii. The Abomination to the Lord

Another frequently found expression involving the divine name is *tôʿăbat YHWH* "abomination to the Lord." This phrase occurs 12 times (including *tôʿăbat napšô* in 6:16) in Proverbs, all in collections I and II.[207] It is noted in the OT that the noun *tôʿēbâ* occurs more frequently in three books, Ezekiel (43 times), Proverbs (21 times), and Deuteronomy (17 times). According to R. E. Clements and M. Weinfeld, the use of *tôʿēbâ* in Deuteronomy and Ezekiel is to express the divine feeling of abhorrence in connection with alien cultic objects and practices.[208] However, it is significant to note that the exact phrase *tôʿăbat YHWH* is found only in Deuteronomy (8 times) and Proverbs (11 times) in the entire OT, even though many instances of *tôʿēbâ* in Ezekiel also refers to God's abomination. The notable use of *tôʿēbâ* in connection with idolatry and wisdom in the three books directs us to suggest that cult and wisdom are the two realms in which divine displeasure is understood as the ultimate disapproval of human conducts.[209] Because of the frequent occurrence of the expression in Proverbs, it is suggested that the sage tries to achieve the goal of wisdom education by using the divine abhorrence on the one hand and the deed-consequence principle on the other hand.

As for the use of *tôʿăbat YHWH* in Proverbs, it is noted that four negative themes are mentioned as the objects of God's displeasure: bad human behaviors/characters, dishonest trading practices, judicial corruption, and unacceptable sacrifice. The human behaviors or characters which are abominable to the Lord are comprehensively listed in 6:17–19: proud eyes, a lying tongue, hands shedding innocent blood, heart devising evil thoughts, swift feet to run to evil, a lying witness, and a man who causes strife among brothers (cf. 3:32; 11:20; 12:22; 15:9, 26; 16:5). It is interesting that, among many crimes in society, the Lord is particularly displeased by the use of dishonest scales (11:1; 20:10, 23). Clements also appears to be curious about this phenomenon when he attempts to explain the use of *tôʿăbat YHWH* in connection with the dishonest scales. According to him, punitive actions could hardly be taken against the dishonest trading practices because obtaining proof of such practices was extremely difficult. As a result, this type of crime "cannot readily be dealt with by any other means of social sanction than reproof."[210] Therefore, the sage relies on the divine condemnation against the elusive crime. Weinfeld offers a different understanding of the use of the phrase. According to his understanding of the use of the phrase in Deuteronomy, the reason that dishonest weights and measures are abominable to the Lord is because the dishonesty is characterized as two-facedness or hypocritical attitude, a feature that is also found in idolatry and sacrifice of blemished animals.[211] Another possible explanation for the divine abhorrent feeling toward the dishonest scales may be found in Prov 16:11 and Isa 40:12. It is understood in these two texts that the weights and scales are God's work to reflect divine justice, and that, more importantly, the Lord himself is a user of a balance (*peles*) and the scales (*mōʾznayim*) to weigh mountains and hills. This direct connection of the Lord to the scales may be the reason for the strong divine abhorrence when the tools are willfully misused for unrighteous gains. Similarly, the use of *tôʿăbat YHWH* in reference to the abuse of justice in the law court (17:15) and the sacrifice offered by the wicked (15:8) can be understood in the context of divine justice and worship.

In his discussion of the concept of abomination, Clements points out that *rāṣôn* "favor, acceptability" denotes an opposite concept of abomination.[212] If the ultimate condemnation is the divine abomination, then the ultimate favor or acceptance is the *rāṣôn* that comes from the Lord (8:35; 12:2; 18:22). The blessing of having a (wise) wife is that the husband will obtain *rāṣôn* from the Lord (8:35; 18:22).

iii. The Divine Retribution

The divine name *YHWH* is also frequently found in the sayings which deal with the theme of divine retribution.[213] Like the expression "abomination to the Lord," the notion of divine retribution is intended to encourage positive conducts and to deter negative ones in the wisdom context. The positive aspects of the divine retribution are: he rewards one who is kind to the poor (19:17), rewards him who loves his enemies (26:22), blesses those who trust him (28:25; 29:25), does not allow the righteous to be hungry (10:3), and saves him who waits for him (20:22). On the other hand, God's dealings with morally negative people are: he takes punitive actions against the wicked and proud (3:33; 15:25), is far from the wicked (15:29), and does not intervene when a sinner falls into a disaster (22:14).

iv. The Human Way and Divine Way

What is meant by this heading is that, no matter what humans plan or do, it is the Lord's will that prevails at the end. In this sense, the sayings which contain the idea of the Lord's sovereignty nullifying human intentions can be understood as expressing the limitations of wisdom.[214] In the wisdom context, the sovereignty of God in human affairs are shown in the following ways: walking belongs to man, but he does not understand his way because man's steps come from the Lord (20:24), humans plan many things, but the realization comes from the Lord (16:1), humans cast lots, but the outcome of the casting is determined by the Lord (16:33), many seek favor from a human ruler, but justice of man comes from the Lord (29:26), and, finally, humans bequeath houses or wealth to their descendants, but a prudent wife comes from the Lord (19:14).

v. The Lord as Creator

The theme that the Lord is the Creator of the world and humanity is found in collections I, II, and V (3:19; 8:22; 16:4; 20:12; 22:2; 29:13). Westermann's view about God's creation is that there are two traditions of God's creation in the OT: the creation of humanity and the creation of the material world. He agrees with P. Doll who points out that the theme of world creation is prominent in Proverbs 1–9 (especially in 3 and 8) while the theme of human creation is frequent in Proverbs 10–29. Of the two traditions, Westermann says that "human creation belongs to an older line of tradition and that material creation is reflective of a younger tradition."[215] If his view was applied to Proverbs, it could be said that collection I belongs to the younger tradition while collections II and V belong to the older tradition. However, even if the wisdom material in collection I was considered late, the creation sayings in Proverbs 3 and 8 would not be suitable to be used for dating because their main concern is not about material creation but about the role of wisdom in God's creation.[216]

The Lord as Creator is portrayed in collections I, II, and V in the following ways: the Lord created the world with wisdom, understanding, and knowledge (3:19–20), he created everything for its purpose (16:4),[217] he is the creator of every constituent member of society (22:2; 29:13), and he is the creator of every part of the human body (20:12).

vi. The Lord's Knowledge

In three instances the Lord is the subject of the verbs, *bḥn* "to test" and *tkn* "to examine," to convey the notion that he alone knows the true motivation of the human heart. He tests (*bḥn*) human hearts (17:3) and examines (*tkn*) human spirits and hearts (16:2; 21:2; cf. 24:12). The same concept of God is also found in 5:21 and 15:3 where God's eyes are featured as seeing all the ways of the good and the bad. God's omniscient attribute is also indicated in connection with Sheol or Abaddon, the most inaccessible and mysterious realm of the dead (15:11).

vii. Trusting the Lord

Crenshaw appears perfect when he defines wisdom as "knowing and doing the right thing," a definition that seems broader than the definitions offered by others.[218] In the wisdom context, "right" can be understood as "suitable" for a particular condition, occasion, or place. In other words, wisdom is a skill to get the job done in an appropriate way. When one understands wisdom in this way, the sage's teaching to trust in the Lord is remarkable because trusting the Lord is deviant in the world of wisdom where one is expected to steer his or her own life by the sense of appropriateness. In this sense, the sayings about trusting the Lord are considered uniquely Israelite. Trusting the Lord is an act of faith which transcends the realm of wisdom with no self-reliance. This point is well made in 3:5 where the son is admonished not to rely on his own discernment (*bînâ*) but to trust the Lord with all his heart. What is implied in this saying is not the denial of wisdom but the recognition of the limitations of wisdom. It is also said in 3:24–26 that the human fear of sudden disaster, which must have been great in ancient society, is to be overcome by the confidence in the Lord. The sage clearly declares that the purpose of his teaching is to make the student put his trust in the Lord (22:19). Finally, the sage promises that he who trusts in the Lord will have prosperity (16:20; 28:25; 29:25).

viii. The Lord and Wisdom

The last theme to be examined in connection with the Lord is the relationship between the Lord and wisdom. In the relationship between the two, the Lord is portrayed as the giver and patron of wisdom. Wisdom, knowledge, and understanding are his gifts to humans (2:6). He stores up sound wisdom for the upright (2:7), and protects the paths of justice and his faithful people so that those who are already on the right path may remain on it (2:8).[219] The eyes of the Lord preserve knowledge (22:12). It becomes clear from these sayings that wisdom is not independent of God and it alone is not a guarantee of success.[220] The sage in fact says that there is no wisdom, no understanding, and no counsel against the Lord (21:30). Even though humans make many plans, only the Lord's purpose will stand (19:21).

Another theme to be considered additionally in the discussion of the God-sayings is the monotheistic view of Proverbs. In his discussion of the concept of God, J. L. Crenshaw points out that the image of God as a jealous God, the un-paralleled feature of Yahwism, does not appear in wisdom literature.[221] It is true that there is no explicit prohibition or condemnation of worshiping idols in Proverbs, but there are several elements that could be understood in connection with Israelite monotheistic belief. First of all, the comparison of the three Wis-dom books with regard to divine names (cf. Table 1.15) indicates that Proverbs is clearly separated from Job and Ecclesiastes by the consistent use of the divine name *YHWH* throughout the book. This unique feature of Proverbs must be understood as the intention of the book to identify the Lord as the only deity related to wisdom. Secondly, the angry language of Wisdom in 1:24–28 is remi-niscent of God's complaint in prophetic messages. Because of people's disre-gard of her call, Wisdom promises the same treatment to them: she will laugh at their disaster, they will call her but will not get an answer, and they will seek her but will not find her. God also expresses his deepest disappointment at Israel's idolatry, and promises the same punishment for the failure to respond to his call (Isa 50:2; Jer 7:13; Mic 3:4). The vengeful reaction of Wisdom in 1:24–28 comes close to representing the jealous image of God. This is one of the simi-larities by which S. Harris seeks to establish a close relationship between Prov-erbs and Jeremiah.[222] Thirdly, the father admonishes his son in 3:4 not to rely on his understanding but to trust in the Lord with all his heart (*bĕkol lēb*). Here, trusting the Lord with all the heart is to be taken in the context of monotheistic faith because "with all the heart" appears frequently in Deuteronomy to connote the undivided loyalty for God (e.g., Deut 4:29; 6:5; 10:12; 11:13; 13:4).[223]

B. Ḥokmâ "wisdom" (42 times)[224]

Ḥokmâ occurs 153 times in the OT, 88 of which are in Wisdom books (42 times in Proverbs, 28 times in Ecclesiastes, and 18 times in Job). It is a well-known fact that outside Wisdom books *ḥokmâ* refers to technical knowledge and skills required by various professions, and that the *ḥākām* is a person who can perform special functions with such knowledge and skills. Thus *ḥokmâ* is used in refer-ence to the sailors (Ps 107:27), professional wailing women (Jer 9:16), and snake charmers (Ps 58:6). The craftsmen to whom Moses and Solomon en-trusted the projects of building the Tabernacle and Temple were therefore called "the wise men" (Ex 28:3; 31:3, 6; 1 Kgs 7:14).[225] In Proverbs various wisdom terms appear in synonymous parallelism with *ḥokmâ*. The synonymous words are *tĕbûnâ* (2:2, 6; 3:13, 19; 5:1; 8:1; 21:30; 24:3), *bînâ* (4:5, 7; 7:4; 9:10; 16:16; 23:23), *daʿat* (2:6, 10; 14:6; 30:3), *mûsār* (23:23), *tôrâ* (31:26), and *yōšer* (4:11).

Even those who maintain the view that wisdom is international and secular in character must think that the integration of wisdom and Israelite religion in Proverbs is a remarkable accomplishment of the Israelite sage. The sage does not portray wisdom and its synonyms as autonomous principles apart from God, nor does he claim that wisdom is the only answer for human success. Rather, he often indicates that there are certain aspects of human life in which wisdom is ineffective, and that the course of life is ultimately determined by God no matter what humans do.[226] The relationship of wisdom to God would be summarized in the following ways: wisdom is given by the Lord (2:6), the fear of the Lord precedes learning wisdom (1:7; 9:10), the discipline of wisdom in fact is the fear of the Lord (15:33), and no wisdom, understanding, or plan can stand against the Lord (21:30). A correct understanding of wisdom in relationship with God is crucially important because the OT does not recognize any significance of wisdom apart from God. It is important to consider the fact that the OT condemns international wisdom as a symbol of pride against God (e.g., Egyptian wisdom in Isa 19:11–12; Babylonian wisdom in Isa 47:10; and Tyrian wisdom in Ezek 28:4–7; cf. 1 Cor 1:20–21). Jeremiah regards the rejection of God's word by the wise as an act with no wisdom at all (Jer 8:9). We are therefore compelled to understand the value of wisdom only within its relationship to God. Only in that context wisdom is better than precious stones (8:11; 16:16), finding wisdom leads to blessed life (3:13; 14:8), walking with wisdom means safety (28:26), and one who loves wisdom will bring joy to his father (29:3).

Despite the introduction (1:2–6) in which one of the purposes of Proverbs is stated as to give knowledge and wisdom to naive fools and young men, attaining wisdom seems not possible for everyone. Wisdom appears to be out of reach for three types of fool. First, the *ʾĕwîl* cannot possess wisdom because he despises it (1:7), and because wisdom is located too high for him to reach (24:7). The second type of fool is the *lēṣ* whom Shupak considers incorrigible and worse than *petî* and *kĕsîl*.[227] The *lēṣ* may try to seek wisdom, but he will not acquire it, probably because of his scornful attitude (14:6). The third type of fool is the *kĕsîl*. He too may try to acquire wisdom with money, but his heart does not desire it (17:16). Whybray points out that the last example (17:16) has been used by some commentators as evidence for the existence of private education in ancient Israel.[228]

The relationship between wisdom and fools is sharply contrasted with the relationship between wisdom and intellectual people. Prominent is the intimacy of wisdom to those who have the ability of understanding represented by the words derived from the root *byn*: the *nābôn*, *mēbîn*, and a man of *tĕbûnâ*. Wisdom is found on the lips of the *nābôn* "intelligent man" (10:13),[229] and rests in his heart (14:33). Wisdom is with the face of the *mēbîn* "discerning man" (17:24), and is for the man of *tĕbûnâ* "discernment" (10:23). The association of wisdom with the lips (10:13) and mouth (10:31) indicates that speech is the favorite domain of wisdom to show its effectiveness in human life. Wisdom is close to those who possess a humble attitude: wisdom is with the *ṣānûaʿ* "humble man" (11:2) and the *nôʿāṣ* "he who takes advice" (13:10).

The use of *ḥokmâ* in the six collections may be summarized as follows: the association of wisdom with God in collections I and II (2:6; 3:19; 9:10; 15:33;

21:30), with *tĕbûnâ* in collections I, II, and III (2:2, 6; 3:13, 19; 5:1; 8:1; 21:30; 24:3), with *bînâ* in collections I, II, and III (4:5, 7; 7:4; 9:10; 16:16; 23:23), and with *da ʿat* in collections I, II, and VI (2:6, 10; 14:6; 30:3). The theme of wisdom in connection with fools appears in collections I, II, and III (1:7; 14:6; 17:16; 24:7), and parental admonition to gain wisdom is found in collections I and III (2:2; 4:5, 7, 11; 5:1; 7:4; 23:33; 24:14).

C. *Melek* "king" (32 times)[230]

In Proverbs *melek* occurs more frequently in chapters 16, 20, 25, 30, and 31. As for the image of the king, notable is his close relationship to God. First of all, the king is described as being subjected to God and as the one who needs his care. Although a king is an absolute figure whose heart is unsearchable like the high sky and the deep earth (25:3), the Lord can direct his heart wherever he pleases, as a farmer controls irrigation channels (21:1). As a human, a king too needs God's protection. It is said in 20:28a, "Loyalty and faithfulness guard the king." Due to the great resemblance between this saying and the two texts from Psalms, it may be possible to understand the meaning of Prov 20:28a in light of the texts from Psalms.

Prov 20:28a   *ḥesed we ʾĕmet yiṣṣĕrû melek*
               "Loyalty and faithfulness guard a king"
Ps 61:8   *ḥesed we ʾĕmet man yinṣeruhû*
               "Appoint loyalty and faithfulness; let them guard him (king)"
Ps 40:12   *ḥasdĕkā wa ʾămittĕkā tāmîd yiṣṣĕrûnî*
               "Your loyalty and faithfulness always guard me (David)"

What is common in the three texts is the royal context in which personified *ḥesed* and *ʾĕmet* guard a king. Although humans also practice *ḥesed* and *ʾĕmet*, it is clearly understood in the Psalms texts that the two guardian attributes are divine not human. The human practice of loyalty and faithfulness is modeled after the divine qualities, and it is exactly the meaning of 20:28b, "and he (king) makes his throne secure by (his own) loyalty." Commentators generally agree that the personified loyalty and faithfulness in Prov 20:28a belong to God who wants to preserve the king, and that the loyalty in the second half of the verse refers to the king's practice.[231]

Second, Proverbs employs God's absolute image to describe the same image of the king in his kingdom. In 24:21 the father teaches his son that the Lord and the king are the two objects to fear. In 25:2 God's glory and the king's glory are compared by their contrasting actions: God's glory is being mysterious, but the king's glory is revealing (25:2). This may explain why a revelatory oracle is assigned to the lips of the king (16:10). Like God, the king has the power of life and death (16:14, 15).

Third, the king is described as a key figure to secure the well-being of the nation by suppressing evil and promoting good. He sits on the throne of judgment (20:8). It is an abomination for the king to act wickedly (16:12). Instead, he has to make the nation stand firm by removing the wicked (20:26) and practicing justice (29:4, 14). The mother of a king admonishes him to refrain from associating with women and drinking wine (31:3, 4) because women and wine will cause him to neglect royal duties.

At this point of our discussion, it would be appropriate to examine W. Zimmerli's statement about the king in Wisdom books. He says, "Proverbs and Ecclesiastes speak more than once about the king. But the king is never the anointed king of God's people Israel and the son of David, who received God's special promise."[232] It is true that in 32 instances of *melek*, the king is identified neither as the king of Israel nor as the son of David, except Solomon in 1:1 and Hezekiah in 25:1. However, the absence of such specific information does not warrant that the king in Proverbs is a non-Israelite figure. It would be more natural to say that he is an Israelite than to say that he is a non-Israelite, because other characters who are frequently mentioned in Proverbs (such as the father, mother, son, the strange woman, the wicked, and the righteous) are clearly Israelites without specific national identifications. Wisdom also is depicted as an Israelite who speaks in the traditional prophetic language.[233] The same can said of the ideal wife in chapter 31. If Israel had its own wisdom tradition developed within the family or clan,[234] and if the royal proverbs in the Old Testament originated in the Israelite folk culture,[235] it would be possible that what is indicated in the royal proverbs in Proverbs may represent the sage's desire for Israelite kings to be righteous.

In order to have a better understanding of the king in Proverbs, it is necessary to take a closer look at the literary milieu in which the king is mentioned. No one would deny that in the OT the most important promise of God to Israelite kingship is the dynastic oracle in 2 Sam 7:1–17. The main feature of the promise is the permanent stability of the Davidic dynasty, and this eternal notion of kingship is expressed in 2 Sam 7:13 and 16 with three key words, *kwn* "to establish," *kissē'* "throne," and *'ōlām* "eternity." It appears that the theme of the permanent throne of David is drawn from the image of God's throne because the three words are commonly used to describe both the divine and Davidic thrones (e.g., Ps 93:2, "your [God's] throne [*kissē'*] is established [*kwn*] long ago, you are from eternity [*'ōlām*]").[236] The same theme is also found in Prov 29:14 in reference to a king who judges the poor with truth: *kis'ô lā'ad yikkôn*"his throne will be established forever."

In addition to this, the king's throne described in Prov 25:5 (cf. 16:12) resembles God's throne that is founded on righteousness and justice (Pss 89:15; 97:2):

Prov 25:5   *yikkôn baṣṣedeq kis'ô*
               "his throne is established by righteousness"

Ps 89:15   *ṣedeq ûmišpāṭ mĕkôn kis'ekā*
               "righteousness and justice are the foundation of your throne"

It is also significant to note the similarity between Prov 20:28 and Isa 9:6 in which the most ideal Davidic kingship is mentioned in reference to the Messiah. The common structure between the two texts is the use of the verb *s'd* "to sustain" and the noun *kissē*' "throne" followed by the preposition "with":

> Prov 20:28b   *wĕsā'ad baḥesed kis'ô*
>   "and he *sustains* his *throne with* loyalty"
> Isa 9:6   *'al kissē' dāwid . . . ûlĕsa'ădāh bĕmišpāṭ*
>   "on the *throne* of David . . . and to *sustain* it *with* justice"

On the basis of the comparison of the three thrones (divine, Davidic, and the king's in Proverbs), we suggest that, like other characters in Proverbs, the king presented by the Israelite sage is to be understood as an Israelite.

(11) The Relationship
between Collections I, II, III, and VI

בוז	14/8	to despise	I-2	II-3	III-2	VI-1
בִּינָה	37/14	discernment	I-10	II-1	III-2	VI-1
יסף	212/14	to add	I-4	II-7	III-2	VI-1
כָּזָב	31/9	falsehood	I-1	II-6	III-1	VI-1
מות	780/8	to die	I-1	II-5	III-1	VI-1
מנע	29/5	to withhold	I-2	II-1	III-1	VI-1

Collection VI is usually considered an appendix in Proverbs, which is divided into two parts (30:1–14 and 15–33). The position retained in this study is to take the entire chapter as a cohesive unit because of the unity that runs from the first to the second part. This unity will be explained later in the discussion of collection VI. In regard to the exclusive words, six words occur only in collections I, II, III, and VI, and among them the use of *bînâ* and *kāzāb* will be discussed below.

A. *Bînâ* "discernment, understanding" (14 times)[237]

Bînâ occurs 37 times in the OT, 23 of which are in two Wisdom books (14 times in Proverbs and 9 times in Job). Because of its high frequency in Proverbs and Job, Whybray ascribes the occurrence of *bînâ* in late OT passages to the influence of wisdom tradition (or intellectual tradition).[238] According to him, the close semantic relationship between *bînâ* and *ḥokmâ* is seen in the fact that they are synonymous in 16 instances in the OT, being virtually interchangeable each other.[239] In Proverbs the peculiar usage of *bînâ* is that it is a favorite wisdom term in collection I (10 of 14 times). *Bînâ* occurs in synonymous parallelism with *ḥokmâ* (1:2; 4:5, 7; 7:4; 9:10; 16:16; 23:23), *mûsār* (1:2; 4:1; 23:23), and *tĕbûnâ* (2:3). The theological importance of *bînâ* is indicated in its relationship to the Lord. As in the case of *ḥokmâ*, the sage defines the relationship between the Lord and *bînâ* in a similar way: one must trust the Lord with all his heart, not his own *bînâ* (3:5), the knowledge of the Holy One is *bînâ* (9:10), and one can understand the fear of the Lord through *bînâ* (2:3, 5).

As for the use of *bînâ* in Proverbs, consistency is seen in collections I, II, and III in which the noun occurs in association with the verb *qnh* "to acquire" (4:5, 7; 16:16; 23:23).

B. *Kāzāb* "lie, falsehood" (9 times)[240]

Kāzāb occurs 31 times in the OT: 13 times in Prophets, 9 times in Proverbs, 6 times in Psalms, twice in Judges, and once in Daniel. Although Whybray does not include *kāzāb* in his intellectual vocabulary because it is not found in Job and Ecclesiastes while occurring non-wisdom books, close relationship between *kāzāb* and wisdom is implied when Shupak points out that biblical terms denoting deceit and falsehood frequently appear in the wisdom phraseology.[241]

As for the meaning of *kāzāb*, Delitzsch offers an interesting semantic distinction between *kāzāb* and *šeqer*. According to him, *kāzāb* is a lie characterized as fiction and *šeqer* is a lie intended to distort actual facts.[242] This aspect of *kāzāb* is highlighted in the fact that the noun occurs seven times in Ezekiel to characterize the speeches and visions of false prophets. The Lord condemns the false prophets because they speak *kāzāb* and *šāwĕʾ* "falsehood."[243] Although *kāzāb* appears 31 times in nine books of the OT, its usage in Proverbs is distinctive, separating Proverbs from other books. It is noted elsewhere in the OT that the verb *dbr* or *ʾmr* is used to speak a lie (*kāzāb*).[244] It is, however, only in Proverbs that the verb *pwḥ* "to blow, breathe" is used to speak a lie (*kāzāb*).[245] Due to this peculiar phenomenon, it is possible that the association of *kāzāb* and *pwḥ* is a wisdom diction used among the wisdom circles reflected in Proverbs.

It is significant to note that *kāzāb* occurs in connection with *ʿēd šeqer*, *ʿēd ʾĕmûnîm* and *ʿēd ʾĕmet* (6:19; 14:5, 25). This usage implies that *kāzāb* sometimes denotes perjury in legal matters. The collocation of *šāwĕʾ* "falsehood" and *kāzāb* in the prayer of a man in 30:7–9 is reminiscent of Ezekiel where the two words occur together seven times in reference to false prophets. Collections I and II are linked by the identical sayings in 6:19 and 14:5 and the use of *kāzāb* in association with the verb *pwḥ*.

(12) The Relationship
between Collections I, II, IV, and V

חֶסֶר	15/13	needy	I-4	II-7	IV-1	V-1
מַחְסוֹר	13/8	poverty	I-1	II-5	IV-1	V-1
מִשְׁפָּט	424/20	judgment	I-4	II-12	IV-1	V-3
עבר	547/12	to pass over	I-5	II-3	IV-1	V-3
עֵד	69/11	witness	I-1	II-8	IV-1	V-1
עָצֵל	14/14	lazy	I-2	II-7	IV-1	V-4
פָּנִים	2040/18	face	I-3	II-6	IV-2	V-7
רֵעַ	187/32	neighbor	I-6	II-14	IV-1	V-11

Eight words are exclusive to collections I, II, IV, and V, and the use of three words (*ʿāṣēl*, *ḥāsēr*, and *mišpāṭ*) will be discussed below. The significance of the examination is implied by the fact that, while collections I, II, and V are attributed to Solomon, collection IV is a non-Solomonic and the smallest collection consisting of only 12 verses (24:23–34).

A. *ʿāṣēl* "sluggard" (14 times)[246]

ʿāṣēl is unique in two aspects: it is the only word in biblical Hebrew to designate a sluggard, and is found only in Proverbs. Since it is the only word for its kind, Whybray reasonably speculates that it must have been in common use even though it is not found outside Proverbs.[247] In Proverbs *ʿāṣēl* appears in antithetic parallelism with *ḥārûṣ* "diligent" (13:4) and *yāšār* "upright" (15:19) and in synonymous parallelism with the phrase *ḥăsar lēb* "senseless" (24:30). The three instances indicate that the *ʿāṣēl* refers to not only a sluggish person but a morally and intellectually negative person.

The lazy aspect of the *ʿāṣēl* is vividly delineated in several areas of life: eating, sleeping, and field work. In eating food, the *ʿāṣēl* is so lethargic that his hand cannot take food from the dish to the mouth (19:24; 26:15). Excessive sleeping is a conspicuous feature of the *ʿāṣēl*. Several sayings indicate that getting out of bed is a very difficult task for him (6:9; 26:14; cf. 19:15; 24:33). Considering his lazy character, it is natural to expect that the sluggard does not plow the field at a proper time (20:4). As a result, his field and vineyard are in a dreadful condition: weeds grow all over the field and the stone wall is broken down (24:30–31). It is, however, surprising to note that the laziness of the *ʿāṣēl* has no effect on his reasoning ability. He is able to justify his lifestyle: he explains that he does not go out from the house because there is a lion outside (22:13; 26:13). More surprising than this is his confidence in his own wisdom: he considers himself wiser than seven wise men (26:16). The two instances of

ʿāṣēl in 26:16 and 24:30 indicate that the sage considers the ʿāṣēl a type of fool. The sluggard is also unreliable, and the sage warns about the unreliability of the ʿāṣēl as a messenger: sending the ʿāṣēl as a messenger will cause pain to the sender (10:26). The ironical aspect of the ʿāṣēl is that the sluggard has strong desires for many things but, since he does not want to act, his desires eventually become the cause of his self-destruction (21:25; 13:4).

The descriptions of the ʿāṣēl in collections I, II, IV, and V show consistency: collections I and V commonly describe the sleeping problem of the sluggard (6:9; 26:14), and collections II and V depict his sluggishness in eating (19:24; 26:15) and his attitude to find a pretext for inactivity (22:13; 26:13). Collections I and IV are linked by the occurrence of ʿāṣēl in the similar sayings (6:6–11 and 24:30–34) that contain two identical verses (6:10–11=24:33–34).

B. Ḥāsēr "lacking" (13 times)[248]

Ḥāsēr occurs 16 times in the OT: 13 times in Proverbs, once each in 1 Samuel, 2 Samuel, and Ecclesiastes. A survey of the 16 instances shows that ḥāsēr is used in two ways in the OT: in 12 instances (all in Proverbs) it is used in two fixed expressions, ḥăsar lēb (11 times) and ḥăsar tĕbûnâ (once), to indicate the lack of intellect or cognitive faculties, and in the remaining four instances it indicates lack of food (2 Sam 3:29; Prov 12:9), lack of madmen (1 Sam 21:16), and lack of things (Eccl 6:2). That the fixed expression, ḥăsar lēb, is found only in Proverbs (11 times) to refer to a type of fool indicates that the expression is sapiential.[249]

Shupak puts the ḥăsar lēb and petî on the top of her list of fools as the mildest or the most positive fool,[250] but, as we shall see later, the gradation of those fools is not a simple matter. In Proverbs the ḥăsar lēb stands in synonymous parallelism with the petî "naive person" (9:4, 16) and the ʿāṣēl "sluggard" (24:30), and in antithetic parallelism with the nābôn "discerning man" (10:13) or the ʾîš tĕbûnâ "man of discernment" (11:12; 15:21). Against the common view that the expression ḥăsar lēb refers to a type of fool, it should be pointed out that, syntactically speaking, the phrase is often adjectival not nominal. For example, it is used attributively in the following instances to modify a person:

7:7	naʿar ḥăsar lēb "senseless lad"
17:18	ʾādām ḥăsar lēb "senseless man"
24:30	ʾādām ḥăsar lēb "senseless man"

The same adjectival function of ḥăsar lēb is apparent when the phrase is used predicatively in the structure, "He who . . ." as in the following examples:

6:32	nōʾēp ʾiššâ ḥăsar lēb
	"he who commits adultery with a woman is *senseless*"

11:12   *bāz lĕrēʿhû ḥăsar lēb*
          "he who despises his neighbor is *senseless*"

12:11   *mĕraddēp rêqîm ḥăsar lēb*
          "he who pursues futilities is *senseless*"

The notable features of the *ḥăsar lēb* are the lack of morality (6:32; 7:7) and discernment (12:11; 15:21; 17:18). Although the *ḥăsar lēb* denotes a person who lacks intellect, he is self-confident despising others (11:12). A sluggard (*ʾîš ʿāṣēl*) is equated with a senseless man (*ʾādām ḥăsar lēb*) in 24:30 because his vineyard is ruined not only because of his laziness but also his lack of understanding.

The phrase *ḥăsar lēb* alone is a sufficient ground to say that collections I, II, and IV are linked by a unique wisdom expression, because the phrase is found only in Proverbs. *Ḥăsar tĕbûnâ* in 28:16 (collection V) is not exactly the same as *ḥăsar lēb*, but the two phrases are similar in the sense that *ḥāsēr* is used in both phrases to express the lack of discernment.

C. *Mišpāṭ* "justice" (20 times)[251]

Although *mišpāṭ* occurs 20 times in Proverbs, it is remarkable to note that it does not have many synonyms or antonyms. This phenomenon may imply that the noun is a technical term whose meaning is difficult to be conveyed by other terms. As in Prophets, the only word that occurs in Proverbs in close relationship with *mišpāṭ* is *ṣĕdāqâ* (or *ṣedeq*): three times *mišpāṭ* is juxtaposed with *ṣedeq* or *ṣĕdāqâ* (1:3; 2:9; 21:3) and twice *mišpāṭ* and *ṣĕdāqâ* occur together in synonymous parallelism (8:20; 16:8). The antonyms of *mišpāṭ* are rarely found: *mirmâ* "deceit" (12:5) and *ʾāwen* "wickedness, deception" (19:28) appear in antithetic parallelism with *mišpāṭ*. The two antonyms suggest that one of the important aspects of *mišpāṭ* is truth or honesty. It is noted in the 20 instances of *mišpāṭ* that the noun never conveys a neutral meaning, such as "custom" in *mišpat hammelek* "the royal custom" (1 Sam 8:9), but that it is always a moral term denoting the right state.

A number of sayings in Proverbs describe the relationship between *mišpāṭ* and the Lord in various ways. First of all, the Lord guards the paths of *mišpāṭ* for his people (2:8). Fox offers an insightful interpretation of the passage: "Once they step on to the right path, God helps them remain on it. He protects them by guarding their behavior."[252] Another important aspect of the relationship between God and *mišpāṭ* is that the ultimate decision (*mišpāṭ*) for human affairs comes from the Lord (16:33; 29:26). The use of dishonest scales in the commercial transaction has been a common problem in ancient and modern times. In an attempt to warn against and to correct the dishonest business practice, the sage declares that the honest (*mišpāṭ*) scales and weights belong to the Lord, and that they are his work (16:11). The sage echoes the message of prophets in 21:3 when he defines the meaning of true worship: "The practice of justice and right-eousness is far more acceptable to the Lord than the sacrifice." *Mišpāṭ* is mentioned in the context of the judicial court (18:5; 17:23; 19:28; 24:23) and in connection with the king's responsibility to use justice to stabilize the land (29:4; 16:10). Practicing *mišpāṭ* is a joy to the righteous, and the thoughts of the righteous are *mišpāṭ* (21:15; 12:5), but the wicked and evil neither practice nor understand *mišpāṭ* (21:7; 28:5).

The use of *mišpāṭ* in collections I, II, IV, and V is consistent: the occurrence of the noun in Lord-sayings is common to collections I, II, and V (2:8, 9; 16:11, 33; 21:3; 28:5; 29:26), collections II and IV are tied by *mišpāṭ* in the court setting (18:5; 24:23), and the association of *mišpāṭ* with the king is common to collections II and V (16:10; 29:4).

(13) The Relationship between Collections I, II, IV, V, and VI

| יכח | 59/10 | to rebuke | I-4 | II-2 | IV-1 | V-2 | VI-1 |

Ykḥ "to rebuke" (10 times)[253]

Ykḥ is the only word that is exclusive to the five collections. The verb occurs 59 times in the OT, and its strong association with wisdom is indicated by the frequent occurrence of the verb in two Wisdom books: 17 times in Job and 10 times in Proverbs. For this reason, Shupak considers that *ykḥ* is one of the seven verbs related to teaching and education in Wisdom books.[254]

A survey of the instances of *ykḥ* in Proverbs shows that two prepositions are used in connection with the verb. First, the object of reproof (*ykḥ*) is often marked with the preposition *l-* (9:7, 8; 15:12; 19:25): for example, "Reprove (*hôkaḥ*) a wise man (*lĕḥākām*) and he will love you" (9:8). When the object is marked with *b-*, the intention of the reproof (*ykḥ*) appears not to be educational but to prove one's guilt: for example, "Do not add to his words, lest he convict you (*yôkîaḥ bĕkā*) and you will be proved a liar" (30:6). God's reproof denoted by *ykḥ* serves two purposes in Proverbs: it is a sign of love for his children (3:12) and it is to condemn sinners (30:6).

Since the nature of reproof entails condemnation on one hand and demand for correction on the other, the fool not only rejects it but hates the one who reproves him (9:7, 8; 15:12). In contrast to this, there are several types of people who are willing to be wise (or wiser) by the method of reproof. The first type is the wise. When the *ḥākām* "wise man" is reproved, he loves the one who reproves (9:8b). Also, reproof makes the *nābôn* "discerning man" gain more knowledge (19:25). In the world of wisdom, nothing could be more ideal than a wise man whose reproof is cherished by others. What is described in 25:12 may be a wise man's wish to have such an ideal wisdom environment: "A gold earring and an ornament of fine gold are a wise man's reproof to a listening ear." In another instance, the sage expresses his belief that reproof brings good outcomes (28:23).

The verb *ykḥ* is used in collections I, II, IV, V, and VI in two ways, to educate and to condemn. In most of the instances the purpose of reproof is educational (3:12; 9:7, 8, 8; 15:12; 19:25; 24:25; 25:12; 28:23), but in collections IV and VI (24:25; 30:6) the verb is used in the sense of condemnation.

(14) The Relationship between Collections I, II, IV, V, VI, and VII

יָד	1617/31	hand	I-8	II-14	IV-1	V-3	VI-2	VII-3
רֵישׁ	7/7	poverty	I-1	II-2	IV-1	V-1	VI-1	VII-1

Rêš "poverty" (seven times)[255]

Only two words, *yād* and *rêš*, occur exclusively in the six collections, and the use of *rêš* in those collections will be examined below.

Rêš occurs seven times in the OT, all in Proverbs. The exclusive occurrence of the noun in Proverbs along with its two instances in Ben Sira (11:14; 31:7) implies that *rêš* belongs to the wisdom vocabulary. It is interesting to note that the word occurs in the six collections in three slightly different forms:

rēʾš	Collections I and VI (6:11; 30:8)
rêš	Collections II and IV (10:15; 13:18; 24:34)
rîš	Collections V and VII (28:19; 31:7)

Although not certain, the different spellings involving *ʾālep* and *yôd* may reflect the different pronunciations, probably in different wisdom circles. *Rêš* is used in synonymous parallelism with *maḥsôr* "poverty" (6:11; 24:34), *qālôn* "disgrace" (13:18), and *ʿāmāl* "toil" (31:7), and the last two words indicate that humiliation and hardship are the aspects of poverty. On the other hand, the three antonyms of *rêš*, *hôn* "wealth" (10:15), *ʿōšer* "wealth" (30:8), and *leḥem* "bread" (28:19), confirms that poverty denotes lack of material things.

Proverbs does not say that poverty is always attributed to human causes.

For example, when Agur prays to God to give him neither poverty nor wealth (30:8), it is understood that poverty can come from God. However, the sayings in which *rêš* occurs show that poverty is the result of negative human conducts. Three human factors are considered to be the causes of poverty: excessive sleep (6:11; 24:34), rejecting instruction (13:18), and pursuing vain things (28:19).

The fact that *rêš* is not found elsewhere in the OT indicates that collections I, II, IV, V, VI, and VII are linked by the unique notion of poverty denoted by the noun.

(15) The Relationship between Collections I, II, and V

a. Verbs (14)

אהב	208/25	to love	I-8	II-15	V-2
חפשׂ	23/3	to search	I-1	II-1	V-1
כבד	113/7	to be heavy	I-3	II-3	V-1
נחל	59/6	to possess	I-2	II-3	V-1
נקה	44/7	to be clean	I-1	II-5	V-1
סור	300/17	to turn aside	I-6	II-9	V-2
עזב	208/11	to forsake	I-6	II-2	V-3
ענה	316/7	to answer	I-1	II-3	V-3
פוח	15/7	to breathe	I-1	II-5	V-1
פרע	16/6	to let go	I-3	II-2	V-1
צפן	32/9	to hide	I-5	II-2	V-2
קשׁב	46/8	to incline	I-6	II-1	V-1
רבה	176/11	to be much	I-3	II-2	V-6
שׁגה	21/6	to go astray	I-3	II-2	V-1

b. Adjectives/Nouns (36)

אח	629/8	brother	I-1	II-6	V-1
אשׁר	45/8	blessedness	I-3	II-3	V-2
בֶּגֶד	215/4	garment	I-1	II-1	V-2
בַּעַד	105/4	separation	I-2	II-1	V-1
בֶּצַע	23/3	gain	I-1	II-1	V-1
חָמָס	60/7	violence	I-2	II-4	V-1

חֵן	69/13	favor	I-6	II-5	V-2
יָשָׁר	118/25	upright	I-4	II-18	V-3
כָּבוֹד	199/15	glory	I-3	II-6	V-6
כִּסֵּא	135/6	chair	I-1	II-3	V-2
כֶּסֶף	403/13	silver	I-5	II-4	V-4
מָקוֹר	18/7	spring	I-1	II-5	V-1
מַרְפֵּא	16/8	healing	I-2	II-5	V-1
מָשָׁל	39/6	proverb	I-2	II-1	V-3
נָדִיב	26/5	noble	I-1	II-3	V-1
סוֹד	21/5	counsel	I-1	II-3	V-1
סֵתֶר	35/3	covering	I-1	II-1	V-1
עִיר	1042/4	city	I-1	II-2	V-1
עֵץ	329/6	tree	I-1	II-3	V-2
עֵצָה	88/10	counsel	I-3	II-6	V-1
עִקֵּשׁ	11/7	twisted	I-2	II-4	V-1
פִּנָּה	30/4	corner	I-2	II-1	V-1
פֶּתִי	19/15	simple	I-9	II-5	V-1
קָהָל	122/3	congregation	I-1	II-1	V-1
קִנְאָה	43/3	jealousy	I-1	II-1	V-1
קָצִיר	54/5	harvest	I-1	II-2	V-2
רֶגֶל	243/15	foot	I-11	II-1	V-3
רְחוֹב	43/5	open place	I-3	II-1	V-1
רַךְ	16/3	tender	I-1	II-1	V-1
שַׂר	421/3	chief	I-1	II-1	V-1
שֶׁמֶן	193/5	oil	I-1	II-2	V-2
תּוֹכַחַת	24/16	rebuke	I-6	II-7	V-3
תֹּם	23/7	integrity	I-1	II-5	V-1
תָּמִיד	103/4	continuity	I-2	II-1	V-1
תָּמִים	91/6	perfect	I-2	II-2	V-2
תִּפְאָרָה	51/6	beauty	I-1	II-4	V-1

A total of 50 words (14 verbs and 36 adjectives/nouns) occur exclusively in the three major collections, and, considering the relevance to wisdom, the use of the following five words will be examined below: *tôkaḥat* "reproof," *petî* "simple," *marpēʾ* "healing," *māqôr* "spring," and *ʿēṣâ* "counsel."

A. *Tôkaḥat* "reproof" (16 times)[256]

Tôkaḥat occurs 24 times in the OT (not including the four instances of *tôkēḥâ*): 16 times in Proverbs, three times in Psalms, twice each in Job and Jeremiah, and once in Habakkuk. According to Shupak, *tôkaḥat* is one of the main terms to denote instruction and teaching in wisdom material.[257] As for the usage of the term, Fox points out that *tôkaḥat* is always critical and negative with no explicit demand for repentance.[258] However, in view that both the root *ykḥ* and *tôkaḥat* have a connotation "to put in the right," and that *tôkaḥat* sometimes clearly conveys the notion of change in Proverbs, his explanation of the term as mere criticism is difficult to understand.[259] For example, in 29:1, the person to whom a reproof (*tôkaḥat*) is addressed is called "one who hardens the neck" (*maqšê ʿōrep*). Outside Proverbs the expression "hardening the neck" is found ten times, and it is an exclusive expression to depict the stubborn attitude of the Israelite kings and people who refuse to change.[260] A good example for the case would be Jer 17:23, "and they hardened (*wayyaqšû*) their necks (*ʿorpām*) not to hear and not to take instruction." Therefore, it is certain that the act of hardening the neck by the "man of reproofs" (*ʾîš tôkāḥôt*) in Prov 29:1 means resisting the demand for change which is included in the reproof. Also, that the connotation of *tôkaḥat* is more than mere criticism is evident in the two expressions, *tôkēḥôt mûsār* "instructive reproofs" (6:23) and *tôkaḥat ḥayyîm* "reproof of life" (15:31). Both phrases clearly imply that reproof denoted by *tôkaḥat* is educational to save one from premature death. The educational aspect of *tôkaḥat* is also shown in the sayings where *mûsār* "discipline" occurs in synonymous parallelism with *tôkaḥat*. It is significant to note that the two words occur together frequently (3:11; 5:12; 6:23; 10:17; 12:1; 13:18; 15:5; 15:32). The synonymous relationship between *tôkaḥat* and *ʿēṣâ* "counsel" also highlights the educational aspect of the term (1:25, 30): for example, "You let go all my *counsel*, and did not accept my *reproof*" (1:25).

That *tôkaḥat* includes the element of repentance is also indicated by its use in association of the three verbs (*šmʿ* "to hear," *šmr* "to keep," and *šwb* "to turn"): for example, "he who listens to reproof" (15:32), "he who keeps reproof" (13:18), and "Turn to my reproof!" (1:23). It is understood in these three examples that a demand for change or repentance is inherent in reproof. On the other hand, the attitude of a person who rejects *tôkaḥat* is denoted by the following verbs: *nʾṣ* "to contemn" (1:30; 5:12), *śnʾ* "to hate" (12:1; 15:10), *qwṣ* "to abhor" (3:11), *ʿzb* "to leave" (10:17), and *ʾbh* "to accept" with *lōʾ* "not" (1:25). A significant phenomenon in regard to the use of *tôkaḥat* is that the noun always occurs in the same sentence structure in collection II, separating the collection from collections I and V. In all its seven instances in collection II, *tôkaḥat* appears in the following structure: "He who (participle) + *tôkaḥat* + consequence."[261] A good example to illustrate the structure would be 12:1b: "he who hates reproof is foolish." The use of *tôkaḥat* in association with a rod in collection V (29:15) brings out a forceful oral aspect of reproof in education: "A rod and *reproof* will give wisdom" (29:15). Another instance of *tôkaḥat* in collection V shows the value of sincere reproof: "An open reproof is better than hidden love" (27:5). *Tôkaḥat* is used in collection I in reference to God, Wisdom, and the father to pay attention to their reproofs (1:23, 25, 30; 3:11; 5:12).

A survey of the instances of *tôkaḥat* in collections I, II, and V shows that the noun refers to the reproof of Wisdom, the Lord, or the father in collection I, while it denotes reproof in general in collections II and V. As pointed out above, the sentence structure in which *tôkaḥat* occurs is unique in collection II. *Tôkaḥat* in the context of youth education is common to collections I and V (3:11; 5:12; 29:15).

B. *Petî* "simple" (15 times)[262]

As Whybray points out, the use of *petî* is not exclusive to wisdom material (e.g., Ps 116:6; Ezek 45:20),[263] The noun occurs 19 times in the OT, but its predominant occurrence in Proverbs (15 times) and its occurrence in two Wisdom psalms (19:8; 119:130) strongly indicates that it belongs to the wisdom vocabulary. The plural form of *petî* shows three variations in Proverbs: *pĕtā'yim* (1:4; 7:7; 8:5; 9:6; 14:18; 27:12), *pĕtāyim* (1:22, 32), and *pĕtāyîm* (22:3). Interestingly, Psalms also displays two of the three variant forms (*pĕtā'yim* in 116:6 and *pĕtāyîm* in 119:130). The situation which involves the plural form of *petî* is similar to the case of *rêš* as we have seen before: in both cases *'ālep* is involved as a silent letter. In the case of *petî*, since the differences between the three forms are hardly discernible in sound, it might be possible that the forms reflect different scribal practices.[264]

According to Shupak and Fox, the *petî* is a "positive" or "corrigible" fool, because he is capable of learning, and because his folly is due to his lack of knowledge and experience.[265] The association of the *petî* with the *na'ar* "youth" (1:4) and the *ḥăsar lēb* "senseless" (9:4; 9:16) in synonymous parallelism supports the view that wicked nature is not inherent in the *petî*. The view is also supported by the fact that the *'ārûm* "shrewd" occurs four times in antithetic parallelism with the *petî* (14:15, 18; 22:3; 27:12), highlighting the naive quality of the *petî* in contrast with the cunning personality of the *'ārûm*. It is therefore clear that the *petî* refers to a fool who easily believes everything without careful examination, as is described in 14:15. In contrast to him, a cunning person (*'ārûm*) knows how to avoid a dangerous situation before experiencing the consequence. The *petî* lacks such foresight and eventually pays for his folly (22:3; 27;12). It appears that the effective way to educate the *petî* is to make him learn from the punishment of other fools. So it is said in 19:25 and 21:11 that, when the mocker (*lēṣ*) is punished, the *petî* becomes wise.

Two things are noticeable with regard to the use of *petî* in collections I, II, and V. First, as shown below, *petî*-sayings are often repeated:

Collection I   9:4 parallel to 9:16
Collection II   19:25 parallel to 21:11
Collections II-V   22:3 parallel to 27:12

Second, it is observed in each of the three collections that the *petî* is frequently associated with the words that are derived from the root ʿ*rm*: ʿ*rm*, ʿ*ārûm*, and ʿ*ormâ* (1:4; 8:5; 14:15, 18; 19:25; 21:11; 22:3; 27:12). The purpose of the collocation of ʿ*rm*-words and the *petî* in those instances is to emphasize the contrasting qualities between the two or to indicate that the *petî* is in need of the type of wisdom denoted by ʿ*rm*-words.

A connection between collections II and V is indicated by the presence of the repeated sayings (22:3; 27:12), and the use of *petî* in association with ʿ*rm*-words in collections I, II, and V shows that the use of the noun in the three collections is consistent.

C. *Marpē ʾ* "healing" (eight times)[266]

Marpē ʾ occurs 16 times in the OT: eight times in Proverbs, four times in Jeremiah, twice in 2 Chronicles, and once each in Malachi and Ecclesiastes. The use of *marpē ʾ* outside Proverbs is always figurative, not referring to the actual healing of a disease (except 2 Chr 21:18). In a figurative sense, *marpē ʾ* seems to share some of the semantic range with *šālôm* "soundness." In Jeremiah *marpē ʾ* occurs three times in connection with *šālôm*, denoting the state of peace (e.g., "We hoped for peace [*šālôm*] but no good, for a time of *marpē ʾ* but only terror" (Jer 8:15; 14:19; cf. 33:6). The understanding of the figurative use of *marpē ʾ* is important because it is used in the same way in Proverbs, mainly in the sense of "calmness" or "relief."

A survey of the use of *marpē ʾ* in Proverbs shows that the term occurs in synonymous parallelism with *ḥayyîm* "life" (4:22) and *mātôq* "sweetness" (16:24) while it appears in antithetic parallelism with *rāqāb* "rottenness" (14:30), *madqārâ* "piercing" (12:18), and *selep* "crookedness" (15:4). An important aspect of *marpē ʾ* is its close relationship with human speech: the father's words or pleasant words (*dābār* and *ʾōmer*) are *marpē ʾ* to the body and bones (4:22; 16:24), the tongue, especially the tongue of the wise, brings *marpē ʾ* (12:18; 15:4), and a faithful messenger is *marpē ʾ* (13:17).

The negative phrase *ʾên marpē ʾ* "no healing," which occurs five times in the OT (Jer 14:19; 2 Chr 21:18; 36:16; Prov 6:15; 29:1), conveys the notion that the given situation is an irreversible divine judgment. There are two cases in Proverbs, in which *marpē ʾ* is not available (*ʾên marpē ʾ* "no healing"). The worthless man in 6:12 is portrayed as going around with crooked mouth and evil heart, and destruction is sudden to such a person with "no healing" for him (6:15). The same fate applies to a "man of reproofs" who hardens his neck

(29:1).

Collections I and V are linked together by the identical cola in 6:15 and 29:1 ("he will be suddenly broken and no remedy"), and the figurative use of *marpē'* in association with speech is common to collections I and II (4:22; 12:18; 12:17; 15:4; 16:24).

D. *Māqôr* "spring" (7 times)[267]

Māqôr occurs 18 times in the OT. Outside Proverbs *māqôr* denotes the source of water (Jer 51:36; Hos 13:15), blood (Lev 12:7; 20:18), tears (Jer 8:23), and Israel (Ps 68:27). Twice God is called *mĕqôr mayim ḥayyîm* "the spring of living water" in Jeremiah (2:13; 17:13). The spring in Zech 13:1, which will be opened for the house of David to cleanse the sins of Israel, clearly refers to the future Messiah, and in Ps 36:10 the spring of life belongs to God.

In Proverbs *māqôr* appears four times in the phrase "spring of life" (*mĕqôr ḥayyîm*), all in collection II (10:11; 13:14; 14:27; 16:22):

10:11	Spring of life is the mouth of the righteous
13:14	Spring of life is the instruction of the wise
14:27	Spring of life is the fear of the Lord
16:22	Spring of life is prudence to its possessors

It is observed in the four instances that three times the "spring of life" is associated with wisdom (10:11; 13:14; 16:22) while the fear of the Lord is mentioned once as the spring of life in 14:27.

The use of *māqôr* in collections I, II, and V is not consistent: in collection I it is used allegorically in reference to the loving wife (5:18), in collection II it is used in the formulaic expressions such as "spring of life" or "spring of wisdom" (18:4), and in collection V it is used in a literal sense "polluted spring" (25:26).

E. *'ēṣâ* "counsel" (ten times)[268]

'ēṣâ occurs 88 times in the OT, mainly in the following six books: 10 times in 2 Samuel, 18 times in Isaiah, 8 times in Jeremiah, 11 times in Psalms, 9 times in Job, and 10 times in Proverbs. Second Samuel is distinctive among the six books with regard to the usage of *'ēṣâ*. All the ten instances of *'ēṣâ* in 2 Samuel are confined to chapters 15–17, the Ahithophel-Absalom story, and in those chapters the term always refers to the *advice* of Ahithophel except in 17:14 (the *advice* of Hushai). The frequent use of *'ēṣâ* in connection with the two royal advisors in 2 Samuel seems to have prompted McKane to suggest that the term refers to political advice or policy.[269] He continues to suggest that in Israel the *'ēṣâ* of a counselor and the *dābār* of a prophet (and priest) were the two sources of politi-

cal guidance available to the king. Despite their common function, there is significant difference between the two sources. The difference is that the first (*ʿēṣâ*) is a purely human product from empirical sagacity, while the second (*dābār* of a prophet) is the revealed word of God. Whybray, however, rejects McKane's understanding of *ʿēṣâ* as political advice. He explains that such a specialized meaning of *ʿēṣâ* is not found in Wisdom books (Proverbs and Job), although it could be possible that the term became a technical term in political circles during the monarchy.[270]

In Proverbs *ʿēṣâ* frequently occurs in synonymous parallelism with the following wisdom terms: *tôkaḥat* "reproof" (1:25, 30), *taḥbûlâ* "guidance" (20:18), *mûsār* "discipline" (19:20), *tûšiyyâ* "sound wisdom" (8:14), and *maḥăšābă* "plan" (19:21). In 21:30 *ʿēṣâ* appears with two other important wisdom terms (*ḥokmâ* and *tĕbûnâ*) to express the limit of human wisdom in relation to the Lord: "No wisdom, no discernment, and no counsel against the Lord."

As pointed out above, Whybray understands, in opposition to McKane's view, that *ʿēṣâ* is an intellectual faculty belonging to all, and that in the OT the term is the most common word with the meaning "advice" which must have been in common use.[271] This broad use of *ʿēṣâ* is confirmed in Proverbs when the term is found in association with the Lord (19:21), Wisdom (1:25, 30; 8:14), and men in general (12:15; 19:20; 20:5, 18; 21:30; 27:9). The occurrence of *ʿēṣâ* in 19:21 in association with the Lord is to emphasize the divine sovereignty over human wisdom: "Many thoughts are in a man's heart, but it is the Lord's *ʿēṣâ* that will stand." The three instances of *ʿēṣâ* in collection I refer to the speeches of Wisdom, who complains that humans have rejected her *counsel* (1:25, 30; 8:14). The counsel that belongs to the human domain is described as deep water from the human heart (20:5) and as sweet to one's friend (27:9).[272] That *ʿēṣâ* is a thought deeper than *maḥăšābâ* "plan" is seen in the fact that the latter is established by the assistance of the former (20:18).

No clear links between collections I, II, and V are indicated by the use of *ʿēṣâ*: in collection I counsel always belongs to Wisdom (1:25, 30; 8:14), and counsel in God-sayings is found only in collection II (19:21; 21:30).

(16) The Relationship
between Collections I, II, V, and VI

אֵשׁ	379/5	fire	I-1	II-1	V-2	VI-1
בָּרַךְ	256/6	to kneel	I-2	II-2	V-1	VI-1
דָּם	360/8	blood	I-4	II-1	V-2	VI-1
חֶרֶב	411/4	sword	I-1	II-1	V-1	VI-1
יָצָא	1067/11	to go out	I-1	II-3	V-3	VI-4

יָרַד	379/7	to go down	I-3	II-2	V-1	VI-1
מַיִם	580/14	water	I-5	II-4	V-3	VI-2
קַיִץ	20/4	summer	I-1	II-1	V-1	VI-1
רוּחַ	389/21	spirit	I-1	II-13	V-6	VI-1
שָׂבַע	97/19	to be sated	I-3	II-6	V-6	VI-4
שָׂנֵא	112/26	to hate	I-7	II-10	V-8	VI-1

Eleven words (five verbs and six nouns) exclusively occur in the four collections, and among them the use of *rûaḥ* will be examined below.

Rûaḥ "wind, spirit" (21 times)[273]

Rûaḥ occurs 389 times in the OT, and 76 of them are in Wisdom books (21 times in Proverbs, 31 times in Job, and 24 times in Ecclesiastes). *Rûaḥ* has many shades of meaning in the OT, and it is often difficult to decide which fits best in a given context. The basic notion of the word is probably "air in motion," as implied in the following meanings: breath, wind (more than 100 times), wind from the four sides of the world (used with the "east, west, south, and north"), spirit, mind, the Spirit of God/the Lord, and the Holy Spirit.[274]

In Proverbs *rûaḥ* occurs mainly in collections II (13 times) and V (6 times), while it is found once each in collections I and VI. Four times *rûaḥ* denotes the wind in nature (25:14, 23; 27:16; 30:4). The meaning of *rûaḥ* in a given saying is often decided by the word or phrase standing in parallelism. For example, the phrase, *'erek 'appayim* "one who is slow to anger," in 14:29 and 16:32 indicates that *rûaḥ* in the two places is to be understood as "temper." On the basis of parallelism, *rûaḥ* sometimes denotes a person: *ne'ĕman rûaḥ* "a trustworthy person" (in parallel to *rākîl* "slanderer" in 11:13), *qar rûaḥ* "one who is cool" (in parallel to *ḥôśēk 'ămārayw* "one who restrains his words" in 17:27), and *šĕpal rûaḥ* "a humble man" (in parallel to *ga'ăwat 'ādām* "pride of a man" in 29:23). *Rûaḥ* is frequently understood as "mind, heart" which is indistinguishable from *lēb* (15:4; 16:2, 18, 19; 18:14; 25:28), but, when the two words occur together, it is clear that *rûaḥ* refers to the innermost element of a human being (e.g., in 15:13, "in the pain of the heart [*lēb*] the spirit [*rûaḥ*] is crushed"). In two other instances the expression *rûaḥ nĕkē'â* "a crushed spirit" describes the deepest trouble of a person: "a crushed spirit, who can bear?" (18:14), and "a crushed spirit dries up the bones" (17:22).

The use of *rûaḥ* in collections I, II, V, and VI shows consistency: it means wind in collections II, V, and VI (11:29; 25:14, 23; 27:16; 30:4), anger in collections II and V (14:29; 29:11), and spirit in collection I, II, and V (1:23; 15:4, 13; 16:2, 18, 19, 32; 17:22, 27; 18:14, 14; 25:28; 29:23). The expression "humble spirit" (*šĕpal rûaḥ*) occurs in collections II and V (16:19; 29:23), and the phrase "crushed spirit" (*rûaḥ nĕkēʾā*) is found three times within collection II (15:13; 17:22; 18:14).

(17) The Relationship between Collections I, II, V, and VII

אבד	184/10	to perish	I-1	II-6	V-2	VII-1
בטח	120/10	to trust	I-1	II-4	V-4	VII-1
חַיִּים	150/33	life	I-12	II-19	V-1	VII-1
יסר	42/5	to discipline	I-1	II-1	V-2	VII-1
לָשׁוֹן	109/19	tongue	I-2	II-12	V-4	VII-1
פְּרִי	118/10	fruit	I-2	II-5	V-1	VII-2
צֶדֶק	119/9	righteousness	I-5	II-2	V-1	VII-1
רַב	485/25	many	I-1	II-15	V-8	VII-1
רָחוֹק	85/4	far, distant	I-1	II-1	V-1	VII-1
שֶׁקֶר	113/20	falsehood, lie	I-2	II-13	V-4	VII-1
תּוֹרָה	220/13	instruction	I-6	II-1	V-5	VII-1
תמך	21/9	to grasp	I-4	II-2	V-2	VII-1

Twelve words (four verbs and eight adjectives/nouns) occur exclusively in the four collections, and the use of two words, *ḥayyîm* and *šeqer*, will be examined below.

A. *Ḥayyîm* "life" (33 times)[275]

Ḥayyîm, the plural form of *ḥay* "life," denotes the abstract idea of the qualities of a living being.[276] *Ḥayyîm* occurs 150 times in the OT, and about one-third (52 times) of the instances are in Wisdom books: 33 times in Proverbs, 12 times in Ecclesiastes, and 7 times in Job. This distribution implies that, although *ḥayyîm* is not a wisdom term, its use in Wisdom books is significant.

In Proverbs *ḥayyîm* occurs mainly in collections I and II (31 of 33 times). One significant aspect of the use of *ḥayyîm* in Proverbs is that the term frequently occurs in fixed expressions. It forms four different phrases in conjunction with *ʾōraḥ* "way," *ʿēṣ* "tree," *māqôr* "fountain," and *šānâ* "year," and their occurrences are restricted to collections I and II:

ʾōraḥ ḥayyîm	2:19; 5:6; 10:17; 15:24; cf. 6:23	(I, II)
mĕqôr ḥayyîm	10:11; 13:14; 14:27; 16:22	(II)
ʿeṣ ḥayyîm	3:18; 11:30; 13:12; 15:4	(I, II)
šĕnôt ḥayyîm	3:2; 4:10; 9;11	(I)

The first expression *ʾōraḥ ḥayyîm* "way of life" is found in collections I
and II (2:19; 5:6; 10:17; 15:24; cf. *derek ḥayyîm* in 6:23). The way of life means
a way which leads to life, and therefore it is important to know where the way is
and how to walk in it. However, there are some people who will never reach the
way of life. They are those who go to the strange woman and the strange woman
herself (2:19; 5:6). The reason why the strange woman and her associates cannot
find the way of life is clearly indicated in 5:5: it is because she walks in the path
to death, and because her house and her ways lead to the realm of death. Where
and how can one find the way of life? The sage's answer is that keeping instruction and reproof is the way of life (6:23; 10:17).[277]

The second expression *mĕqôr ḥayyîm* "fountain of life" is found only in
collection II (10:11; 13:14; 14:27; 16:22). Whatever mythological origins are
implied by the expression, it is clear that the sage uses the well-known expression as a figure of speech to denote the vitality which can be imparted by wisdom. With regard to the two expressions, "tree of life" and "fountain of life,"
McKane rightly points out that the Mesopotamian mythology supposedly related
to the expressions is "moribund in the book of Proverbs."[278] This understanding
of *mĕqôr ḥayyîm* as a figure of speech with no mythological implication is important to interpret the four sayings in which the phrase appear. The identity of
the fountain of life differs in the four sayings: the fountain of life refers to the
mouth of the righteous (10:11), the instruction of the wise (13:24), the fear of
the Lord (14:27), and prudence (16:22). If one is to interpret the four sayings
with an mythological understanding of *mĕqôr ḥayyîm* no congruity will be
found among the four different identities of the fountain of life. However, as a
figure of speech to denote the vitality of life, the multiple identity of
mĕqôr ḥayyîm means that humans can gain strength for living from different
sources. Also, in light of Isa 11:2, the mention of wisdom and the fear of the
Lord as different sources of vitality must not be taken as incongruous (for example, the view that God-sayings are to correct or reinterpret the old wisdom).
Isaiah prophesies in 11:2 that the Spirit of the Lord will rest on the Messiah,
along with the Spirit of *wisdom*, the Spirit of *understanding*, the Spirit of *counsel*, the Spirit of *power*, and the Spirit of *knowledge*. Striking is to note that the
Spirit of the Lord can coexist, without tension, with the Spirit associated with
the major wisdom terms. All the qualities of wisdom become congruous and
coherent with the Spirit of the Lord in the Messiah. Regarding the tendency to
separate wisdom from Israelite religion, Murphy says that "the separation of
Yahwism from wisdom is an academic, theoretical, separation," and that "wisdom and Yahwism are a blend, not two entities one imposed on the other."[279]

The third expression, "tree of life" (*ʿēṣ ḥayyîm*), is found in collections I
and II (3:18; 11:30; 13:12; 15:4). Again, it is important to understand that the
phrase is devoid of mythological notions in Proverbs. Like *mĕqôr ḥayyîm*, it
also denotes vitality, not any kind of an actual tree. Four things are identified
with the tree of life: wisdom (3:18), fruit of the righteous (11:30), a fulfilled
desire (13:12), and a soothing tongue (15:4). The reason that they are called

"tree of life" is because they bring happiness and joy in life.

The last expression *šĕnôt ḥayyîm* "years of life," is found only in collection I. The phrase occurs in the context where a long life and prosperity are promised by the father and Wisdom: the father affirms that the son will enjoy a long life if he obeys to the father's instruction (3:2; 4:10), and Lady Wisdom also promises a long life to the *petî* and *ḥăsar lēb* (9:11). The promise of a long life is reminiscent of the Fifth Commandment of the Decalogue, and, in view of the commandment, the father and Wisdom, both as the figures of authority in Proverbs, are certainly entitled to give the promise whose fulfillment is guaranteed by God.

The use of *ḥayyîm* in Proverbs is considered consistent at least in collections I and II. The noun forms four frequently found phrases in connection with *ʾōraḥ*, *ʿēṣ*, *māqôr*, and *šānâ* in collections I and II. On the other hand, the two collections show their distinctive use of *ḥayyîm*: the expression *šĕnôt ḥayyîm* is found only in collection I (3:2; 4:10; 9:11), and *mĕqôr ḥayyîm* appears exclusively in collection II (10:11; 13:14; 14:27; 16:22). The association of *ḥayyîm* with the tongue and mouth to denote the life-giving power of speech is also found only in collection II (10:11; 15:4; 18:21). *Ḥayyîm* occurs once each in collections V and VII and the single occurrence is not sufficient to find any link to other collections.

B. *Šeqer* "lie" (20 times)[280]

Table 1.16
Words for Deception

Word	Freq.	Meaning	I	II	III	IV	V	VI	VII
bgd	49/9	to be unfaithful	1	6	1		1		
khš	22/1	to deceive						1	
kzb	16/2	to lie		1			1		
kāzāb	31/9	lie	1	6	1		1		
mašš'ôn	1/1	deception					1		
mirmâ	39/8	deception		7			1		
rmh	8/1	to deceive					1		
šeqer	113/20	lie	2	13			4		1

Table 1.16 shows that *šeqer* is the most frequent word for deception in Proverbs, occurring in the three major collections (I, II, and V) and collection VII. A survey of the instances of *šeqer* shows that the term often occurs in antithetic parallelism with the nouns which are derived from the root *ʾmn* "to be firm": it occurs with *ʾĕmet* "faithfulness" (11:18; 12:19), *ʾĕmûnâ* "faithfulness" (12:17, 22),

and *'ēmûn* "faithfulness" (14:5). This phenomenon implies that inconsistency or unreliability is the nature of *šeqer*. The survey also shows that *šeqer* is frequently associated with speech organs of the human body or terms related to speech. The close relationship between *šeqer* and speech is seen in the following phrases that are found in collections I, II, and V:

lĕšôn šeqer	"lying tongue"	6:17; 12:19; 21:6; 26:28	(I, II, V)
'ēd šeqer	"false witness"	6:19; 12:17; 14:5; 19:5, 9; 25:18	(I, II, V)
śiptê šeqer	"lying lips"	10:18; 12:22; 17:7	(II)
dĕbar šeqer	"false word"	13:5; 29:12	(II, V)

The first expression *lĕšôn šeqer* is included in the list of the seven abominations to the Lord (6:17), and it indicates that telling a lie, along with pride, violence, and evil, is the object of the Lord's strong displeasure. It is not difficult to conjecture from 21:6 that the main motivation of cheating is to gain material things. The sage likens the act of acquiring treasures by a lying tongue to the act of seeking one's own death (21:6). The cruel nature of a lying tongue is seen in its hatred toward the already crushed victims (26:28).

The phrase *'ēd šeqer* is the most frequent expression among the four, and the context involving the *'ēd šeqer* is considered judicial or public, a setting in which the judge relies heavily on the testimony of a witness. For this reason, the instances of the phrase in Proverbs are reminiscent of the Ninth Commandment of the Decalogue. The following comparison of Ex 20:16 and Prov 25:18 indicates a strong possibility that the similarity between the two texts is not accidental:

Ex 20:16   *lō' ta'ănê bĕrē'ăkā 'ēd šeqer*
              "You shall not answer as a false witness against your neighbor"
Prov 25:18   *'îš 'ōnê bĕrē'ēhû 'ēd šeqer*
              "A man answering as a false witness against his neighbor"

The occurrences of the *lĕšôn šeqer* and *'ēd šeqer* in the list of the seven abominations to the Lord (6:16–19) indicates that the two expressions of falsehood are to be differentiated: the first as general and the second as specific. Although it is not specifically mentioned, the setting of the sayings in which *'ēd šeqer* occurs are likely judicial (6:19; 12:17; 14:5; 19:5, 9; 25:18). In Israelite society where the testimony of a witness was a crucial factor in judgment, a false witness could do great harm to others. Such harmful effects of a false witness are compared to a club, sword, and sharp arrow in 25:18. The notion that the *'ēd šeqer* is destined to be punished is expressed in 19:5 and 9.

Of the two remaining expressions, *śiptê šeqer* and *dĕbar šeqer* the first ("lying lips") occurs in a God-saying as an abomination to the Lord (12:22). It also occurs in reference to a noble man as an improper quality for him to possess. Similarly, a righteous person and a king is admonished to dissociate themselves from *děbar šeqer* "deceitful word" in 13:5; 29:12, because when a king listens to lies (*děbar šeqer* without discernment, his officials will become wicked (29:12).

Except for human speech, the use of *šeqer* is rare in Proverbs. In only four of the 20 instances of the word, it is used with regard to earning (11:18), bread (20:17), gift (25:14), and beauty (31:30).

The fact that the expressions *lěšôn šeqer* and *'ēd šeqer* are common to collections I, II, and V indicates coherent wisdom elements in the three collections. The single instance of *šeqer* in collection VII (31:30) is insufficient to establish a link to other collections, but the occurrence of *šeqer* in association with *hebel* in 21:6 (II) and 31:30 (VII) shows resemblance.

(18) The Relationship between Collections I, II, and VI

אָוֶן	77/9	trouble	I-2	II-6	VI-1
לָעַג	18/3	to mock	I-1	II-1	VI-1
נָשָׂא	650/9	to carry	I-2	II-4	VI-3
עָצוּם	31/3	mighty	I-1	II-1	VI-1
עֹשֶׁר	37/9	wealth	I-2	II-6	VI-1
צַעַד	14/4	step	I-2	II-1	VI-1
רוּם	166/6	to be high	I-2	II-3	VI-1
רָחַק	57/6	to be far	I-2	II-3	VI-1

Eight words (four verbs and four adjectives/nouns) occur exclusively in the three collections. Among these, the use of *'āwen* and *'ōšer* will be examined below.

A. *'āwen* "trouble, sin" (nine times)[281]

The occurrence of *'āwen* in the OT is not balanced. It occurs 77 times in the OT, but most of its instances are in three types of books: 29 times in Psalms, 22 times in Wisdom books (13 times in Job and 9 times in Proverbs), and 23 times in Prophets. Whybray points out that *'āwen* always occurs in poetry with the exception of Ezek 11:2.[282] The semantic range of *'āwen* is somewhat broad, including meanings such as "sin," "misery," and "idolatry."[283] For example, *'āwen* is frequently juxtaposed with *'āmāl* to denote "misery, toil" (Hab 1:3; Pss 10:7; 55:11; 90:10). In the phrase *pō'ălê 'āwen* (16 times in Psalms), however, it denotes "sin, iniquity."

In Proverbs, three times ʾāwen denotes a sin committed by speech (6:12; 17:4; 19:28). Although 19:28 reads "the mouth of the wicked swallows evil (ʾāwen)," the act of swallowing must be an output not an input because the saying refers to the testimony of the wicked in the court setting, as McKane suggests.[284] The instance of ʾāwen in 6:12 also means a sin which is related to speech, because the ʾîš ʾāwen goes around with the crooked mouth. In 12:21 ("No ʾāwen befalls the righteous") and 22:8 ("One who sows injustice harvests ʾāwen"), ʾāwen appears to denote "trouble, misery." In 30:20 the term is employed by an adulteress in her denial of adultery. Metaphorically, she wipes away any fragment of food from her mouth, and says, "I have not done ʾāwen."

A similar literary environment is indicated by the use of ʾāwen with bĕliyyaʿal in 6:12 (collection I) and 19:28 (collection II), and the association of ʾāwen with the verb pʿl in 10:29; 21:15; 30:20 indicates the usage of the noun in collections II and VII is consistent.

B. ʿōšer "wealth" (nine times)[285]

ʿōšer occurs 37 times in the OT. Although the noun is not considered as a wisdom term, the close relationship of "wealth" with wisdom is indicated by the fact that it occurs 15 times in the Wisdom books (9 times in Proverbs and 6 times in Ecclesiastes) and 6 times in the story of Solomon's wisdom (1 Kgs 3:11, 13; 10:23; 2 Chr 1:21, 12; 9:22).

In Proverbs ʿōšer and kābôd "honor" occur together four times in synonymous parallelism or juxtaposition (3:16; 8:18; 11:16; 22:4). The juxtaposition of "wealth and honor" is found 12 times in the OT as an expression to connote the most ideal state of success. A survey of those 12 instances shows that it occurs in two different contexts, royalty and wisdom. Four Israelite kings are reported to have possessed "wealth and glory": David (1 Kgs 29:28; 1 Chr 29:12), Solomon (1 Kgs 3:13; 2 Chr 1:12), Jehoshaphat (2 Chr 17:5; 18:1), and Hezekiah (2 Chr 32:27). In the wisdom context, wealth and honor are a reward from the Lord (Prov 22:4; Eccl 6:2),[286] and they are also found in the hand of Wisdom (Prov 3:16; 8:18). However, when ʿōšer occurs alone, the notion of wealth is often negative in Proverbs. The negative understanding of wealth is shown in three instances: "He who trusts in his *wealth* will fall" (11:28), "A (good) name is more desirable than much *wealth*" (22:1), and "Give me neither poverty nor *wealth*" (30:8).

The phrase ʿōšer wĕkābôd "wealth and honor" is common to collections I and II (3:16; 8:18; 22:4), and the negative understanding of wealth is common to collections II and VI (11:28; 22:1; 30:8).

(19) The Relationship
between Collections I, II, and VII

גָּמַל	37/3	to deal fully	I-1	II-1	VII-1
חֶסֶד	246/10	love, mercy	I-1	II-8	VII-1
נֶדֶר	60/3	vow	I-1	II-1	VII-1
פְּנִינִים	6/4	coral, rubies	I-2	II-1	VII-1
שָׁלָל	75/3	spoil	I-1	II-1	VII-1

Five words (one verb and four nouns) occur exclusively in the three collections, and, of the five, the use of *pĕnînîm*, a term used to indicate the value of wisdom, will be examined below.

Pĕnînîm "corals, rubies" (four times)[287]

Pĕnînîm occurs six times in three books of the OT: four times in Proverbs and once each in Job and Lamentations. The occurrence of the word in Proverbs, Job, and Ben Sira (three times) indicates its close relationship to wisdom. The meaning of the word is obscure. Delitzsch proposes "corals" as its basic meaning because its cognate in Arabic means "branch," and because the color "red" is attributed to *pĕnînîm* in Lam 4:7. According to him, the basic meaning "corals" has become generalized to include "pearls" into the shades of its meaning.[288] In Proverbs *pĕnînîm* is used in reference to wisdom (3:15; 8:11), "lips of knowledge" (20:15), and the ideal wife (31:10). For those who identify the ideal wife with the personified Wisdom in chapters 1–9, the use of *pĕnînîm* in reference to the wife in 31:10 is one of the key elements for the identification.[289]

Pĕnînîm combined with the preposition *min* (*mippĕnînîm*) is often used for comparison (Job 28:18; Prov 3:15; 8:11; 31:10; Lam 4:7), and the use of the combined form in reference to Wisdom in collection I (3:15; 8:11) and the ideal wife in collection VII (31:10) is considered consistent. Also, the four instances of the rare term in collections I, II, and VII are to be taken as a coherent wisdom element in the three collections.

(20) The Relationship
between Collections I and III

בְּאֵר	38/2	well, pit	I-1	III-1
גִּיל	45/5	to rejoice	I-1	III-4
חֵךְ	18/3	palate	I-2	III-1

כָּנָף	109/2	wing	I-1	III-1
כשל	62/5	to stumble	I-3	III-2
כתב	223/3	to write	I-2	III-1
לחם	6/4	to eat	I-2	III-2
מוֹעֵצָה	7/2	counsel, plan	I-1	III-1
מֵישָׁר	19/5	uprightness	I-3	III-2
מִשְׁכָּב	46/2	bed	I-1	III-1
פִּתְאֹם	25/4	suddenness	I-2	III-2
קיץ	22/2	to awake	I-1	III-1
קנא	34/4	to be jealous	I-1	III-3

Thirteen words (six verbs and seven nouns) occur exclusively in the two collections, and among the 13 words, the use of two verbs (*lḥm* and *qn*ʾ) and two nouns (*môʿēṣâ* and *mêšārîm*) will be examined below.

A. *Lḥm* "to eat" (four times)[290]

Table 1.17
Verbs for Eating

Verb	Freq.	Meaning	I	II	III	IV	V	VI	VII
ʾbs	2/1	to feed			1				
ʾkl	807/15	to eat	1	3	3		4	3	1
lḥm	6/4	to eat	2		2				
śbʿ	97/18	to eat one's fill	2	6			6	4	

According to Table 1.17, the frequency of *ʾkl* is far greater than that of *śbʿ* in the OT (807 times to 97 times). However, as shown in the table, the verb *śbʿ* occurs more frequently in Proverbs than *ʾkl* (18 times to 15 times). Proverbs is in fact the only book in the OT, where *śbʿ* is more common than *ʾkl*. This unusual phenomenon may be explained by the fact that in Proverbs the verb *śbʿ* is used to denote both in an actual and a metaphorical sense for the actions of seeing or visiting. Of the usage of the four verbs listed in the table, *ʾbs* is used to feed animals (1 Kgs 5:3; Prov 15:17), *ʾkl* denotes eating of humans, animals, and inanimate things (e.g., the sword and fire), and *śbʿ* denotes sufficiency of eating, seeing (27:20), or visiting (25:17).

The last verb *lḥm* has its own unique aspect. The uniqueness of *lḥm* is that all its six instances in the OT are in poetry: four times in Proverbs and once each in Deuteronomy (32:24) and Psalms. In Proverbs *lḥm* occurs twice each in collections I and III. In collection III, the verb appears in the opening lines of two units that deal with table manners: eating with a ruler (23:1–3) or eating with a stingy man (23:6–8). In collection I the verb occurs in Wisdom's invitation to her banquet (9:5) and in the description of the wicked eating the bread of wickedness (4:17). What is common in all the four instances is the notion that the eating takes place in a banquet setting or in a place where food is plenty. In the last instance (4:17), the wicked eat the bread of wickedness and drink the wine of violence, as if their strength to continue doing wickedness and violence is provided by the evil food. Although Toy offers a slightly different interpretation that wickedness and violence are the food and drink for the wicked,[291] the point to make is that food shortage is not in view in 4:17: the wicked can eat and drink to their fill. In his discussion of the metaphor "Life as a Banquet," Fox considers the description in 4:17 as one of the two types of banquet in life,[292] and his view supports our understanding of *lḥm* to denote eating in a banquet setting with plenty of food (cf. Ps 141:4). Another aspect of *lḥm* is that in three instances (9:5; 23:1, 6) the verb denotes eating by invitation. These two aspects of the verb are common to Collections I and III.

B. *Mô'ēṣâ* "counsel" (twice)[293]

Mô'ēṣâ occurs seven times in the OT: three times in Prophets (Jer 7:24; Mic 6:16; Hos 11:6) and twice each in Psalms (5:11; 81:13) and Proverbs (1:31; 22:20). The noun has two distinctive aspects in its usage: it always appears in the plural, and outside Proverbs it always denotes human counsel in disobedience to God's instruction. The instance of *mô'ēṣâ* in Prov 1:31 also refers to the counsel of those who have rejected the fear of the Lord and the instruction of Wisdom. The other instance of the noun in Proverbs is in 22:20, the verse which contains the controversial word *šlšwm* ("Have I not written to you *šlšwm* ... ?"). Significant is that, no matter how *šlšwm* is translated, *mô'ēṣâ* in the verse is to be understood in a positive sense. Then, this is the only instance of *mô'ēṣâ* in the OT for positive use. Scott L. Harris pointed out that there are numerous similarities between Prov 1:20–33 and Jeremiah chapters 7 and 20.[294] In view of his suggestion, it is possible that the negative use of *mô'ēṣôt* in 1:31 is in line with the prophetic tradition, while the positive use of the term in 22:20 reflects the positive understanding of *mô'ēṣâ* in the wisdom circles.

As far as the use of *mô'ēṣâ* is concerned, collections I and III are not coherent. This incoherence could be attractive to those who maintain a strong Egyptian connection of collection III.

C. *Mêšārîm* "uprightness" (five times)[295]

Mêšārîm occurs 19 times in the OT, always in the plural as a plural of amplification to intensify the meaning of the root.[296] The noun is found seven times in Psalms, five times in Proverbs, three times in Isaiah, twice in Song of Songs, and once each in Daniel and 1 Chronicles. A survey of the instances of *mêšārîm* shows that the noun tends to be associated with certain words:

   a. With *ṣdq*-words—Pss 9:9; 58:2; 98:9; Prov 1:3; 2:9; Isa 26:7; 33:15; 45:19
   b. With *mišpāṭ*—Pss 17:2; 99:4; Prov 1:3; 2:9
   c. With "to judge" (*špṭ* or *dyn*)—Pss 9:9; 58:2; 75:3; 96:10; 98:9
   d. With "to speak" (*dbr* or *ngd*)—Isa 33:15; 45:19; Prov 8:6; 23:16

The association of *mêšārîm* with *ṣdq*–words and *mišpāṭ* indicates that it is one of the key words to convey the notion of "rightness." It is in Psalms that *mêšārîm* predominantly occurs with the verb "to judge" denoted by *špṭ* or *dyn*. This phenomenon may be due to the understanding that judgment must be carried out by means of *mêšārîm* in both human and divine realms (e.g., Ps 9:9 "he will judge peoples with *mêšārîm*"). When *mêšārîm* is "spoken," it refers to the truthful content in human speech. Remarkable is the use of *mêšārîm* in Prov 23:31 and Song 7:10 where the term occurs with *yayin* and *hlk* to describe the smooth movement of wine from the mouth into the throat. The identical context of Prov 23:31 and Song 7:10 that contains *mêšārîm*, *yayin*, and *hlk* points to the possibility that, besides its association with the judicial setting, *mêšārîm* may have belonged to the domain of drinking in ancient Israel.

In Proverbs *mêšārîm* occurs twice in juxtaposition with *ṣedeq* "righteousness" and *mišpāṭ* "justice" (1:3; 2:9). It also occurs twice in association with speech (8:6; 23:16). The use of *mêšārîm* in 23:31 in connection with wine is quite different from its use in the four sayings in Proverbs, indicating a neutral meaning of the term with no moral value.

The use of *mêšārîm* in collections I and III appears consistent because of the association of the term with *śāpâ* "lip" in 8:6 and 23:16.

D. *Qn'* "to be jealous" (four times)[297]

Qn' occurs 34 times in the OT to denote an emotional state caused by envy, rivalry, zeal, or jealousy. The verb is used in reference to a man's zeal for God (e.g., Elijah's zeal for God in 1 Kgs 19:10, 14; cf. Num 25:12, 13), jealousy between women (Gen 30:1), jealousy between a husband and wife (Num 5:14, 30), jealousy between brothers (Gen 37:11), and rivalry between nations or individuals (Isa 11:13; Ps 106:16). God becomes jealous when his people worship idols (Deut 32:16, 21; I Kgs 14:22; Ezek 8:3). Unlike its diverse usage elsewhere in the OT, the usage of *qn'* in Proverbs is remarkably one dimensional. It

is used only for one theme: to envy morally negative people, such as envying a
violent man (3:31), sinners (23:17), the evil (24:1), or the wicked (24:19). Naturally, this kind of envy is always prohibited in Proverbs by a negative command
"Do not envy . . . ." Another interesting aspect of *qn³* is that the use of the verb
for envying the wicked is found only in Proverbs and Psalms (37:1). Since
Psalm 37 is classified as a wisdom psalm, it can be said that the use of *qn³* in the
context of envying the success of the wicked may belong to the realm of wisdom.

Although the four sayings in the Proverbs (3:31; 23:17; 24:1, 19) do not
clearly mention the success of the morally negative people, it is probable from
the context that such is the case. If the wicked can be prosperous, how does the
sage persuade the reader not to envy their prosperity? The following examples
indicate that the sage's reasons for the prohibition are religious:

3:31a	Prohibition	"Do not envy (*qn³*) a violent man,"
3:32–34	Reason	"for the perverse is an abomination to the Lord . . . the curse of the Lord is on the house of the wicked."
23:17a	Prohibition	"Do not let your heart envy (*qn³*) sinners,"
23:17b–18	Reason	"but (let it be zealous) for the fear of the Lord all the day, for if there is a future, your hope will not be cut off."
24:19b	Prohibition	"Do not envy (*qn³*) the wicked,"
24:20	Reason	"for the evil will have no future, and the lamp of the wicked will go out."

It is clear in the examples that the sage's solution for the problem of inverse
phenomenon (the prosperity of the wicked) is religious or theological. According to him, one must not envy the prosperity of the wicked because it is an
abomination to the Lord or an object of his curse. Also, the sage appears religious when he says that the evil will have no future. This seems that he has faith
in God's judgment in future. The future (*³aḥărît*) mentioned in 23:18 and 24:20
is not to be taken in the eschatological sense of Christian doctrine, but it may
represent the sage's belief in divine judgment in future, possibly a sapiential
expression of the idea of eschatology. At any rate, it is apparent that the sage
appeals to the Lord whenever the limitation of wisdom is felt in a given situation.

The use of the verb *qn³* to forbid the envy of morally negative people in
collections I and III is consistent.

(21) The Relationship
between Collections I and IV

חִבֻּק	2/2	folding	I-1	IV-1	
נְבֹחַ	4/2	straightness	I-1	IV-1	
נעם	8/3	to be pleasant	I-2	IV-1	
נשׁק	32/2	to kiss	I-1	IV-1	
תְּנוּמָה	5/3	slumber	I-2	IV-1	

Five words (two verbs and three nouns) occur exclusively in the two collections. Of these five, the use of the two words, *ḥibbuq* and *těnûmâ*, will be examined together because the two words appear together in the repeated sayings (6:10; 24:33).

Ḥibbuq "folding" (twice) and
Těnûmâ "slumber" (three times)[298]

While the verb *ḥbq* occurs 13 times in the OT, the noun *ḥibbuq* occurs only twice in the OT (in Proverbs). Because the verb *ḥbq* means to embrace someone or something,[299] *ḥibbuq* is understood in Proverbs as preparation for sleep by putting two hands on the chest as if embracing oneself (cf. Eccl 4:5).

Table 1.18
Words for Sleep

Word	Freq.	Meaning	I	II	III	IV	V	VI	VII
yšn	25/1	to sleep	1						
šenâ	23/7	sleep	5	1		1			
nûmâ	1/1	drowsiness			1				
těnûmâ	5/3	slumber	2			1			
rdm	7/1	to sleep deeply		1					
tardēmâ	7/1	deep sleep		1					

The table shows that in Proverbs the occurrence of the words for sleep is restricted to the first four collections (I, II, III, and IV). The table also shows that sleep is represented by three roots, *yšn*, *nwm*, and *rdm*. The frequency indicates that the words to denote sleep are relatively rare in the OT. For this reason, James G. S. S. Thomson points out that in the Old Testament references to sleep are incidental and not numerous.[300] In Proverbs it is in collection I that words for sleep are found more frequently, and in this regard collection I is distinguished from other collections.

The Old Testament knows four different nouns for sleep, *nûmâ, tĕnûmâ, šēnâ,* and *tardēmâ,* and, according to Thomson who investigated the use of the last three words, *tĕnûmâ* is the first stage of sleep.[301] The significance of Proverbs about sleep is that it is the only book in the OT where all the four terms are found.

Because *ḥibbuq* and *tĕnûmâ* occur in the two identical sayings (6:10–11; 24:33–34), a connection between collections I and IV is evident. With regard to the phenomenon of repetition in 6:10–11 and 24:33–34, one of the more compelling questions would be whether the repetition is due to a direct borrowing from one to the other. Daniel C. Snell, who has thoroughly examined the phenomenon of repetition in Proverbs, suggests that 6:1–19 may have existed, as an independent unit before the composition of collection I.[302] In that case, the question about a direct borrowing between collections I and IV is not relevant. Instead, it is possible that the repetition is due to the independent drawings of the two collections from a common source. Delitzsch, however, suggests that, if collection IV was written in the time of Hezekiah, the author of collection I may have borrowed the saying from collection IV.[303] Toy, while acknowledging that both explanations (drawing from a common source and a direct borrowing) are possible, does not choose either of the two, but explains that the composition of 6:6–11 is better than that of 24:30–34.[304] Although Toy's view that 6:9 is necessary to introduce 6:10–11 is reasonable, one can argue that the relationship between 24:32 and 24:33–34 is equally smooth and excellent in meaning. Considering the nature of a "collection," it is more likely that the repetition is due to drawing from a common source. The repeated saying (6:10=24:33) in 6:6–11 and 24:30–34 may have been a two-verse, independent saying on its own which was in circulation among wise men. It was then taken up later by two different composers in the process of composing longer sayings about the sluggard.

(22) The Relationship between Collections I, IV, and VI

מָגֵן   63/4   shield   I-2   IV-1   VI-1

Māgēn "shield" (four times)[305]

Māgēn is the only word that occurs exclusively in the three collections. It occurs twice in collection I, once in reference to God as a shield for those who walk with integrity (2:7) and the other in reference to poverty which comes to the sluggard like an armed man ("man of the shield," 6:11). Interestingly, the first theme of the shield is repeated in 30:5 and the second in 24::34 as follows:

2:7	The Lord as a shield
30:5	God (*ĕlôah*) as a shield
6:11	Poverty like an armed man
24:34	Poverty like an armed man

The repeated themes of the shield indicate the coherent usage of *māgēn* in collections I, IV, and VI.

(23) The Relationship
between Collections I and V

a. Verbs (13)

אוֹר	43/2	to be light	I-1	V-1
חוּל	40/4	to whirl	I-2	V-2
חזק	293/4	to be strong	I-3	V-1
חלק	9/4	to be smooth	I-2	V-2
חתה	4/2	to snatch up	I-1	V-1
ירה	79/4	to throw	I-3	V-1
נהם	5/2	to growl	I-1	V-1
פחד	25/2	to dread	I-1	V-1
פרץ	49/2	to break out	I-1	V-1
רנן	54/3	to cry aloud	I-2	V-1
רפס	5/2	to tread	I-1	V-1
שׁבר	148/3	to break	I-1	V-2
שׁוה	21/4	to resemble	I-2	V-2

b. Adjectives/Nouns (25)

אֶחָד	970/2	one	I-1	V-1
אַחֵר	166/2	another	I-1	V-1
אֹרֶךְ	96/3	length	I-2	V-1
בּוֹר	64/3	pit	I-2	V-1
בֹּקֶר	214/2	morning	I-1	V-1
גַּחֶלֶת	18/3	coal	I-1	V-2
גַּנָּב	17/2	thief	I-1	V-1

דֶּלֶת	87/2	door	I-1	V-1
הַר	547/2	mountain	I-1	V-1
חָלָק	12/2	smooth	I-1	V-1
חֵץ	53/3	arrow	I-1	V-2
יָמִין	139/3	right hand	I-2	V-1
לָצוֹן	3/2	scorning	I-1	V-1
מָחָר	52/2	tomorrow	I-1	V-1
מַעְיָן	23/3	spring	I-2	V-1
מְאֵרָה	5/2	curse	I-1	V-1
נָגִיד	44/2	leader	I-1	V-1
עֹמֶק	2/2	depth	I-1	V-1
פַּעַם	115/3	beat, time	I-2	V-1
פֶּתַע	7/2	suddenness	I-1	V-1
צִפּוֹר	40/4	bird	I-2	V-2
קוֹל	505/7	voice	I-5	V-2
קָצִין	12/2	chief, ruler	I-1	V-1
רֶשֶׁת	22/2	net	I-1	V-1
שִׁבְעָה	227/2	seven	I-1	V-1

Two features are noted in the thirty eight words (13 verbs and 25 adjectives/nouns) that occur exclusively in the two collections. First, each of the 38 words displays low frequency in Proverbs. It is remarkable to note that none of the exclusive words has a frequency higher than 4 in Proverbs except *qôl* "voice" that occurs 7 times. This phenomenon implies that the task to establish literary links between the two collections would be difficult due to the very low frequency of the words. Secondly, as we shall see later, the exclusive words rarely occur in the same or similar context in the two collections. Only six of the 38 words occur in similar literary environments. These two features of the exclusive words seem to partially support Snell's conclusion that there is no relation between collections I and V.[306] However, it will be shown below that the two collections share common literary elements, even though they are not great in number.

A. *Peta*ʿ "suddenness" (twice) and *Šbr* "to break" (three times)[307]

*Peta*ʿ and *šbr* occur together in the saying repeated at 6:15b and 29:1b: *peta*ʿ *yiššābēr wĕ'ên marpē'* ("he will be broken suddenly and no healing"). According to Snell's four charts of repeated verses, this colon is the only repeated literary unit between collections I and V.[308] Although the theme of a sudden disaster without a remedy is applied to a sinner ('îš 'āwen in 6:12) in collection I and to a man of reproof ('îš tôkāḥôt in 29:1) in collection V, the repetition of the theme indicates a link between the two collections.

B. Bôr "cistern, pit" (three times)[309]

The two instances of bôr in collection I denote two different things. In 1:12 it denotes a grave in the idiomatic expression yôrdê bôr "those who go down to the pit,"[310] but the use of bôr in 5:15 is allegorical symbolizing one's wife. Although bôr refers to a grave in 28:17 as in 1:12, its context differs from that of 1:12.

C. Ḥālāq "smooth" (twice) and Ḥlq "to be smooth" (four times)[311]

Table 1.19
Words for Smoothness

Word	Freq.	Meaning	I	II	III	IV	V	VI	VII
ḥlq	9/4	to be smooth	2				2		
ḥālāq	12/2	smooth	1				1		
ḥēleq	1/1	smoothness	1						
ḥelqâ	2/1	smoothness	1						

Table 1.19 shows that ḥlq-words are found only in collections I and V in Proverbs, and the use of the words to denote smooth speech is also common in the two collections. Ḥālāq, the first word in our discussion, is used in collection I to describe the smooth talk of the strange woman (5:3) and in collection V the smooth mouth brings disaster (26:28). The usage of the verb ḥlq is also the same in the two collections: the verb is used in connection with the speech of the strange woman in collection I (2:16; 7:5) and the flattery of a man in collection V (28:23; 29:5).

Collections I and V are linked by two common features of the ḥlq-words: the words occur only in the two collections, and the smooth speech denoted by the words functions as a trap to others.

D. *Ḥth* "to snatch up" (twice)[312]

Ḥth occurs only four times in the OT: twice in Proverbs and once each in Isaiah and Psalms. In its three instances the verb denotes the act of taking up fire (Isa 30:14; Prov 6:27; 25:22). In Prov 6:27 taking up fire into one's bosom symbolizes the danger of approaching another man's wife. It is also used metaphorically in 25:22 to describe the effects of a compassionate attitude (offering food and water) toward one's enemy. Although the meaning of putting coals on one's head in 25:22 is difficult to grasp,[313] the rarity of the verb in the OT and its same usage in association with fire point to a coherent aspect between the two collections.

(24) The Relationship between Collections I, V, and VI

| אֱלֹהִים | 2603/5 | God | I-3 | V-1 | VI-1 |
| צָרַר | 36/3 | to bind up | I-1 | V-1 | VI-1 |

ʾĕlōhîm "God" (five times)[314]

Table 1.20
Divine Names in Proverbs

Word	Freq.	Meaning	I	II	III	IV	V	VI	VII
YHWH	6828/87	YHWH	19	55	5		6	1	1
ʾĕlōhîm	2603/5	God	3				1	1	
ʾĕlôah	57/1	God						1	
Qādōš	116/2	Holy One	1					1	
(*ʾēl*)	235/4	God						(2)	(2)

NOTE: In Proverbs *ʾēl* occurs in two personal names, Ithiel (30:1) and Lemuel (31:1, 4).

Although three different divine names and one epithet are used in Proverbs (*ʾēl* does not occur independently but occurs in two theophoric names, Ithiel and Lemuel), it is evident in Table 1.20 that the sage's intention throughout the book is to present the deity as *YHWH*. Considering the size of collection IV (12 verses), the absence of divine names in the collection should not be considered significant.

In collection I *ʾĕlōhîm* occurs three times and *qĕdōšîm* once. It is noted in the collection that both words are easily identified with the Lord by means of the

context and synonymous parallelism. This identification of the Lord is important, because it will help the reader understand the same two terms in collection
VI (30:1–14) as referring to the Lord.[315]

The phenomenon that the divine name *YHWH* is almost exclusively used
in Proverbs raises a question about the presence of other divine names in the
book. As far as *'ĕlōhîm* is concerned, the name occurs in the places where its
use is inevitable. *'ĕlōhîm* occurs five times in Proverbs, and its occurrences in
2:5 and 30:9 are demanded by parallelism:

> 2:5   Then, you will understand the fear of the Lord (*YHWH*),
>   and you will find the knowledge of God (*'ĕlōhîm*).
> 30:9   And I will say "Who is the Lord (*YHWH*)?"
>   and I will blaspheme the name of my God (*'ĕlōhîm*).

In two other instances, the use of *'ĕlōhîm* also appears necessary in order to
make a contrast between a divine being and a human being in a generic sense
(*'ĕlōhîm* and *'ādām'* in 3:4) and between divine authority and human authority
(*'ĕlōhîm* and *melek* in 25:2). In 2:17 *'ĕlōhîm* occurs as the God of the strange
woman. As Fox correctly points out, since she is an Israelite woman, her God
must be *YHWH*.[316] However, two factors possibly prevented the sage from using the divine name *YHWH* in 2:17. First, the expression "her youth" in the first
colon may have compelled "her God" to appear in the second colon. The second
factor is theological. It may have been offensive for the sage to use the divine
name *YHWH* in connection with the adulterous woman. In that case, it can be
said that the same editorial principle which explains the occurrence of *'ĕlōhîm*,
instead of the expected "the Lord God," in the dialogue between the serpent and
Eve (Gen 3:1–5) is operative in Prov 2:17.

When the five occurrences of *'ĕlōhîm* in collections I, V, and VI are understood as necessary, it becomes more evident that the sage's intention was to present the Lord as the only divine name throughout the book.

(25) The Relationship
between Collections I and VI

גָּנַב	40/3	to steal	I-2	VI-1
חָקַק	19/4	to decree	I-3	VI-1
לָמַד	86/2	to learn	I-1	VI-1
מָלַךְ	347/2	to be king	I-1	VI-1
נָאַף	31/2	to commit adultery	I-1	VI-1
נְמָלָה	2/2	ant	I-1	VI-1
עַפְעַף	10/4	eyelid	I-3	VI-1
קָדוֹשׁ	116/2	holy	I-1	VI-1

Eight words (five verbs, three adjectives/nouns) occur exclusively in the two collections, and the use of the three words (*nĕmālâ*, *ʿapʿap*, and *nʾp*) will be examined below.

A. *Nĕmālâ* "ant" (twice)[317]

The ant is mentioned only twice in the entire OT, in Prov 6:6 and 30:25. In the two instances the ant symbolizes discipline, diligence, and wisdom. W. F. Albright points out that one of the Amarna letters written by a man named *Labʾayu* of Shechem contains a proverbial saying that features the ant: "If ants are smitten, they do not accept [the striking] quietly, but they bite the hand of the man who smites them."[318] He continues to suggest that the origin of Prov 6:6 and 30:25 should not be dated later than the Canaanite letter. Although the appearance of the ant in a proverbial saying is common to the Amarna letter and Proverbs, the militant image of the insect in the letter is significantly different from its diligent image in Proverbs. The different images imply that a connection between Proverbs and the letter may not be probable.

Another interesting thing about the ant-saying in Prov 6:6–8 is the difference between the MT and LXX. The ancient Greek version has three additional lines after 6:8, featuring the bee as a model of diligence. With regard to the appearance of the bee in the LXX, Johann Cook points out that the ant and bee are also mentioned in Aristotle's *Historia Animalium* in the same order as in the LXX.[319] It may be possible that the additional lines about the bee in the LXX may be ascribed to the influence of the Aristotle's book, but the two insects have been known universally as symbols of diligence and wisdom.

In regard to the use of the ant in collections I and VI, a connection between the two is suggested based on the following observations: the description of *nĕmālâ* in 6:6 and 30:25 is almost the same: it is weak but wise, storing up its food in the summer, the ant is mentioned only in the two texts in the entire OT, and both 6:8 and 30:25 commonly contain the three words, *kwn*, *qayiṣ*, and *leḥem*.

B. *ʿapʿap* "eyelid, eye" (four times)[320]

ʿapʿap occurs ten times in the OT, always in the plural: four times in Proverbs, three times in Job, twice in Psalms, and once in Jeremiah. As M. Dahood points out,[321] the use of the word in 4Q184 ("and she wantonly raises her pupils [*ʿpʿpyh*] to gaze upon a just man") is very similar to the use of the same word in reference to a harlot in Prov 6:25 ("Do not let her take you with her pupils [*ʿapʿapêhā*]"). In the OT *apʿap* occurs six times in synonymous parallelism with *ʿayin* "eye," and three of them are in Proverbs with *ʿapʿap* always in the second colon (4:25; 6:4; 30:13). The usage of *ʿap ʿap* in Proverbs shows that Proverbs is closer to Psalms than Job (Ps 132:4 and Prov 6:4 are almost identical).

The occurrence of the rare word *ʿap ʿap* in collections I and VI indicates a common aspect of the two collections. As for the usage of the noun in the two collections, *ap ʿap* plays a role to reinforce the meaning of *ʿayin* by means of synonymous parallelism. This common usage also indicates a coherent aspect of the two collections.

C. *Nʾp* "to commit adultery" (twice)[322]

The verb *n ʾp* occurs 31 times in the OT, 21 of which are in Prophets (eight times in Jeremiah, six times in Ezekiel, five times in Hosea, and once each in Isaiah and Malachi). The predominant use of the verb in the Prophetic books is to characterize Israel's unfaithful relation to the Lord as adultery. Of the definition of adultery, the most commonly quoted one seems that "the man can only commit adultery against a marriage other than his own, the woman only against her own."[323]

In Proverbs the verb is used twice, once of a man and the other of a woman, and, the definition of adultery helps us understand that each of the two cases involves at least one married person. In 6:32 the father says, "He who commits adultery with a woman is a senseless fool, he does it for his own destruction." Although the father appears to speak about adultery in general, it is apparent that his true intention is to warn his unmarried son against the seductive woman who is married (6:24–26).[324] In 30:20 the verb is used of an adulterous woman (*ʾiššâ měnāʾāpe*). Even if she was an amoral woman rather than an immoral one,[325] it is implied by the designation (*ʾiššâ měnāʾāpet*) that she is a married woman.

As mentioned earlier, a thorough study about the relationship between the Decalogue and Proverbs is yet to appear. However, since the verb *n ʾp* represents the Seventh Commandment, it would be appropriate to see if there is any connection between the Decalogue and the two texts in Proverbs (6:32; 30:20). In their explanation of the relationship between the Decalogue and Prophets, Freedman and Willoughby take Hos 4:2 and Jer 7:9 as examples to explain the adaptation of the Decalogue by the prophets.[326] According to the two scholars, the prophets used the Decalogue as means to measure the social and religious sins of Israel. In doing so, they appear to have exercised a certain degree of freedom in selecting and ordering the commandments and using terminology, depending on need. The texts, Hos 4:2 and Jer 7:9, show that each prophet quotes five commandments from the Decalogue in different order: Hosea quotes "cursing, lying, murder, stealing, and adultery," and Jeremiah, "stealing, murder, adultery, false swearing, and worshiping Baal." In Proverbs a similar phenomenon is observed in connection with the Seventh Commandment. When one considers the literary environment of 6:32, it is noted that the theme of adultery in 6:32 is preceded by the theme of stealing (*gnb*) in 6:30–31. Similarly, in chapter 30 a saying about dishonoring parents comes immediately before the numerical saying (30:18–20) in which an emphasis is placed on adultery. In other words, in Proverbs the first instance of *n᾽p* comes after the Eighth Commandment (stealing) and the second instance after the Fifth Commandment (honoring parents). Considering the central role of the Decalogue in Israelite religion and society, it would be difficult to deny that the sage was aware of the Decalogue when he spoke of certain fundamentally important themes, such as fearing the Lord, honoring the parents, false witnessing, and adultery.

The two instances of the verb *n᾽p* in collections I and VI are insufficient to establish a link between the two collections.

(26) The Relationship between Collections I and VII

חֵפֶץ	40/3	delight	I-2	VII-1
יֳפִי	19/2	beauty	I-1	VII-1
לַיְלָה	227/3	night	I-1	VII-2
מַרְבַד	2/2	coverlet	I-1	VII-1
סַחַר	7/3	traffic, gain	I-2	VII-1
רָזַן	6/2	to be weighty	I-1	VII-1
שָׁכַח	102/5	to forget	I-3	VII-2

Two verbs and five nouns occur exclusively in the two collections. Of these, the use of the following four words will be examined below: *sahar*, *rzn*, *marbad*, and *layĕlâ*.

A. *Sahar* "trading profit" (three times)[327]

The noun *sahar* occurs seven times in the OT; four times in Isaiah and three times in Proverbs. The fact that it always occurs either with a pronominal suffix (four times) or in the construct state (three times) but never in the absolute state indicates that *sahar* refers to a profit that is produced by a person or thing. Of the meaning of the verb *shr* in Genesis, E. A. Speiser argues that, although the meaning of the participial form *sōhēr* is undoubtedly "trader," the verb *shr* in Genesis means "to wander" or "to journey" without any connotation of trading.[328] He suggests that the participial form may have become a technical term in a later period to mean a trader who goes around. In the OT *sahar* occurs in synonymous parallelism with *yāgîaʿ* "product of labor, acquisition" (Isa 45:14) and *tĕbûʾâ* "income" (Isa 23:3; Prov 3:14). The three instances of *sahar* in Proverbs are to refer to the profit of wisdom, silver, and the ideal wife (3:14 [twice]; 31:18). T. P. McCreesh, one of those who identify the personified Wisdom in chapters 1–9 with the ideal wife in chapter 31, points out that there are thematic and linguistic features which are common to Wisdom (chapters 1–9) and the wife (chapter 31).[329] Considering that the phrase *ṭôb saḥrāh* (3:14; 31:18) also is used in reference to Wisdom and the ideal wife, and that *saḥar* occurs only in the two places in Proverbs (3:14; 31:18), the noun must be added to McCreesh's list as a common literary feature to both characters.

The occurrence of the phrase *ṭôb saḥrāh* in 3:14 and 31:18 is taken as one of the links between the two collections.

B. *Rzn* "to be weighty" (twice)[330]

The root *rzn* occurs seven times in the OT, once as a noun (*rāzôn* "ruler" in Prov 14:28) and six times as a plural participle with the meaning "ruler, dignitary" (twice in Proverbs and once each in Judges, Isaiah, Habakkuk, and Psalms). Several linguistic features are observed in the six instances of the participle plural form *rôzĕnîm*: the word is found only in poetic texts, it occurs in synonymous parallelism mainly with *mĕlākîm* "kings" (Judg 5:3; Hab 1:10; Ps 2:2; Prov 8:15; 31:4) and once with *šōpĕṭîm* "judges" (Isa 40:23), and, significantly, it always refers to rulers in an international context outside Proverbs. The last feature of *rôzĕnîm* compels to understand the context of Prov 8:15 and 31:4 also to be international.

It is interesting to note in Prov 8:15–16 that five different terms are employed to designate various types of rulers (*mĕlākîm, rôzĕnîm, śārîm, nĕdîbîm,* and *šōpĕṭîm*), and that Wisdom declares that she is the one who enables all of them to exercise their power effectively. The mention of the five types of rulers indicates that wisdom is an essential quality particularly for national leaders.

In 31:4 *rôzĕnîm* is used to admonish a king (Lemuel) about the danger of intoxication: "Drinking wine is not for kings, nor is strong drink for rulers (*rôzĕnîm*)." Although the invitation of Wisdom to her banquet includes drinking wine (9:5), wine is often mentioned in a negative way in Proverbs, mainly because of its effects on drinkers to neglect their responsibilities (cf. 20:1; 23:29–35; 31:4).

The rarity of the root *rzn* in the OT and the international flavor in 8:15–16 and 31:4 in which *rôzĕnîm* occurs indicate that the use of the participial form of the root in collections I and VII is coherent.

C. *Marbad* "coverlet" (twice) and *Layĕlâ* "night" (three times)[331]

Even though *layĕlâ* is a common word in the OT with no significance in wisdom material, its use in Proverbs will be examined here along with the use of *marbad*, because *marbad* and *layĕlâ* occur only in two places in Proverbs (chs. 7 and 31) to describe the contrasting lifestyles of the adulterous woman (7:6–23) and the ideal wife (31:10–31). It is remarkable that the affinities and contrasts between 7:6–23 and 31:10–31 have not been noticed by interpreters, although some have mentioned that the rare words for the exotic foreign goods are common to both units.[332]

One of the features that are common to the two units (7:6–23 and 31:10–31) is their location in the collections. The two units are located at the end of collection I and VII: the description of the adulterous woman in chapter 7 is the father's last instruction (the tenth), and the acrostic poem of the ideal wife in ch. 31 is the last part of collection VII as well as the closing unit of the entire book. Another resemblance between the two units is that the adulterous woman and the ideal wife are portrayed within the context of their marriages and homes. However, the relationship between the two women is not about resemblance but about contrast in their lifestyle as a wife. First of all, the adulterous woman does not stay at home most of the time (7:11–12) while the ideal wife is understood as staying at home for her activities. Both women are described as active at night: the adulterous woman to meet a young man (7:9–10) and the ideal wife to continue to work late into the night (31:18). One is worthy of her husband's trust (31:11), but the other is obviously not (7:19–20). Both make their bedrooms romantic using exotic coverlets for their beds, for contrasting purposes (7:16; 31:22). The adulterous woman appears to be an extravagant spender on expensive imported goods (7:16–17),[333] while the ideal wife is a diligent producer and seller of her own products (31:13, 24). One speaks smoothly only to seduce a foolish young man (7:21), while the other opens her mouth with wisdom and instruction (31:26). A man who associates himself with the adulterous woman will lose his own life (7:22–23), but the ideal wife brings honor to her man (31:23). The comparison of the two wives can be summed up with the saying at 12:4: "A capable wife is her husband's crown, but a shameful wife is like rot in his bones."[334]

The two units (7:6–23 and 31:10–31) also contain literary affinities that can be considered not accidental. The first linguistic feature to be discussed is the occurrence of *layĕlâ* and *marbad* in the two units. *Layĕlâ* (or *layil*) occurs 238 times in the OT, and is too common to be considered in connection with wisdom material. However, the remarkable aspect of the use of *layĕlâ* in Proverbs is that the noun is used only in reference to the activities of the two women (7:9; 31:15, 18). In 7:9–10 "night" is the time for the adulterous woman to go out to meet a young man, but the ideal wife gets up while it is still "night" (*layĕlâ*) to provide food for her household (31:15), and she stays up late to work at night (31:18). Far more significant than *layĕlâ* is the occurrence of *marbad* in the two units (7:16; 31:22). The noun is a rare word not found elsewhere in the entire OT. It occurs in both places in the plural form (*marbaddîm*), referring to bed coverlets.[335] In contrast to the strange woman who appears to have purchased the expensive Egyptian coverlets, the ideal wife *makes* such coverlets by herself (31:22). The exclusive use of the rare word (*marbaddîm*) in association with the two women strongly suggests a literary link between 7:6–23 and 31:10–31.

7:16   *Marbaddîm rābadtî ʿarśî hătubôt ʾētûn miṣrāyim* (7:16)
        "I have covered my bed with coverlets, black linen drapes from Egypt."
31:22   *Marbaddîm ʿāśĕtâ lāh śēś wĕʾargāmān lĕbûśāh* (31:22)
        "She makes coverlets for herself, and linen and purple are her clothing."

What is remarkable in the comparison of the two texts is that both are loaded with rare words of fabrics, and that the six words in each text are arranged in an identical structure as shown below.[336]

Table 1.21
Comparison of 7:16 and 31:22

	A term of fabrics	Subj+verb	Pron. suf.	Terms of fabrics
7:16	*marbaddîm*	*rābadtî*	*ʿarśî*	*hătubôt* and *ʾētûn*
31:22	*marbaddîm*	*ʿāśĕtâ*	*lāh*	*śēś* and *ʾargāmān*

The last common linguistic feature to be discussed in the two units (7:6–23; 31:10–31) is the participles, *hōmiyyâ* "boisterous, noisy" in 7:11 and *ṣôpiyyâ* "watchful, vigilant" in 31:27. The significance of *hōmiyyâ* is that the participle represents the identical character of the adulterous woman in 7:11 (*hōmiyyâ hîʾ* "she is boisterous") and Lady Folly in 9:13 (*ʾēśet kĕsîlût hōmiyyâ* "the foolish woman is boisterous"). It is thus reasonable to conclude that Lady Folly in ch. 9 is the personification of the adulterous woman in ch. 7. The common use of *hōmiyyâ* for the two female characters indicates that Lady Folly is a symbolic persona to represent not only the abstract concept of folly but also the adulterous woman. This identification is supported by the fact that the naive fool (*petî*) and the senseless fool (*hăsar lēb*) are the common victims of the adulterous woman and Lady Folly (7:7; 9:16). Subsequently, it can be further concluded that the relationship between Lady Folly and the adulterous woman (ch. 7) is parallel to the relationship between personified Wisdom and the ideal wife (ch. 31).

The peculiar feminine participial pattern of *hōmiyyâ* needs explanation. The participle is derived from the verb *hmh*, and the pattern is not frequent in the OT, although the same pattern is attested in the use of other verbs. The intention of this pattern is understood as to retain the original third radical *yôd*.[337] Remarkable is the fact that the uncommon pattern of the feminine participle

form is found in the two units, *hōmiyyâ* in 7:11 and *ṣôpiyyâ* in 31:27. The occurrence of the two uncommon famine participial forms in the two units
(7:6–23; 31:10–31) also indicates a connection between them.

At this point in our discussion of *hōmiyyâ* and *ṣôpiyyâ* it is necessary to
examine A. Wolters' study on *ṣôpiyyâ* in 31:27. Although the same feminine
participial pattern is represented in *hōmiyyâ*, he focuses only on *ṣôpiyyâ*, and
offers a unique understanding of the word in the context of 31:10–31. The main
point which Wolters attempts to prove in his argument is that the author of the
acrostic poem (31:10–31) wanted to express *sophia* "wisdom" through the Hebrew word *ṣôpiyyâ*.[338] It appears in the beginning of his study that the direction
of the study is indicated by his own two questions: "Why is a participle used in
31:27 while perfect or imperfect forms represent her activities in other places?"
and "Why does the feminine participle take the unusual form?" The two questions are answered in his conclusion that the use of *ṣôpiyyâ* in the Hebrew text is
intended to represent the Greek word *sophia* in sound.

His two questions are considered helpful for the purpose of this study to
establish the contrasting relationship between the adulterous woman in ch. 7 and
the ideal wife in ch. 31. However, it will become evident in the course of our
examination of *ṣôpiyyâ* that his conclusion is difficult to be accepted.

First of all, what Wolters calls unusual regarding *ṣôpiyyâ* is a linguistic
phenomenon to preserve the original *yôd* of the root, resulting in *qôṭillâ* pattern
in which the third radical is doubled to protect the previous short vowel.[339] Although examples for the pattern are not numerous, a handful of the feminine
participles show the same pattern in the OT: e.g., *hōmiyyâ* (Isa 22:2; Prov 1:21;
7:11; 9:13), *ṣôpiyyâ* (Prov 31:27), *bôkiyyâ* "weeping" (Lam 1:16), *pōriyyâ*
"fruitful" (Isa 17:6; 32:12; Ezek 19:10; Ps 128:3), and *'ōtiyyôt* "things to come"
(Isa 41:23; 44:7; 45:11). In light of these examples, it becomes obvious that his
question, "Why does the feminine participle take the unusual form?," loses a
significant amount of relevance with regard to the form. If his question were
legitimate to ask in 31:27, the same question should be also legitimate in Prov
7:11 and 9:13 where the same unusual form *hōmiyyâ* is found (cf. *hōmiyyôt* in
1:21). But such a question would not have any legitimacy to be asked in the
three places (7:11; 9:13; 1:21).

Considering that the ideal wife's activities are usually represented by perfect or imperfect forms in the acrostic poem, his second question, "Why a participle in 31:27?" appears to have legitimacy. In his attempt to answer the question, however, he seeks the answer in Crüsemann's study of the participial
hymns. Consequently, he explains *ṣôpiyyâ* in the acrostic poem as a hymnic
participle which, according to him, Crüsemann has failed to include in his list.[340]
As will be shown below, if one considered the usage of the verb *ṣph* "to look
out, keep watch" in the OT, Wolters' understanding of *ṣôpiyyâ* as a hymnic participle would be considered unnecessary.

A survey of the instances of *ṣph* in the OT indicates that any attempt to find
an answer for a question like his must begin with the examination of the usage

of the verb in the OT. *Sph* occurs 27 times in the *qal* in the OT. In relation to Wolters' question about *ṣôpiyyâ*, an important and remarkable aspect of the verb is that in its 27 instances in the *qal*, it occurs 25 times in the participle (24 times as active and once as passive). Another important aspect of the verb is that in most of those instances its participial form denotes the meaning "watchman," or "sentinel." *Sph* occurs 10 times in the historical books (1 and 2 Samuel and 2 Kings) as a participle, with the meaning "sentinel" in the military context. The participial form of *ṣph* in Isaiah, Jeremiah, Ezekiel, and Hosea describes the prophets as spiritual watchmen for Israel. This peculiar usage of *ṣph* continues to be found later in Ben Sira as well, where the verb occurs three times in the *qal*, two of which occur as participles (37:14; 51:3). On the basis of the usage of the verb in the OT, we are thus compelled to disagree to Wolters' explanation of *ṣôpiyyâ* in Prov 31:27 as a hymnic participle. Even if the acrostic poem could be classified as a heroic hymn,[341] it is not the reason that *ṣph* occurs in the participle. It is rather because of the usage of the verb in Hebrew reflected in the OT. The verb almost never occurs in the perfect or imperfect in the *qal*.

This aspect of *ṣph* can be tested in another acrostic poem in the OT. Psalm 37 is an acrostic poem which employs the verb *ṣph* for the verse of the letter *ṣādê*. As expected, in the psalm *ṣph* occurs in the participle to begin the line of *ṣādê* (v.32): "a wicked man is watchful (*ṣôpê*) on a righteous man, seeking to kill him." Although the participles of other verbs also occur in Psalm 37, the *ṣādê* line confirms the usage that *ṣph* occurs almost always in the participle in the *qal*.

In view of this aspect of the verb, it can be concluded that the use of *ṣph* in Prov 31:27 is perfectly in line with its usage in the OT. Moreover, the participle depicts the ideal wife as a sentinel who watches over the affairs of the entire household (31:27a, "she is watchful over the activities of her house"). The image of the ideal wife as a sentinel is also perfectly in line with the usage of the verb in the OT in terms of the meaning.

Another questionable conclusion offered by Wolters is his alternative translation of 31:27. In an effort to support his view that *ṣôpiyyâ* refers to the Greek word *sophia*, he suggests that 31:27 can be translated as follows: "The ways of her household are wisdom (*ṣôpiyyâ*)." In Proverbs, however, such a translation is syntactically unusual with regard to wisdom. *Hokmâ* occurs 42 times in Proverbs, and, although wisdom can be taught, imparted from one to another, or used as a means to accomplish something, the word never occurs in such a defining sentence structure, "Wisdom *is* . . . ," as in the translation suggested by Wolters. In Proverbs the *beginning* of wisdom is defined as the fear of the Lord (9:10), but wisdom itself is never defined nor equated with anything directly.[342] For this reason, if Wolters' alternative translation of 31:27 were to be accepted, it would be the only such case of wisdom in Proverbs. The legitimacy of his study of *ṣôpiyyâ* is also questioned by others: some have recently questioned the appropriateness of Wolters' treatment of *ṣôpiyyâ* with regard to the relationship between Hebrew *ṣādê* and Greek *sigma* and his interpretation of

31:27.[343] The similarity of the sound between *ṣôpiyyâ* and *sophia* is remarkable, but it is dangerously deceptive. Wolters' whole reasoning in his study seems to have been triggered by the similarity of the sound of the two words.

Returning to our discussion of the relationship between the adulterous woman in ch. 7 and the ideal wife in ch. 31, the occurrence of *hōmiyyâ* in 7:11 and *ṣôpiyyâ* in 31:27 can be taken as another literary phenomenon to connect the two units. If a link between 7:6–23 and 31:10–31 is granted, the peculiar pattern of *ṣôpiyyâ*, instead of the usual pattern *ṣôpâ*, can be explained as having been influenced by the three instances of *hōmiyyâ* in 7:11; 9:13; 1:21.

The literary and thematic similarities between 7:6–23 and 31:10–31 are substantial, and they suggest the involvement of the same editor in the final forms of collection I and the acrostic poem (31:10–31). The coherent relationship between collection I and VII is indicated by the similarities between the two texts and, in addition to these, by the theme of the fear of the Lord (31:30).

2. The Relationship between Collection II and Other Collections

The total number of words that occur exclusively in collection II and other collections is 415 (165 verbs and 250 adjectives/nouns), and these words are distributed in the 19 different groups of the collections as shown below:

II	242	II-III-VI-VII	1	II-V	90
II-III	19	II-III-VII	1	II-V-VI	3
II-III-IV	2	II-IV	2	II-V-VII	3
II-III-V	16	II-IV-V	6	II-VI	14
II-III-V-VI	2	II-IV-V-VI	1	II-VI-VII	1
II-III-V-VII	1	II-IV-V-VI-VII	1	II-VII	9
II-III-VI	1				

(1) Characteristic Exclusive Words in Collection II

a. Verbs (89)

אבס	2/1	to feed	אזל	4/1	to go away
אזן	42/1	to listen	אטם	8/2	to shut up
אכף	1/1	to press, urge	אנה	6/1	to encounter
באש	18/1	to stink	בזה	43/3	to despise
בחל	1/1	to gain by greed	בחן	28/1	to examine
בטה	4/1	to speak rashly	בקר	7/1	to inquire
ברח	65/1	to flee	גבה	34/2	to be high
גלע	3/3	to expose	גרר	5/1	to drag away
גרש	47/1	to drive out	דחה	8/1	to push
הדף	11/1	to thrust, push	הפך	94/2	to overturn
זכה	8/1	to be clean	זעף	4/1	to be enraged

זרע	56/2	to sow	חלץ	27/2	to rescue
חנך	5/1	to train up	חפץ	86/2	to delight in
חפר	17/2	to search for	חרך	1/1	to set in motion
חרש	47/2	to be silent	טול	13/1	to hurl, cast
טהר	93/1	to be clean	יבש	61/1	to be dry
יעל	23/2	to profit	ירא	4/1	to pour
כאב	8/1	to be in pain	כול	38/1	to sustain
כפה	1/1	to subdue	כפר	101/2	to cover
כתר	6/1	to surround	לבט	3/2	to thrust down
לוה	14/3	to borrow	לון	71/2	to lodge, abide
לעע	3/1	to talk wildly	מוש	20/1	to depart
מעל	35/1	to act unfaithfully	מעט	22/1	to be small
מרק	4/1	to scour, polish	משך	36/1	to draw, drag
נדף	9/1	to drive	נוב	4/1	to bear fruit
נחת	10/1	to go down	סלף	7/4	to twist, pervert
סעד	12/1	to support	ספה	21/1	to sweep
עוה	17/1	to bend, twist	עור	80/1	to awake
עכר	14/4	to stir up	עמל	11/1	to labor
עצה	1/1	to shut	ערם	5/2	to be shrewd
פזר	10/1	to scatter	פטר	5/1	to separate
פנה	135/1	to turn	פקד	223/1	to visit, muster
פקח	20/1	to open eyes	פרד	26/5	to divide
פרח	25/2	to bud	פרר	50/1	to break
פשק	2/1	to open wide	צדק	41/1	to be just
קבל	13/1	to receive	קוה	47/1	to wait for
קלה	7/1	to be dishonored	קצר	34/1	to reap
קצר	15/1	to be short	רגע	6/1	to disturb
רדם	7/1	to be in sleep	רחב	25/1	to be wide
רצח	16/1	to murder	רקב	2/1	to rot
רשע	35/2	to be wicked	שבר	21/1	to buy grain
שבת	71/2	to cease	שחה	172/1	to bow down
שחח	22/1	to bow	שלם	15/1	to make peace
שמד	90/1	to be destroyed	שקט	41/1	to be quiet
תור	25/1	to seek out			

b. Adjectives/Nouns (153)

אֵבוּס	3/1	crib	אֹהֶל	345/1	tent
אוֹן	13/1	vigor, strength	אוֹפָן	35/1	wheel
אֵימָה	17/1	terror, dread	אֵיפָה	40/2	ephah
אֵיתָן	14/1	perennial	אֹכֶל	44/1	food
אַלְמָנָה	56/1	widow	אֶלֶף	8/1	cattle
אֹמֶן	8/3	faithfulness	אֲרֻחָה	6/1	meal
אַרְמוֹן	32/1	citadel	אָשׁוּר	7/1	step, going
אָשָׁם	46/1	guilt	בּוּז	11/2	contempt
בָּחוּר	44/1	young man	בַּר	13/1	grain
בַּר	7/1	pure	בְּרִיחַ	40/1	bar
גֵּאֶה	9/2	proud	גָּבֹהַּ	40/1	high
גֹּבַהּ	17/1	haughtiness	גֵּהָה	1/1	healing
גּוֹי	556/1	nation	גְּמוּל	19/2	dealing
גְּעָרָה	15/3	rebuke	דְּאָגָה	6/1	anxiety
דָּבֵק	3/1	clinging	הֲדָרָה	5/1	adornment, glory
הַוָּה	16/4	destruction	הֲפַכְפַּך	1/1	crooked
וָזָר	1/1	guilty	זֵד	13/1	arrogant
זָדוֹן	11/3	insolence	זַךְ	11/3	pure, clean
זֵכֶר	23/1	remembrance	זַעַף	7/1	raging, rage
זְעָקָה	18/1	cry	זֶרַע	229/1	sowing, seed
חַבּוּרָה	7/1	stripe, blow	חֵדֶק	2/1	brier
חֲזִיר	7/1	swine	חֹטֶר	2/1	branch, twig
חָנֵף	13/1	profane	חֶסֶד	2/1	shame
חָצָץ	2/1	gravel	חָרֵב	2/1	dry
חָרוּץ	5/5	sharp	חֹרֶף	7/1	harvest time
טוּב	32/1	good things	טוֹבָה	62/1	welfare
יָהִיר	2/1	proud	יְסוֹד	20/1	foundation
יָפֶה	42/1	beautiful	יְקָר	17/1	preciousness
יָרָק	5/1	herbs	יֶתֶר	96/1	excess
כְּלִמָּה	30/1	reproach	כִּשָּׁלוֹן	1/1	a stumbling
מֵאָה	581/1	hundred	מָאוֹר	19/1	luminary
מֹאזְנַיִם	15/3	scales	מִגְדָּל	34/1	tower
מְגוֹרָה	3/1	fear	מִדְבָּר	271/1	wilderness
מַדְקָרָה	1/1	piercing	מְהוּמָה	12/1	confusion
מַהֲלֻמָה	2/2	blows	מוֹתָר	3/2	abundance

Hebrew	Ref	Meaning	Hebrew	Ref	Meaning
מַחֲלָה	2/1	sickness	מַחְסֶה	20/1	refuge
מְחִתָּה	11/7	terror, ruin	מַכָּה	44/1	blow
מָלֵא	63/1	full	מַלְאָךְ	212/3	messenger
מַלְקוֹשׁ	8/1	spring-rain	מֶמֶר	1/1	bitterness
מַס	23/1	laborer	מְסִלָּה	27/1	highway
מָעוֹז	33/1	refuge	מַעֲלָל	41/1	deed
מַעֲרָךְ	1/1	arrangement	מַצָּה	3/2	contention
מָצוֹד	4/1	net	מִצְעָד	3/1	step
מָרָה	1/1	bitterness	מְרִי	23/1	rebellion
מֵרֵעַ	8/2	friend	מְשֻׂכָה	1/1	hedge
מַשְׁחִית	11/1	ruin, destroyer	מִשְׁתֶּה	46/1	feast, drink
מַתָּן	5/3	gift	מַתָּנָה	17/1	gift
נַהַם	2/2	growling	נַחֲלָה	221/3	inheritance
נִיר	5/1	lamp	נִיר	3/1	fallow ground
נָכֵא	3/3	stricken	נֶצַח	45/1	perpetuity
נְשָׁמָה	24/1	breath	סֶלֶף	2/2	crookedness
עָב	31/1	dark cloud	עֶבְרָה	34/5	rage, fury
עַוְלָה	29/1	injustice	עָלֶה	19/1	leaf, leafage
עָמֵל	9/1	laborer	עֲנָוָה	7/3	humility
עֹנֶשׁ	2/1	fine, indemnity	עַצֶּבֶת	5/2	hurt, pain
עַצְלָה	1/1	sluggishness	עֵקֶב	15/1	reward, gain
עָרֵב	2/1	sweet	עֲרוּבָה	2/1	pledge
עָרִיץ	20/1	terrifying	עָשָׁן	25/1	smoke
פֶּלֶס	2/1	scale	פְּעֻלָּה	14/2	work
צוּף	2/1	honey-comb	צַיִד	19/1	hunting
צֵן	2/1	thorn?	צָנוּעַ	1/1	modest
צָרֵב	1/1	burning	קֹדֶשׁ	477/1	holiness
קֶסֶם	11/1	divination	קָצֶה	95/1	end
קָצֵר	5/2	short	רִאשׁוֹן	140/2	former, first
רָזוֹן	1/1	ruler	רַחֲמִים	39/1	compassion
רָכִיל	6/2	slanderer	רְמִיָּה	5/4	laxness
רִנָּה	33/1	cry, shout	רָקָב	5/2	rottenness
רִשְׁעָה	14/2	wickedness	שֹׂבַע	8/1	plenty
שְׂחוֹק	16/2	laughter	שֵׂיבָה	19/2	gray hair, old
שֶׂכֶר	2/1	hire, wages	שִׂמְחָה	94/8	joy
שֶׁבֶר	44/4	breaking	שֶׁבֶת	3/1	cessation

שַׁכּוּל	6/1	bereaved	שָׁלֵם	27/1	complete
שֶׁפֶט	16/1	judgment	שֹׁרֶשׁ	33/2	root
תַּאֲוָה	20/8	desire	תּוּגָה	4/3	grief
תּוֹחֶלֶת	6/3	hope	תַּחֲנוּן	18/1	supplication
תֻּמָּה	5/1	integrity	תַּעֲנוּג	5/1	luxury
תַּרְדֵּמָה	7/1	deep sleep			

The number of the words that are found only in collection II is 242 (89 verbs and 153 adjectives/nouns). A survey of the exclusive words shows that a considerable number of words are synonymous sharing common semantic areas among them. Of the various synonymous words, the words whose meanings are considered more relevant to wisdom have been grouped together under one meaning for each group. Since these words are exclusive to collection II, it can be said that some of the characteristics of collection II are represented by the groups of the synonyms.

The following five groups of synonyms are considered more relevant to wisdom, and their use in collection II will be examined below according to the semantic categories:

a. Words for Arrogance   *gēʾê, gbh, gāboah, gōbah, zēd, zādôn, yāhîr*
b. Words for Desire   *qwh, hawwâ, taʾăwâ, tôhelet*
c. Words for Perversity   *hpk, hăpakpak, slp, selep, ʿwh*
d. Words for Anger   *zʿp, zaʿap, ʿebrâ*
e. Words for Measurement   *ʾêpâ, môʾzĕnayim, peles*

A. Words for Arrogance
gēʾê, gbh, gāboah, gōbah, zēd, zādôn, yāhîr

Table 2.1
Words for Arrogance

Word	Freq.	Meaning	I	II	III	IV	V	VI	VII
gēʾâ	1/1	arrogance	1						
gēʾê	9/2	arrogant		2					
gaʾăwâ	19/2	arrogance		1			1		
gāʾôn	49/2	arrogance	1	1					
gbh	34/2	to be high		2					
gāboah	40/1	haughty		1					
gōbah	17/1	haughtiness		1					
zēd	13/1	presumptuous		1					
zādôn	11/3	presumptuousness		3					
yāhîr	2/1	arrogant		1					

rhb	4/1	to act arrogantly	1	
rûm	6/2	haughtiness	1	1

Table 2.1 shows two aspects of the words for arrogance: the theme of arrogance is confined to the three Solomonic collections (I, II, and V), and most of the words that belong to the semantic category are found in collection II (10 of the 12). This concentrated occurrence of the words in collection II indicates that arrogance is one of the characteristics of the collection. The table also shows that the theme of arrogance in collection II is denoted mainly by the roots, *gbh* and *zyd*.

i. *Gēʾê* "arrogant" (twice)[1]

The basic meaning of the root *gʾh* is "to be/become high."[2] Eight words are derived from the root (*gēʾ*, *gēʾê*, *gēʾâ*, *gaʾăwâ*, *gāʾôn*, *gēʾût*, *gaʾăyôn*, and *gēwâ*), and four of them are found in Proverbs (*gēʾâ*, *gēʾê*, *gaʾăwâ*, and *gāʾôn*). The fact that the root *gʾh* and its derivatives occur in poetic texts or in elevated prose indicates that the root belongs to the vocabulary of poetry, not to everyday language.[3] *Gēʾê* "arrogant" occurs nine times in the OT: twice each in Isaiah, Psalms, Job, and Proverbs, and once in Jeremiah. In Proverbs the word stands in antithetic parallelism with *ʾalmānâ* "widow" (15:25) and *ʿanî* "poor" (16:19), implying that the arrogant oppress the two powerless classes in society. The two sayings (15:25; 16:19) reflect the sage's two different approaches to the problem of the arrogant in society. Although it is not clearly expressed in 15:25 that the arrogant are those who encroach a widow's land, the sage threatens them that the Lord will tear down their houses (if they do such a thing). This indicates that the sage makes an appeal to God in dealing with the social crime committed by the arrogant. The sage also uses an ethical approach to deal with the arrogant, and it is shown in 16:19 which is a Better-saying: in a comparison of the humble and arrogant, the sage simply gives higher moral value to the humble over the arrogant: "Better is a humble-minded person among the poor than to share plunder with the arrogant."

ii. *Gbh* (twice), *gābōah* (once), and *gōbah* (once)[4]

The root *gbh* means "to be/become high" both in Hebrew and other Semitic languages.[5] Three substantives derive from the root, *gābōah*, *gōbah*, and *gabhût*, and the first two are found in collection II.

The verb *gbh* occurs 34 times in the OT, six of which are in two Wisdom books (four times in Job and twice in Proverbs). It is also noted in Psalms and Prophets that *gbh* is frequently found in a wisdom or proverbial context. This phenomenon suggests that *gbh* and its derivatives are closely related to wisdom.[6] Another aspect of *gbh* is that it occurs frequently in association with the heart, indicating that haughtiness is a deep-seated human inclination (Ezek 28:2, 5, 17; Ps 131:1; 2 Chr 17:6; 26:16; 32:25; Prov 18:12).

In Proverbs the verb *gbh* occurs twice to denote the haughtiness of the heart (18:12) and one's pride symbolized by his high gate (17:19). Interesting is the occurrence of *šeber* "destruction" in the two sayings in connection with haughtiness. The collocation of *gbh* and *šeber* in the two sayings is intended to give a warning that haughtiness or arrogance results in one's destruction. The adjective *gābōah* occurs in 16:5 in association with the heart, "every proud heart (*kol gĕbah lēb*) is an abomination to the Lord," and the noun *gōbah* also occurs in 16:18 to denote a proud spirit (*gōbah rûaḥ*). The association of the *gbh*-words with the heart (15:5; 18:12) and spirit (16:18) indicates that haughtiness is an attitude problem located in the innermost place of a human being, and the association of the same words with destruction (17:19; 18:12), stumbling (16:18), and divine abomination (16:5) indicates that haughtiness results in self-destruction.

iii. *Zēd* "Presumptuous" (once) and *zādôn* "presumptuousness" (three times)[7]

The last two words for arrogance to be examined are *zēd* and *zādôn*, both derived from the root *zyd*.[8] The root and its derivatives basically denote pride related to presumptuousness and rebellion.[9] The adjective *zēd* occurs 13 times in the OT, always in the plural (*zēdîm*) except the instance in Prov 21:24. A survey of the instances of *zēd* reveals several features of the presumptuous. In Isa 13:11 the Lord says that he will stop the pride of the presumptuous (*gĕʾôn zēdîm*). The juxtaposition of *gāʾôn* and *zēd* in the text implies that the main element of presumptuousness is the sense of self-importance or self-exaltation denoted by *gāʾôn*. In Isa 13:11 and Ps 86:14, *zēd* occurs in synonymous parallelism with *ʿārîṣ* "violent," also implying that the presumptuous often achieve their goals by means of force. Proverbs 21:24 is loaded with three words related to arrogance and two words for a fool: "A presumptuous (*zēd*) and proud person (*yāhîr*), his name is a mocker (*lēṣ*), behaving with the outburst (*ʿebrâ*) of pride (*zādôn*)." Despite the syntactical difficulty, the intent of the saying is clearly to say that a mocker is a possessor of extreme arrogance. The same relationship between presumptuousness and mocking is also found in Ps 119:51, "the presumptuous mock me very much." The presumptuous are characterized not only as violent but also as deceitful in their behavior. The psalmist complains in Ps 119: 69 and 78 that the presumptuous suppress him with lies.

The noun *zādôn* occurs 11 times in the OT, referring to an abstract idea or a person. In Proverbs *zādôn* occurs three times to show what negative consequences it can bring to a presumptuous person and to others: presumptuousness is inevitably followed by shame (11:2), brings strife among others (13:10), and makes a mocker act furiously (21:24).

B. Words for Desire: *qwh, hawwâ, ta'ăwâ, tôhelet*

Table 2.2
Words for Desire

Word	Freq.	Meaning	I	II	III	IV	V	VI	VII
qwh	47/1	to wait for	1						
tiqwâ	32/8	hope		4	2		2		
'wh	26/6	to desire		3	3				
ta'ăwâ	20/8	desire		8					
hawwâ	16/4	desire, ruin		4					
ḥmd	18/4	to desire	2	2					
tôhelet	6/3	hope		3					

Table 2.2 shows that the theme of desire is another characteristic of collections II. All the seven words for desire occur in collection II, and four of them are exclusive to the collection.

i. *Qwh* "hope, wait for" (once)[10]

The etymological origin of *qwh* is uncertain, but Westermann points out that the basic meaning "to be tense" corresponds well to the use of *qwh* in the *pi'el*.[11] The verb *qwh* occurs 47 times in the OT: 6 times in the *qal* and 41 times in the *pi'el* with the meaning "to hope." The significance of the verb is that the Lord is the object of hope in 28 of the 47 instances. According to Westermann, the Hebrew usage of hope conveys both the process of hoping and the object of hope, while Greek *elpis* denotes only the object of hope.[12] The only instance of the verb *qwh* in Prov 20:22 emphasizes the Lord as the object of hope, "Wait for the Lord, and he will deliver you." The saying admonishes the victim of a wrongdoing to wait for the Lord, instead of taking justice into his own hand.

ii. *Hawwâ* "desire, ruin" (four times)[13]

The noun *hawwâ* occurs 16 times in the OT: eight times in Psalms, four times in Proverbs, three times in Job, and once in Micah. The problem related to the meaning of *hawwâ* is that it means "desire" in a few instances and "destruction, ruin" in others.[14] S. Erlandsson points out that the root *hwy* has several different meanings in Semitic languages, such as "to be," "to fall," and "to love, desire."[15] However, he does not suggest the possibility that the two different meanings of *hawwâ* derive from two separate roots. Rather, he understands the negative meaning "ruin" as the consequence of evil desire.[16] In Proverbs the meaning "desire" fits well in the context of 10:3 and 11:6 but not in 17:4 and 19:13. In the last two sayings, *hawwâ* denotes a negative meaning "destruction" or a meaning similar to that. In Proverbs "desire" denoted by *hawwâ* is associated only with morally negative people: the Lord will thwart the *desire* of the wicked (10:3) and the faithless are caught by their own *desire* (11:6). This phenomenon supports Erlandsson's view that the negative meaning of the noun is the consequence of evil desire.

iii. *Ta'ăwâ* "desire" (eight times)[17]

Ta'ăwâ occurs 20 times in the OT: eight times each in Psalms and Proverbs and once each in Genesis, Numbers, Isaiah, and Job. Although it is sometimes difficult to distinguish between the desire aroused by outside factors and the desire arising from inner need, all the eight instances in Proverbs seem to refer to the desire related to inner need. Unlike *hawwâ*, *ta'ăwâ* occurs in collection II in connection with the righteous (10:24; 11:23), a sluggard (21:25), and a man in general (19:22), indicating that *ta'ăwâ* is a morally neutral term. However, the consequence of desire is determined by the moral character of one who desires. While the desires of the righteous are good and therefore they are granted (10:24; 11:23), the desire (*ta'ăwâ*) of the sluggard is the cause of his own death because his hands refuse to work (21:25). In several sayings, the important psychological effects of fulfilled or unfulfilled desire is well depicted: a fulfilled desire is the tree of life and sweet to the soul (13:12b, 19a), whereas a delayed hope (*tôhelet*) can cause the heart to be sick (13:12a).

iv. *Tôhelet* "hope" (three times)[18]

Tôhelet occurs six times in the OT: three times in Proverbs and once each in Psalms, Job, and Lamentations. In Proverbs the word occurs in synonymous parallelism with *tiqwâ* "hope" (10:28; 11:7) and *ta'ăwâ* "desire" (13:12). The usage of *tôhelet* is the same as that of *ta'ăwâ* in the sense that both words are used with no specified object of hope or desire, and that it is used neutrally in reference to a positive ("the hope of the righteous" in10:28), negative ("the hope of [a wicked man's] power" in 11:7), or any person ("deferred hope" in 13:12).

C. Words for Perversity: *hpk, hăpakpak, slp, selep, 'wh*

Table 2.3
Words for Perversity

Word	Freq.	Meaning	I	II	III	IV	V	VI	VII
hpk	94/2	to overturn		2					
hăpakpak	1/1	crooked		1					

tahpukâ	10/9	perversity	4	4	1	
lwz	6/5	to turn aside	4	1		
lāzût	1/1	crookedness	1			
slp	7/4	to twist		4		
selep	2/2	crookedness		2		
ʿqš	5/2	to twist		1		1
ʿiqqēš	11/7	perverse	2	4		1
ʿiqšût	2/2	perversity	2			
ʿwh	17/1	to bend		1		
ptl	5/1	to twist	1			

The table shows that the theme of perversity is found predominantly in collections I and II, and that six of the 12 words are exclusive to collection II.

i. *Hpk* "to overturn" (twice)[19]

The verb *hpk* occurs 94 times in the OT, in the *qal*, *nifʿal*, and *hitpaʿel*. K. Seybold explains the basic meaning of *hpk* as an action that brings about a sudden change, often a reversal of what is normal.[20] In Proverbs *hpk* occurs twice, as an infinitive absolute (12:7) and a participle in the *nipʿal* (17:20). In light of the frequent use of the infinitive absolute as a divine command in the OT, Waltke interprets the overturn denoted by *hāpôk* in 12:7 as related to God's future judgment.[21] The *nifʿal* participial form of *hpk* in 17:20 denotes the perversity of speech ("he who is perverse of tongue").

ii. *Hăpakpak* "crooked" (once)[22]

The adjective *hăpakpak*, formed by the reduplication of the second and third radicals of the root, is found only once here in the entire OT. Seybold points out that the derivatives of *hpk* are more precisely defined as bearing the notion of perversion than the root.[23] The use of *hăpakpak* in connection with *derek* "way" in Prov 21:8 presents a picture of the crooked path of a guilty man.[24]

iii. *Slp* "to twist" (four times)[25]

The root *slp* occurs nine times in the OT: seven times as a verb and twice as a noun. The semantic range of *slp* is similar to that of *hpk*, both denoting the acts of twisting and ruining. As a verb, *slp* occurs four times in Proverbs to denote an act of twist: in 13:6 wickedness twists sin (to make it worse), in 19:3 folly twists a foolish man's way, in 21:12 the Lord twists the wicked, and in 22:12 the Lord twists (or overturns) the words of the treacherous. The instances of the verb show that, regardless of the subject, the effect of twisting is always against a negative object.

iv. *Selep* "crookedness" (twice)[26]

The noun *selep* is found twice only in Proverbs in the OT. Its antithetic relationship with *tummâ* "integrity" (11:3) and *marpē ʾ* "healing" (15:4) implies that the semantic range of *selep* includes unfaithfulness and unsoundness. These two negative notions of *selep* are further highlighted by the association of the noun with *bôgĕdîm* "the faithless" (11:3) and *šeber* "breaking" (15:4).

v. *ʿwh* "to bend" (once)[27]

ʿwh occurs 17 times in the OT. The basic meaning of the verb is "to twist," which is developed to the meaning "to go astray" or "to do wrong," in the *qal* and *hipʿil*.[28] The notion of deviation from what is right is strongly reflected in its instances when *ʿwh* is juxtaposed with *ḥtʾ* "to miss the mark, sin" and *ršʿ* in the *hipʿil* "to act wickedly" (Ps 106:8; 2 Chr 6:37; Dan 9:5; cf. 2 Sam 7:14). When the verb *ʿwh* is used in reference to *nĕtîbâ* "path" (Lam 3:9) and *derek* "way" (Jer 3:21), it clearly means "to twist" or "to pervert." The verb occurs in Prov 12:8 as a participle in the *nifʿal* in reference to the heart (*naʿăwê lēb* "one who is perverted with regard to the heart").

D. Words for Anger: *zʿp, zaʿap, ʿebrâ*

Table 2.4
Words for Anger

Word	Freq.	Meaning	I	II	III	IV	V	VI	VII
ʾap	277/16	anger, nose		8	2		4	2	
zʿm	12/3	to be indignant		1		1	1		
zʿp	4/1	to be enraged	1						
zaʿap	7/1	rage		1					
hēmâ	125/8	heat, rage	1	5	1		1		
ḥrh	93/1	to be kindled			1				
ḥrr	10/1	to be hot					1		
kaʿas	21/4	vexation		3			1		
ʿebrâ	34/5	rage		5					

Table 2.4 shows that words for anger occur more frequently in collections II, III, and V than other collections. Also, on the basis of the table, one can expect the theme of anger to be found more frequently in collection II than other collections because of the higher number and frequency of the words in it.

i. $Z^{c}p$ "to be enraged" (once)[29]

The verb $z^{c}p$ is a rare word in the OT, occurring only four times: once each in Genesis, Daniel, Proverbs, and 2 Chronicles. In Gen 40:6 and Dan 1:10, $z^{c}p$ clearly means "to look sickly, emaciated" rather than "to be enraged." This different meaning of the verb in the two texts implies that it may come from a different root.[30] The other two instances of the verb deal with human anger against God and priests. In Prov 19:3 a fool who has been led astray by his own folly is angry to the Lord.

ii. $Za^{c}ap$ "rage" (once)[31]

The noun $za^{c}ap$ occurs seven times in the OT: three times in 2 Chronicles and once each in Isaiah, Micah, Jonah, and Proverbs. In Prov 19:12 $za^{c}ap$ refers to a king's anger which is compared to a lion's growling.

iii. $^{c}ebrâ$ "rage" (five times)[32]

The noun $^{c}ebrâ$ occurs 34 times in the OT, mainly in Prophetic books (19 times) and Wisdom books (7 times). A survey of the instances of the noun shows that it often occurs in fixed expressions, such as $^{c}ebrat\ YHWH$ "the wrath of the Lord" (Ezek 7:19; Zeph 1:18; Isa 9:18; 13:13), $yôm\ ^{c}ebrâ$ "the day of wrath" (Zeph 1:15, 18; Prov 11:4; Ezk 7:19; Job 21:30), and $^{5}ēš\ ^{c}ebrātî$ "the fire of my wrath" (Ezek 21:36; 22:21, 31; 38:19). $^{c}ebrâ$ is used more often to refer to divine wrath (23 times) than human wrath (11 times). In Proverbs $^{c}ebrâ$ occurs five times, and three of them refer to a king's wrath (14:35), a mocker's anger (21:24), and the anger of one who sows iniquity (22:8). The instances of the noun in 11:4 and 11:23 require explanation. In 11:4 ("Wealth is of no profit on the day of wrath") $^{c}ebrâ$ occurs in the expression "on the day of wrath" ($bĕyôm\ ^{c}ebrâ$). Some commentators note that "the day of wrath" in the saying is reminiscent of the same phrase used by prophets (Ezek 7:18; Zeph 1:15, 18), and they interpret the expression in Prov 11:4 as referring to the Lord's wrath.[33] Although it is not certain whether the expression conveys an eschatological notion in Proverbs, it certainly implies the judgment of God. The sage warns that ill-gotten wealth has no effect on God's judgment day. Similarly, the instance of $^{c}ebrâ$ in 11:23 is also understood as referring to God's wrath as in 11:4 ("the hope of the wicked is wrath"). When one considers the use of the expression "on the day of wrath" in Prophetic books and Proverbs, it becomes clear that the expression occurs in a context in Prophetic books while the same expression is a formula without a context in Proverbs. This observation implies the possibility that some prophetic expressions were used in wisdom material without the indication of the setting or context because of the familiarity of the expressions.

E. Words for Measurement: *'êpâ, mō'zĕnayim, peles*

Table 2.5
Words for Measure and Weight

Word	Freq.	Meaning	I	II	III	IV	V	VI	VII
'eben	269/11	stone, weight		7		1	3		
'êpâ	40/2	ephah		2					
mō'zĕnayim	15/3	scales		3					
peles	2/1	scale		1					
pls	6/3	to make level	3						
tkn	18/3	to weigh		2	1				

Table 2.5 shows that most of the terms related to a scale or weight occur in collection II (three of the six terms are exclusive to collection II). A survey of the instances of *'eben* shows that the term is used in Proverbs in two ways: it means a stone in general or a measuring weight for a scale. Although *'eben* occurs in three collections (II, IV, and V), collection II differs from the other two in the use of *'eben*: the noun always denotes a weight of a scale in collection II (except once in 17:8), while it always means a stone in collections IV and V. The table also shows that the verb *pls* occurs three times in collection I, but it is always used in association with the way (*ma'gāl* and *'ōrah*) not the scale. Therefore, it is safe to say that the words for measure and weight are almost exclusive to collection II.

i. *'êpâ* "ephah" (twice)[34]

'êpâ occurs 40 times in the OT, 25 of which are in the Prophets. As for the origin of the name "ephah," Zech 5:6–10 is often cited to indicate that the name of the measure *'êpâ* was taken from a basket called *'êpâ*. The noun occurs twice in Prov 20:10, and, in light of Deut 25:13–16, the double occurrence of *'êpâ* alongside *'eben wā'eben* in the saying is understood as signifying "a large and a small" measuring containers for dishonest transactions in selling and buying grains. In Prov 20:10 the falsification of measures and weights is strongly condemned as an abomination to the Lord.

ii. *Mō'zĕnayim* "scales" (three times)[35]

Mō'zĕnayim occurs 15 times in the OT: eight times in Prophetic books, five times in Wisdom books, and once each in Leviticus and Psalms. The two expressions, *mō'zĕnê mirmâ* "scales of deceit" (Hos 12:8; Amos 8:5) and *mō'zĕnê reša'* "scales of wickedness" (Mic 6:11) in the messages of the 8th century prophets, indicate that the use of falsified scales was common both in Israel and Judah during the time of the prophets. The term *mō'zĕnayim* occurs three times in Proverbs, all in the God-sayings (11:1; 16:11; 20:23). In the three sayings, dishonest scales (*mō'zĕnê mirmâ*) are mentioned twice as an abomination to the Lord (11:1; 20:23), and the sage says in 16:11 that honest scales (*mōzĕnê mišpāṭ*) belong to the Lord. The strong association of the scales with the Lord implies that divine condemnation is the only effective way to correct the dishonest business practice.

iii. *Peles* "scale" (once)[36]

Peles is another rare term to denote a scale in the OT, occurring only twice (Isa 40:12; Prov 16:11). In both places *peles* and *mō'zĕnayim* occur together to convey the entirety of the scale. According to Prov 16:11, the scales and weights are understood as part of the Lord's creation. Therefore, the honest use of the instruments by humans is necessary to reflect divine justice in society.

It is remarkable to note that, in collection II, the three exclusive terms for measure and weight (*'êpâ*, *mō'zĕnayim*, and *peles*) always occur in God-sayings (11:1; 16:11; 20:10, 23), and that the occurrence of the verb *tkn* is also confined to God-sayings, always the Lord as its subject (16:2; 21:2; 24:12).[37]

(2) The Relationship
between Collections II and III

a. Verbs (12)

אוה	26/6	to desire	II-3	III-3
איב	281/2	to be hostile to	II-1	III-1
דעך	9/3	to be extinguished	II-2	III-1
זקן	18/2	to be old	II-1	III-1
חדל	59/3	to cease	II-2	III-1
חלה	75/3	to be weak	II-2	III-1
חשׂך	27/6	to withhold	II-5	III-1
יעץ	65/5	to advise	II-4	III-1
נכה	504/6	to smite	II-3	III-3
סוג	24/3	to move away	II-1	III-2
שׁדד	43/3	to ruin	II-2	III-1
תכן	18/3	to measure	II-2	III-1

b. Adjectives/Nouns (7)

גְּבוּל	240/3	boundary	II-1	III-2
זִמָּה	29/3	evil device	II-2	III-1
מִלְחָמָה	316/3	war	II-2	III-1
עָמֹק	20/4	deep	II-3	III-1
שֹׁד	25/2	violence	II-1	III-1
שׁוּחָה	5/2	pit	II-1	III-1
תְּשׁוּעָה	34/3	deliverance	II-2	III-1

Nineteen words (12 verbs and 7 adjectives/nouns) occur exclusively in the two collections, and the use of the following five words ($\check{s}\hat{u}\underline{h}\hat{a}$, $d^{\,c}k$, ʾwh, zimmâ, and tkn) in the two collections will be examined below.

A. Šûḥâ "pit" (twice)[38]

$\check{S}\hat{u}\underline{h}\hat{a}$ occurs five times in the OT: three times in Jeremiah and twice in Proverbs. Jeremiah uses $\check{s}\hat{u}\underline{h}\hat{a}$ in a figurative way to describe the threat of his people to him (e.g., "they dug a pit for me" in 18:20, cf. 18:22). In Proverbs the word occurs in two sayings in reference to morally negative women: the mouth of the strange women is a deep *pit* (22:14), and an adulteress is a deep *pit* (23:27). In Proverbs a well (*bôr*) or a pit ($\check{s}\hat{u}\underline{h}\hat{a}$) is often used metaphorically to symbolize a woman (e.g., 5:15–20; 22:14; 23:27), but it is apparent in 22:14 and 23:27 that the "deep pit" ($\check{s}\hat{u}\underline{h}\hat{a}$ $^{c}\check{a}muqq\hat{a}$) signifies death or a grave.[39]

Collections II and III are clearly linked by the use of the common phrase "deep pit" ($\check{s}\hat{u}\underline{h}\hat{a}$ $^{c}\check{a}muqq\hat{a}$) in 22:14 and 23:27 to symbolize the danger of the infamous woman in Proverbs.

B. Dᶜk "to be extinguished" (three times)[40]

The verb $d^{\,c}k$ occurs nine times in the OT, seven of which are in Wisdom books (four times in Job and three times in Proverbs). In all the instances (except in Job 6:17), the verb is used in connection with a lamp or a wick. The extinguished lamp denoted by the verb $d^{\,c}k$ in those instances always signifies the terminated life of negative characters, such as the pursuing Egyptian armies (Isa 43:17), a son who curses his parents (Prov 20:20), the wicked (Prov 13:9; 24:20; Job 18:5, 6; 21:17), and the enemies of the psalmist (Ps 118:12). The frequent use of $d^{\,c}k$ in Wisdom books indicates that an "extinguished lamp" may have been a popular figure of speech in wisdom circles to describe the end of the wicked.

In Proverbs $d^{\,c}k$ is used in reference to the wicked (13:9; 24:20) and a son who curses his father and mother (20:20). Collections II and III are linked by the identical saying at 13:9b and 24:20b ("the lamp of the wicked will be extinguished").

C. ʾwh "to desire" (six times)[41]

The verb ʾwh occurs 26 times in the OT: 11 times in the pi ʿel and 15 times in the hitpa ʿel. The main difference between the pi ʿel and hitpa ʿel in using ʾwh is that, when the verb is used in the pi ʿel, the subject of the act of desiring is usually nepeš, denoting a desire from the innermost place of a human being, but the use of the verb in the hitpa ʿel denotes "to desire selfishly, crave."[42] In Proverbs ʾwh occurs five times in the hitpa ʿel (13:4; 21:26; 23:3, 6; 24:1) and once in the pi ʿel (21:10), and collections II and III do not show any similarity in regard to the use of the verb. In collection III the verb is always used in a negative command ("Do not desire . . . .") to prohibit the desire for food or the desire for friendship with the wicked (23:3, 6; 24:1). On the other hand, the verb is used three times in collection II in connection with the desire of the negative characters, the sluggard and the wicked (13:4; 21:10, 26).

D. Zimmâ "(evil) plan" (three times)[43]

Zimmâ is found 29 times in the OT. The noun occurs frequently in Ezekiel (14 times) to describe the lewd conducts of Israel and Judah. According to S. Steingrimsson, the noun means "evil plan" in six instances (Prov 10:23; 21:27; 24:9; Isa 32:7; Ps 119:50; Job 17:11) and "wickedness, lewdness" in other instances.[44] In Proverbs zimmâ is associated with the wicked or a fool. It is said in 10:23 that making an evil plan (zimmâ) is like a joke to a fool (kĕsîl). According to 21:27, the sacrifice offered by the wicked is even more abominable because of an evil plan (zimmâ) attached to it. In 24:9 the plan (zimmâ) of folly (ʾiwwelet) is equated with sin. Murphy explains that the phrase "the plan of folly" in 24:9 means a plan made by a fool.[45] The association of zimmâ with a fool (kĕsîl in 10:23 and ʾiwwelet in 24:9) links collections II and III.

E. Tkn "to weigh, measure" (three times)[46]

The verb tkn is considered a variant of tqn, with the basic meaning "to allocate, determine according to size or weight."[47] Tkn occurs 18 times in the OT: three times in the qal, ten times in the nip ʿal, four times in the pi ʿel, and once in the pu ʿal. Of these, all the three instances in the qal are in Proverbs, and nine of the ten instances in the nip ʿal are in Ezekiel in reference to the way (derek) of the Lord and Israel. In Proverbs the subject of tkn is always the Lord and the objects of his weighing are the spirits (16:2) and hearts (21:2; 24:12) of human beings. The Lord's act of weighing the human spirit and heart occurs in the context where people believe their ways are pure and straight. Therefore, the intention of the three sayings is to emphasize that the Lord is the one who knows the true motives behind all human acts, even when people say with pretended ignorance, "We did not know this," (24:12). The expression *tōkēn libbôt* "weighing the heart" which occurs in collections II (21:2) and III (24:12) is not found elsewhere in the OT. The three features of *tkn* (occurrence in the *qal*, the Lord as its subject, and the unique expression) clearly point to the linkage between collections II and III.

(3) The Relationship
between Collections II, III, and V

a. Verbs (6)

חָקַר	27/4	to search	II-1	III-1	V-2
חָשַׁב	123/5	to think	II-3	III-1	V-1
מוֹט	37/4	to totter	II-2	III-1	V-1
יָלַד	468/7	to bear, beget	II-3	III-3	V-1
עָשַׁר	17/6	to be rich	II-4	III-1	V-1
רָעָה	95/6	to associate	II-3	III-1	V-2

b. Adjectives/Nouns (10)

דְּבַשׁ	54/4	honey	II-1	III-1	V-2
דַּל	47/15	needy, poor	II-7	III-2	V-6
מִבְטָח	15/4	confidence	II-2	III-1	V-1
מוֹקֵשׁ	27/8	snare	II-5	III-1	V-2
מָתוֹק	12/3	sweetness	II-1	III-1	V-1
פֶּצַע	8/3	bruise, wound	II-1	III-1	V-1
פַּת	14/3	fragment, bit	II-1	III-1	V-1
שֵׁבֶט	190/8	rod, staff	II-4	III-2	V-2
שְׁנַיִם	516/6	two	II-3	III-1	V-2
תִּקְוָה	32/8	hope	II-4	III-2	V-2

Sixteen words (6 verbs and 10 nouns) occur exclusively in collections II, III, and V, and the use of six words (*pesaʿ*, *dal*, *tiqwâ*, *ʿšr*, *môqēš*, and *šēbet*) in the three collections will be examined below.

A. *Peṣaʿ* "wound" (three times)[48]

Peṣaʿ appears eight times in the OT to denote a physical wound: three times in Proverbs, twice in Exodus, and once each in Genesis, Isaiah, and Job. In Proverbs the noun occurs three times in the three collections, and the literary environments in which the noun occurs do not show any linguistic resemblance between the collections. Rather, some affinities involving *peṣaʿ* are found between Proverbs and other books in the OT. For example, the juxtaposition of *ḥabbûrâ* "blow" and *peṣaʿ* in Prov 20:30 is also found in Isa 1:6 and Ex 21:25. The two words also occur in synonymous parallelism in Gen 4:23. The expression "wounds for no reason" (*pĕṣāʿîm ḥinnām*) is found in Prov 23:29 and Job 9:17. Nevertheless, the occurrences of *peṣaʿ* in Prov 20:30 and 27:6 show a similar functional aspect of the noun, that is, a correctional or purifying function of wound: *peṣaʿ* cleans away evil (20:30) and *peṣaʿ* motivated by love is trustworthy (27:6).

B. *Dal* "poor" (15 times)[49]

Table 2.6
Words for Poverty

Word	Freq.	Meaning	I	II	III	IV	V	VI	VII
ʾebyôn	61/4	poor		1				1	2
dal	47/15	poor		7	2		6		
ḥsr	25/2	to lack		1					1
ḥāsēr	15/13	lacking	3	8		1	1		
ḥeser	2/1	poverty					1		
maḥsôr	13/8	poverty	1	5		1	1		
ʿānāw	21/3	bowed	1	2					
ʿānî	75/5	poor		1	1			1	2
ʿŏnî	36/1	oppressed							1
rwš	24/16	to be poor		12			4		
rîš	7/7	poverty	1	2		1	1	1	1

The table shows that each collection contains at least two or more terms for poverty, and this fact indicates that poverty is one of the main concerns in Proverbs. It is observed in the table that the theme of poverty is represented more frequently by the three roots, *ḥsr* (24 times), *rwš* (23 times), and *dll* (15 times).

Dal is found 15 times in Proverbs: seven times in collection II, six times in collection V, and twice in collection III. The noun appears in synonymous par-

allelism with *'ebyôn* (14:31), *'ānî* (22:22), and *rāš* (28:3). Of these four words
for poverty (*dal*, *'ebyôn*, *'ānî*, and *rāš*), Whybray concludes that there is virtually no semantic distinction between them.[50] Although *dal* is consistently used in
Proverbs for the people who are in poor economic standing, the word is also
used elsewhere in the OT in reference to animals and houses to describe the
weak or declining state of power.[51] For example, the physical state of the seven
thin cows in the Pharaoh's dream (Gen 41:19) is described as "poor" (*dallôt*),
and in 2 Sam 13:4 Jonadab asks Amnon, who has become sick on account of
love for his half-sister Tamar, "Why are you so 'poor' (*dal*) morning after
morning?" In 2 Sam 3:1 the dragging war between the house of Saul and the
house of David makes the house of Saul "weaker and weaker"
(*hōlēkîm wĕdallîm*).

A survey of the *dal*-sayings in Proverbs indicates that the sage's intent in
many of the sayings is to protect the poor by promising rewards to those who
show kindness to them or by warning those who oppress them for punishment.
The sage's deep concern for the poor is clearly demonstrated in two God-
sayings: in 14:31 the oppression of the poor is equated with dishonoring their
Creator, and in 19:17 helping the poor is likened to a loan to the Lord, a loan
that will be repaid by the Lord himself. The same protective tone for the poor is
heard in other sayings: he who gives to the poor from his own food will be
blessed (22:9), the wealth acquired by charging interests will be given to those
who are kind to the poor (28:8), and a king who judges the poor with honesty
will enjoy the long stability of his throne (29:14). The sayings that convey the
notion of retribution are obviously intended to deter the oppression of the poor
in society: he who covers his ears "not to hear" the cry of the poor will "not be
heard" when he cries (21:13), and he who oppresses the poor in order to be rich
will end up being poor (22:16). The protection of the poor is unambiguously
expressed in 22:22: "Do not rob a poor person because he is poor" (22:22).
However, the reality of poverty is objectively described in two sayings with no
intended moral lesson: the poor have no friends (19:4), and poverty is the ruin of
the poor (10:15).

Collections II and V are linked by two common phrases: *hōnēn dal* "he who
is kind to the poor" (19:17; 28:8) and *'ōšēq dal* "he who oppresses the poor"
(14:31; 22:16; 28:3), while the two occurrences of *dal* in 22:22 (collection III)
are insufficient to establish any linkage to other collections. Thematically, the
protection of the poor is common to all the three collections.

C. *Tiqwâ* "hope" (eight times)[52]

Tiqwâ is found 32 times in the OT, 21 of which are in two Wisdom books (13
times in Job and 8 times in Proverbs). As for the usage of the verb *qwh* and the
noun *tiqwâ*, G. Waschke points out that Psalms and Prophetic books tend to use
the verb, while Wisdom books tend to use the noun.[53] However, his view that

tiqwâ often refers to "dashed" or "destroyed" hope is partially correct as far as Proverbs is concerned.[54] In Proverbs two sayings mention the hope of the wicked as destined to perish (10:28; 11:7), and in 11:23 the hope of the wicked is implied as the object of (divine) wrath. Waschke's understanding of *tiqwâ* as often referring to dashed hope appears to have some relevance in regard to these three sayings (10:28; 11:7; 11:23), but the noun in other sayings connotes hope in a positive sense. In 23:18 the son is admonished not to envy sinners but to have hope for future which will not be cut off. The same future hope is expressed in connection with wisdom in 24:14: if one finds wisdom, he will have future and his hope will not be cut off. In 19:18 a father is instructed to discipline his son because (or while) there is hope for the child. The remaining two instances of hope in Proverbs are related to two undesirable characters in the wisdom context: a person who is wise in his own eyes (26:12) and a person who is hasty in speech (29:20). The two sayings sarcastically point out that a fool has more hope than both of them.

An examination of the use of *tiqwâ* in the OT shows that the noun often occurs with the verb *'bd* "to perish" and the particle *yēš* "there is . . . ." The use of *tiqwâ* in association with *'bd* denotes hope that has been terminated before fulfillment (Prov 10:28; 11:7; Ps 9:19; Job 8:13; 14:19; Ezek 19:5; 37:11), and the expression *yēš tiqwâ* ("there is hope . . . .") denotes hope in future, especially, eschatological hope in some texts (Jer 31:17; Prov 19:18; Job 11:18; 14:7; Ruth 1:12; Lam 3:29). The same futuristic or eschatological aspect is conveyed by the association of *tiqwâ* with *'aḥărît* "end" (Jer 31:17; 29:11; Prov 23:18; 24:14).

It is significant to note that in Proverbs the dictions which involve *tiqwâ* are highly formulaic. The expression "your hope will not be cut off" occurs twice as a main clause after the conditional clause "if there is future . . . ." (23:18; 24:14). Another expression "a fool has more hope than him" also repeats twice in sentences that begin with "Do you see a man . . . ?" (26:12; 29:20). As shown below, *tiqwâ* occurs in a distinctive literary environment in each collection:

Collection II   *tiqwâ* + *rāšā'* + *'bd* (10:28; 11:7; cf. 11:23)
Collection III   *tiqwâ* + *yēš* *'aḥărît* (23:18; 24:14; cf. 19:18)
Collection V   *tiqwâ* + "Do you see a man who is . . . ." (26:12; 29:20)

D. *'šr* "to be rich" (six times)[55]

The verb *'šr* occurs 17 times in the OT. What is significant with regard to *'šr* is that the 17 instances of the verb could present an integrated biblical understanding of wealth. On one hand, *'šr* is used to emphasize the Lord as the agent who makes one rich. According to the song of Hannah, it is the Lord who makes one poor or rich: "The Lord makes poor and makes rich" (1 Sam 2:7). A similar understanding of being rich is found in Prov 10:22, where it is said that the Lord's blessing makes one rich, not human toil.[56] Two sayings in Proverbs, on the other hand, indicate that riches and poverty are the consequences of human activity. In the antithetic parallelism of 10:4, poverty is described as the consequence of laziness and becoming rich as the consequence of diligence. It is also warned in 21:17 that an extravagant lifestyle leads to poverty. The two sayings show that one is responsible for his own poverty. A different biblical understanding of wealth is found in 23:4 and 28:20. Both sayings serve as a warning against human desire to be rich. One is admonished in 23:4 to use his discernment to stop the struggle to be rich. The verb used in 23:4 to describe the struggle is yg ʿ "to be/become weary" in the sense of bodily fatigue.[57] The exhausting struggle to be rich in 23:4 is an "unbridled pursuit of riches" which is senseless.[58] This attitude toward wealth can be characterized as ungodly because it does not recognize the relationship of wealth to the Lord (cf. 10:22). The intention of 23:4 is not to idealize poverty but to teach that riches cannot be gained through labor apart from the Lord. The same can be said of 28:20 in which a person who is in haste to be rich is condemned. It is reasonably conjectured in the text that, when one is obsessed by a strong desire to get rich quickly, he will not be innocent because he will become insensitive to wrongdoing.

In collections III (23:4) and IV (28:20) the verb ʿšr is used in the context that denounces an excessive human effort to be rich with no room to consider the Lord as the source of riches, while in collection II the Lord's blessing and human diligence are mentioned as two factors to be rich (10:4, 22; cf. 21:17).

E. *Môqēš* "snare" (eight times)[59]

Môqēš occurs 27 times in the OT, always figuratively except in Amos 3:5 and Job 40:24. Although it is certain that *môqēš* denotes an ancient hunting tool, no agreement has been made on its precise meaning.[60] In its figurative use *môqēš* signifies one's role to make others stumble as seen in the following relationships:

    a. Canaanite gods as *môqēš* to Israel (Exod 23:33; Deut 7:16; Judg 2:3; Ps 106:36)
    b. Canaanite peoples as *môqēš* to Israel (Exod 34:12; Josh 23:13)
    c. The Lord as *môqēš* to the people in Jerusalem (Isa 8:14)
    d. Moses (or Israel) as *môqēš* to Egyptians (Exod 10:7)
    e. Saul's use of his daughter Michal as *môqēš* to David (1 Sam 18:21)

In Psalms the psalmist frequently complains that his enemies have hidden snares for him (Pss 64:6; 140:6; 141:9; cf. Job 34:30).

The use of *môqēš* in Proverbs is distinctive in the sense that the noun is frequently associated with human speech. According to 12:13, when an unrighteous person (implied so by parallelism) speaks unjustly, his own speech will become an evil snare (*môqēš*) to himself. Similarly, the lips of a fool are a snare for his own life (18:7). The close relationship between *môqēš* and speech is also seen in a religious context in 20:25. It is implied in the text that a worshiper makes a vow to God in a careless manner before having a full awareness of his action. In that case the vow becomes a snare to him. Besides human speech, sin can function as *môqēš*: "A snare (*môqēš*) is in the transgression of an evil man" (29:6). Significant is the relation of *môqēš* to human fear as a sign of not trusting in God: while a person who trusts in the Lord enjoys security, one who has fear will feel that his own fear is a trap to him (29:25). A snare of death is undoubtedly the ultimate snare which everyone must avoid, and Proverbs teaches how one can avoid snares of death (*môqēšê māwet*): one must have the fear of the Lord, which is the fountain of life, to turn from the snares of death (14:27). Also, one must listen to the instruction of wisdom to avoid the snares of death (13:14), because the function of wisdom's teaching is to lead to the fear of the Lord.(15:33).

In 12:13 and 29:6, *môqēš* appears in a sentence, "A *snare* is . . . in the transgression of . . . ," indicating the consistent use of the noun in collections II and V.

F. *Šēbet* "rod" (eight times)[61]

Šēbet occurs 191 times in the OT. Of the 191 instances, the word means "tribe" in 144 instances and "staff, rod" in the remaining 47 instances.[62] It is noted that, when *šēbet* denotes a "rod," it often occurs in association with God who uses it as a disciplinarian.[63] For example, in Isa 10:5 the Lord uses Assyria as the rod of his anger to discipline Israel. Although a strict distinction between the beating for punishment and the beating for correction is difficult, the use of the rod in Proverbs can be divided in two ways, punitive (10:13; 26:3) and educational (13:24; 22:15; 23:13, 14; 29:15). In the punitive context, a rod is used to punish two types of fool: in 10:13 a rod is for the back of the *ḥăsar lēb*("senseless fool"), and in 26:3 for the back of the *kĕsîl*. On the other hand, using a rod for pedagogical purposes is strongly advocated in Proverbs. Encouragement for child discipline is found in 13:24 where a father who spares the rod is considered hating his own son.

Physical punishment was undoubtedly universal in ancient education, and Proverbs is not exceptional in this regard. It appears that Proverbs supports beating as a main educational method because of the understanding of human nature in the Israelite wisdom context and because of the merits of physical punishment. The understanding of human nature that justifies beating as a method of education is seen in 22:15 where folly is considered inherent in the mind of a youth and the rod of discipline (*šēbet mûsār*) appears to be the only way to eradicate it from him. As for the merits of beating in education, the sage seems to believe that discipline with a rod has a preventative or salvific function, and that a youth can be wise through such physical discipline. The father is instructed in 23:13–14 to use a rod for his child because beating will save him from premature death. It seems harsh, but, according to 29:15, wisdom is imparted to the youth by means of a rod and rebuke. According to 13:24, a father's love or hatred toward his son can be measured by his discipline or no discipline of his son.

The use of *šēbet* for educational purposes is common to collections II, III, and V (13:24; 22:15; 23:13, 14; 29:15), and collections II and V are linked further by the expression "a rod for the back of . . . " (*šēbet lĕgēw*) in 10:13 and 26:3.

(4) The Relationship
between Collections II, III, VI, and VII

עָנִי   75/5   poor, afflicted   II-1   III-1   VI-1   VII-2

ʿānî "poor" (five times)[64]

ʿānî is the only word that occurs exclusively in the four collections. Although it is difficult to distinguish between *ʿānî* and *ʿnāw* in regard to their meaning and plural forms (*ʿăniyîm* and *ʿănāwîm*), the three instances of *ʿănāw* (3:34; 4:21; 16:19) are not included in our discussion (see Table 2.6 for the distribution of the words for poverty in Proverbs). The five instances of *ʿānî* in Proverbs show two aspects of the poor: economic destitution and suffering from oppression. The economically unbearable condition of the poor is described in 15:15a as follows: "All the days of a poor person are evil." However, the poor are advised in 15:15b that the miserable external circumstances can be overcome by a cheerful heart.[65] The poor sometimes find those who are kind to them. For example, the ideal wife in 31:10–31 is praised because she is generous to the *ʿānî*, the economical destitute (31:20). Several sayings reveal the second aspect of the poor that they are vulnerable to oppression and exploitation. The negative command in 22:22 prohibits the oppression of the poor: "Do not rob a poor person (*dal*) because he is poor, and do not crush the needy (*ʿānî*) at the gate." The gate in the text indicates the oppression of the poor in the judicial court. Because the court is a place where the poor suffer easily, the mother of a king admonishes her son to be a protector of the poor in the court (31:9). The oppression of the poor is highlighted in 30:14 in which the poor are devoured by the cruel people whose teeth are compared to sharp swords.

The message of the five sayings about the poor can be summarized in the following way: the poor must try to overcome painful external conditions with inner joy, no one should mistreat the poor simply because they are powerless, and the poor must be protected by authorities, especially in the court of law. It is significant to note that the command to protect the poor is given to both ordinary people (22:22) and the king (31:9), indicating that the protection of the poor is the responsibility of the entire community.

The use of ʿānî in collections VI and VII appears consistent in the sense that ʿānî and ʾebyôn are always juxtaposed in the three sayings (30:14; 31:9, 20).

(5) The Relationship between Collections II and IV

| לְאֹם | 35/4 | people, nation | II-3 | IV-1 |
| קבב | 13/2 | to curse | II-1 | IV-1 |

Two words occur exclusively in collections II and IV, the largest (II) and the smallest collection (IV) in Proverbs. Of the two words, we will examine the use of *lěʾōm* in the two collections.

Lěʾōm "nation, people" (four times)[66]

Lěʾōm occurs 35 times in the OT: 14 times in Psalms, 11 times in Isaiah, four times each in Genesis and Proverbs, and once each in Jeremiah and Habakkuk. H. D. Preuss pointed out several features of the word: *lěʾōm* is an archaic or archaizing word, the singular occurs only 4 times in the OT, and the plural always appears in poetic parallelism.[67] In Proverbs *lěʾōm* occurs twice in the singular and twice in the plural, denoting peoples and nations in a general sense. The intention of the four sayings seems to underscore the power of public opinion or the importance of ordinary people. In 11:26 the curse and blessing of people (*lěʾōm*) are mentioned in reference to merchants who probably do not open their grain stores, especially, in a time of famine.[68] A serious warning is issued to a king in 14:28 not to neglect the well-being of his people, because royal glory and downfall are directly dependent on his people. In 24:24 judges who invert justice are threatened to be condemned by peoples or nations (*lěʾummîm*). In 14:34 the effects of righteousness and sin are mentioned in relation to a nation: righteousness exalts a nation, but sin would be the shame of peoples (*lěʾummîm*).

The theme of the people's curse is common to 11:26 and 24:24 in which both the verb *qbb* "to curse" (the other exclusive word) and *lěʾōm* occur. Although the curse of the people in the two sayings is directed two different groups of people (store owners in 11:26 and judges in 24:24), the theme and the occurrence of *qbb* in the two sayings indicate that the use of *lĕʾōm* in collections II and IV is consistent.

(6) The Relationship
between Collections II and V

a. Verbs (38)

אוץ	10/4	to hasten	II-2	V-2
אמן	100/5	to confirm	II-2	V-3
ארך	34/3	to be long	II-1	V-2
בוש	109/6	to be ashamed	II-5	V-1
גלה	113/7	to uncover	II-3	V-4
גלל	16/2	to roll	II-1	V-1
גרה	14/4	to stir up stripe	II-1	V-3
דלה	6/2	to draw	II-1	V-1
דשן	11/4	to be fat	II-3	V-1
חבל	23/3	to bind	II-2	V-1
חלק	56/3	to divide	II-2	V-1
חנן	78/6	to show favor	II-4	V-2
חרף	39/3	to reproach	II-2	V-1
טמן	31/2	to hide	II-1	V-1
טרד	2/2	to pursue	II-1	V-1
ישע	205/2	to deliver	II-1	V-1
כרה	15/2	to dig	II-1	V-1
להם	2/2	to swallow	II-1	V-1
מלט	95/3	to slip away	II-2	V-1
נגד	369/2	to tell	II-1	V-1
נוח	143/3	to rest	II-2	V-1
סתר	82/5	to hide	II-1	V-4
עבד	289/2	to work, serve	II-1	V-1
עבר	8/3	to be angry	II-2	V-1
עלץ	8/2	to rejoice	II-1	V-1
עמד	521/4	to stand	II-1	V-3
ענש	9/4	to fine, punish	II-3	V-1
עקש	5/2	to twist	II-1	V-1
עשק	37/4	to oppress	II-2	V-2

פָּגַשׁ	14/3	to meet	II-2	V-1
פָּשַׁע	40/2	to transgress	II-1	V-1
קָבַץ	127/2	to gather	II-1	V-1
רָגַן	7/4	to murmur	II-2	V-2
רָדַף	144/8	to pursue	II-6	V-2
רוּשׁ	24/16	to be poor	II-12	V-4
רָעַע	8/2	to break	II-1	V-1
שָׂגַב	20/3	to be high	II-2	V-1
שָׁנָה	9/2	to repeat	II-1	V-1

b. Adjectives/Nouns (52)

אֲבַדּוֹן	6/2	underworld	II-1	V-1
אֲדָמָה	225/2	ground	II-1	V-1
אֱמוּנָה	49/3	firmness	II-2	V-1
אֲרִי	35/3	lion	II-1	V-2
אָרֵךְ	17/4	long	II-3	V-1
גַּאֲוָה	19/2	pride	II-1	V-1
גַּג	30/2	roof	II-1	V-1
גֵּו	6/3	back	II-2	V-1
גֶּרֶם	5/2	bone	II-1	V-1
דֹּב	12/2	bear	II-1	V-1
דִּבָּה	9/2	evil report	II-1	V-1
דֶּלֶף	2/2	dropping (rain)	II-1	V-1
זָהָב	387/7	gold	II-4	V-3
חֶבֶר	7/2	association	II-1	V-1
חוֹמָה	133/2	wall	II-1	V-1
חֹמֶץ	6/2	vinegar	II-1	V-1
חֹסֶן	5/2	wealth	II-1	V-1
טַעַם	13/2	taste, judgment	II-1	V-1
כּוּר	9/2	furnace	II-1	V-1
כְּלִי	324/2	utensil	II-1	V-1
כֵּן	22/3	right, honest	II-2	V-1
כַּעַס	21/4	vexation, anger	II-3	V-1
כְּפִיר	31/3	young lion	II-2	V-1
מְחִיר	15/2	price, hire	II-1	V-1
מַעֲנֶה	8/5	answer	II-4	V-1
מַצְרֵף	2/2	crucible	II-1	V-1

מָקוֹם	401/3	place	II-1	V-2
מִרְמָה	39/8	deceit	II-7	V-1
מַשְׂכִּית	6/2	imagination	II-1	V-1
מֶתֶק	2/2	sweetness	II-1	V-1
נָאוֶה	10/3	comely, fair	II-2	V-1
נֶזֶם	14/2	ring	II-1	V-1
סוּס	137/2	horse	II-1	V-1
עַד	47/2	perpetuity	II-1	V-1
עָרוּם	11/8	shrewd	II-7	V-1
עֵשֶׂב	33/2	herb	II-1	V-1
עָשִׁיר	23/9	rich	II-7	V-2
פֶּשַׁע	93/12	transgression	II-6	V-6
צִיר	6/2	messenger	II-1	V-1
צַלַּחַת	4/2	dish	II-1	V-1
קַר	3/2	cool	II-1	V-1
קֶרֶב	227/3	inward part	II-2	V-1
קָרוֹב	78/2	near	II-1	V-1
קִרְיָה	29/5	town, city	II-4	V-1
רוּם	6/2	haughtiness	II-1	V-1
רָחָב	20/2	wide	II-1	V-1
רֵיק	14/2	empty	II-1	V-1
שָׂבֵעַ	10/2	satisfied	II-1	V-1
שִׂנְאָה	17/4	hatred	II-3	V-1
שְׁמוּעָה	27/2	report	II-1	V-1
שָׁפָל	18/2	low	II-1	V-1
תְּפִלָּה	77/3	prayer	II-2	V-1

Ninety words (38 verbs and 52 adjectives/nouns) occur exclusively in collections II and V, and the use 20 words (4 verbs and 16 nouns) in the two collections will be examined below.

A. Maṣrēp "melting pot" (twice) and kûr "furnace" (twice)[69]

The instances of maṣrēp and kûr are examined here together because the two words occur in the parallel sayings at 17:3 and 27:21. Before examining the use of maṣrēp in Proverbs, we will survey the use of the verb ṣrp "to melt" in the

OT. The verb occurs 33 times in the OT, 24 of which are in Prophetic books and Psalms (16 times in Prophets and 8 times in Psalms). Although the meaning of *ṣrp* is related to metal work, a survey of the 33 instances of the verb shows an interesting aspect in its usage. *Ṣrp* is used 16 times in the context of testing or purifying humans (Judg 7:4; Isa 1:25; 48:10; Jer 6:29, 29; 9:6; Zech 13:9, 9; Mal 3:2, 3; Pss 17:3; 26:2; 66:10, 10; Dan 11:35; 12:10), and the verb is used six times to denote the purity of God's word (2 Sam 22:31; Pss 12:7; 18:31; 105:19; 119:140; Prov 30:5).

The noun *maṣrēp* is found only in Proverbs (twice) in the OT, and like the verb it also is used for testing humans. *Maṣrēp* occurs twice in a repeated half-verse, "The melting pot (*maṣrēp*) is for silver and the furnace (*kûr*) for gold" (17:3; 27:21). In 17:3 the melting pot and furnace are compared to the Lord who examines the human heart for a true motivation. In 27:21 the same half-verse is paired with another theme but still in connection with a man: this time a man is tested by the praise (or respect) that he receives from others.

Kûr "furnace," the second word under discussion, also occurs twice in Proverbs in juxtaposition with *maṣrēp* in the repeated half-verse saying (17:3a; 27:21a). *Kûr* occurs seven times elsewhere in the OT: five times in Prophetic books and once each in Deuteronomy and 1 Kings. The usage of *kûr* indicates that the noun is always used in a metaphorical way: a furnace as a place for punishment or affliction. Three times *kûr* refers to Egypt as an iron-smelting furnace (*kûr habbarzel*), where Israelites experienced miseries as slaves of the nation (Deut 4:20; 1 Kgs 8:51; Jer 11:4). The notion of punishment is expressed by *kûr* in Ezek 22:18, 20, and 22, where Jerusalem is compared to the furnace to be destroyed by the wrath of the Lord.

Collections II and V are clearly linked by the occurrences of *maṣrēp* and *kûr* in the repeated half-verses (17:3a; 27:21a).

B. *Delep* "dropping" (twice) and *ṭrd* "to drip continually" (twice)[70]

Twice these two words occur together in the phrase *delep ṭôrēd* "continuous drip" in 19:13 and 27:15. The root *dlp* basically denotes the dripping of rain or tears.[71] The two occurrences of *delep* in Proverbs are the only occurrences of the noun in the entire OT. In 19:13 and 27:15 *delep* and the verb *ṭrd* are used to describe the annoying aspect of the contentious wife. The man in 19:13 suffers from two unhappy relationships: as a father he has a foolish son, and as a husband he has to live with a quarrelsome wife. Although 19:13b and 27:15 are very similar in meaning, the emphasis expressed by "continuous drip" is placed on different objects in the sayings: while the annoying drip of rain is compared to the *quarrels* of a wife in 19:13b, the *wife* annoys the husband like a continual dripping on a rainy day in 27:15. G. Dalman explains from his own experience that a dripping on a rainy day in Palestine is very unpleasant.[72]

Of the meaning of *trd*, J. C. Greenfield agrees that the basic meaning of the verb is "to drip continually." However, on the basis of its usage in MH, he points out that its meaning includes "to drive."[73] Thus the use of *trd* in connection with *delep* underscores the durative aspect of the dripping of rain, a metaphor referring to the "incessant talk" of the contentious wife.[74] According to Greenfield, another attractive interpretation of the phrase *delep tôrēd* is Rashi's translation as "annoying rain," on the basis of the Arabic equivalent to *trd*.[75]

As mentioned above, a close look at the syntax of 19:13 and 27:15 reveals that the emphases of the two sayings are slightly different:

19:13b   A constant dripping is the *contentions* of a wife
27:15   A constant dripping on a rainy day and a contentious *wife* are alike

Besides 19:13 and 27:15, the theme of the contentious wife (*ʾēšet midwānîm*) is also found in three other sayings in collections II and V (21:9, 19; 25:24). The fact that the theme is frequently found only in collections II and V (19:13; 21:9, 19; 25:24; 27:15) is a clear indication of coherence between the two collections.

C. *Rgn* "to grumble" (four times) and *lhm* "to devour greedily" (twice)[76]

The two verbs, *rgn* and *lhm*, also occur together in the repeated saying at 18:8 and 26:22. *Rgn* occurs seven times in the OT: four times in Proverbs and once each in Deuteronomy, Isaiah, and Psalms. In its three instances outside Proverbs it always describes the grumbling attitude of Israelites: Israelites grumble after hearing the reports from the twelve spies (Deut 1:27; Ps 106:25), and the grumbling Israelites will learn a lesson after witnessing God's salvation (Isa 29:24). In Proverbs *rgn* always occurs as a participle in the *nipʿal*, denoting a slanderer (16:28; 18:8; 26:20, 22). The four sayings show two features of a slander or gossip. In the repeated saying (18:8=26:22) the words of a gossip are described as delicious food that goes down deep into the stomach. The saying presents a picture in which two persons share the joy of speaking and hearing gossip. The second feature of gossip is its effect to destroy the unity of the community. Van Leeuwen describes the nature of gossip in the following way: "Gossip is like junk food, delicious to taste before it settles inside to do its destructive work."[77] Interesting is that *nirgān* "slanderer" occurs in 16:28 in synonymous parallelism with *ʾîš tahpukôt* "man of perversity." This synonymous relationship between the two helps understand the meaning of *nirgān* not only as one who spreads rumors but also as one who distorts truth, consequently separating friends from one another.[78] In 26:20 the essential relationship between wood and fire is mentioned in reference to the same kind of essential relationship between a gossiper and strife. As fire does not exist without wood, strife does not happen without a gossiper. This saying emphasizes the damaging effect of gossip to the community.

Lhm, the second verb to be discussed, occurs twice only in Proverbs in the entire OT. It appears along with *rgn* in 18:8 and 26:22 as a participle in the *hitpaʿel* to denote "bits greedily swallowed" or "delicacies."[79]

The link between collections II and V is indicated by the repeated saying (18:8=26:22).

D. *ʿārûm* "shrewd" (eight times) and *ʿnš* "to punish" (four times)[80]

ʿārûm and *ʿnš* are another pair of words in the sense that they occur together in a saying repeated in collections II and V: (in 22:3 and 27:12). The consensus for the root *ʿrm* and its two derivatives, *ʿārûm* and *ʿormâ*, is that they belong to the wisdom vocabulary.[81] *ʿārûm* occurs 11 times in the OT: eight times in Proverbs, twice in Job, and once in Genesis. A survey of the instances of *ʿārûm* shows a peculiar phenomenon. The *ʿārûm* always occurs in antithetic parallelism to be compared to one of the three types of fool: *ʾĕwîl* (12:16), *kĕsîl* (12:23; 13:16; 14:8), and *pĕtî* (14:15, 18; 22:3; 27:12). As far as Proverbs is concerned, the *ʿārûm* can be characterized as a savvy person who knows how to achieve his goals, or a person whose actions are marked with prudence. For example, his prudence is shown in his hiding of knowledge (12:23) or overlooking an insult (12:16). With his prudence, he hides himself to avoid a foreseeable disaster (22:3; 27:12). The *ʿārûm* knows how to use *daʿat* "knowledge" to achieve his goals (13:16; 14:18), and "understands" (*byn*) what he does (14:8, 15).

The verb *ʿnš* occurs nine times in the OT: four times in Proverbs, twice in Exodus, and once each in Deuteronomy, Amos, and 2 Chronicles. Outside Proverbs, *ʿnš* consistently denotes fines imposed on a guilty party for wrongdoing (Ex 21:20, 20; Deut 22:19; 1 Chr 36:3; Amos 2:8 [wine]). In Proverbs, however, it is not certain whether the punishment denoted by *ʿnš* involves a fine. According to 21:11, a naive fool becomes wise when he observes a mocker who is being punished (*baʿnoš*). In this case, it is more likely that the punishment is physical beatings because the implication is that the naive fool is frightened by seeing the punishment. Also, the fact that *ʿnš* appears in synonymous parallelism with *nkh* "to smite" (17:6) supports the view that *ʿnš* may denote physical punishment in Proverbs (cf. 22:3; 27:12).

Collections II and V are linked by the repeated saying (22:3=27:12) in which *ʿārûm* and *ʿnš* occur.

E. Ṣallaḥat "dish, bowl, pot" (twice)[82]

Ṣallaḥat occurs only four times in the OT: twice in Proverbs and once each in 2 Kings and 2 Chronicles. In 2 Chr 35:13 the ṣallaḥat is understood as a cooking-pot to boil food. Based of his excavation, J. L. Kelso describes the ṣallaḥat as a medium sized ring-burnished bowl without handles, and confirms the use of the ṣallaḥat as a cooking-pot.[83] In Proverbs, however, the word probably denotes a dish or bowl instead of a cooking-pot, because the sluggard can put his hand in the ṣallaḥat to bring food to his mouth. His problem is that he is so languid that he cannot bring his hand back to his mouth (19:24; 26:15).

Collections II and V are linked by the two sayings (19:24; 26:15) that are practically the same.

F. *Rwš* "to be poor" (16 times)[84]

The root *rwš* occurs 31 times in the OT: once as a finite verb, 23 times as a participle, and seven times as the noun *rîš*. A significant aspect of the root shown in its occurrence in the OT is that *rwš*-words are found only in five books but predominantly in Proverbs: once in 1 Samuel, three times in 2 Samuel, twice in Psalms, 23 times in Proverb, and twice in Ecclesiastes. Although the meaning of the root has no direct bearing on wisdom, the fact that it occurs predominantly in Proverbs and all the seven occurrences of the noun *rîš* are only in the book suggests that *rwš*-words may have been favorite words to denote the idea of poverty in wisdom circles. A survey of the 31 instances of the root shows two features of *rwš*. First, its frequent occurrence as a participle (23 times) indicates that the use of the root in the OT is mostly substantive. Secondly, the noun and participial forms of *rwš* exhibit spelling variations: the noun appears as *rîš*, *rêš*, or *rēʾš*, and the participle as *rāʾš* or *rāš* in the singular and as *rāʾšîm* or *rāšîm* in the plural.

In Proverbs the root *rwš* occurs 16 times, always as a participle. The participial forms are used ten times to show a contrast between the poor and four different groups of people: the poor and the rich (*ʿšr* or *ʿāšîr*, 10:4; 13:7; 14:20; 18:23; 22:2, 7; 28:6), the poor and one who has perverted lips (*ʿiqqēš śĕpātāyw*, 19:1), the poor and a liar (*ʾîš kāzāb* 19:22), and the poor and an oppressor (*ʾîš tĕkākîm*, 29:13). These contrasts present a picture of the righteous poor.

As pointed out earlier, Proverbs emphasizes the protection of the poor, and the idea is clearly understood in the three God-sayings which involve the verb *rwš*. In 17:5, mocking a poor person or laughing at his misery is theologically interpreted as reproaching his Creator, the Lord. The right of the poor to live side by side with the rich is emphasized by the fact that the Lord is the Creator of both (22:2). That the Lord is the life-giver of both the poor and oppressor aims to teach the oppressor that the life of the oppressed is as important as his (29:13). Three Better-sayings idealize the state of poverty in comparison to morally negative persons: a poor man with integrity is better than a foolish man with perverted lips (19:1), a poor man is better than a liar (19:22), and a poor man with integrity is better than a rich man whose ways are perverted (28:6). On the other hand, two sayings objectively highlight the realistic aspect of the poor. The reality for a poor person to face in life is that he will be rejected by his friends and even by his own brothers (14:20; 19:7).[85] However, the adjacent sayings, 14:21 ("he who is kind to the poor is blessed") and 19:6 ("everyone is a friend to a gift-giver"), appear to correct such social trends. As far as the root *rwš* is concerned, poverty as a result of laziness is mentioned only once in 10:4, "He who works with a slack hand is a poor man."

Collections II and V are linked by the repeated half-verse in 19:1 and 28:6 ("Better is a poor person walking with his integrity") and the similar theme that the Lord is the Creator of two contrasting groups of people (22:2; 29:13).

G. *Gēw* "back" (three times)[86]

It is most likely that *gēw* is a variant of *gaw* which also denotes "back." According to F. M. Cross and T. O. Lambdin, the two nouns are closely related to *gĕwiyyâ* "body" or similar cognate words in Aramaic which have the etymological base *gaww*-.[87] *Gaw* is always used with the verb *šlk* "to throw" to denote the notion of rejection. Israel throws God or his law behind their backs (*gaw*) in 1 Kgs 14:9; Ezek 23:35; Neh 9:26. *Gēw* is also used in the same way. In Isa 38:17 God throws (*šlk*) Hezekiah's sin behind his back (*gēw*) as a sign of forgiveness. *Gēw* occurs six times in the OT: three times in Isaiah and three times in Proverbs, and the usage of the noun in the two books is consistent: *gēw* denotes an area on the body, especially for beating (Isa 50:6; Prov 10:13; 19:29; 26:3). Those texts suggest that beating of a fool on his back may have been a common practice in ancient Israel. Beating is mentioned three times in Proverbs (10:13; 19:29; 26:3), and Murphy aptly interprets the point of those sayings in the following way: beating is "the only language that a fool can understand."[88]

Collections II and V are linked by the expression "a rod is for the back of (fools)" in 10:13 and 26:3.

H. *Gerem* "bone" (twice)[89]

Gerem occurs five times in the OT: twice in Proverbs, once each in Genesis, 2 Kings, and Job. The meaning of *gerem* "bone" is supported by its cognates in Aramaic and Arabic. However, in Gen 49:14 and 2 Kgs 9:13, the meaning "bone" does not fit well in the context. Some have attempted to solve the difficulty by either emending the text or giving a different meaning to the noun. For example, S. I. Feigin emends *ḥămôr gerem* in Gen 49:14 to *ḥămôr gārim* and translates the words as "castrated ass."[90] J. Gray thinks that *gerem* in 2 Kgs 9:13

is a rare architectural term with the root meaning "to cut," and translates the term as "top."[91] However, *gerem* with the meaning "bone" creates no difficulty in the context of Proverbs. Like its synonym *ʿeṣem* which is a more common term for the bone in the OT (108 times), *gerem* denotes the seat of vitality in the human body: "A crushed spirit dries up the bones" (17:22). In 25:15 the effectiveness and power of gentle speech is highlighted by the sharp contrast between a soft tongue and a hard bone: "A soft tongue breaks a bone."

Although *gerem* occurs in different contexts in collections II and V, the occurrence of the rare noun in the two may reflect the same wisdom climate of the two collections.

I. Ṣîr "messenger" (twice)[92]

Ṣîr also is a rare term occurring only six times in the OT: four times in Prophetic books (twice in Isaiah, once each in Jeremiah and Obadiah) and twice in Proverbs. The use of *ṣîr* in Isaiah, Jeremiah, and Obadiah is distinctive in the sense that the noun always refers to a messenger between nations, never between individuals. However, the same international setting of *ṣîr* is not clear in Proverbs. In 13:17 a faithful messenger (*ṣîr*) is compared to "healing" to his sender, and is contrasted with an evil messenger (*malʾāk*). The life-giving effect of a faithful messenger is emphasized again in 25:13: a faithful messenger is compared to the coolness of snow on a hot harvesting day.

The almost identical expression "faithful messenger" (*ṣîr ʾĕmûnîm* in 13:17 and *ṣîr neʾĕman* in 25:13) and reviving effect of the *ṣîr* in the two proverbs indicate that the use of *ṣîr* in collections II and V is coherent.

J. Pešaʿ "transgression" (12 times)[93]

Table 2.7
Words for Sin

Word	Freq.	Meaning	I	II	III	IV	V	VI	VII
ʾšm	36/1	to be guilty						1	
ʾāšām	46/1	guilt		1					
ḥṭʾ	238/6	to miss, sin	1	5					
ḥaṭṭāʾt	221/7	sin	1	5	1				
ḥaṭṭāʾ	19/3	sinner	1	1	1				
ʿāwôn	229/2	iniquity	1	1					
pšʿ	41/2	to transgress		1			1		
pešaʿ	93/12	transgression		6			6		

The table reveals some distinctive features of the words for sin in Proverbs. The first notable phenomenon is that the sin represented by the root *ḥṭ*ʾ occurs only in collections I, II, and III, while the sin represented by the root *pš*ʿ is found only in collections II and V. It is also interesting that, although collection V is one of the three main collections, it contains only one type of sin denoted by the root *pš*ʿ.

The noun *pešaʿ* occurs 93 times in the OT. About the meaning of *pešaʿ*, R. Knierim does not agree to the traditional view that the meaning of *pešaʿ* is "dispute" or "rebellion." He explains that the meaning of the term has developed from referring to specific (legally definable criminal acts within social and international relations) to comprehensive sin (unidentifiable sin in a cultic setting).[94] His position that *pešaʿ* denotes unidentifiable sin is supported in Proverbs. In all its 12 instances in the book, *pešaʿ* refers to wrongdoings in a general sense except in 28:24 in which a specific criminal act is implied (robbing one's parents).

It is significant to note that in Proverbs love is emphasized as an act of forgiving or overlooking *pešaʿ*. According to 10:12, love is to cover over all offenses (*kol pěšāʿîm*), and in 17:9 one who covers over an offense is understood as seeking love. In 19:11 the glory of a prudent man is to overlook sin (*pešaʿ*). The frequent association of *pešaʿ* with the verb *ksh* "to cover" (10:12; 17:9; 28:13) implies that as far as Proverbs is concerned *pešaʿ* is forgiven by an act of concealing or covering over. The antithetic parallelism in 17:9 further elucidates that "covering" means not repeating: "One who covers over an offense seeks love, but one who repeats a matter separates intimate friends." However, "covering" of one's offense must be done by others, not by the guilty person himself. It is warned in 28:13 that, if anyone conceals (*ksh*) his own sin, he will not prosper.

Although *pešaʿ* is usually understood as unidentified sin, the following two sayings indicate that it sometimes refers to a verbally committed sin: "*pešaʿ* does not stop in many words" (10:19), and "An evil snare is in *pešaʿ* of lips" (12:13; cf. 29:6). Other sayings show that three types of people are prone to commit *pešaʿ*: one who loves strife (17:19), the wicked (29:16), and an angry person (29:22).

Collections II and V are linked by several common expressions: "covering over sin" (*ksh* + *pešaʿ* in 10:12; 17:9; 28:13), "snare" and "sin" (*môqēš* + *pešaʿ* in 12:13; 29:6), and "sin in much . . ." (*běrōb/birěbôt . . . pešaʿ* in 10:19; 29:16).

K. *Nāʾwê* "beautiful, suitable" (three times)[95]

K.-M. Beyse points out that it is not certain whether *nāʾwê* is a participle in the *nipʿal* or an adjective of *nʾh*.[96] *Nāʾwê* occurs ten times in the OT: four times in Song of Songs, three times in Proverbs, twice in Psalms, and once in Jer 6:2

(including the variant *nāwâ*). It is interesting to note that in the OT the term is used in three different ways: aesthetic use, cultic use, and ethical use. In Song of Songs and Jeremiah it is used in reference to the beautiful appearance of a woman or city (Song 1:5; 2:14; 4:3; 6:4; Jer 6:2). In the cultic setting it describes the appropriateness of praise in worshiping the Lord (Pss 33:1; 147:1). The use of the term in Proverbs is clearly ethical. It occurs three times in the book in a negative formulaic expression ". . . not fitting (*lō' nā'wê*) for a fool . . ." to connote impropriety (17:7; 19:10; 26:1): fine speech, luxury, and glory are not fitting for a fool (*nābāl* or *kĕsîl*).

The negative expression, *lō' nā'wê likĕsîl* "not fitting for a fool" is common to collections II and V (19:10; 26:1), indicating coherence between the two.

L. Ḥeber "association, spell" (twice) and gāg "roof" (twice)[97]

Ḥeber and *gāg* are discussed together here because of their occurrence in the repeated saying (21:9=25:24). About the root *ḥbr* and its meaning, H. Cazelles explains that several different Semitic roots involving *ḫbr* and *ḥbr* have been coalesced in Hebrew and West Semitic *ḥbr*, making the situation complex with regard to the meaning and root.[98] The noun *ḥeber* occurs seven times in the OT: twice each in Isaiah and Proverbs, and once each in Deuteronomy, Hosea, and Psalms. On the basis of the Akkadian root *ḫbr* ("sound, noise"), J. J. Finkelstein says that all the instances of *ḥeber* in the OT, except Hos 6:9, must be related to the Akkadian root. He rejects the earlier view that the meaning of *ḥeber* is "storehouse," and offers his own translation of Prov 21:9 and 25:24 as follows: "It is better to live on the edge of a roof than with a contentious wife and *a noisy household* (*bêt ḥeber*)."[99] McKane, after reviewing the related texts in Akkadian and Ugaritic, concludes with some reservation that the translation of the LXX ("a common house") makes a right sense in the context.[100] Whether *bêt ḥeber* is "a noisy household" or "a house of association" shared with a quarrelsome wife, the sense of the saying is not affected. *Gāg*, the second word in our discussion, occurs 30 times in the OT, and its meaning "roof" is undisputed, requiring no further explanation.

It is remarkable that the theme of a contentious wife occurs five times in Proverbs: three times in association with the husband's desire to be far from her (21:9, 19; 25:24) and twice in comparison with continual drippings on a rainy day (19:13; 27:15). The fact that all the five sayings are confined to collections II and V and four of the five are involved in repetition (21:9=25:24 and 19:13b=27:15) affirms the linkage between the two collections.

M. *ʾărî* "lion" (3 times), *kĕpîr* "young lion" (3 times), and *dôb* "bear" (twice)[101]

Table 2.8
Words for the Lion and Bear

Word	Freq.	Meaning	I	II	III	IV	V	VI	VII
ʾărî	35/3	lion	1				2		
dôb	12/2	bear	1				1		
kĕpîr	31/3	young lion	2				1		
layiš	3/1	lion						1	
šaḥal	7/1	young lion					1		

The Old Testament employs seven different words for a lion (*ʾărî*, *ʾaryê*, *gûr*, *kĕpîr*, *lābî ʾ*/*lĕbiyyaʾ*, *layiš*, and *šaḥal*), and Table 2.8 shows that four of the seven lion terms occur in Proverbs. It is also observed in the table that the lion-sayings in Proverbs are almost exclusively found in collections II and V. Considering the disappearance of the wild beasts and kingship in Israel in later periods, it is reasonable to suggest that the sayings which mention the lion in connection with a human king (e.g., 19:12; 20:2) belong to the earlier strata of the wisdom sayings in Proverbs.

A lion or a bear is mentioned in Proverbs to illustrate certain aspects of humanity. For example, in 19:12 and 20:2 the king's anger is compared to the lion's (*kĕpîr*) roar to emphasize the fear of the royal wrath, and similarly, a wicked ruler in 28:15 is likened to a roaring lion (*ʾărî*) and rampant bear (*dôb*) to depict him as a predatory animal. Although it may not be common for lions to roam in the streets of a town, the sluggard (*ʿāṣēl*) refuses to go out from the house with an excuse that a lion (*ʾărî* and *šaḥal*) is outside in the street to kill him (22:13; 26:13). The danger of meeting a fool is described in an exaggerated way in 17:12: one should rather meet a bear robbed of her cubs than meet a fool (*kĕsîl*) with his folly.

A link between collections II and V is clearly indicated by the lion theme and the parallel sayings (22:13; 26:13) in the two collections.

(7) The Peculiar Relationship between Collections II and V

The examination of the 20 exclusive words (4 verbs and 16 nouns) in collections II and V reveals two peculiar aspects of the relationship between the two collections, which require an additional explanation. The first peculiar and remarkable phenomenon is that most of the exclusive words (17 of the 20 words), as shown in the examination, occur in the repeated verses between collections II and V (see Table 2.9 below). This means that the themes which are represented in the repeated sayings are unique to collections II and V.

Secondly, if we borrow the terminology used by Daniel C. Snell, some of the repeated sayings between collections II and V are called "whole-verse repetition." Snell's exhaustive study of the repeated sayings in Proverbs shows that the phenomenon of whole-verse repetition is frequent within a collection (e.g., more than 20 verses are involved in the whole-verse repetition within collection I) but not frequent between collections.[102] It is noted in his study that the phenomenon of the whole-verse repetition between collections is restricted almost exclusively to collections II and V. Exceptions to this phenomenon are only two, 6:10–11=24:33–34 and 8:35=18:22 (I=IV and I=II). Snell lists 22 verses (11 pairs) from collections II and V as wholly repeated. This phenomenon indicates that the relationship between collections II and V is far more peculiar than between other collections, and that the linkage between the two collections is affirmed by numerous words and phrases. Since the whole-verse repetition is almost exclusively restricted to collections II and V, an explanation of the phenomenon may help one understand the nature of the relationship between the two collections.

As an attempt to have an overall view of the repeated verses between collections II and V and to find out the pattern or nature of repetition, the repeated verses have been classified according to the type of repetition (e.g., thematic, half-verse, and whole-verse repetition), and have been compiled in the following table.[103]

Table 2.9
Repeated Verses in Collections II and V

Repetition	Collection II	Collection V	Exclusive Word
Thematic	10:1a	27:11a	
Half-verse	10:13b; 19:29b	26:3b	*gēw*
Thematic	11:13a; 20:19a	25:9b	*glh*
Thematic	11:14a	29:18a	
Thematic	12:10a	27:23a	
Whole-verse	12:11	28:19	*ʾădāmâ, rdp, rêq*
Whole-verse	12:13	29:6	*pešaᶜ*
Thematic	13:17b	25:13b	*sîr, ʾmn*
Half-verse	15:18a	29:22a (cf. 28:25a)	*grh*
Half-verse	16:12b (cf. 20:28b)	25:5b; 29:14b	
Half-verse	17:3a	27:21a	*maṣrēp, kûr*
Half-verse	17:7a; 19:10a	26:1b	*nāʾwê*
Whole-verse	18:8	26:22	*rgn, lhm*
Half-verse	18:9b	28:24b	

Whole-verse	19:1	28:6	rwš
Half-verse	19:13b	27:15	delep, ṭrd
Whole-verse	19:24	26:15	ṭmn, ṣallaḥat
Whole-verse	20:16	27:13	ḥbl
Whole-verse	21:9 (cf. 21:19)	25:24	gāg, ḥeber
Thematic	22:2	29:13	rwš, pgš
Whole-verse	22:3	27:12	ʿārûm, str, ʿnš
Whole-verse	22:13	26:13	ʾărî

As mentioned above, a significant phenomenon which is shown in the table is that most of the verses involved in repetition contain at least one or more words which are exclusive to collections II and V. A further examination of the table shows that all the repeated verses classified as whole-verse repetition contain one or more exclusive words. Another significant aspect of the phenomenon of repetition shown below is that repetition is not a partial phenomenon involving only certain chapters but a total phenomenon involving all the chapters in the two collections (except ch. 14):

Collection II	ch. 10 (2 verses)	ch. 11 (2 verses)	ch. 12 (3 verses)
	ch. 13 (1 verse)	ch. 15 (1 verse)	ch. 16 (1 verse)
	ch. 17 (2 verses)	ch. 18 (2 verses)	ch. 19 (3 verses)
	ch. 20 (1 verse)	ch. 21 (1 verse)	ch. 22 (3 verses)
Collection V	ch. 25 (4 verses)	ch. 26 (5 verses)	ch. 27 (6 verses)
	ch. 28 (3 verses)	ch. 29 (5 verses)	

It has been pointed out by some that 16:1–22:16 and chapters 25–29 share a large number of similar and identical sayings,[104] but Table 2.9 shows that similarities are found in chapters 10–15 also. One of the immediate questions in dealing with the phenomenon of repetition in Proverbs would be how to explain the presence of repeated sayings between two given collections. Although the complex nature of Proverbs in terms of the composition and collection of sayings would not allow any simple answer, as far as collections II and V are concerned, the presence of the repeated verses in the two collections may not be the result of direct borrowing from one to the other.

Agreeing with Snell who says that whole-verse repetition is more important than any other types of repetition,[105] we will attempt to explain the relationship between collections II and V, mainly on the basis of whole-verse repetition. The following comparisons of the repeated verses show that the degree of repetition varies among the nine pairs of the whole verses repeated in collections II and V: one pair (18:8 and 26:22) shows exact repetition, three pairs show minor differences, and five pairs show various differences in words and word order.

i. Exact Repetition

18:8=26:22   *dibrê nirgān kĕmitlahămîm wĕhēm yārĕdû hadrê bāten*
              "The words of a gossip are like delicacies,
                  and they go down to the chambers of the belly."

This is one of the two sayings in Proverbs which are identical (the other is
14:12=16:25, a repetition within collection II).

ii. Minor Differences

21:9   *tôb lāšebet ʿal pinnat gāg mēʾēšet midyānîm ûbêt hāber*
         "Better to stay in the corner of a roof,
             than a contentious wife and a shared house."
25:24   *tôb šebet ʿal pinnat gāg mēʾēšet midyānîm ûbêt hāber*
         "Better to stay in the corner of a roof,
             than a contentious wife and a shared house."

The difference between 21:9 and 25:24 involves the preposition *l-* in *lāšebet*. A
survey of the infinitive of the verb *yšb* shows that *lāšebet* is far more frequent
than *šebet* in the OT (40 times to 8 times, both without suffixes). However, the
situation is reversed in a comparative or an exclamatory clause which begins
with *tôb*. In such a clause *tôb* is followed by *šebet* three times (Ps 133:1; Prov
21:19; 25:24) but followed by *lāšebet* only once (Prov 21:9). Since both expressions (*tôb lāšebet* and *tôb šebet*) occur in the same chapter (21:9, 19) in collection II, the difference represented by the preposition between collections II and
V appears to be stylistic with no significance.

20:16   *lĕqah bigĕdô kî ʿārab zār ûbĕ ʿad nokrîm* (K) *hablēhû*
         "Take his garment for he has given surety for a stranger,
             and seize it, because of foreigners."
27:13   *qah bigĕdô kî ʿārab zār ûbĕ ʿad nokriyyâ hablēhû*
         "Take his garment for he has given surety for a stranger,
             and seize it, because of a strange woman."

There are two differences between 20:16 and 27:13: *lĕqah* (20:16)/*qah* (27:13)
and *nokrîm* (K, 20:16)/*nokriyyâ* (27:13). In view of the fact that the Kethib
nokrîm in 20:16 has no reason to be replaced with the Qere (*nokriyyâ*),[106] it is
likely that the intention of the Qere is to harmonize *nokrîm* in 20:16 with
nokriyyâ in 27:13, or that the Qere may have been influenced by the numerous
references of the strange woman in chapters 1–9.[107] If the repetition had been the
consequence of borrowing, the direction of the borrowing would not have been
from collection V (20:16) to collection II (27:13) for two reasons: (a) the im-
perative form *lĕqah* (20:16) is much less frequently used than *qah* (27:13) in the
OT (3 times to 121 times), and (b) *nokriyyâ* in 27:13 is more at home in Prov-

erbs than *nokrîm* (Kethib) in 20:16 (one would change the former to the latter after borrowing the sentence). However, the nature of the differences between the two suggests that the two sayings are independent of each other.

22:3   *ʿārûm rāʾâ rāʿâ wĕissātēr* (K)   *ûpĕtāyim ʿābĕrû wĕne ʿĕnāšû*
         "A clever man sees trouble and hides himself,
                but the simple ones go on and suffer."
27:12   *ʿārûm rāʾâ rāʿâ nistār   pĕtāʾyim ʿābĕrû ne ʿĕnāšû*
         "A clever man sees trouble, he hides himself,
                the simple ones go on, they suffer."

Three minor differences are noted between 22:3 and 27:12, *wĕyissātēr* (K) and *nistār*, the conjunction *wāw* (*wĕne ʿĕnāšû* and *ne ʿĕnāšû*), and the conjunction and spelling (*ûpĕtāyim* and *pĕtāʾyim*). The comparison of the two parallel sayings indicates that 27:12 is terser and more poetic than 22:3. An inferior poetic character of 22:3 is also indicated by the inconsistency in using the verbs: while the first colon has the sequence, perf. + conj. + impf., the sequence in the second colon is perf. + conj. + perf. It is therefore possible that the Qere in 22:3 (*wĕnistār*) may have been motivated by the intention to make the sequence of the verbs consistent. Another possibility for the Qere is that the scribe may have been encouraged to correct the awkward verbal sequence in 22:3 by his knowledge of the sequence in 27:12. The second difference between 22:3 and 27:12 is the presence and absence of the conjunction in three places: the conjunction is used three times in 22:3, but it is completely absent in 27:12. As pointed out above, the verbs in 22:3 are connected twice by the conjunction *wāw*, but the same verbs in 27:12 are arranged in an asyndetic structure without the help of the conjunction "and." Although the phenomenon of asyndeton is not easy to translate, it is understood that the coordinate relationship of verbs without a conjunction is terse but more vigorous and bolder in a poetic text.[108] Consequently, it is suggested that the sentence structure of 27:12 reflects originality with a more powerful poetic style. With regard to the spelling difference between *pĕtāyim* (22:3) and *pĕtāʾyim* (27:12), the function of *ʾālep* is understood as to soften *yôd*.[109] On the basis of this understanding, one can suggest that *pĕtāʾyim* may be later in time than *pĕtāyim*, although the coexistence of the two forms is possible at any given time.

Because of the three inferior linguistic aspects of 22:3 (the verbal sequence, the use of the conjunction, and the spelling), if there had been borrowing between 22:3 and 27:12, the direction should have been from 22:3 (II) to 27:12 (V), not the other way around. However, it is difficult to think that such changes were made in the course of borrowing, and that 27:12 is an improved product of 22:3. Rather, more probable is that the two sayings are originals with no interaction or dependence between the two.

iii. Other Differences

> 12:11 *ʿōbēd ʾadmātô yiśbaʿ lāhem   ûmĕraddĕp rēqîm ḥăsar lēb*
> "One who works his land will be satisfied with food,
>   but one who follows vain things is a fool."
>
> 28:19 *ʿōbēd ʾadmātô yiśbaʿ lāhem   ûmĕraddĕp rēqîm yiśbaʿ rîš*
> "One who works his land will be satisfied with food,
>   but one who follows vain things will be filled with poverty."

As we continue the comparison of the remaining five pairs of whole-verse repetition, we encounter more substantial differences between two parallel texts. The
difference between 12:11 and 28:19 is noted in the last two words of the sayings. While the person who follows vain things is called *ḥăsar lēb* "senseless
man" in 12:11, the same person in 28:19 is warned that "he will have plenty of
poverty" (*yiśbaʿ rîš*). As far as parallelism is concerned, 28:19 is better than
12:11 because *yiśbaʿ rîš* in 28:19b is paired with *yiśbaʿ lehem* in 28:19a in perfect antithetic parallelism, but *ḥăsar lēb* in 12:11b does not match well with its
counterpart *yiśbaʿ lehem* in 12:11a. In view of the perfect parallelism in 28:19,
if there had been borrowing between the two collections, it should have been
from collection II (12:11) to collection V (28:19). Another important factor that
makes the direction of borrowing from collection V to collection II improbable
is the presence of *ḥăsar lēb* in 12:11. *Ḥăsar lēb* is a stock phrase in collections I
(4 times) and II (6 times), but is never found in collection V. It is difficult to
imagine that a collector or an editor of collection II changed *yiśbaʿ lehem* to
ḥăsar lēb destroying the perfect parallelism. It is probable that the difference
between 12:11 and 28:19 did not stem from direct borrowing, but that the two
sayings were formed independently from a common subject matter. Whybray
also supports the view that variant sayings are originals on which the editors of
different collections were able to draw.[110]

> 12:13 *bĕpeśaʿ śĕpātayim môqēš rāʿ   wayyēṣēʾ miṣṣārâ ṣaddîq*
> "An evil snare is in the transgression of lips,[111]
>   but a righteous man gets out of trouble."
>
> 29:6 *bĕpeśaʿ ʾîš rāʿ môqēš   wĕṣaddîq yārûn wĕśāmēaḥ*
> "A snare is in the transgression of an evil man,
>   but a righteous man shouts and rejoices."

Although the difference between the two sayings involve three words and the
word order, it is certain that the sense of the two sayings is the same. The first
colon of 12:13 has been interpreted in three different ways due to the ambiguous
relationship between *môqēš* and *rāʿ*: "an evil snare is in the transgression of
lips," "the snare of an evil man (subjective genitive) is in his malicious speech,"
and "an evil man is ensnared by the transgression of his lips."[112] Although 29:6a
does not render much assistance in clearing up the ambiguity in 12:13a, the
wording of 29:6a indicates that the half verse has relevance to 12:13a. In 29:6a

rā occurs before *môqēš*, modifying *ʾîš*: "A snare is in the transgression of an evil man." If *rā*ʿ in 12:13a is understood as *ʾîš rā*ʿ "an evil man" as in 29:6a, then the snare is understood as being set up by the evil man, which supports the second interpretation: "The snare of an evil man (subjective genitive) is in (his) malicious speech."

The second halves of 12:13 and 29:6 display greater difference, suggesting that they may have been composed separately but in a similar way in connection with the same first half. Although the theme is the same, direct borrowing between 12:13 and 29:6 is a remote possibility. The two sayings are independent.

> 19:1   *ṭôb rāš hôlēk bĕtummô   mēʿiqqēš śĕpātāyw wĕhûʾ kĕsîl*
>   "Better a poor man who walks with his integrity,
>   than a man whose lips are perverse and he is a fool."
> 28:6   *ṭôb rāš hôlēk bĕtummô   mēʿiqqēš dĕrākayim wĕhûʾ ʿāšîr*
>   "Better a poor man who walks with his integrity,
>   than a man whose double ways are perverse and he is rich."

The nature of difference between 19:1 and 28:6 is similar to that of the difference between the two previous sayings (12:13; 29:6). The first halves of the two sayings are exactly the same, but the second halves show differences in two words. Nevertheless, the second halves show the same structure, "than . . . and he is . . . ," pointing to the similarity between them. Commentators note the unusual dual form *dĕrākayim* "two ways" in 28:6, and think that it is either a scribal error or a later interpretation of the consonantal text to refer to the metaphor of "two ways" in Proverbs.[113] However, the fact that the same dual form of *derek* also occurs in 28:18 in connection with *ʿqš* excludes the possibility of a scribal error. From a literary point of view, 28:6 is superior to 19:1 for two reasons: the contrast between the poor and rich in 28:6 is better than the contrast between the poor and fool in 19:1, and, similarly, the relationship between "walk" and "ways" in 28:6 is more natural than the relationship between "walk" and "lips" in 19:1. As for the comparison of the second halves, any borrowing between 19:1b and 28:6b would be improbable. More likely is that the two sayings have been composed independently using a common, self-contained theme, "poverty with integrity is better." This understanding appears to support O. Eissfeldt's view that one-line proverbs were the forerunners of two-line wisdom sayings.[114] Although Eissfeldt's view is not able to explain more complex cases in Proverbs,[115] it has relevance to the problem of repeated sayings. In order to illustrate the possibility of the expansion from one-line saying to two-line saying, we will take one example from half verses repeated. The first halves of 17:3a and 27:21a are an identical proverb: "The crucible for silver, the furnace for gold," but the second halves of the two verses bear no resemblance: "and the Lord tests hearts" (17:3b) and "and a man is according to his praise" (27:21b) The complete difference between the two second halves does not allow any speculation on the possibility of dependence between 17:3 and 27:21. It is rather certain that newly composed lines were separately added to the already existing self-contained one-line proverb, transforming it, on one hand, into a God-saying (17:3), and, on the other hand, into an ethical wisdom saying (27:21). We now return to 19:1 and 28:6, and conclude that the two sayings are separate originals which may have been built on a common theme "a poor man walking with his integrity."

19:24   *tāman ʿāṣēl yadô bassalāhat gam ʾel pîhû loʾ yĕšîbennâ*
         "A sluggard dips his hand in the dish,
              he will not even bring it back to his mouth."
26:15   *tāman ʿāṣēl yadô bassalāhat   nilʾâ lahăšîbāh ʾel pîw*
         "A sluggard dips his hand in the dish,
              he is too tired to bring it back to his mouth."

The pattern of difference between 19:24 and 26:15 is the same as in the previous instances: whereas the first halves of the two verses are exactly the same, the second halves differ each other. The second half of 19:24 displays a linguistic feature which belongs mainly to collection II. The adverb *gam* is used 23 times in Proverbs, 17 times in collection II, 3 times in collection V, and once each in collections I, III, and IV. A survey of the usage of *gam* in Proverbs shows that the adverb occurs in two places in a clause. It occurs in the middle of a clause immediately before the word to be emphasized (e.g., *gam šĕnêhem* "even two of them," 20:12). *Gam* also occurs at the beginning of a clause for the purpose of emphasis, inverting the normal word order (e.g., *gam biśĕhôq yikʾab lēb* "Even in laughter, the heart is sad," 14:13). In 19:24b *gam* stands at the beginning of the second colon to emphatically portray the laziness of a sluggard, and this verse is one of the 12 such instances in collection II (14:13, 20; 16:4, 7; 17:26, 28; 18:9; 19:2; 20:11; 21:13; 22:6). Elsewhere in Proverbs, *gam* occurs only three times at the beginning of a clause or sentence (24:23; 25:1; 28:9), and two of them are in the titles (*gam ʾēllê* "These are also . . ." in 24:23; 25:1). Based on the instances of the adverb, we suggest that the frontal positioning of *gam* in a clause is a linguistic feature of collection II. On the other hand, 26:15b also contains its own distinctive element. The verb *lʾh* "to be weary" in 26:15b is a low frequency verb occurring 19 times in the OT (once in Proverbs). These linguistic features in 19:24b and 26:15b suggest that the two sayings are variants of one original saying.

22:13   *ʾāmar ʿāṣēl ʾărî bahûṣ bĕtôk rĕhōbôt ʾērāṣēah*
         "A sluggard says, 'There is a lion outside!
              I will be killed in the middle of the plazas'"
26:13   *ʾāmar ʿāṣēl šahal badārek   ʾărî bên hārĕhōbôt*
         "A sluggard says, 'There is a young lion in the street!
              A lion in the plazas!'"

These two sayings are the last pair of whole-verse repetition in our discussion. Despite the three different words between the two sayings, the resemblance is undeniable because of the same beginning "A sluggard says . . ." followed by the direct speech "the lion is in the street." As far as parallelism is concerned, 26:13 appears better than 22:13, and the more polished poetic style of 26:13 implies that the direction of borrowing from 26:13 to 22:13 is unlikely. A main difference between 22:13 and 26:13 is that two different terms for the lion are used in the second saying: while *ʾărî* alone occurs in 22:13a, *šahal* (26:13a) and *ʾărî* (26:13b) are used synonymously in 26:13. Elsewhere in the OT, *šahal* is found six times (3 times in Job, 2 times in Hosea, and once in Psalms), indicating that it belongs to poetic language. In those six instances, *kĕpîr* "young lion" occurs three times, always as a B-word, in synonymous parallelism with *šahal* (Hos 5:14; Ps 91:3; Job 4:10). In this sense, the pairing of *šahal* and *ʾărî* in Prov 26:13 is somewhat unusual in the light of the more common pair of *šahal* and *kĕpîr*. Although it is not certain whether the use of *ʾărî* instead of *kĕpîr* in 26:13 was due to the influence of 22:13, the substantial difference between *šahal badderek*(26:13a) and *ʾărî bahûṣ* (22:13a) indicates that there is no direct influence between 22:13 and 26:13.

Having examined the differences of the nine pairs of whole-verse repetition between collections II and V, a summary of the examination is offered in the following way. First of all, a pattern of difference emerges from the five parallel pairs that show more considerable differences (12:11//28:19; 12:13//29:6; 19:1//28:6; 19:24//26:15; 22:13//26:13): the main difference between two parallel sayings is always located in the second colon, never in the first. For example, in the three pairs (12:11//28:19; 19:1//28:6; 19:24//26:5) the first halves are exactly the same, but the second halves contain difference. This phenomenon implies that in the process of composing a two-colon saying the first half, a self-contained proverb, was regarded as a chief constituent of a saying while the second half was an element to be adapted to a specific need. The comparison of the following two pairs points to this possibility: the differences located in the second halves of 12:11 and 19:1 may be due to the emphasis of the fool in collection II:

12:11	"One who works his land will be satisfied with food,
	but one who follows vain things is *a fool*."
28:19	"One who works his land will be satisfied with food,
	but one who follows vain things *will be filled with poverty*."

19:1	"Better a poor man who walks with his integrity,
	than a man whose lips are perverse and he is *a fool*."
28:6	"Better a poor man who walks with his integrity,
	than a man whose double ways are perverse and he is *rich*."

Another interesting phenomenon is that, as far as whole-verse repetition is concerned, the sayings in collection V are superior to their counterparts in collection II in terms of parallelism and poetic style (e.g., 28:19//12:11; 26:13//22:13; 28:6//19:1). Although no firm conclusion can be drawn from the phenomenon, the examination of the parallel sayings indicates that direct borrowing or direct influence from one to the other is not probable. Rather, the existence of the one identical pair (18:8=26:22) and three almost identical pairs (20:16//27:13; 21:9//25:24; 22:3//27:12) point to the possibility that the editors of the two collections drew those sayings from a common source, and that the differences are the results of adaptation to the purpose of emphasis.

It has been pointed out in our earlier discussion that Eissfeldt's expansion theory (from one line to two lines) is feasible to explain some of repeated sayings but not in other cases. His view (also the view of this study) seems possible when the first line is a self-contained saying, but, when it is incomplete or subordinate in sense, the expansion theory reveals its weakness. For example, Snell lists 22:2 and 29:13 as a pair under the heading, "Whole Verses Repeated with Four or More Dissimilar Words."[116] Although the difference between the two sayings is great, it is difficult to deny the resemblance between them because of the three common key words ("the poor," "meet," and "the Lord") and the structure ("A and B meet"). In view that the first halves of the two sayings ("A and B meet") do not make a complete sense without the second lines, it is difficult to use the expansion theory to explain this type of repeated sayings.

Before attempting to offer an explanation for the phenomenon of repetition between collections II and V, we want to present a set of two lists in which the verses involved in repetition (whole-verse, half-verse, and thematic) between the two collections have been tabulated in two ways: the first two left columns show the repeated verses in the ascending order in collection II, and the last two columns show the repeated verses in the ascending order in collection V.

Table 2.10
The Sequential Order of Repeated Verses in Collections II and V

Repetition	Collections II-V	Repetition	Collections V-II
Thematic	10:1a//27:11a	Half-verse	25:5b//16:12b
Half-verse	10:13b//26:3b	Thematic	25:9b//11:13a//20:19a
Thematic	11:14a//29:18a	Thematic	25:13b//13:17b
Thematic	12:10a//27:23a	Whole-verse	25:24//21:9
Whole-verse	12:11//28:19	Half-verse	26:1b//17:7a//19:10a
Whole-verse	12:13//29:6	Half-verse	26:3b//10:13b//19:29b
Thematic	13:17b//25:13b	Whole-verse	26:13//22:13
Half-verse	15:18a//29:22a	Whole-verse	26:15//19:24
Half-verse	16:12b//25:5b//29:14b	Whole-verse	26:22//18:8
Half-verse	17:3a//27:21a	Thematic	27:11a//10:1a

Half-verse	17:7a//26:1b		Whole-verse	27:12//22:3
Whole-verse	18:8//26:22		Whole-verse	27:13//20:16
Half-verse	18:9b//28:24b		Half-verse	27:15//19:13b
Whole-verse	19:1//28:6		Half-verse	27:21a//17:3a
Half-verse	19:10a//26:1b		Thematic	27:23a//12:10a
Half-verse	19:13b//27:15		Whole-verse	28:6//19:1
Whole-verse	19:24//26:15		Whole-verse	28:19//12:11
Half-verse	19:29b/26:3b		Half-verse	28:24b//18:9b
Whole-verse	20:16//27:13		Whole-verse	29:6//12:13
Thematic	20:19a//25:9b		Thematic	29:13//22:2
Whole-verse	21:9//25:24		Half-verse	29:14b//16:12b
Thematic	22:2//29:13		Thematic	29:18a//11:14a
Whole-verse	22:3//27:12		Half-verse	29:22//15:18a
Whole-verse	22:13//26:13			

The purpose of the table is to point out two features of the repetition. First, the repetition between collections II and V involves all the chapters of the two collections (except chapter 14). Secondly, it is observed in the table that repeated verses are more heavily concentrated in certain places. For example, repeated verses are found in succession in 12:10–13; 18:8–9; 22:2–3 (collection II), and in 27:11–15; 29:13–14 (collection V). In the comparison of the nine pairs of the repeated sayings between collections II and V, we have suggested that the phenomenon of repetition between the two collections is not the result of direct borrowing from one to the other but the result of separate drawings by the editors from commonly available sources to them. It may be possible that, in the process of incorporating sayings from a common source into a collection, one editor may have located them in one place while the other may have scattered them within a collection, depending on certain necessities such as the context or continuation of thought.

Regardless of the probability of this suggestion, one thing is certain: the frequent and almost exclusive phenomenon of whole-verse repetition between collections II and V proves that the connection between the two is a more substantial than the connections between other collections, and that the two are more closely related each other in the process of collecting sayings than other collections.

(8) The Relationship
between Collections II, V, and VI

אֶפֶס	43/3	end	II-1	V-1	VI-1
עֶבֶד	799/10	servant	II-6	V-2	VI-2
שֵׁן	55/3	tooth	II-1	V-1	VI-1

Three words ('*epes*, '*ebed*, and *šēn*) occur exclusively in collections II, V, and VI, and among these the use of '*ebed* will be examined below.

'*ebed* "servant, slave" (ten times)[117]

In general '*ebed* designates a person who is subordinated to someone else without freedom. However, the setting of subordination or the relationship between the '*ebed* and his master is not always the same. The ten instances of '*ebed* in Proverbs can be divided into three groups according to the context. It is understood in five of the ten instances that the master of the '*ebed* is an ordinary person (12:9; 17:2; 29:19, 21; 30:10). One of the five sayings implies that possessing a slave was so common in Israel that even a socially insignificant person could have a slave: "Better to be slighted but to have a slave" (12:9). Several sayings reveal a remarkably humane aspect in the slave-master relationship: a prudent slave ('*ebed maśkîl*) could take the place of a shameful son in dividing family inheritance (17:2), a master is warned not to be overly kind and generous to a slave boy by pampering him from childhood (29:21), and a master is informed that a slave is not easily disciplined by mere words (29:19). Fairness to slaves is emphasized in 30:10 in which free people are admonished not to slander a slave to his master.

Although W. M. W. Roth takes '*ebed* in 30:22 as a slave on the grounds of the chiastic relationship between '*ebed* and *šiphâ* "female slave" (30:23),[118] it is possible that the '*ebed* in 14:35, 19:10, and 30:22 refers to a member of the royal court in various positions. In 14:35 the king's favor or wrath falls on the '*ebed* depending on his competence in serving the king. Twice '*ebed* occurs in the context of the reversal of normal power in society (19:10; 30:22), a theme which Van Leeuwen calls "a world upside down."[119]

It is well known that slaves came from mainly two sources in ancient society: prisoners of war and free persons who were in debt. It has been pointed out that debt slaves enjoyed far better status in Mesopotamia because they were not slaves in the normal sense.[120] It is also implied in the context of 22:7 how free people could become debt slaves of other citizens: "the rich rule over the poor, and the borrower is a slave to a lender" (cf. 11:20).[121] The last example (22:7) confirms that debt slavery was a universal phenomenon in the ancient world.

Although no literary affinities are found among the sayings in which '*ebed* occurs, the three collections contain common themes of the slave. The theme of the upside-down social order involving the slave is found in collections II and VI (19:10; 30:22), and humane treatment of slaves in a family setting is common to all the three collections (17:2; 29:19, 21; 30:10). However, debt slavery is found only in collection II (11:29; 22:7) and the discipline of the slave only in collection V (29:19, 21).

(9) The Relationship
between Collections II, V, and VII

דִּין	19/5	judgment	II-2	V-1	VII-2
הלל	150/9	to be boastful	II-2	V-4	VII-3
פָּרַשׂ	67/3	to spread out	II-1	V-1	VII-1

Three words occur exclusively in the three collections, and among these the use of the verb *hll* will be examined below.

Hll "to praise" (nine times)[122]

The verb *hll* occurs mainly in the *piʿel* (113 out of 150 occurrences), mostly to praise God, his name, and his word, and is rarely used to praise humans or things.[123] In Proverbs the verb occurs four times in the *piʿel* (27:2; 28:4; 31:28; 31:31), once in the *puʿal* (12:8), and four times in the *hitpaʿel* (20:14; 25:14; 27:1; 31:30). The use of *hll* in Proverbs is distinctive in the sense that God is not the object of the verb in the book. Two sayings point out the functional aspect of praise in measuring one's true reputation: "A man is praised according to his prudence" (12:8), and "Let another praise you, not your own mouth" (27:2). The point of these two sayings is well reflected in the life of the ideal wife who is praised by her husband and her own deeds (31:28, 31).

Hll appears 23 times in the *hitpaʿel* in the OT, and a survey of the 23 instances shows that the verb is used mainly with a preposition: 18 times with the preposition *b-* and once with the preposition *ʿim-* (Ps 106:5). In the *hitpaʿel* the basic meaning of *hll* with *b-* is "to boast about" or "to rejoice in" the thing or person that comes after the preposition, and without the preposition the meaning is still the same.[124] In Proverbs *hll* occurs four times in the *hitpaʿel* (20:14; 25:14; 27:1; 31:30), and twice the verb is followed by the preposition *b-* (25:14; 27:1). In the last two instances the function of the preposition *b-* is to introduce the ground of boasting (*hll*): boasting about a false gift (*bĕmattat šeqer*) in 25:14 and boasting about tomorrow (*bĕyôm māḥār*) in 27:1.

At this point we want to suggest a reconsideration of the meaning of the phrase *mattat šeqer* "gift of deception" in 25:14 in connection with the use of *hll*. Delitzsch pointed out that Hitzig and Heidenheim had incorrectly interpreted *mattat šeqer* in 25:14 as a falsely promised gift to be received.[125] Since Delitzsch, commentators have interpreted *mattat šeqer* as a falsely promised gift to give, not to receive. For example, McKane translates the second colon of 25:14 as "a man who boasts about a non-existent gift," and interprets the meaning of the line as follows: a man, posing as a great benefactor, promises to give a gift but in the end he does not carry out his promise.[126] However, the discarded view seems to deserve reconsideration. First of all, it has to be pointed out that *mattat* can denote a gift that has been received as well as a gift given to others. In the six instances of *mattat* in the OT, three times it denotes a gift to be given to others. In 1 Kgs 13:7 King Jeroboam invites a prophet from Judah to his home, saying, "I will give you a gift (*mattat*)," and in Ezek 46:5 and 11 *mattat* denotes unspecified quantity of grain offering which is to be offered to God. On the other hand, *mattat* can mean a gift that has been received. According to Eccl 3:13 and 5:18, everyone must eat, drink, and find pleasure in his toilsome life because life is a *gift* from God. Therefore, *mattat šeqer* can be a false gift either to give or to receive, and consequently the phrase can be understood in two ways in the context of 25:14b: a man who boasts about a gift but never gives or a man who foolishly boasts about a gift that he never receives.

In addition, if we agree with M. A. Klopfenstein who distinguishes *šqr* from *kzb*, a gift that was promised but never given would be *mattat kĕzābim* According to him, *šeqer* in phrases like *lĕšôn šeqer* "lying tongue" or *śiptê šeqer* "lying lips" does not indicate falsehood or incorrectness, but it means "aggressive deceit intended to harm the other."[127] Although he later acknowledges the semantic development of *šeqer* from the strong "breach of faith" to the weakened meaning "deception" or "nothingness,"[128] considering the comparison of a "false witness" (*'ēd šeqer*) to lethal weapons (a hammer, sword, and a sharp arrow) in 25:18, a stronger meaning of *šeqer* seems appropriate in the phrase *mattat šeqer* in 25:14. Since *leḥem šeqer* "bread of falsehood" in 20:17 means material profit gained by a dishonest way,[129] and *zera' šeqer* "seed of falsehood" is synonymous with *yildê peša'* "children of transgression" in Isa 57:4, we suggest that *mattat šeqer* be understood in a similar way: a gift motivated by dishonesty to pervert truth or a gift intended to accomplish morally negative purposes. Being understood in this way, the phrase denotes a gift to which strings are attached. Also, in this sense, *mattat šeqer* is similar to *šōḥad* "bribe." In fact, *mattan*, a synonym of *mattat*, and *šōḥad* occur together in synonymous parallelism in 21:14, "A gift (*mattan*) in secret averts anger, and a bribe (*šōḥad*) in the bosom, strong wrath." The meaning of the two lines of 25:14 is characterized by the same idea (nothingness or emptiness): as clouds and wind without rain are nothing, so is a man who boasts about receiving a bribe-like gift intended to bend justice. Another possible understanding of 25:14b is: a person who rejoices in receiving a gift of bribery will end up being nothing.

Although 12:8 and 27:2 show resemblance in meaning that true praise comes from another not from oneself, no clear links between collections II, V, and VII are indicated by the use of the verb *hll*.

(10) The Relationship
between Collections II and VI

בְּהֵמָה	190/2	cattle	II-1	VI-1
בַּעַר	5/2	brutishness	II-1	VI-1
גְּבוֹר	159/3	strong	II-2	VI-1
חסה	37/2	to seek, refuge	II-1	VI-1
טָהוֹר	95/3	clean, pure	II-2	VI-1
יטב	101/5	to be good	II-3	VI-2
כזב	16/2	to lie	II-1	VI-1
נָבָל	18/3	foolish	II-2	VI-1
נַחַל	137/2	wadi, stream	II-1	VI-1
עַז	23/3	strong	II-2	VI-1
פעל	56/4	to do	II-3	VI-1
קלל	79/4	to be slight	II-2	VI-2
שׁאל	172/2	to ask	II-1	VI-1
שֵׁם	864/7	name	II-4	VI-3

Fourteen words (6 verbs and 8 adjectives/nouns) occur exclusively in the two collections, and the use of *ba'ar* and *nābāl* in the two collections will be examined below.

A. *Ba'ar* "brutish, stupid" (twice)[130]

Both the verb *b'r* and the substantive *ba'ar* derive from *bĕ'îr* "cattle, beast."[131] The substantive *ba'ar* is a rare term occurring only five times in the OT: three times in Psalms and twice in Proverbs. Its usage in the OT is unique in the sense that it always occurs in association with the words that belong to wisdom vocabulary, such as *yd'*, *da'at*, *byn*, *bînâ*, *ḥākām*, *ḥokmâ*, *kĕsîl*, *lmd*, *mûsār*, and *tôkaḥat*. This aspect of *ba'ar* clearly indicates that it also belongs to the wisdom domain with a notion "the unwise" in a broad sense.[132] In Proverbs the *ba'ar* refers to a person who hates reproof (12:1). Agur explains in 30:2–3 that he calls himself *ba'ar* because he does not have discernment, wisdom, or the knowledge of the Holy One. Although no literary resemblance is found between 12:1 and 30:2–3, the usage of *ba'ar* in collections II and VI is considered coherent because of the use of the word in connection with wisdom.

B. *Nābāl* "fool" (three times)[133]

The close relationship between collections II and VI with regard to the words for fools is implied by the fact that *ba'ar* and *nābāl*, the two least used terms for a fool in Proverbs, are found only in the two collections (cf. Table 1.13).

Of the meaning of *nābāl*, W. M. W. Roth points out that the traditional understanding of the word as "fool" is partly because of the influence of the LXX where *nābāl* is often rendered as ἄφρων. He subsequently suggests on the basis of Job 30:1–8 that *nābāl* denotes an outcast.[134] It appears that Roth's view is feasible in Prov 17:7 and 30:22. In 17:7, where *nābāl* occurs in parallelism with *nādîb* "nobleman," the parallelism requires *nābāl* to denote a person of a lowly social status, not a person of lowly intellectual ability. Whybray accepts Roth's definition of *nābāl* in his comment on 30:22, and interprets the second colon as a depiction of an outcast who enjoys prosperity.[135] In 17:21, however, the meaning of *nābāl* as an outcast is not natural in the context. Roth interprets *ʾăbî nābāl* in 17:21 as "a father of an ostracized member of society,"[136] but in view of the synonymous relationship between *yōlēd kĕsîl* and *ʾăbî nābāl*, it would be more natural to understand the *nābāl* as an intellectually inferior person.

Despite no literary resemblance, the exclusive occurrence of *nābāl* in collections II and VI may reflect a coherent wisdom element of the two collections.

(11) The Relationship
between Collections II, VI, and VII

אֶבְיוֹן   61/4   needy, poor   II-1   VI-1   VII-2

ʾebyôn "poor" (four times)[137]

ʾebyôn, one of the terms to denote the poor in Proverbs, is the only word that occurs exclusively in the three collections. As far as Proverbs is concerned, the poor can be divided into two groups: the poor denoted by the roots *ḥsr* or *rwš* and the poor denoted by the substantives, *dal*, *'ānî*, and *ʾebyôn*. The reason for the division in Proverbs is the negative or positive connotations conveyed by the terms in the context. For example, poverty as a consequence of laziness is denoted by the words derived from the roots *ḥsr* and *rwš* (*rēʾš* and *maḥsôr* in 6:11, *rāʾš* in 10:4, and *rîš* and *maḥsôr* in 24:34). One who ignores discipline will be rewarded with poverty (*rîš*) and disgrace (13:18), and it is said in 28:19 that one who pursues worthless things will be filled with poverty (*rîš*). Also, the poor man denoted by *rwš* in 28:3 (*geber rāš*) is a negative figure because he oppresses other poor people (*dallîm*). Nevertheless, the poor represented by the root *rwš* also enjoy God's protection because the Lord is their Creator (17:5; 22:2; 29:13), and they walk in integrity (19:1; 28:6). The positive and negative images of the poor represented by the root *rwš* indicate that the root is used to denote the poor in general.

However, a distinctive aspect of the poor is represented by the second group of the words (*dal*, *ʿānî*, and *ʾebyôn*). A remarkable aspect of the three words is that they are never associated with negative themes such as laziness, ignoring discipline, or oppressing others. In this sense the three terms may represent the "innocent" or "righteous" poor. In connection with our discussion of the terms for the poor in Proverbs, it is significant to note that in Psalms *ʾebyôn* occurs 23 times while *rāš* occurs only once. The predominant use of *ʾebyôn* in Psalms (e.g., "I am poor" in 40:18; 70:6) supports the view that a poor person represented by *ʾebyôn* is innocent or righteous, especially in the worship setting. In Proverbs *ʾebyôn* occurs four times, three times in juxtaposition with *ʿānî* (30:14; 31:9, 20) and once with *dāl* (14:31). The common aspect of the *ʾebyôn* implied in all the four instances in collections II, VI, and VII is that the *ʾebyôn* is a poor person who needs protection.

(12) The Relationship
between Collections II and VII

דרשׁ	164/2	to seek	II-1	VII-1
הֶבֶל	73/3	vapor, breath	II-2	VII-1
הָדָר	30/2	splendor, honor	II-1	VII-1
זָקֵן	187/3	old	II-2	VII-1
חַיִל	244/5	strength	II-2	VII-3
חסר	25/2	to lack	II-1	VII-1
מַעֲשֶׂה	234/3	deed, work	II-2	VII-1
צפה	36/2	to look out	II-1	VII-1
שֵׁכָר	23/3	strong drink	II-1	VII-2

Nine words (3 verbs and 6 adjectives/nouns) occur exclusively in the two collections, and the use of *šēkār*, *ṣph*, and *ḥayil* in the two collections will be examined below.

A. *Šēkār* "strong drink" (three times)[138]

Šēkār occurs 23 times in the OT, almost always in juxtaposition or synonymous parallelism with *yayin* "wine" (exceptions are Num 28:7 and Ps 69:13). A

striking phenomenon about the relationship between *šēkār* and *yayin* is that
šēkār completely disappears in late biblical books, making *yayin* occur alone in
those books. Thus *šēkār* is not found at all in Ruth, Song of Songs, Ecclesiastes,
Lamentations, Esther, Daniel, Ezra Nehemiah, and 1 and 2 Chronicles, while
yayin is found 32 times in those books. A. Hurvitz takes the juxtaposed relationship in *yayin wěšēkār* "wine and strong drink" (16 times in the OT) as an hendiadys to signify one unified concept, and concludes that *yayin* is the standard
word for drink in BH, and that *šēkār* belongs to poetic language.[139]

In Proverbs *šēkār* always occurs with *yayin*, and the three instances of *šēkār*
in collections II and VII provide an integrated understanding of the functional
aspect of wine. In 31:4 kings and rulers are admonished not to drink *yayin* and
šēkār because of the subversive and forgetful effects of the drinks. According to
20:1, *yayin* and *šēkār* make a person unwise (20:1). On the other hand, the forgetful effect of wine could be a temporary consolation to those who are in pain
and misery (31:6). No linkage is indicated by the use of *šēkār* between collections II and VII.

B. *Ṣph* "to watch attentively, guard" (twice)[140]

One of the characteristics of the verb *ṣph* has been pointed out earlier when A.
Wolters' view on *ṣôpiyyâ* in 31:27 was examined.[141] In the OT the verb is used
almost always as a participle (25 out of 27 instances in the *qal*). The active participle of *ṣph* often denotes a literal or figurative sentinel in the military and prophetic contexts. The two instances of *ṣph* in Proverbs also are participial forms.
It is said in 15:3 that the eyes of the Lord are everywhere watching (*ṣôpôt*) both
the good and evil, and in 31:27 the ideal wife is watching over (*ṣôpiyyâ*) the
affairs of her household. Whybray points out that the verb is used in the same
sense in both instances.[142] Wolters did not consider the participial use of the
verb in the OT, and drew an invalid conclusion on the basis of the similarity of
the sound between *ṣôpiyyâ* and *sophia*.[143]

The two instances of *ṣph* in collections II and VII are insufficient to establish a link between the two collections.

C. *Ḥayil* "wealth, strength" (five times)[144]

Ḥayil occurs 245 times in the OT with a great range of meaning. Although *ḥayil*
is synonymous with *kōaḥ*, its use is restricted to human beings, while *kōaḥ* is
used to describe the power of both God and humans.[145] However, on the basis of
Ps 59:12 in which *ḥayil* appears to have been used of God (*běḥêlěkā* "with your
[God] power"), H. Eising concludes that at least in that single instance *ḥayil*
refers to one of God's attributes.[146]

In Proverbs *ḥayil* is used in reference to three different types of people: it denotes the ability of a wise woman (12:4; 31:10, 29), the wealth of a sinner (13:22), and the strength of a king (31:3). *Ḥayil* is one of the key words for those who propose to read Proverbs in a unified way. According to the view, the phrase *'ēšet ḥayil* "a capable wife" in 12:4 and 31:10 is understood as the author's intention to present the wife as Lady Wisdom depicted in chapters 1–9, and the occurrence of *ḥayil* in 31:3 and 29 is one of the literary elements to unify chapter 31.[147]

On the basis of the unified reading of Proverbs, *'ēšet ḥayil* in 12:4 and 31:10 indicates a link between collections II and VII.

3. The Relationship between Collection III and Other Collections

A total of 57 words (24 verbs and 33 adjectives/nouns) occur exclusively in collection III and other collections as shown below:

Collection III	44 words	Collections III-V	3 words
Collections III-IV-V	2 words	Collections III-VI	2 words
Collections III-IV-V-VII	1 word	Collections III-VII	5 words

(1) Characteristic Exclusive Words in Collection III

a. Verbs (15)

אדם	10/1	to be red		אחר	17/1	to be behind
אלף	5/1	to learn		גאל	60/1	to redeem
דכא	18/1	to crush		הלם	8/1	to smite
חרה	93/1	to be kindled		יגע	26/1	to toil
יצב	47/2	to take one's stand		נשך	16/1	to bite
סבא	6/2	to imbibe		עלז	16/1	to exult
פרש	1/1	to pierce		קבע	6/2	to rob
שער	1/1	to calculate				

b. Adjectives/Nouns (29)

אֲבוֹי	1/1	alas		גִּיל	9/1	rejoicing
הֶרֶג	5/1	slaughter		חֵבֶל	1/1	mast
חַכְלִילוּת	1/1	dullness (eye)		חָזָק	56/1	strong

חָשֹׁךְ	1/1	obscure, low	חֶרֶף	1/1	prey
יָתוֹם	42/1	orphan	כּוֹס	31/1	cup
כִּלְיָה	31/1	kidneys	לֹעַ	1/1	throat
מָהִיר	4/1	quick	מַטְעָם	8/2	tasty food
מִלָּה	38/1	word	מִמְסָךְ	2/1	mixed drink
מַשָּׁאָה	2/1	loan, pledge	נוּמָה	1/1	slumber
נָעִים	13/3	pleasant	פִּיד	4/1	ruin
צִפְעוֹנִי	4/1	serpent	צַר	41/1	narrow
קֶרַע	4/1	rag, torn piece	קֹשְׁטְ	1/1	truth
רָאמֹת	3/1	corals	רֵבֶץ	4/1	dwelling place
שִׂיחַ	14/1	complaint	שַׂכִּין	1/1	knife
שִׁלְשׁוֹם	25/1	? (K)			

Forty-four words (15 verbs and 29 adjectives/nouns) occur exclusively in collection III. A survey of the exclusive words reveals several aspects of the vocabulary. First, in Proverbs collection III has the highest rate of the occurrence of *hapax legomena* in proportion to the size, as shown below (the first percentage refers to the size of a collection and the second percentage refers to the rate of the *hapax legomena*).[1]

Col I (28%)	16 words (22%)	Col V (15.1%)	21 words (28%)
Col II (41%)	18 words (24%)	Col VI (3.6%)	4 words (5%)
Col III (7.7%)	11 words (15%)	Col VII (3.4%)	3 words (4%)
Col IV (1.2%)	1 word (1%)		

Secondly, among the 31 chapters in Proverbs, chapter 23 (collection III) contains more *hapax legomena* (9 words) than any other chapters.[2] Thirdly, seven of the nine *hapax legomena* in chapter 23 occur in two units, one dealing with dining manners (23:1–8) and the other describing a drunken man (23:29–35). This phenomenon is because the table manner and intoxication are rare subjects in the OT.[3]

Collection III is considered peculiar in employing various exclusive words related to drinking and the human body, and the use of the words belonging to the two categories will be examined below.

A. Words Related to Drinking (23:20–21, 29–35)

Of the 44 exclusive words in collection III, the words which are related to drinking wine are found in two passages, 23:20–21 and 23:29–35. The two passages contain 16 exclusive words (36%) and five of them are *hapax legomena* (ʾăbôy, ḥibbēl, ḥaklîlût, nûmâ, prš).

The two passages describe the undesirable consequences of drinking wine. The son is admonished in 23:20–21 not to associate himself with excessive drinkers and gluttons of meat because those people will become poor in the end. The second passage (23:29–35) is a sort of caricature of a drunkard, which is intended to admonish "Do not look at wine when it is red" (23:31).[4] Of the 16 exclusive words in the two passages, we will examine the use of nine words occurring in the context of drinking wine.

a. Sbᵓ "to imbibe" (twice)[5]

Sbᵓ occurs only six times in the OT: twice each in Proverbs and Nahum and once each in Deuteronomy and Isaiah. M. Weinfeld notes that the instances of sbᵓ in Deut 21:20 and in Prov 23:20–21 show affinity.[6] In both instances sbᵓ occurs with zll "to be thoughtless" in reference to a son who is required to obey his parents. In Deut 21:20 the parents who have a rebellious son are instructed to testify before elders, saying, ". . . he does not listen (šômēaᶜ) to our voice. He is worthless (zôlēl) and drunken (sôbēᵓ)." The three words (šmᶜ, zll, and sbᵓ) also occur in the text of Proverbs: šmᶜ occurs in the beginning of Prov 23:19, "Listen (šĕmaᶜ), you, my son . . . ," and is followed by sôbēᵓ and zôlēl twice in verses 20 and 21. The occurrences of sbᵓ with zll in Deut 21:20 and Prov 23:20–21 clearly indicate that drinking by youth was a problem in the family.

b. Qeraᶜ "pieces of cloth, rags" (23:21)

Qeraᶜ is a rare word occurring only four times in the entire OT, always in the plural (1 Kgs 11:30, 31; 2 Kgs 2:12; Prov 23:21). In the three instances in 1 and 2 Kings, qeraᶜ occurs with the cognate verb qrᶜ "to tear" which reinforces the state of being torn off. For example, in 1 Kgs 11:30–31 Ahijah tears (qrᶜ) his new cloak into twelve pieces (qĕrāᶜîm) to ask Jeroboam to take ten qĕrāᶜîm. In the light of the three instances of qĕrāᶜîm in 1 and 2 Kings, the "rags" in Prov 23:21 is understood as a cloak torn into pieces, signifying one's poverty.

c. Nûmâ "slumber" (23:21)

Nûmâ is a hapax legomenon in the OT. The root nwm occurs six times as a verb and five times as the noun tĕnûmâ. Because of the fact that the verb occurs in Prophets and Psalms, and that tĕnûmâ occurs only in Psalms and Wisdom books, J. Schüpphaus suggests that nwm and tĕnûmâ belong to poetic language.[7] According to James G. S. S. Thomson, nwm is one of the three roots (two others are yšn and rdm) to denote sleep in Hebrew. He explains that the three nouns, tĕnûmâ, šēnâ, and tardēmâ which are derived from the three roots, represent the three stages of sleep, tĕnûmâ as the first stage and tardēmâ as the deepest sleep.[8] The three stages of sleep proposed by him may be correct in some cases, but the usage of the three nouns in poetic texts indicates that it is difficult to distinguish such stages. For example, in Ps 76:6 the verb *nwm* is used with the noun *šēnâ* in the following way: "they sleep (*nāmû*) their sleep (*šēnātām*)," suggesting the indistinguishable usage between the two roots. In Job 33:15 *tardēmâ* is mentioned in synonymous parallelism with *tĕnûmâ* as means for divine revelation. It is not natural to think in Job 33:15 that God's revelation comes after one has moved from the deepest sleep (*tardēmâ*) back to the shallow first stage of sleep (*tĕnûmâ*). Rather, both terms appear to denote deep sleep with no sharp distinction between them. Also, the inconsistent word order between *nwm*-words and *yšn*-words in parallelism indicates that strict distinction between the synonymous terms may not be possible at least in poetic texts (e.g., *lōʾ yānûm wĕlōʾ yîšān* in Psalm 121:4 and *mĕʿaṭ šēnôt mĕʿaṭ tĕnûmôt* in Prov 6:10).[9] If *nûmâ* in Prov 23:21 refers to the state of sleeping after heavy drinking or voracious eating of meat, the notion of "light sleep" is not appropriate in the context. We rather picture here a person who is unconscious in a torn garment after heavy drinking or eating.

d. *Śîaḥ* "complaint" (23:29)

Śîaḥ occurs 14 times in the OT, 11 of which are in poetic books (five times in Psalms, five times in Job, and once in Proverbs). According to J. Hausmann, the main issue in connection with *śîaḥ* is whether it refers to inner, mental activity (proposed by S. Mowinckel) or whether it involves the acoustic expression of emotion (proposed by H.-P. Müller).[10] Agreeing with Müller, Hausmann interprets most instances of *śîaḥ* as the expressions of emotion (e.g., lament, praise, and uncontrolled chattering), except the instances in Psalm 119 where he accepts the meaning suggested by Mowinckel.[11] A peculiar phenomenon noted in the instances of *śîaḥ* is that a pronominal suffix is always attached to the word, except for a problematic instance in 1 Kgs 18:27.[12] Eleven times *śîaḥ* appears with the first person singular "my" and once with the third person singular "his." Although the word occurs in the absolute state in Prov 23:29, the question "Who has *śîaḥ*?" indicates that it also must belong to someone.

The significance of this phenomenon (*śîaḥ* + a pronominal suffix) is that, barring the questionable passage in 1 Kgs 18:27, *śîaḥ* denotes an activity, mental or verbal, which always requires an identifiable agent. In other words, *śîaḥ* is not an absolute idea that can exist without an agent.[13] And the predominant use of the first person pronominal suffix with *śîaḥ* (11 out of 13 instances) indicates that outside Proverbs *śîaḥ* denotes a complaint expressed in the direct relationship between "I" and "You" (in all the 11 instances "my complaint" is directed to God as "You"). The third person pronominal suffix in "his *śîaḥ*" in 2 Kgs 9:11 also must be understood in the relationship of "I" and "You" because the complaint belongs to the prophet (I) who spoke directly to Jehu (You).

Of the meaning of *śîaḥ* in the book of Job, N. C. Habel comments that Job's *śîaḥ* is not a traditional cry of lament but a "formal legal complaint against his God."[14] In view of Habel's suggestion and the fact that *śîaḥ* occurs in synonymous parallelism with *midyānîm* "strife" in Prov 23:29,[15] the usual meaning of *śîaḥ* as "lament" or "complaint" seems to be weak in the context of 23:29. The various views on *śîaḥ* reflected in *HALOT* also point to the possibility that the basic meaning of the word needs an elaboration to fit in a given context. We thus offer an interpretation of *śîaḥ* in 23:29 as follows: the word denotes a complaint in the form of an "altercation" or a "squabble" in the "I-You" confrontation. If this understanding of *śîaḥ* is sustained in 23:29, we can suggest that the six questions in 23:29 can be divided into three groups to portray the three gradually developing stages of drinking:

Beginning of Drinking:	"Who has woe (*'ôy*)?"
	"Who has alas (*'ăbôy*)?"
State of Intoxication:	"Who has quarrels?"
	"Who has altercations?"
Aftermaths of Intoxication:	"Who has wounds without cause?"
	"Who has dim eyes?"

In the first two questions, the two words, *'ôy* and *'ăbôy* (*hapax legomenon*), are interjections most probably bursting out of the drinker's mouth, like "Woe to me!" The interjection *'ôy* occurs 24 times in the OT, and is almost always followed by the preposition *l-* (21 times),[16] In the context of drinking, the interjections may function as self-motivation to drink and forget troubles in life (cf. 31:7). The last four questions are easily understood in sequence as describing a drunkard's fight with others and the consequences of the fight and drinking.

e. *Ḥaklîlût* "dullness" (23:29)

Ḥaklîlût is a *hapax legomenon* in the OT, and it is one of the eight feminine abstract nouns with the *-ût* ending in Proverbs (cf. Table 5). Like the other abstract nouns in Proverbs, *ḥaklîlût* is formed on the adjectival form *ḥaklîl* by adding the abstract ending *-ût*. In his study of the word *taršîš*, C. H. Gordon explains the adjectival pattern of *ḥaklîl* and *taršîš* (*qaṭlîl* pattern) as denoting color, and continues to explain that the Hebrew root *ḥkl* is connected to the Akkadian cognate *ekêlu* "to be dark" and that *taršîš* is connected to Hebrew *tîrôš* "wine."[17] On the basis of the formation of the two words and their connection to the Akkadian cognates, he concludes that both *ḥaklîl* and *taršîš* refer to a color "wine-dark." His conclusion differs from the view that *ḥaklîlî* (Gen 49:12) and *ḥaklîlût* (Prov 23:29) are derived from the root *kḥl* "to paint (the eyes)."[18] From a linguistic point of view, the second view (*kḥl* as the root) is more complex than the first (*ḥkl* as the root) in explaining the formation of *ḥaklîlî* and *ḥaklîlût*, because the second view requires the transposition of the first and second consonants followed by the reduplication of the last consonant of the root. Although metathesis is found in a few roots (e.g., *kebeś* and *keśeb*, both, "young ram"), *ḥkl* appears to be the root of *ḥaklîlî*.

It is remarkable to note that Gen 49:12 contains the three key elements, dark color denoted by *ḥkl*, eye, and wine, which also occur in Prov 23:29–30. This strongly suggests that both texts commonly reflect the language that belongs to the domain of drinking.

f. *Mimsāk* "mixed drink, mixing bowl" (23:30)

Mimsāk occurs only twice in the OT, in Prov 23:30 and Isa 65:11. The two passages display resemblance in using not only the rare word *mimsāk* but also the same structure (plural participle + *l-* + *mimsāk*):[19]

Isa 65:11	*hamĕmal'îm lamĕnî mimsāk*
	"those who fill the jug of mixed wine for Fate"
Prov 23:30	*(ha)bbā'îm laḥqōr mimsāk*
	"those who come to search the jug of mixed wine"

The meaning of *mimsāk* has been understood as "mixed wine," due to the verb *msk* "to mix," but some have proposed "jug of mixed wine" as its meaning on the ground of Ugaritic *mmskn* "bowl" and the translation of the Peshitta.[20] Considering the association of *mimsāk* with verbs *ml'* "to fill" (Isa 65:11) and *ḥqr* "to search" (Prov 23:30), the meaning "jug of mixed wine" fits better in both Isa 65:11 and Prov 23:30 than the meaning "mixed wine."

g. *'dm* "to be red" (23:31)

'dm occurs ten times in the OT to denote the red color of the skin or symbolically the sin of Israel, but the use of *'dm* for wine color in Proverbs is unique. The expression *ntn . . . 'ayin* "to give an eye" in 23:31 to convey the notion of sparkling wine is also unique in the OT.

h. *Nšk* "to bite" (23:32)

Nšk occurs 16 times in the OT, ten of which are in reference to a snake biting. The verb is also used five times figuratively to denote "to charge interest." According to A. S. Kapelrud, the notion of interest as "biting" was common in the ancient Near East.[21] However, apart from Prov 23:32, the use of biting (*nšk*) to signify the negative effects of wine is not found elsewhere in the OT.

i. Ṣip ʿōnî "viper" (23:32)

Ṣip ʿōnî occurs only four times in the OT: twice in Isaiah and once each in Jeremiah and Proverbs. It is one of the nine terms for real and visible serpents in the OT, and designates a venomous serpent.[22] Ṣip ʿōnî occurs in Prov 23:32 in synonymous parallelism with nāḥāš "serpent" to reinforce the biting effects of wine.

At this point, we want to add one observation to the discussion of the words related to drinking. It is observed that the texts which deal with drinking in Genesis, Deuteronomy, and Isaiah contain the same expressions that are found in Proverbs. The following are the comparisons between Proverbs and the texts from the three books:

ḥkl + ʿayin	(Gen 49:12; Prov 23:29)
ʿrk + šulḥān	(Isa 65:11; Prov 9:2)
sb ʾ + zll	(Deut 21:20; Prov 23:21)
ʾḥr in connection with wine	(Isa 5:11; Prov 23:30)
pl. ptcp. + l- + mimsāk	(Isa 65:11; Prov 23:30)

The comparisons suggest that the text of Proverbs is a fuller text of the vocabulary and expressions related to drinking wine, and that such vocabulary and expressions were well known to the people of all classes in society, including prophets.

B. Words for the Parts of the Body

a. Kilyâ "kidneys" (23:16)

Kilyâ occurs 31 times in the OT, always in the plural kĕlāyôt "kidneys." The word is used for human (13 times) and non-human kidneys (18 times). While kĕlāyôt always refers to the kidneys of animals in Exodus (twice) and Leviticus (14 times), all of the 13 instances of kĕlāyôt in Jeremiah (four times), Lamentations (once), Psalms (five times), Job (twice), and Proverbs (once) denote human kidneys as one of the most important internal organs. It is significant to note in the 13 instances that God is frequently mentioned in connection with human kidneys: God examines them (bḥn in Jer 11:20; 17:10; Ps 7:10), sees them (r ʾh in Jer 20:12), refines them (ṣrp in Ps 26:2), creates them (qnh in Ps 139:13), and pierces them with an arrow (Job 16:13; Lam 3:13). In three instances the kidneys are related to human emotions (Ps 73:21; Job 19:27; Prov 23:16). The instance of kĕlāyôt in Prov 23:16 is unique in the sense that it is the only place in the OT where the kidneys are mentioned as the seat of human joy: the father's kidneys will rejoice when his son speaks honestly.

b. Lōaʿ "throat" (23:2)

Proverbs 23:1–8 deals with table manners, and is loaded with rare words. Lōaʿ is a *hapax legomenon* in the OT, and is one of the five rare words in the text. Of the five rare words, three are *hapax legemona* (*śakkîn* "knife," *lōaʿ* "throat," and *śʿr* "to calculate") and the remaining two are *lḥm* "to eat" which occurs six times in the OT (four times in Proverbs) and *maṭʿām* "tasty food" occurring eight times in the OT (six times in Gen 27 and twice in Prov 23). In connection with *lōaʿ*, several OT passages in which *lḥm* and *maṭʿām* occur deserve a comparison with Prov 23:1–8. The verb *lḥm* occurs in Proverbs (4 times), Deuteronomy (once), and Psalms (once), and the occurrence of *lḥm* in Psalm 141 attracts our attention because the psalm shows similarities to Prov 23:1–8. In Ps 141:3–4 the psalmist expresses the desire to cut off his association with the wicked by guarding his mouth and not eating their delicacies. Although one may say that putting a knife to the throat in Prov 23:2 is not comparable to guarding the mouth in Ps 141:3 because the first is concerned with food and the second with speech, eating delicacies of others is clearly the common theme in the two passages.[23] Especially, the use of the rare verb *lḥm* in connection with "delicacies" (*manʿammîm* in Ps 141:4 and *maṭʿammîm* in Prov 23:3) in both places points to the possibility that the resemblance between the two texts is not accidental. The noun *maṭʿām* in Prov 23:3 is peculiar in two aspects: it always occurs in the plural (eight times) and it occurs only in two places in the OT (twice in Prov 23:3–6 and six times in Genesis 27). E. A. Speiser, saying that there is similarity between Gen 27:2 and Mesopotamian texts, explains that Gen 27 is an account of great antiquity which is to be understood in the context of a death-bed statement of a dying man (Isaac) with legal binding.[24] In Genesis 27 Isaac tells Esau to prepare "tasty food" (*maṭʿām*) for him so that he may bless him before his death (27:4). In view of Speiser's argument for the Mesopotamian background of Gen 27 and the popularity of the root *ṭʿm* in Aramaic indicated by its 30 occurrences in Daniel and Ezra, it is possible that *maṭʿām* is an Aramaic term and that its six occurrences in Gen 27 is to add a Mesopotamian flavor to the story.[25] Based on Speiser's understanding of *maṭʿām*, a comparison of the three texts is presented below to suggest a connection between Prov 23:1–8 and Ps 141:3–4:

Prov 23:6	ʾal + lḥm . . . maṭʿām
Ps 141:4	bal + lḥm + manʿām
Gen 27	maṭʿām

It is noted in the comparison that *maṭʿām* is employed in Gen 27 and Prov 23:6, but *manʿām* "delicacy" is used in Ps 141. On the basis of the same *maqṭāl* formation and the same meaning of the two words, we suggest that the use of *manʿām* in Ps 141:4 is a Hebrew counterpart of *maṭʿām* which is probably an Aramaic word. The fact that *lōaʿ* and *śakkîn* (both *hapax legomena*) in Prov 23:2 are considered by some commentators as borrowed from Aramaic reinforces the possibility that *maṭ ʿām* is an Aramaic word, and that in Ps 141:4 the psalmist intentionally replaced the word with a Hebrew word of the same meaning and of similar sound.[26]

(2) The Relationship
between Collections III, IV, and V

חזה	55/3	to see	III-1	IV-1	V-1
שׁית	85/4	to put, place	III-1	IV-1	V-2

Two verbs occur exclusively in collections III, IV, and V, and we will examine the use of *ḥzh* in the three collections.

Ḥzh "to see" (three times)[27]

The verb *ḥzh* is considered an Aramaic loanword.[28] A. Jepsen explains that the borrowing of the root *ḥzh* from Aramaic was originally due to prophets and their modes of receiving revelation from God. According to him, the use of *ḥzh* and its derivatives in the OT is restricted to denoting the prophetic perception of a divine voice, usually at night but not in dream.[29] The three instances of the verb *ḥzh* in Proverbs, however, have no notion related to prophets or receiving revelation. In 22:29 and 29:20, the verb denotes perception through the sight of the eye in the normal sense: in both places it begins a question "Do you see (*ḥāzîtā*) a man . . . ?" The use of the verb *rʾh* in the same way in 26:12 ("Do you see [*rāʾîtā*] a man . . . ?") indicates that no distinction between *ḥzh* and *rʾh* (13 times in Proverbs) is possible in Proverbs. In addition to this, *ḥzh* occurs in synonymous parallelism with *rʾh* in 24:32.

A link between collections III and V is indicated by the same beginning, "Do you see a man . . . ?" in 22:29 and 29:20.

(3) The Relationship
between Collections III and V

זלל	11/3	to be light	III-2	V-1
עוף	26/3	to fly	III-2	V-1
קיא	9/2	to vomit up	III-1	V-1

Three verbs occur exclusively in collections III and V, and the use of *zll* and *qyʾ* in the two collections will be examined.

A. *Zll* "to be thoughtless, worthless" (three times)[30]

Zll is a rare word occurring seven times in the OT with the meaning "to be thoughtless" (this meaning is questionable in Jer 2:36). In Proverbs the verb occurs three times, all in the father-son context. In 23:20–21 the father admonishes his son to avoid association with drunkards and gluttons (*zôlălê băśăr*) because poverty is their destiny. *Zll* in 28:7 is also used in the father-son context. Considering the fact that the verb *zll* is never used in the father-son context elsewhere in the OT except in Deut 21:20,[31] the use of *zll* in collections III and V is considered consistent.

B. *Qyʾ* "to vomit" (twice)[32]

The verb *qyʾ* occurs nine times in the OT: four times in Leviticus, twice in Proverbs, and once each in Jeremiah, Job, and Jonah. It is noted in those instances that the use of the verb outside Proverbs is always figurative, except the instance in Jonah 2:11 in which the fish vomits the prophet onto the land. In the figurative use of the verb, land vomits out people (Lev 18:25, 28 [2x]; 20:22), nations drink from the symbolic cup of God's wrath and also symbolically vomit (Jer 25:27), and an evil man swallows wealth and vomits it out (Job 20:15). In Proverbs, however, vomiting is a real act connected to eating the meal of an insincere host (23:8) and excessive eating of honey (25:16). The two instances are not sufficient to establish any link between the two collections.

(4) The Relationship
between Collections III and VI

| נָחָשׁ | 31/2 | serpent | III-1 | VI-1 |
| נֶשֶׁר | 26/3 | eagle | III-1 | VI-2 |

Năḥăš "serpent" (twice)
and *nešer* "eagle" (three times)[33]

"Serpent" and "eagle" are the only two words that occur exclusively in collections III and VI. *Năḥăš* occurs twice in Proverbs: in 23:32 the effect of wine is compared to the biting of a serpent (*năḥăš*) and in 30:19 the way of a serpent (*năḥăš*) on a rock is mentioned as one of four incomprehensible things.

Nešer appears three times in Proverbs. The flight of the eagle (*nešer*) in 23:5 is figurative to represent the transience of wealth. In 30:17 the eagle appears as a scavenging bird over the dead body of a disobedient son, and in 30:19 the way of the eagle in the sky is mentioned as a mystery.

Although the serpent and eagle are mentioned only in collections III and VI, no resemblance is found in the usage of the two nouns in the two collections.

4. Exclusive Words in Collection IV

גָּדֵר	14/1	wall	חָרוּל	3/1	kind of weed
עתד	2/1	to be ready	קִמָּשׂוֹן	1/1	thistles

Four words (1 verb and 3 nouns) occur exclusively in collection IV, and the three nouns, *qimmāšôn, ḥārûl, gādēr*, are found in one text (24:31). The text is part of the sage's teaching on laziness (24:30–34), in which he describes his observation of the sluggard's field and vineyard that were covered with over-grown weeds and the stone wall was in ruin. Whybray points out that there are similar teaching stories in the OT, and that those stories share common features and a common vocabulary.[1] Of the four exclusive words in collection IV, the use of the three nouns in 24:31 will be examined below.

A. Words for Weeds: *ḥārûl* and *qimmāšôn* (24:31)

Table 4.1
Words for Weeds

Word	Freq.	Meaning	I	II	III	IV	V	VI	VII
ḥēdeq	2/1	brier	1						
ḥôaḥ	10/1	brier					1		
ḥārûl	3/1	weed				1			
ṣēn	2/1	thorn	1						
qimmāšôn	1/1	weed				1			

Table 4.1 shows that the five words for weeds are rare in the OT, especially, four of them occurring three times or less. The occurrence of words for weeds in Proverbs is confined to three collections (II, IV, and V). A survey of the instances of the five terms in the OT shows that they occur only in poetic texts. One common aspect of the five words is indicated in their use in Proverbs: they are always used in connection with four undesirable types of people to describe the dire consequences of their laziness or crookedness:

ḥēdeq with ʿāṣēl "sluggard" (15:19)
ḥôaḥ with šikkôr "drunkard" (26:9)
ḥārûl with ʿāṣēl "sluggard"/ḥăsar lēb "mindless fool" (24:30–31)
ṣēn with ʿeqqēš "crooked" (22:5)
qimmāšôn with ʿāṣēl "sluggard"/ḥăsar lēb "mindless fool" (24:30–31)

The comparison shows that the sluggard (ʿāṣēl) is more frequently associated with weeds (ḥēdeq, ḥārûl, and qimmāšôn).

B. Gādēr "stone wall" (24:31)

Gādēr occurs 14 times in the OT to refer to a stone wall built without using mortar.[2] Various types of walls are called gādēr in the OT: a wall around a vineyard (Num 22:24; Ps 80:13; Isa 5:5), a city wall for protection (Ezek 13:5; 22:30; Mic 7:11; Ezr 9:9), walls in the temple area (Ezek 42:7, 10), a wall that a man can break easily (Eccl 10:8), and a wall to confine a person (Hos 2:8). In Prov 24:31 gādēr occurs in a self-explanatory phrase, geder ʾăbānāyw "wall of its (vineyard) stones," indicating that the wall is made with stones only, without using mortar. The stone wall is intended to protect the plants and their fruits in the vineyard from being devoured or trampled down by animals.[3]

5. Exclusive Words in Collection V

a. Verbs (42)

אנח	12/1	to sigh, groan	בהל	39/1	to be disturbed
בוס	12/1	to trample	דלק	9/1	to burn
הגה	4/2	to remove	הדר	6/1	to honor
חדד	2/2	to sharpen	חסד	1/1	to be ashamed
חרר	11/1	to be hot	ידה	117/1	to give thanks
יקר	11/1	to be precious	כלם	38/2	to be humiliated
כתש	1/1	to pound	לאה	19/1	to be weary
להלה	1/1	to amaze	מעד	8/1	to slip, slide
נדד	27/1	to retreat, flee	נוד	26/1	to wander
נוס	157/2	to flee	סבב	162/1	to go around
סחף	2/1	to prostrate	עדה	9/1	to pass on
עלם	27/1	to conceal	עתק	9/1	to move
עתר	2/1	to be abundant	פנק	1/1	to indulge
צלח	55/1	to prosper	צפה	47/1	to lay over
קצה	5/1	to cut off	קשה	28/2	to be hard
רחם	47/1	to love	רמה	8/1	to deceive
שׂכר	20/2	to hire	שׁבח	3/1	to soothe
שׁיר	86/1	to sing	שׁכם	66/1	to start early
שׁנן	9/1	to sharpen	שׁפל	30/2	to be low
שׁקה	61/1	to cause to drink	שׁקק	3/1	to run
שׁרת	62/1	to serve	שׁתק	4/1	to be silent

b. Adjectives/Nouns (87)

אָחוֹר	41/1	backwards	אַכְזְרִיּוּת	1/1	cruelty
אָלָה	37/1	oath	אֹפֶן	1/1	circumstance
בַּרְזֶל	76/2	iron	גֶּשֶׁם	35/2	rain

דַּי	39/2	sufficiency	דַּךְ	4/1	crushed
דְּרוֹר	2/1	swallow	זֵק	3/1	sparks, missile
דֶּשֶׁא	14/1	herb, grass	חָבֵר	12/1	companion
חוֹחַ	10/1	brier	חוֹל	23/1	sand
חָזוֹן	35/1	vision	חֲלִי	2/1	ornament
חֲמוֹר	96/1	donkey	חֶסֶר	2/1	poverty
חָצִיר	22/1	green grass	חֵקֶר	12/2	searching
חֲרָדָה	9/1	fear, anxiety	כָּבֵד	41/1	heavy
כֹּבֶד	4/1	heaviness	כֶּבֶשׂ	107/1	lamb
כֶּלֶב	32/2	dog	כֶּתֶם	9/1	gold
מִדְחֶה	1/1	stumbling	מַהֲלָל	1/1	praise
מִטָּה	29/1	bed	מָטָר	38/2	rain
מַכְתֵּשׁ	2/1	mortar	מָנוֹן	1/1	grief?
מַעֲדָן	3/1	delight	מַעְצָר	1/1	control
מַעֲשַׁקָּה	2/1	extortion	מֵפִיץ	1/1	disperser
מַפֵּלָת	11/1	overthrow	מַרְגֵּמָה	1/1	sling
מַשָּׁאוֹן	1/1	guile	מֶתֶג	5/1	bridle
מַתָּת	6/1	gift	נֵזֶר	25/1	crown
נַחַת	5/1	rest	נֵטֶל	1/1	burden, weight
נֹעַר	4/1	youth	נָשִׂיא	4/1	vapor, mist
נְשִׁיקָה	2/1	kiss	נֶשֶׁךְ	12/1	interest
נֶתֶר	2/1	soda	סַגְרִיר	1/1	steady rain
סִיג	7/2	dross	עֵדֶר	38/1	flock, herd
עָוֶל	21/1	injustice	עֵז	74/1	goat
עָיֵף	17/1	faint, weary	עֱלִי	1/1	pestle
עֹרֶף	33/1	neck	עַתּוּד	29/1	goat
פֶּחָם	3/1	coal	פִּסֵּחַ	14/1	lame
צֹאן	273/1	flock	צִיר	1/1	hinge
צָמֵא	9/1	thirsty	צִנָּה	1/1	coolness
צָפוֹן	152/1	north	קָא	1/1	vomit
קְלָלָה	33/2	curse	קֵן	13/1	nest
קָרָה	5/1	cold	רַב	1/1	archer?
רִיפָה	2/1	grain? fruit?	רָעֵב	21/2	hungry
שׁוֹט	11/1	whip	שׁוֹק	19/1	leg
שְׁחוּת	1/1	pit	שַׁחַל	7/1	lion

שַׁחַת	23/1	pit	שֶׁטֶף	7/1	flood
שִׁיר	77/1	song	שִׁכּוֹר	13/1	drunken
שָׁכֵן	18/1	neighbor	תַּפּוּחַ	6/1	apple
תְּאֵנָה	39/1	fig-tree	תְּכָכִים	1/1	oppression
תָּם	15/1	complete	תַּרְבִּית	6/1	interest
תְּרוּמָה	76/1	contribution			

A total of 129 words (42 verbs and 87 adjectives/nouns) are exclusive to collection V. Of the 129 words, words that belong to animals and rain are considered peculiar to collection V, and the use of those words will be examined below.

A. Words for Animals
Table 5.1
Animals in Proverbs

Word	Freq.	Meaning	I	II	III	IV	V	VI	VII
děrôr	2/1	swallow					1		
nešer	26/3	eagle			1			2	
ʿōrēb	10/1	raven						1	
ṣippôr	40/4	bird	2				2		
zarzîr	1/1	rooster?					1		
němālâ	2/2	ant	1				1		
ʾarbê	24/1	locust					1		
ʾelep	8/1	cattle			1				
běhēmâ	190/2	cattle			1		1		
ʿēder	38/1	flock					1		
ṣōʾn	273/1	flock					1		
kebeś	107/1	lamb					1		
yaʿălâ	1/1	female goat	1						
ʿēz	74/1	goat					1		
ʿattûd	29/1	male goat					1		
tayiš	4/1	male goat						1	
keleb	32/2	dog					2		
ḥăzîr	7/1	swine			1				
ḥămôr	96/1	donkey					1		
sûs	137/2	horse			1		1		
šôr	79/3	bull	1	2					
nāḥāš	31/2	serpent				1		1	
ṣipʿônî	4/1	serpent				1			
śěmāmît	1/1	lizard						1	

'ayyālâ	11/1	doe	1		
ṣĕbî	12/1	gazelle	1		
'ălûqâ	1/1	leech			1
šāpān	4/1	rock-badger			1
dōb	12/2	bear	1	1	
'ărî	35/3	lion	1	2	
kĕpîr	31/3	young lion	2	1	
layiš	3/1	lion			1
šaḥal	7/1	lion		1	

Table 5.1 shows that 33 words for various animals occur in Proverbs. The animals in the table can be divided into five groups: birds, insects, domestic animals, reptiles, and wild animals. Table 5.1 shows that collections V and VI contain more terms of animals than other collection. If one considers the size of each collection of Proverbs, collection VI, a one-chapter collection, is outstanding among all the collections because of the heavy concentration of the animals terms in it (12 terms). The heavy concentration of those words in collection VI is due to the numerical sayings in which various animals are mentioned as vehicles to convey the meanings of wisdom sayings. Before discussing the significance of Collection V in regard to the words for animals, the use of animals in Proverbs will be surveyed briefly.

The significance of domestic animals in the wisdom context is that a person's wisdom and righteousness are measured not only by his sagacious dealings with other human beings but also by his proper relationship with his own animals: "A righteous man knows the need of his flock" (12:10). The wild animals (the lion and bear) are used in Proverbs to signify great fear and terror: a fool refuses to go out from the house because a lion ('ărî and šaḥal) is in the streets (22:13; 26:13), a roaring lion ('ărî) and rampant bear (dōb) are the image of a wicked ruler over poor people (28:15), and a king's wrath in 19:12 and 20:2 is comparable to the roar of a lion (kĕpîr). Also, two types of lion represented by kĕpîr and layiš are mentioned to convey fearless confidence (28:1; 30:30). In 17:12 the danger of encountering a fool is comically exaggerated by saying that such an encounter is more dangerous than meeting a bereaved bear.

It is noted in the instances of animal terms that the sage takes advantage of certain features of animals to highlight human foolishness. The more common animal features utilized by the sage for the purpose are insensitivity to danger, stubbornness, and habitual repetition. A naive young man who goes after an adulteress is compared to an ox (šôr) to be slaughtered and a bird (ṣippôr) flying into a trap (7:21–23). In this comparison the three (the naive young man, ox, and bird) share one common feature: they are not aware of the immanent death that awaits them. The flight of a bird (ṣippôr) and swallow (dĕrôr) is sometimes taken as a symbol of an aimless or wandering attitude (26:2; 27:8). Despite the many good qualities of a dog (keleb), the sage has observed one of its negative

behaviors (habitual repetition) which could be applied to the fool for a pedagogical purpose: "As a dog returns to its vomit, so a fool repeats his folly"
(26:11). In 26:3 the control of a fool is compared to the control of a horse (sûs)
or a donkey (ḥămôr): "A whip for the horse and a bridle for the donkey, and a
rod for the backs of fools." Whybray aptly describes the common element between the three in the following way: "What fools have in common with the
horse and the ass is lack of understanding: persuasion is ineffective for them,
and coercion is the only fitting treatment."[1]

The following presentation is an attempt to summarize the use of the animals in Proverbs according to the features of the animals:

    a.   Valuable animals
        šôr (14:4; 15:17), ʾelep (14:4), bĕhēmâ (12:10), ʿēder (27:23), ṣōʾn
        (27:23), kebeś (27:26), ʿēz (27:27), ʿattûd (27:26)
    b.   Animals as symbol of fear
        ʾărî (22:13; 26:13; 28:15), kĕpîr (19:12; 20:2), šaḥal (26:13), dōb
        (17:12; 28:15), keleb (26:17)
    c.   Animals associated with wisdom
        nĕmālâ (6:6; 30:25), šāpān (30:26), śĕmāmît (30:28), ʾarbê (30:27)
    d.   Animals representing confidence
        kĕpîr (28:1), layiš (30:30), zarzîr (30:31), tayiš (30:31)
    e.   Animals associated with fools
        ṣippôr (7:23), šôr (7:23), ḥăzîr (11:22), keleb (26:11), sûs (26:3),
        ḥăămôr (26:3)
    f.   Animals capable of escaping from danger
        ṣippôr (6:5), ṣĕbî (6:5)
    g.   Birds symbolizing wandering
        ṣippôr (26:2; 27:8), dĕrôr (26:2)
    h.   Animals symbolizing a loving wife
        ʾayyalâ (5:19), yaʿălâ (5:19)
    i.   Scavenging birds
        ʿōrēb (30:17), nešer (30:17)
    j.   Serpents associated with wine
        nāḥāš (23:32), ṣipʿōnî (23:32)
    k.   An animal with an unending appetite
        ʿălûqâ (30:15)

The significance of collection V with regard to animals is that more than
one-third of the animal terms in Proverbs are found in the collection (14 of 33).
Considering that collection V is shorter than collections I and II, the presence of
the 14 animal terms in collection V appears to be one of its characteristics. Of
the 14 animals mentioned in collection V, eight are domestic animals and three
are lions. The eight domestic animals are viewed as valuable household properties which require the caring attention of the owner because they supply neces-

sities for the whole family.[2] For example, the strength of an ox (*šôr*) is said to produce abundant income (14:4), and in 27:23–27 one is instructed to pay attention to his flock (*ṣoʾn*) and cattle (*ʿēder*) because lambs (*kebeś*) provide wool for clothing, male goats (*ʿattûd*) can be used to buy land, and goats (*ʿēz*) provide milk for the whole household.[3]

The mention of the lion and bear in Proverbs is to be considered significant because of the fact that those animals once roamed in ancient Israel before the deforestation of the land.[4] For this reason, lion- or bear-sayings may have been composed in an earlier period of Israel. This view becomes more reasonable when one considers that the terms for the lion and bear are almost exclusive to two Solomonic collections (II and V).

B. Words for Rain

One of the features of collection V is the frequent sayings involving agriculture and weather. Whybray's explanation of the use of the agricultural terms in collection V is that the sayings which reflect agricultural life had originally been independent and self-contained proverbs before becoming wisdom sayings through the editorial process.[5] His view seems to be valid if one considers the fact that those terms mainly occur in similes and metaphors. The peculiarity of the agricultural terms, such as the terms for domestic animals, grass, and temperature, is that many of them occur only in collection V.[6] The words for rain which will be discussed below are part of the agricultural vocabulary found only in collection V. Four words are employed in Proverbs to denote rain: *sagrîr*, *gešem*, *māṭār*, and *malqôš*, and the first three are exclusive to collection V.

a. *Sagrîr* "persistent rain" (27:15)

Sagrîr is a *hapax legomenon* in the OT. Delitzsch points out that the word was in common use in postbiblical Hebrew and Jewish Aramaic.[7] His description of *sagrîr* as continuous and heavy rain is similar to the continuous rain which G. Dalman describes in detail from his experience in Palestine in 1900.[8] The implication in 27:15 is that the annoying dripping from the roof is caused by the heavy and unbroken rain represented by *sagrîr*.

b. *Gešem* "rain" (25:14, 23)

Gešem is one of the 15 words to refer to rain in the OT, and is the second most general term (35 times) for rain next to *māṭār* (38 times). It is said in Gen 7:12 that God sent *gešem* to the earth for 40 days and nights to start the flood. It is also noted that *gešem* is more favored than *māṭār* in Prophetic books (16 times to 7 times). In Proverbs *gešem* occurs twice in association with wind (25:14, 23): if clouds and wind do not produce rain (*gešem*), it is a very unusual and disappointing phenomenon (25:14), and a north wind usually brings rain (25:23). The sage observed the two natural phenomena, and utilized them in wisdom sayings to bring out relevant moral lessons.

c. *Māṭār* "rain" (26:1; 28:3)

R. B. Y. Scott points out that *māṭār* is the most general term for rain in the OT.[9] Its distribution in the OT shows that the authors of Deuteronomy and Job preferred it over *gešem* (in Deuteronomy *māṭār* 6 times but no occurrence of *gešem* and in Job *māṭār* 7 times and *gešem* twice). As in the case of *gešem*, two natural phenomena involving *māṭār* prompted the sage to compose sayings in reference to a fool (26:1) and the oppression of the poor (28:3). According to Scott, rain showers in April and early May are rare in Palestine, so if they come, they are regarded as a gift from God,[10] but snow in summer and rain (*māṭār*) in harvest time are extremely unfit phenomena. This irregular phenomenon is used by the sage to point out the unfitting relationship between a fool and honor in 26:1. In 28:3 a poor man oppressing other poor men (possibly by stealing food) is compared to disastrous torrential rain that sweeps away food.

6. The Exclusive Words and Unity of Collection VI

a. Verbs (13)

אָשֵׁם	36/1	to be guilty	כחשׁ	22/1	to deceive
בעל	16/1	to marry	חצץ	3/1	to dive
טרף	25/1	to tear	יהב	33/2	to give
יכל	193/1	to be able to	לשׁן	2/1	to slander
נבל	25/1	to be foolish	נקר	6/1	to pick, bore
פלא	27/1	be wonderful	רחץ	72/1	to wash
תפשׂ	65/2	to grasp			

b. Adjectives/Nouns (33)

אֱלוֹהַּ	57/1	God	אַלְקוּם	1/1	troop?
אִמְרָה	37/1	word, speech	אַרְבֶּה	24/1	locust
אַרְבַּע	154/5	four	גְּבֶרֶת	15/1	lady, queen
הֵיכָל	80/1	palace	זָרְזִיר	1/1	girded?
חֶמְאָה	11/1	curd	חֹפֶן	6/1	palm of hand
יְקָהָה	2/1	obedience	לַיִשׁ	3/1	lion
מַאֲכֶלֶת	4/1	knife	מִיץ	3/3	squeezing
מְתַלְּעוֹת	3/1	jawbone	נְאֻם	373/1	utterance
סֶלַע	56/1	crag, cliff	עֲלוּקָה	1/1	leech
עַלְמָה	7/1	young woman	עֹצֶר	3/1	restraint
עֹרֵב	10/1	raven	צֹאָה	5/1	filth
צוּר	74/1	rock	קָטֹן	101/1	small
רֶחֶם	32/1	womb	שִׂמְלָה	29/1	garment
שְׂמָמִית	1/1	lizard	שָׁוְא	53/1	emptiness
שָׁלוֹשׁ	430/4	three	שִׁפְחָה	63/1	maid-servant

202

שָׁפָן   4/1   rock-badger   שְׁתַּיִם   252/2   two
תַּיִשׁ   4/1   goat

Forty-six words (13 verbs and 33 adjectives/nouns) occur exclusively in collection VI. The peculiarity of collection VI in connection with the exclusive words is that it has the highest rate of exclusive words in proportion to its size. The following are the ratios of the exclusive words and verses of the collections:

Collection I	256 verses	169 exclusive words	(one in 1.5 verse)
Collection II	375 verses	243 exclusive words	(one in 1.5 verse)
Collection III	70 verses	44 exclusive words	(one in 1.6 verse)
Collection IV	12 verses	4 exclusive words	(one in 3 verses)
Collection V	138 verses	129 exclusive words	(one in 1.1 verse)
Collection VI	33 verses	46 exclusive words	(one in 0.7 verse)
Collection VII	31 verses	26 exclusive words	(one in 1.2 verse)

The presence of more exclusive words in collection VI seems mainly due to the subject matter. The five numerical sayings in 30:15–33 employ various terms for animals, numbers, and persons, and many of them are not found in other collections. For example, it is surprising that the three basic numbers in counting, two (feminine form), three, and four, are not found elsewhere in Proverbs except collection VI. Other categories of the exclusive words in collection VI are the terms to denote various types of people (*šipḥâ* "maid-servant," *gĕberet* "lady," *'almâ* "young woman," and *'alqûm* "troop of soldiers?"), the terms for the parts of the body (*raḥab* "womb," *ḥôpen* "hollow of the hand," and *mĕtallôt* "jawbone"), and the terms related to speech (*'imrâ* "word," *nĕ'um* "utterance," and *lšn* "to slander").

At this point, we want depart from the discussion of the exclusive words in order to consider the literary unity of collection VI (chapter 30). The argument for the unity of chapter 30 is necessary for this study in establishing a connection between collections VI and VII later. Although there is only one heading for chapter 30, it is a common practice among the interpreters of Proverbs to divide the collection at least into two units, 30:1–14 and 30:15–33. Two factors justify this division. First, the LXX separates the text in that way by placing 30:1–14 between collections III (22:17—24:22) and IV (24:23–34). Secondly, a different type of wisdom sayings (numerical sayings) appears from v. 15, marking a departure from the first unit (30:1–14). Interpreters are further divided on how many verses in the first unit (30:1–14) actually belong to Agur, a character mentioned in the heading (30:1). According to Whybray, there are four different views on the extent of Agur's authorship: vv. 1–3, vv. 1–4, vv. 1–9, and vv. 1–33.[1] Since many commentators approach 30:1–14 as a collection of miscellaneous sayings, it is difficult for them to discover any continuity or progression of thought in the unit. However, there are some who attempt to read 30:1–14 as one unit or even the entire chapter as one unit. For example, R. J. Clifford, who considers the division of chapter 30 in the LXX not as significant as others think, offers a coherent reading of 30:1–14, and takes the entire chapter as a unit.[2] According to him, Agur is the speaker of vv. 2–10, and vv. 11–14 functions as a bridge between vv. 1–10 and 15–33. Instead of the view that holds the chapter as a collection of unrelated sayings, a coherent reading like the one offered by Clifford would do justice to the editor of the MT, because, when he placed the sayings under one heading, his intention may have been to present them as a unit. Therefore, the efforts to find the genuine sayings of Agur would be less meaningful than the efforts to find the principles by which the editor had arranged the sayings as a whole. The legitimacy of the second position is supported by the view that the order of the text in the MT is superior to the order in the LXX.[3] If the division of chapter 30 in the LXX is an indication that the order of the material was not yet fixed at the time of the translation, it is compelling for us to look for the reasons why the editor of the MT joined the two units together (30:1–14 and 15–33).

First of all, one can find the common linguistic features between 30:1–14 and 30:15–33, and it is possible to suggest that such verbal affinities encouraged the editor of the MT to connect the two units together. Some of the common linguistic features between 30:1–14 and 15–33 are as follows:

1. *yaqê* and *yĕqāhâ* (vv. 1 and 17)[4]
2. The first person singular subject "I" (vv. 2, 7–9, and 18)
3. "I do not know" ([*lō˒*] *˒ēda˓* in v. 3 and *lō˒ yĕda˓tîm* in v. 18)
4. *šĕttayim* (vv. 7 and 15)[5]
5. *pen/lō˒* + *śb˓* ... *˒mr* (vv. 9 and 15–16)
6. *tpś* (only in vv. 9 and 28 in Proverbs)
7. *˒āb* + *˒ēm* (vv. 11 and 17)
8. "Washing filth" and "wiping the mouth" (vv. 12 and 20)
9. "Haughty eyes" and "mocking eyes" (vv. 13 and 17)
10. The repetition of a key word (vv. 11–14, 21–23, 33)

There are also two important literary elements in 30:1–14, which demand to read the unit (vv. 1–14) as a whole: two questions about God (vv. 4 and 9) and the identical structure of vv. 6 and 10:[6]

    v.4   *mah šĕmô ûmāh šem bĕnô*
         "What is his name and the name of his son?"
    v.9   *mî YHWH* ... *šēm ˒ĕlōhāy*
         "Who is the Lord? ... the name of my God"
    v.6   *˒al tôsp* ... *pen yôkîah bĕkā wĕnikzabtā*
         "Do not add ..., lest he reprove you and you be proved a liar"
    v.10 *˒al talšēn* ... *pen yĕqallelĕkā wĕ˒āšamtā*
         "Do not slander ... lest he curse you and you be held guilty"

In a coherent reading under the title, "The Words of Agur" (30:1), it is possible to understand that the intention of v. 9 is to provide the answer to the question in v. 4. One may think that linking the two verses in such a way is not probable because Agur was a foreigner. However, when we consider the pious foreigners in the OT, like Balaam, Job, and his three friends, it is not impossible to think that the intention of the editor was to present Agur as a pious believer of the Lord by recasting him in the context of Israelite religion. For two reasons, it is suggested that Agur is presented in Proverbs as a pious Gentile who knows the Lord. First, the resemblance between 9:10 and Agur's speech in 30:3 strongly implies that he is expected to know the Lord:

> 9:10 *tĕhillat ḥokmâ yir'at YHWH wĕda'at qĕdōšîm bînâ*
> "Fear of the Lord is the beginning of wisdom,
>   and the knowledge of the Holy One is understanding"
> 30:3 *wĕlō' lāmadtî ḥokmâ wĕda'at qĕdōšîm 'ēdā'*
> "I have not learned wisdom,
>   and I do not know the knowledge of the Holy One"

It is noted in the comparison of 9:10 and 30:2–3 that three main wisdom terms, *ḥokmâ*, *da'at*, and *bînâ*, and the divine epithet *qĕdōšîm* occur in both texts. Significant is the occurrence of the uncommon phrase *da'at qĕdōšîm* in 9:10 and 30:3. This phrase referring to the Lord is found nowhere else in the entire OT. The resemblance between 9:10 and 30:2–3 is too great to be coincident. The occurrence of *YHWH* and *qĕdōṣîm* as pair words in 9:10 implies that a person who knows one of the two terms is expected to know the other. It is thus suggested that the resemblance between 9:10 and 30:2–3 is the evidence for the transformation of Agur by the editor to place him in the context of Israelite religion.

Secondly, the significant similarities between Proverbs 30 and the book of Job also suggest that the editor's intent was to present Agur as a pious Gentile who knew the Lord. It is a well-known fact that Agur's speech in Proverbs 30 bears resemblance to other biblical books. Interpreters commonly point out that the language of Prov 30:1–6 alludes to the passages in the following books: Num 24:3, 15; 2 Sam 23:1; Ps 18:31 (=2 Sam 22:31); Ps 73:22; Deut 4:2; 30:11–14; Isa 40:12–14.[7] However, as we shall see below, the degree of the thematic and literary similarities of Proverbs 30 to Job is far greater than to any other biblical books in the OT. The two most significant common features in Proverbs 30 and Job are: (a) the main figures are foreigners and (b) various divine names are used in both places. It is well known that Prov 30:1–9 is the only place in Proverbs where no less than five different divine names are used: *'ēl*, *qādôš*, *'ĕlôah*, *YHWH*, and *'ĕlōhîm*. Significantly, all these five names also occur in Job. The notable difference between Prov 30:1–9 and Job in using divine names is that *šadday* is lacking in Proverbs while it is frequently used in Job (see

Table 1.15). The following is a summary of the similarities between Proverbs 30 and Job, which are considered significant:

1. Agur as a foreign sage (Job and his friends)
2. Agur's seemingly humble but assertive attitude (Job and his friends)
3. Questions expecting the Lord as the only answer
   (Prov 30:4; Job 38–41)
4. Use of a variety of divine names (Prov 30:1–9; Job 1–41)
5. Request for two things (Prov 30:7; Job 13:20)
6. Teeth (*šēn*)/jawbones (*mĕtallôt*) devouring the poor
   (Prov 30:14; Job 29:17)
7. "Too wonderful from me . . . . I do not know" (Prov 30:18; Job 42:23)
8. Putting the hand over the mouth as a reaction of surprise
   (Prov 30:32; Job 40:4)

A more detailed discussion of resemblance between Proverbs 30 and Job is beyond the scope of this study, but on the basis of the summary alone, it is certain that Proverbs 30 is closer to Job than to any other books in the OT.

We now return to the discussion of 30:1–14 to examine the relationship between 30:6 and 10. Some commentators think that verse 10 is an orphan in the chapter because of its unrelated theme in the context. If the view was correct, then, it would be the only independent single verse among the multi-verse sayings in 30:1–14. It is, however, inconceivable that an editor or a collector would place a short saying between two long units (30:7–9 and 30:11–14), without any connection to the previous or following unit. Some interpreters connect v. 10 to v. 11, using the principle of catchword ("curse" in vv. 10 and 11), in order to explain the presence of v. 10 in the context of 30:1–14. However, the presence of v. 10 in the current place in connection with v. 6 would be better explained on the basis of the structure and context of the two verses.[8] First of all, v. 10 shows great resemblance to v.6. Both verses have an identical structure (*'al* + impf. + indirect/direct obj. + *pen* + impf. + pro. suf. + pf.). Also, the two verses are similar in the sense that they are about the amplifying character of human speech: adding to God's word (v.6) and slandering a servant to his master (v. 10). More significant is the possibility of the interpretation that v. 10 is connected to the previous verses in the context. Although we do not agree with Crenshaw's view that v. 10 is a warning issued by a third speaker to defend Agur from the attack of a second speaker in vv. 7–9,[9] we do agree with him on the point that the servant and Master in v. 10 refer to Agur and God respectively. Since the chapter begins with three words which usually belong to the vocabulary of prophecy (*dibrê*, *maśśā'*, and *nĕ'um*), Agur appears to have been a figure like Balaam, a foreign prophet or sage with the knowledge of YHWH.[10] Then, v. 10 is understood as a warning that, if anyone slanders Agur (God's servant) to his Master, the person will be cursed by the Lord (his Master).

It is now appropriate for us to present another important clue for a coherent reading of the entire chapter (ch. 30).[11] As previously pointed out, the occurrences of the 12 animal terms in collection VI are concentrated in 30:15–33. Although no animals are mentioned in the first half of the chapter (30:1–14), there is an important word in 30:1–14, which relates to the animals in 30:15–33. In 30:2 Agur says, "I am more a beast (*ba 'ar*) than a man" (McKane's translation), and confesses that he does not possess human discernment. *Ba 'ar* which is derived from *bĕ 'îr* "cattle" occurs in Ps 73:22 in a synonymous parallelism with *bĕhēmâ*, a collective noun to denote domestic and wild animals. Although Agur appears humble when he says that he is more a beast than a man, and that he does not possess wisdom and the knowledge of the Holy One, the following questions and the overall context of the unit clearly indicate that he is speaking in a tongue-in-cheek way. When one opens his/her speech, saying "I do not know anything, but . . . ," the ignorance admitted by the speaker is rarely genuine. In most cases, such a humble confession is mere rhetoric to dramatize the knowledge of the speaker, which will be revealed after the confession. It is obvious in the case of Agur that his humility also is rhetoric. Then, what kind of knowledge does he intend to reveal to surprise others? It is implied in 30:4c ("What is his name? What is his son's name if you know?") that he is the one who knows the answers to the questions as well as the other questions in 30:4.

However, if one considers that Agur identifies himself with *ba 'ar*, and that various animals are mentioned in the following numerical sayings, it is probable that the editor's intention was to connect the two units, 30:1–14 and 30:15–33, with the theme of animal. If anyone claims that he is an animal as Agur does, who would be more qualified to discuss about the animal kingdom than the person? In a unified reading of chapter 30, Agur must be understood as a foreign sage who knows God, with the ability to discuss the affairs of humans and animals.

In one place in chapter 30, we wonder whether there is an underlying message when he praises the wisdom of certain animals. After humbly confessing that he is more an *animal* than a man and that he has not learned *wisdom* (30:2–3), he paradoxically points out that four animals are small but extremely *wise* (30:24–28). Is it possible that Agur here implies that he is wiser than others?

On the basis of this observation, we may conclude that the editor's intention in chapter 30 is to let the pious foreign prophet/sage figure praise the sovereignty of the Lord and condemn the disobedient, proud, cruel, greedy, immoral, and upside-down human world, using his knowledge of the animal kingdom.

Another aspect of Proverbs 30 which calls for an attention is that there are elements which echo the Decalogue in the chapter. Since the subjects, such as honoring the parents, murder, adultery, theft, and false witnessing, are common in wisdom material, it is difficult to determine which sayings in Proverbs actually refer to the Decalogue. For example, when the author says in Prov 1:8, "My son, listen to your father's instruction, and do not forsake your mother's teaching," it would be difficult to tell if the author had the Fifth Commandment in his mind. One may deny any connection between Prov 1:18 and the Decalogue because such a parental instruction is common in international wisdom. However, when Ben Sira explains that children must obey their parents because it is the order in the family established by God, he clearly refers to the Fifth Commandment:

> Children, pay heed to a father's right;
>   do so that you may live.
> For the Lord sets a father in honor over his children;
>   a mother's right he confirms over her sons. (Sir 3:1–2)[12]

In view that Ben Sira combined wisdom and the religion of Israel in his book, it is reasonable to understand that, when Israelite wise men composed sayings about honoring parents, the Fifth Commandment was operative in wisdom as paradigm. Also, it is certain that the Decalogue has played the central role in Israel as the guideline for every sector of life. P. D. Miller implies the versatility of the Decalogue to govern the life of Israelites when he points out the character of the Decalogue in the following way: the Commandments can be summarized, elaborated, and used as a kind of trajectory in other parts of the Bible.[13] It is this adaptable aspect of the Decalogue that is reflected throughout Proverbs. With the understanding of the central role played by the Decalogue in Israel, some of the sayings in Prov 30 can be connected to the Decalogue in the following way:

1. "Do not add to his words" (vv. 5–6)	Commandments I and II[14]
2. Šāwĕʾ . . . šēm ʾĕlōhāy (vv. 8–9)	Commandment III
3. Dĕbar kāzāb (v. 8) and	
"Do not slander . . ." (v. 10)	Commandment IX
4. Gānabtî (v. 9)	Commandment VIII
5. Cursing the parents (vv. 11, 17)	Commandment V
6. Devouring the poor (v. 14)	Commandment VI[15]
7. An adulterous woman (v.20)	Commandment VII

7. Exclusive Words in Collection VII and the Relationship between VI and VII

---

a. Verbs (6)

דִּין	25/1	to judge	זָכַר	222/1	to remember
חָגַר	43/1	to gird	טָעַם	11/1	to taste
נָטַע	58/1	to plant	סָחַר	20/1	to trade

b. Adjectives/Nouns (20)

אַחֲרוֹן	51/1	coming after	אִלֵּם	6/1	dumb
אַרְגָּמָן	38/1	purple	בַּר	4/3	son
הֲלִיכָה	6/1	going, doing	זְרוֹעַ	91/1	arm
חָגוֹר	3/1	belt, girdle	חֲלוֹף	1/1	vanishing
טֶרֶף	22/1	prey, food	כִּישׁוֹר	1/1	distaff
כְּנַעֲנִי	4/1	trader	מֶכֶר	3/1	value
סָדִין	4/1	linen wrapper	עֳנִי	36/1	affliction
עַצְלוּת	1/1	sluggishness	פֶּלֶךְ	2/1	spindle
פֵּשֶׁת	16/1	linen, flax	צֶמֶר	16/1	wool
שָׁנִי	42/1	scarlet	שֵׁשׁ	38/1	linen

Twenty-six words (6 verbs and 20 nouns) occur exclusively in collection VII. Of the 20 nouns, four occur in the first unit (31:1–9) and 16 in the second unit (31:10–31). The 11 of the 16 nouns that appear in 31:10–31 show a common

feature: they are terms related to fabrics and weaving instruments. The following
table shows that textile terms are concentrated in two places in Proverbs (collections I and VII):

Table 7.1
Words for Cloths and Weaving Instruments

Word	Freq.	Meaning	I	II	III	IV	V	VI	VII
ʾēṭûn	1/1	linen	1						
ʾargāmān	38/1	purple							1
beged	215/4	garment	1	1			2		
ḥăgôr	3/1	girdle							1
ḥăṭubâ	1/1	colored cloth	1						
kĕnaʿănî	74/1	tradesman							1
lĕbûš	31/3	garment					1		2
marbad	2/2	coverlet	1						1
sādîn	4/1	linen wrapper							1
pēšet	20/1	linen, flax							1
ṣemer	16/1	wool							1
śimlâ	29/1	garment						1	
šît	2/1	garment	1						
šānî	42/1	scarlet							1
šēš	38/1	linen							1
kîšôr	1/1	distaff							1
pelek	2/1	spindle-whorl							1

It has been pointed out earlier that *marbad*, an expensive bedspread mentioned
only twice in the OT, appears in Proverbs in reference to the adulterous woman
(chapter 7) and the ideal wife (chapter 31), connecting collections I and VII. The
linkage between the two collections is also indicated by other words for cloths
which occur exclusively in the two. Table 7.1 shows that the words for cloths
predominantly occur in collections I and VII. A further investigation reveals that
four of the five terms that occur in collection I are found in the story of the
adulterous woman in 7:10–16. As a result, it can be concluded that, except
beged and *śimlâ*, all the words for cloths and weaving instruments in Proverbs
are associated with either the adulterous woman or the ideal wife.

Before discussing about the relationship between collections VI and VII, it
is necessary to discuss about the unity of collection VII. Like collection VI (ch.
30), collection VII (chapter 31) also is customarily divided into to parts because
of the easily recognizable dividing line between 31:1–9 (a royal instruction by a
queen mother) and 31:10–31 (an acrostic poem describing the achievements of

an ideal wife). Moreover, the order of the text in the LXX strongly suggests that the two parts were originally separate units: in the LXX, collection V (chs. 25–29) stands between 31:1–9 and 31:10–31. If chapter 31 was originally one unit, it would be unlikely that the translator is responsible for dividing the chapter into two.[1] Rather, the order of the text of Proverbs in the LXX implies the existence of a different type of Hebrew text of Proverbs in which the acrostic poem (31:10–31) follows collection V (chs. 25–29).[2] Therefore, as in chapter 30, it is likely that the direct connection of 31:1–9 to 31:10–31 in the MT is a result of the editorial work carried out on certain principles. Recently, building upon the studies of M. H. Lichtenstein and T. P. McCreesh,[3] Victor A. Hurowitz has pointed out that chapter 31 can be read coherently on the basis of the chiastic chain of terms and the chiastic structure of themes in the chapter. According to him, it is possible that the two units (31:1–9 and 10–31) have been subjugated to an attempt to form a continuous composition, and therefore the title in 31:1 should be taken as referring to all of chapter 31.[4] The chiastic arrangement of the terms that Hurowitz has discovered indicates that there are literary links between 31:1–9 and 31:10–31. Since Hurowitz and others have already argued for the cohesiveness of chapter 31, our primary concern here is to examine chapters 30 and 31 in search for possible links between the two chapters (collections VI and VII). If there exists any discernible thematic or literary link between the two chapters, it will be possible to explain the editorial principles by which the editor arranged chapters 30 and 31 as the closing of the book.

First of all, it is noted that the headings of both chapters begin with *dibrê* "words of," which Crenshaw points out as the opening word to introduce either a prophetic utterance or wisdom instruction.[5] Regardless of how the word is understood, it is expected that the contents of the two chapters are the same type of material because in chapters 30 and 31 *dibrê* is followed by *maśśā᾿*, another technical term in the prophetic context. It is striking to note that two personal names which contain a divine name *᾿ēl* "God" appear in the two headings, *᾿îtî᾿el* in 30:1 and *lĕmû᾿ēl* in 31:1. It may be reasonable to conjecture that the religious piety implied in the two names (*᾿îtî᾿ēl* "God is with me" and *lĕmû᾿ēl* "Belonging to God") and the excellent moral contents of the sayings may have facilitated the entry of the two units into the book of Proverbs.

The next common element in the two chapters is a series of questions beginning with "Who" or "What." In 30:4 "Who" is used four times and "What" twice, while "What" appears three times in 31:2. In the two chapters those questions are followed by prohibitions which feature the same structure, *᾿al . . . pen* (30:6, 10; 31:3–5). It is remarkable to note that Agur requests *two* things from God in prayer (30:7–9), while the queen mother forbids *two* things from her son (31:3–4). In ch. 30 a unit (30:11–14) in which each of the four verses begins with the same word *dôr* "generation" follows Agur's request for two things.

The last line of the first half of ch. 30 is 30:14, in which the current generation is described as devouring the needy (*῾ānî*) and the poor (*᾿ebyôn*). Significant is the fact that, when the queen mother admonishes the king in ch. 31 to protect the needy (ʿānî) and the poor (ʾebyôn), the two words (ʿānî and ʾebyôn) appear in the same order in 31:9 which marks the end of the first half of chapter 31.

The second halves of the two chapters also share two common features. First, they are distinctive in their own styles: 30:15–33 is characterized by the numerical sayings and 31:10–31 is characterized by the alphabetic order. Secondly, the two second halves are loaded with their own exclusive terms which belong to the specific domains of the world. In 30:15–33 we find 12 words for animals, 8 of which are found nowhere in Proverbs (cf. Table 5.1). Similarly, we find 12 words for cloths and weaving instruments in 31:10–31, ten of which are not found elsewhere in Proverbs (cf. Table 7.1). On the basis of these observations, the resemblance between chapters 30 and 31 is presented in the following way:

	Chapter 30	**Chapter 31**
I. First Unit		
1. Heading	dibrê . . . maśśāʾ (v. 1)	dibrê . . . maśśāʾ (v.1)
2. Theophoric names	ʾîtîʾēl (v.1)	lĕmûʾēl (v. 1)
3. Questions	mî, mah (v.4)	mah (v.2)
4. Prohibition	ʾal . . . pen (vv. 6, 10)	ʾal . . . pen (vv. 3–5)
5. Two things	Two requests (vv.7–9)	Two prohibitions (vv. 3–4)
a. Poverty	rēʾš (v.8)	riš (v. 7)
b. Deny/forget	khš (v. 9)	škḥ (v. 7)
c. Give	ntn (v. 8)	ntn (v. 6)
6. The poor/needy	ʿānî . . . ʾebyôn (v. 14)	ʿānî and ʾebyôn (v. 9)
II. Second Unit		
1. Distinctive style	Numerical sayings	Acrostic poem
2. Exclusive words	Eight words for animals	Ten words for cloths

Another interesting similarity to be added to the list is the verb mḥh "to wipe" which occurs in 30:20 and 31:3. The verb is used in both texts in connection with women to denote their ability to "wipe out": the adulterous woman in 30:20 *wipes* her mouth to appear as if she did not eat anything (adultery) and in 31:3, despite the difficulty of the text, it is understood that the queen mother warns her son that women can *wipe out* kings.

Having presented the similarities between chapters 30 and 31, we are now in a position to suggest at least two things: first, the two chapters are like twin buildings with the same structure to close the book with the sayings of two pious foreign characters. Second, although the LXX may be a witness to the possibility that the four units, 30:1–14; 30:15–33; 31:1–9; 31:10–31, were originally independent collections, the arrangement of the four units in the MT shows that the editor's intention is to make one read each of the two chapters (chs. 30 and 31) in a unified way. Thus, the book of Proverbs begins and ends with royal sayings: the proverbs of Solomon, King of Israel in the beginning and the words for a foreign king at the end. In addition to this, the editor of Proverbs has compiled the sayings and recast the foreign characters in the context of Israelite religion so that the sayings of different origins (sayings of Solomon, sayings of Israelite and non-Israelite wise men, sayings of Agur, and sayings of a non-Israelite queen mother) could be read as a whole under one heading (1:1).

A Summary and Conclusions

Having examined some of the exclusive words which are considered more significant in the wisdom context, we want to summarize the findings of this study to explain the coherent relationship between collections. In this summary, only the findings which clearly indicate the coherence between the collections will be mentioned.

1. The Relationship between the Three Major Collections (I, II, and V)

(1) Collections I and II

These two collections are evidently linked by the exclusive phrase *tôʿăbat YHWH* "abomination to the Lord" which occurs 11 times in the two collections. The peculiar aspect of the usage of the phrase is indicated by the fact that it is found only in Deuteronomy and Proverbs in the entire OT. This peculiarity of the phrase suggests that its exclusive occurrence in collections I and II is an indication of the coherence between the two collections.

The coherence between the two collections is reinforced by the two other exclusive phrases, *ʾōraḥ ḥayyîm* "way of life" and *ʿēṣ ḥayyîm* "tree of life."

The use of the pair words *ḥārûṣ* "gold" and *kesep* "silver" in connection with the value of wisdom also indicates a coherent aspect of wisdom in the two collections. Other literary elements which are considered significant to support the linkage between collections I and II are:

    a. The use of *qālôn* "shame" with *ḥerpâ* "disgrace"
    b. The use of *leqaḥ* "learning" with the verb *ysp* "to add"
    c. The use of *qrṣ* "to pinch" with *ʿayin* "eye" as a body language

d. The exclusive meaning of *ḥrš* "to devise" and its occurrence in the following phrasing: *lēb* + *ḥrš* + *ra* ⁽

e. The almost exclusive occurrences of the words for perversity (see Table 2.3)

f. The use of *tûšiyyâ* "effective wisdom" and *nĕtîbâ* "path"

g. The use of *kāzāb* "falsehood" in association with the verb *pwḥ* "to breathe."

(2) Collections I, II, and V

The coherence of the three major collections is indicated by two exclusive phrases and four words that belong to wisdom vocabulary. The two phrases are formulaic expressions formed in connection with *šeqer* "lie": *lĕšôn šeqer* "lying tongue" (four times) and ⁽*ēd šeqer* "false witness" (six times). The significance of the four words is twofold: all of them belong to wisdom material and their occurrences in the OT are mainly in the three collections: *tôkaḥat* "reproof" occurs 24 times in the OT, 16 of which are in the three collections, *petî* "naive fool" occurs 19 times in the OT, 15 of which are in the three collections, *kĕsîl* "fool" occurs 70 times in the OT, 49 of which are in the three collections, and ⁽*iqqēš* "twisted" occurs 11 times in the OT, seven of which are in the three collections.

(3) Collections I and V

The 38 exclusive words in the two collections show two peculiarities: the frequencies of the 38 words in Proverbs are very low, ranging from two to four (except *qôl* which occurs seven times), and, of the 38 words, it is rare to find a word that occurs in a similar context. The low frequency of the words suggests less opportunity to find a link between the two collections. This phenomenon appears to support Snell's view in some respects. Based on his study of the repeated sayings in Proverbs, Snell concludes that there is no relation between collections I and V. Although his conclusion may be legitimate as far as the phenomenon of repetition is concerned, the two collections still contain a couple literary elements of coherence. First of all, 6:15b and 29:1b are identical. More significantly, the theme of smooth talk represented by the root *ḥlq* is found only in the two collections (see Table 1.19). No other collections know the danger of the smooth talk represented by the root.

(4) Collections II and V

The close relationship between collections II and V is affirmed by the fact that there are more numerous and substantial similarities between the two than between other collections. The most significant feature that points to the close relationship is the presence of repeated sayings in the two collections. As indicated in Snell's study, the phenomenon of whole-verse repetition is almost exclusive to collections II and V (exceptions are 6:10–11=24:33–34 and 8:35//18:22). This almost unique phenomenon testifies that the relationship between collections II and V is peculiar (see Tables 2.9 and 2.10). It is also significant to note that a considerably large number of key words in the repeated sayings are exclusive to the two collections. This means that the themes which are represented by those words are exclusive to the two collections. For example, the theme of a contentious wife is found five times in Proverbs but only in collections II and V, and lion-sayings also are almost exclusively found in the two collections. The description of the Lord as Creator of the poor and rich is also exclusive to the two collections.

Besides the exclusive words and the numerous sayings of whole-verse repetition, collections II and V share common phrases such as *ḥōnēn dal* "he who is kind to the poor" and *ʿōšēq dal* "he who oppresses the poor." The sin denoted by the words which are derived from the root *pšʿ* (see Table 2.7) also indicates the coherent relationship between the two collections.

One significant thing in connection with whole-verse repetition is that the parallel sayings in collection V show superiority to their counterparts in collection II in terms of poetic style, especially parallelism. It is unlikely that the superior parallelism in collection V is due to the improvement of inferior parallel sayings in collection II. The examination of the parallel saying reveals that there is no possibility of direct borrowing between the two collections. The poorer quality of parallelism in collection II in comparison to collection V may be due to the adaptation of an original saying to emphasize the subject matter in a given context (e.g., 12:11//28:19; cf. *ḥăsar lēb* in 10:13; 11:12; 15:21; 17:18).

2. The Relationship between Other Collections

(1) Collections I, II, and III

A significant exclusive theme that indicates a coherent aspect of the three collections is "fear of the Lord" represented in two ways: the use of the phrase *yirʾat YHWH* and the use of the verb *yrʾ* with *YHWH* as object. The only exception to this phenomenon is 31:30.

The occurrence of several significant wisdom terms in collections I, II, and III also indicates that the three collections contain coherent wisdom elements. The *lēṣ* who is considered the worst fool in Proverbs appears only in the three collections. The verb *tqʿ* occurs four times in the three collections, with the meaning "to clap hands" in the sense to pledge, but never occurs elsewhere in the OT with this technical meaning (except the instance in Job 17:3). *Taḥbulôt*, an important synonym of *ḥokmâ*, occurs only in the three collections. Other words of significance which reflect coherence of the three collections are *ʾōraḥ* "way," *ʾēmer* "word, speech," and the sin denoted by the words derived from the root *ḥṭʾ* (see Table 2.7).

Another important indication for the coherent wisdom climate in collections I, II, and III is the predominant occurrence of wisdom terms in the three. According to Table 1.10, among the 16 words for wisdom in Proverbs, collections I and II each contain 14 words, collection III contains 11, and nine of the 16 words are common to the three collections (four of them are exclusive). This phenomenon clearly indicates the coherent wisdom aspect of the three collections.

(2) Collections I, II, III, and V

The three Solomonic collections (I, II, and V) and collection III of the wise men also share a common wisdom element in regard to folly. The three most frequent terms related to the theme of folly in Proverbs are *kĕsîl* (49 times), *ʾiwwelet* (23 times), and *ʾĕwîl* (19 times), and, significantly, the three terms are exclusive to the four collections (see Table 1.13). This means that the four collections are coherent at least with regard to the theme of folly denoted by the three terms.

(3) Collections I, II, III, and VII

A theme that is common to the four collections is the fear of the Lord which is denoted by *yirʾâ* and *yrʾ* in association with the Lord.

(4) Collections I, II, and IV

The conjoining of *ḥāsēr* and *lēb* creates a unique phrase to refer to a type of fool that is found only in Proverbs in the entire OT. The 11 occurrences of the phrase (*ḥăsar lēb*) in the three collections clearly indicate the coherent wisdom aspect in regard to folly.

(5) Collections I, II, IV, and V

ʿāṣēl is the only word in biblical Hebrew to denote a sluggard, and all of its 14 occurrences in the OT are in the four collections. In this sense, the four collections show coherence.

(6) Collections I, II, IV, V, VI, and VII

Rêš "poverty" is one of the two exclusive words in the six collections. Significant is the fact that the noun is not found elsewhere in the OT. Therefore, it can be said that the six collections are linked by this term.

(7) Collections I, II, and VII

The usage of *pěnînîm* "rubies" in the OT is consistent: the noun is always used in a comparative sense, either to highlight the value of wisdom or the red color of an object. Its consistent usage and the similar context in the three collections indicate the coherent wisdom aspect.

(8) Collections I and III

Collections I and III are linked by the unique usage of the verb *qn'*: the verb always occurs in the negative command not to envy sinners (3:31and 24:1 in which *qn'* occurs are very similar in meaning). Also, the occurrence of the rare verb *lḥm* in the two collections indicates a common wisdom element. The verb denotes eating in a banquet setting with plenty of food.

(9) Collections I and IV

Collection IV is the smallest collection in Proverbs, but is undoubtedly linked to collection I by the identical sayings (6:10–11=24:33–34) embedded in the passage about the *ʿāṣēl* "sluggard."

(10) Collections I and VI

These two collections are the only places in the entire OT where *němālâ* "ant" is mentioned. Moreover, the same literary environment in which the ant is mentioned in association with *kwn*, *qayiṣ*, and *leḥem* in the two collections indicates a coherent wisdom element. Another significant literary element that clearly indicates linkage between collection I and VI is the peculiar phrase *daʿat qědôšîm* "knowledge of the Holy One." As in the case of *němālâ*, the divine epithet *qědôšîm* occurs in a similar literary environment in 9:10 and 30:2–3: the three main wisdom terms (*ḥokmâ*, *bînâ*, and *daʿat*) are commonly found in the two texts. Significant is the fact that the use of the phrase *daʿat qědôšîm* in reference to the Lord is found nowhere else in the OT.

(11) Collections I and VII

It is well known that those who propose a unified reading of Proverbs identify the Lady Wisdom with the ideal wife in chapter 31. It is essential in such a reading to understand that collections I and VII are coherent. Building on this view, this study has emphasized that the thematic and literary affinities between the strange woman in chapter 7 and the ideal wife in chapter 31 are undeniable.

The two ladies are comparable in variously contrasting ways, including the two feminine participles, *hōmiyyâ* and *ṣôpiyyâ*. Significant are the striking similarities between 7:16 and 31:22.

(12) Collections II and III

The coherence of collections II and III is proved by the six pairs of parallel sayings in the two collections (11:14b//24:6b; 13:9b//24:20b; 16:2//21:2//24:12; 20:18b//24:6a; 22:14a//23:27a; 17:18a//22:26a//6:1b). Besides the sayings, the two exclusive expressions, *šûḥâ ʿᾱmuqqâ* "deep pit" (symbolizing the danger of the strange woman) and *tōkēn libbôt* "weighing the heart," also indicate a coherent wisdom aspect of the two collections. It has been pointed out in the examination of the occurrence of *taḥbulôt* "counsel" in 24:6 and 20:18 that 24:6 is composed of 20:18b and 11:14b (20:18b + 11:14b = 24:6). The relationship between the three verses also indicates the link between collections II and III.

(13) Collections II and VI

The frequency of *baʿar* "brutish" and *nᾱbᾱl* "foolish" is low in the OT. The two terms occur exclusively in the two collections in connection with other wisdom terms. This phenomenon suggests a coherent aspect of the collections.

(14) Collections III and V

The verb *zll* "worthless" is used in the two collections in reference to a son in the context where the parents show a serious concern for their disobedient son. Such use of the verb is found nowhere in the OT except its instances in Deuteronomy and Proverbs. The peculiar use of *zll* indicates a link not only between Deuteronomy and Proverbs but also between collections III and V.

(15) Collections I, II, III, and IV

This group of collections includes collection IV which is the smallest in Proverbs (only 12 verses). A significant exclusive word in the four collections is *mûsᾱr* "discipline" which is an important synonym of *ḥokmâ* in Proverbs (cf. 1:2, 7). The noun occurs 30 times (60% of 50 instances in the OT) in the four collections, indicating that the four collections are coherent in using an important wisdom term for education.

(16) Collections VI and VII

One of the major findings of this study is the existence of the close relationship between collections VI and VII. A unified reading of chapters 30 and 31 reveals a striking resemblance between the two chapters in regard to the structure, words, and style. Those literary affinities clearly testify that the two chapters, which had probably existed as four smaller independent units in earlier periods, have been subjected to the same editorial processes in order to appear at the end of Proverbs as twin chapters.

In addition to the close relationship between collections VI and VII, it has been pointed out in this study that the first part of collection VI (30:1–14) contains significant similarities to the book of Job.

3. Religious Aspects of Proverbs

In the absence of serious studies about the relationship between Israelite religion and wisdom, it is not an easy task to select religious terms in Proverbs. However, under the governing principles of this study, which have been proven tenable in Proverbs, it is concluded with caution that most of the traditional religious terms in the OT still retain their religious notions in Proverbs. With regard to the words related to Israelite religion in Table 1.4, it has been emphasized in this study that, when secular and religious meanings are equally possible in the context, it is not necessary to eliminate one in favor of the other. Besides the divine name for the Lord, terms related to religious practices (e.g., prayer, sacrifice, and holiness), terms for various types of sin, terms for blessing and curse, and terms for the notions of righteousness and wickedness can be interpreted in the context of Israelite religion.

Proverbs features various characters, most of whom appear to be Israelites: the parents, the son, and the adulterous woman. Since the Lord is mentioned as the Creator of the poor and rich in the book, they are to be understood as Israelites. The same can be said of the wise men in the book because they frequently appeal to the Lord whenever wisdom is not able to provide solutions for certain moral issues. Although the kings in Proverbs are never called the kings of Israel or Judah (except the instances in 1:1; 25:1), the language used to describe the stability of their thrones is an echo of God's promise to David in 2 Sam 7:13. This also implies that the kings in Proverbs are to be understood as Israelite kings. The insensitive citizen who loudly blesses his neighbor early in the morning is most likely an Israelite (27:14).

Another significant expression to be understood in the context of Israelite religion is *yôm* ʿebrâ "the day of wrath" in Proverbs. Based on the use of the expression in the OT, it has been argued in this study that the expression refers to the Day of the Lord in an eschatological sense. Even when ʿebrâ occurs alone without "day" (11:23), it is most likely that it refers to God's wrath. An eschatological notion is also conveyed by two other expressions, *yēš tiqwâ* "there is hope" (cf. Jer 31:27; Prov 19:18; Job 11:18; 14:7; Ruth 1:12; Lam 3:29) and *ʾaḥărît* "end" + *tiqwâ* "hope" (cf. Jer 31:17; 29:11; Prov 23:18; 24:14).

An integrated understanding of God emerges from the God-sayings in collections I, II, and V: the Lord created the world with wisdom and knowledge, he created everything for its purpose, he is the creator of every constituent member of society, and he is the creator of every part of the human body.

In Proverbs God's omniscience is expressed in three ways: (a) the Lord examines human heart and spirits, (b) the eyes of the Lord see every place, watching the good and evil, and every way of a man is before his eyes, and (c) Sheol (or Abaddon), the most inaccessible and mysterious realm of the dead, cannot be hidden before the Lord.

The sage acknowledges that trusting in the Lord is essential in the world where wisdom alone cannot explain all things. The father admonishes his son not to trust his own understanding but to trust the Lord with all his heart (3:5). The sage says that the goal of his wisdom education is to make the pupil trust in the Lord (22:19).

God is described in Proverbs as the giver and patron of wisdom. Wisdom, knowledge, and understanding are his gifts to humans (2:6). One must learn the fear of the Lord first and everything else afterwards (1:7; 9:10). No human wisdom, understanding, or plan can stand against the Lord (24:30).

Finally, the religious aspect of Proverbs can be affirmed by the relationship of the book to the Decalogue. In view of the central role played by the Decalogue in Israelite society (e.g., the use the Decalogue by prophets), it is difficult to deny that the Decalogue also served as paradigm when the sage composed sayings in regard to obedience to parents and false witness against a neighbor. As an example, the use of the verb *ḥmd* "to desire" in Proverbs has been explained. *Ḥmd* occurs 18 times in the OT, but only in three instances the object of the verb is a woman: twice in the Tenth Commandment (Ex 20:17; Deut 5:21) and once in Prov 6:25. It is, therefore, reasonable to say that, when the father warned his son against the strange woman (another man's wife), he used the language of the Decalogue.

Appendix A

The Groups of the Collections
and the Number of Exclusive Words

I	168	I-V-VII	4
I-II	87	I-VI	8
I-II-III	26	I-VI-VII	2
I-II-III-IV-V	4	I-VII	7
I-II-III-IV	2	II	242
I-II-III-IV-V-VI	7	II-III	19
I-II-III-IV-V-VI-VII	2	II-III-IV	2
I-II-III-IV-V-VII	5	II-III-V	16
I-II-III-V	36	II-III-V-VI	2
I-II-III-V-VI	8	II-III-V-VII	1
I-II-III-V-VI-VII	13	II-III-VI	1
I-II-III-V-VII	7	II-III-VI-VII	1
I-II-III-VI	6	II-III-VII	1
I-II-III-VII	5	II-IV	2
I-II-IV	3	II-IV-V	6
I-II-IV-V	8	II-IV-V-VI	1
I-II-IV-V-VI	1	II-IV-V-VI-VII	1
I-II-IV-V-VI-VII	2	II-V	90
I-II-V	50	II-V-VI	3
I-II-V-VI	11	II-V-VII	3
I-II-V-VI-VII	2	II-VI	14
I-II-V-VII	12	II-VI-VII	1
I-II-VI	8	II-VII	9
I-II-VII	5	III	44
I-III	13	III-IV-V	2
I-III-IV	1	III-IV-V-VII	1
I-III-IV-V	1	III-V	3
I-III-V	5	III-VI	2
I-III-V-VI	1	III-VII	5
I-III-V-VII	1	IV	4
I-III-VI	2	V	129
I-III-VII	2	V-VI	6
I-IV	5	V-VII	5
I-IV-VI	1	VI	46
I-V	38	VI-VII	5
I-V-VI	2	VII	26

Appendix B

Words Occurring Only in Proverbs

1. Verbs

אכף	1	to press, urge	16:26
בחל	1	to get by greed	20:21
גלע	3	to expose	17:14; 18:1; 20:3
חדד	2	to sharpen	27:17, 17
חסד	1	to be ashamed	25:10
חרך	1	to set in motion	12:27
טרד	2	to pursue	19:13; 27:15
כפה	1	to subdue	21:14
כתש	1	to pound	27:22
להלה	1	to amaze	26:18
להם	2	to swallow	18:8; 26:22
עצה	1	to shut	16:30
פוץ	1	to flow	5:16
פנק	1	to indulge	29:21
פרש	1	to pierce	23:32
רבד	1	to deck	7:16
שער	1	to calculate	23:7

2. Nouns

אֲבוֹי	1	Oh!	23:29
אֵטוּן	1	thread, yarn	7:16
אַכְזְרִיוּת	1	cruelty	27:4
אַלְקוּם	1	soldiers	30:31
אֹפֶן	1	circumstance	25:11
גֵּאָה	1	pride	8:13
גֵּהָה	1	healing	17:22
גַּרְגְּרוֹת	4	neck	1:9; 3:3, 22; 6:21
דֶּלֶף	2	dropping (rain)	19:13; 27:15

224

הֲפַכְפַּךְ	1	crooked	21:8
וָזָר	1	guilty	21:8
זַרְזִיר	1	girded	30:31
חֹבֵל	1	mast	23:34
חִבֻּק	2	folding (hands)	6:10; 24:33
חֲטֻבָה	1	dark-hued stuffs	7:16
חַכְלִילוּת	1	dullness (eye)	23:29
חֲלוֹף	1	vanishing	31:8
חֵלֶק	1	smoothness	7:21
חָרוּץ	5	sharp	10:4; 12:24, 27; 13:4; 21:5
חָשֹׁךְ	1	obscure, low	22:29
חֶתֶף	1	prey	23:28
יַעֲלָה	1	goat	5:19
כְּסִילוּת	1	stupidity	9:13
כִּשָּׁלוֹן	1	a stumbling	16:18
כִּישׁוֹר	1	distaff	31:19
לִוְיָה	2	wreath	1:9; 4:9
לָזוּת	1	crookedness	4:24
לֹעַ	1	throat	23:2
לֶכֶד	1	capture	3:26
מִדְחֶה	1	stumbling	26:28
מַדְקָרָה	1	piercing	12:18
מַהֲלָל	1	praise	27:21
מַהֲלֻמָה	2	blows	18:6; 19:29
מִיץ	3	squeezing	30:33, 33, 33
מֶמֶר	1	bitterness	17:25
מָנוֹן	1	trouble?	29:21
מַעְצָר	1	control	25:28
מַעֲרָךְ	1	arrangement	16:1
מֵפִיץ	1	scatterer	25:18
מִפְעָל	1	work	8:22
מִפְתָּח	1	opening	8:6
מַצְרֵף	2	crucible	17:3; 27:21
מַרְבַּד	2	coverlet	7:16; 31:22
מַרְגֵּמָה	1	sling	26:8
מָרָה	1	bitterness	14:10
מְשֻׂכָה	1	hedge	15:19
מַשָּׁאוֹן	1	guile	26:26
מֶתֶק	2	sweetness	16:21; 27:9
נַהַם	2	growling	19:12; 20:2

Hebrew	Count	Meaning	References
נוּמָה	1	slumber	23:21
נֵטֶל	1	burden, weight	27:3
נָכֵא	3	stricken	15:13; 17:22; 18:14
נְמָלָה	2	ant	6:6; 30:25
סַגְרִיר	1	steady rain	27:15
סֶלֶף	2	crookedness	11:3; 15:4
עֱלִי	1	pestle	27:22
עֲלוּקָה	1	leech	30:15
עֹמֶק	2	depth	9:18; 25:3
עָצֵל	14	lazy	6:6, 9; 10:26; 13:4; 15:19; 19:24; 20:4
			21:25; 22:13; 24:30; 26:13, 14, 15, 16
עַצְלָה	1	sluggishness	19:15
עַצְלוּת	1	sluggishness	31:27
עִקְּשׁוּת	2	crookedness	4:24; 6:12
עָתֵק	1	valuable	8:18
פְּתַיּוּת	1	simplicity	9:13
צִיר	1	hinge	26:14
צִנָּה	1	coolness	25:13
צָנוּעַ	1	modest	11:2
צָרֵב	1	burning	16:27
קֵא	1	vomit	26:11
קִמָּשׂוֹן	1	thistles	24:31
קֹשְׁטְ	1	truth	22:21
רָזוֹן	1	ruler	14:28
רֵישׁ	7	poverty	6:11; 10:15; 13:18; 24:34; 28:19; 30:8; 31:7
רִפְאוּת	1	healing	3:8
שַׂכִּין	1	knife	23:2
שְׂמָמִית	1	lizard	30:28
שָׁאֲוָה	1	storm	1:27
שִׁחוּת	1	pit	28:10
תְּכָכִים	1	oppression	29:13

Appendix C

Exclusive Words in the Collections

1. Exclusive Words in Collection I (168)

(1) Verbs (56)

אבה	54/4	to consent	אתה	21/1	to come
בקע	51/1	to cleave	דרך	62/1	to tread
הרג	167/2	to kill	חבק	13/2	to clasp
חמל	41/1	to spare	חמס	8/1	to wrong
חצב	25/1	to hew	טבח	11/1	to slaughter
טבע	10/1	to sink	יסד	42/1	to establish
יקש	10/1	to lure	ישן	25/1	to sleep
יתר	105/1	to remain over	כוה	2/1	to burn
מגן	3/1	to deliver	מהר	64/3	to hasten
מלל	7/1	to rub	מסך	5/2	to mix
מתק	6/1	to be sweet	נבט	69/1	to look
נגע	150/1	to touch, strike	נגף	49/1	to strike, smite
נדח	55/1	to banish	נוע	40/1	to waver
נוף	37/1	to besprinkle	נזל	18/1	to flow, trickle
נטף	18/1	to drop, drip	נסך	26/1	to set, install
נשג	50/1	to overtake	סרר	17/1	to be stubborn
עלס	3/1	to rejoice	ענד	2/1	to bind
ערך	75/1	to arrange	פוץ	1/1	to flow
פלח	5/1	to cleave	פלס	6/3	to weigh
פתל	5/1	to twist	צוד	17/1	to hunt
צעד	8/1	to step, march	קוץ	9/1	to abhor, dread
קרב	291/1	to be near	רבד	1/1	to deck
רהב	4/1	to act proudly	רעף	5/1	to trickle, drip
שטה	6/2	to turn aside	שיח	20/1	to complain
שרף	117/1	to burn	שרר	7/1	to act as prince
שאן	5/1	to be at ease	שוח	5/1	to sink down
שען	22/1	to lean over	שפך	115/2	to pour
שקד	18/1	to watch	שקף	22/1	to look out

(2) Adjectives/Nouns (112)

אָהַב	2/1	love	אֹהַב	2/1	love
אֹהֶל	4/1	perfume	אָחוֹת	114/1	sister
אֵטוּן	1/1	thread, yarn	אַיָּלָה	11/1	doe
אַל	5/1	strength, power	אָמוֹן	2/1	artificer
אָסָם	2/1	storehouse	אֲפֵלָה	10/2	darkness
אֶצְבַּע	31/2	finger	אֶשְׁנָב	2/1	window-lattice
בַּד	158/2	separation	בְּרִית	283/1	covenant
גַּאָה	1/1	pride	גְּבוּרָה	61/1	strength
גִּבְעָה	59/1	hill	גַּף	4/1	body, self
גַּרְגְּרוֹת	4/4	neck	דַּד	4/1	breast
דּוֹד	61/1	beloved, uncle	הוֹד	24/1	splendor, vigor
חֶבֶל	50/1	cord	חַד	4/1	sharp
חֻג	3/1	vault (heaven)	חֲטֻבָה	1/1	dark-hued stuff
חִידָה	17/1	riddle	חַי	239/1	living
חַלּוֹן	31/1	window	חָלָל	91/1	pierced one
חֵלֶק	1/1	smoothness	חֶלְקָה	6/1	smoothness
חָסִיד	32/1	kind, pious	טֶבַח	12/2	slaughter
יָחִיד	9/1	only (one)	יַעֲלָה	1/1	goat
יֶקֶב	15/1	wine-vet	יָקוּשׁ	4/1	fowler
כָּבֵד	14/1	liver	כִּכָּר	55/1	loaf of bread
כֶּסֶא	2/1	full moon	כְּסִילוּת	1/1	stupidity
כֶּסֶל	6/1	confidence	לֵבָב	252/2	heart
לוּחַ	43/2	tablet	לִוְיָה	2/2	wreath
לְזוּת	1/1	crookedness	לֶכֶד	1/1	capture
לַעֲנָה	8/1	wormwood	מַאֲכָל	30/1	food
מָבוֹא	25/1	entrance	מוֹדָע	2/1	kinsman
מוּם	19/1	blemish	מוֹסָד	13/1	foundation
מוֹר	12/1	myrrh	מוֹרֶה	7/1	teacher
מְזוּזָה	19/1	door-post	מַטְמוֹן	5/1	hidden treasure
מְלִיצָה	2/1	satire	מַעְגָּל	16/7	track, way
מִפְעָל	1/1	work	מִפְתָּח	1/1	opening
מָרוֹם	54/3	height	מְשׁוּבָה	12/1	turning back
מִשְׁמָר	22/1	guard, watch	נֹגַהּ	20/1	brightness
נֶגַע	78/1	stroke	נֹכַח	25/2	front (adv/prep)
נְעוּרִים	46/2	youth	נָקִי	43/2	clean, innocent
נָקָם	17/1	vengeance	נֶשֶׁף	12/1	twilight
עֵדָה	149/1	congregation	עַיִן	28/1	spring
עֶכֶס	2/1	anklet	עַמּוּד	111/1	pillar

עֲנָק	3/1	necklace
עִקְּשׁוּת	2/2	crookedness
עָרְמָה	6/3	craftiness
עָתֵק	1/1	valuable
פַּחַד	49/4	dread
צְבִי	12/1	gazelle
צְרוֹר	10/1	bundle, pouch
קִנְיָן	10/1	acquisition
רְפָאוּת	1/1	healing
שְׂמֹאול	54/2	left hand
שׁוֹאָה	13/1	devastation
שַׁחַק	21/2	dust, cloud
שִׁית	2/1	garment
שֶׁלֶם	87/1	peace offering
שִׁקּוּי	3/1	drink
שֵׁשׁ	135/1	six
תְּהוֹם	36/4	abyss, ocean
תְּחִלָּה	22/1	beginning
עָפָר	110/1	dust
עֶרֶב	135/1	evening
עֶרֶשׂ	10/1	couch
פָּז	9/1	gold
פְּתַיוּת	1/1	simplicity
צוּקָה	3/1	distress
קֶדֶם	87/2	front, east
קִנָּמוֹן	3/1	cinnamon
שָׂבָע	8/1	plenty
שָׁאֲוָה	1/1	storm
שׁוּק	4/1	street
שֹׁטֵר	25/1	official
שֻׁלְחָן	71/1	table
שַׁעֲשֻׁעִים	9/2	delight
שֹׁר	3/1	navel-string
תֵּבֵל	36/2	world
תּוֹצָאָה	23/1	outgoing
תִּירוֹשׁ	38/1	new wine

2. Exclusive Words in Collections I and II (87)

(1) Verbs (36)

אגר	3/2	to gather	I-1	II-1		בחר	172/8	to choose	I-4	II-4
בלע	49/3	to swallow	I-1	II-2		בצע	16/2	to gain by evil	I-1	II-1
המה	34/4	to murmur	I-3	II-1		זרה	39/4	to scatter	I-1	II-3
חטא	238/6	to miss, sin	I-1	II-5		חיה	283/4	to live	I-3	II-1
חמד	18/4	to desire	I-2	II-2		חרש	27/7	to device evil	I-3	II-4
ישר	25/5	to be straight	I-3	II-2		כלה	206/3	to complete	I-1	II-2
לוז	6/5	to turn aside	I-4	II-1		לכד	121/4	to capture	I-2	II-2
מאן	41/3	to refuse	I-1	II-2		מאס	76/2	to reject	I-1	II-1
נאץ	31/3	to contemn	I-2	II-1		נבע	11/4	to pour out	I-1	II-3
נחה	39/3	to lead, guide	I-1	II-2		נטש	40/3	to forsake	I-2	II-1
נסח	4/2	to pull away	I-1	II-1		נצב	116/2	to stand	I-1	II-1
סלל	11/2	to lift up	I-1	II-1		עזז	11/3	to be strong	I-2	II-1
ערב	8/2	to be sweet	I-1	II-1		פוק	7/4	to bring out	I-2	II-2
קנה	84/13	to acquire	I-6	II-7		קרץ	5/3	to nip, pinch	I-2	II-1
קשר	44/4	to bind	I-3	II-1		רוה	15/4	to drench	I-2	II-2
רוץ	80/4	to run	I-3	II-1		רעב	12/3	to be hungry	I-1	II-2
שכל	61/13	to be prudent	I-1	II-12		שחר	13/5	to look early	I-3	II-2
שכן	129/5	to abide	I-4	II-1		תעה	50/5	to wander	I-1	II-4

(2) Adjectives/Nouns (51)

אוֹר	122/4	light	I-2	II-2		אוֹצָר	79/4	storehouse	I-1	II-3
אִישׁוֹן	5/3	pupil	I-2	II-1		אַכְזָרִי	8/4	cruel	I-1	II-3
אַלּוּף	69/3	friend	I-1	II-2		בֶּטַח	42/4	trust	I-3	II-1
בְּלִיַּעַל	27/3	uselessness	I-2	II-1		גָּאוֹן	49/2	pride	I-1	II-1
גּוֹרָל	78/4	lots	I-1	II-3		זֶבַח	162/5	sacrifice	I-1	II-4
חֵיק	38/5	bosom	I-2	II-3		חָרוּץ	6/4	gold	I-3	II-1
חֶרְפָּה	73/2	reproach	I-1	II-1		חֹשֶׁךְ	80/2	darkness	I-1	II-1
טַל	31/2	dew	I-1	II-1		יֹשֶׁר	14/5	uprightness	I-2	II-3
כִּיס	5/2	bag, purse	I-1	II-1		כֹּפֶר	13/3	ransom	I-1	II-2
לֶקַח	9/6	learning	I-4	II-2		מַחֲשָׁבָה	50/8	thought	I-1	II-7
מִצְוָה	181/10	command	I-7	II-3		נֶגֶד	151/4	in front of	I-1	II-3
נֹעַם	7/3	loveliness	I-1	II-2		נְתִיבָה	21/6	path	I-5	II-1
סוּפָה	15/2	storm-wind	I-1	II-1		עָוֹן	229/2	iniquity	I-1	II-1
עֲטָרָה	23/5	crown	I-1	II-4		עָנָו	21/3	the afflicted	I-2	II-1
עֶצֶב	6/4	pain, toil	I-1	II-3		עֶצֶם	126/5	bone	I-1	II-4
עֵת	294/5	time	I-3	II-2		פַּח	25/2	bird-trap	I-1	II-1
פֶּלֶג	10/2	channel	I-1	II-1		פֶּתַח	164/6	entrance	I-5	II-1
צְדָקָה	157/18	justice	I-2	II-16		קָלוֹן	17/8	dishonor	I-3	II-5
קֶרֶת	5/4	town	I-3	II-1		רֵאשִׁית	51/5	beginning	I-4	II-1
רְפָאִים	8/3	shades	I-2	II-1		רָצוֹן	56/14	goodwill	I-1	II-13
רֶשַׁע	30/5	wickedness	I-2	II-3		שָׂמֵחַ	21/4	glad, joyful	I-1	II-3
שְׁאֵר	16/2	flesh	I-1	II-1		שׁוֹר	79/3	bull	I-1	II-2
שֹׁחַד	23/4	bribe	I-1	II-3		שַׁלְוָה	8/2	quietness	I-1	II-1
שָׁלוֹם	237/3	peace	I-2	II-1		שָׁנָה	874/5	year	I-4	II-1
תְּבוּאָה	41/8	income	I-3	II-5		תָּוֶךְ	418/8	midst	I-5	II-3
תּוּשִׁיָּה	12/4	wisdom	I-3	II-1						

3. Exclusive Words in Collections I, II, and III (26)

(1) Verbs (11)

ארב	26/6	to ambush	I-3	II-1	III-2
הגה	25/3	to moan	I-1	II-1	III-1
כרת	285/4	to cut off	I-1	II-1	III-2
ליץ	28/18	to mock	I-6	II-11	III-1
מלא	250/7	to be full	I-4	II-2	III-1
נטה	185/12	to stretch	I-8	II-3	III-1
נצל	213/12	to rescue	I-4	II-6	III-2

רעע	93/6	to be evil	I-1	II-3	III-2		
רפה	46/3	to relax	I-1	II-1	III-1		
רצה	56/3	to be pleased	I-1	II-1	III-1		
תקע	68/4	to clap	I-1	II-2	III-1		

(2) Adjectives/Nouns (15)

אֹמֶר	55/22	word	I-14	II-5	III-3		
אֹרַח	59/19	way	I-12	II-6	III-1		
בָּשָׂר	270/4	flesh	I-2	II-1	III-1		
חֹטֵא	19/3	sinful	I-1	II-1	III-1		
חַטָּאת	221/7	sin	I-1	II-5	III-1		
יָקָר	36/5	precious	I-3	II-1	III-1		
יִרְאָה	44/14	fear	I-5	II-8	III-1		
יֵשׁ	138/13	existence	I-2	II-9	III-2		
כֹּחַ	125/5	strength	I-1	II-2	III-2		
מְזִמָּה	19/8	plan	I-5	II-2	III-1		
נָוֶה	32/3	abode	I-1	II-1	III-1		
רֹב	151/12	abundance	I-2	II-9	III-1		
שֵׂכֶל	16/6	prudence	I-1	II-4	III-1		
תַּהְפֻּכָה	10/9	perversity	I-4	II-4	III-1		
תַּחְבֻּלָה	6/5	counsel	I-1	II-3	III-1		

4. Exclusive Words in Collections I, II, III, and IV (2)

| בנה | 373/4 | to build | I-1 | II-1 | III-1 | IV-1 | |
| מוּסָר | 50/30 | discipline | I-13 | II-13 | III-3 | IV-1 | |

5. Exclusive Words in Collections I. II. III. IV, and V (4)

צַדִּיק	206/66	righteous	I-4	II-49	III-3	IV-1	V-9
רָאָה	1299/13	to see	I-2	II-2	III-3	IV-1	V-5
רָשָׁע	263/78	wicked	I-7	II-54	III-4	IV-1	V-12
שָׂפָה	176/46	lip	I-6	II-32	III-3	IV-2	V-3

6. Exclusive Words in Collections I, II, III, IV, V, and VI (7)

אָדָם	561/45	man	I-8	II-21	III-3	IV-1	V-10	VI-2
אִישׁ	2179/90	man	I-10	II-45	III-4	IV-3	V-27	VI-1
אמר	5298/24	to say	I-9	II-4	III-2	IV-2	V-4	VI-3

הָלַךְ	1549/39	to go	I-21	II-12	III-1	IV-1	V-3	VI-1
חָכָם	138/47	wise	I-6	II-28	III-3	IV-1	V-8	VI-1
כּוּן	217/20	to be firm	I-5	II-9	III-2	IV-1	V-2	VI-1
שׁוּב	1059/23	to return	I-3	II-6	III-3	IV-2	V-8	VI-1

7. Words Occurring in all the Collections (2)

דָּבָר	1442/36	word	I-4	II-16	III-2	IV-1	V-9	VI-3	VII-1
לֵב	599/97	heart	I-19	II-51	III-13	IV-2	V-10	VI-1	VII-1

8. Exclusive Words in Collections I, II, III, IV, V, and VII (5)

בּוֹא	2565/33	to come	I-13	II-11	III-4	IV-2	V-2	VII-1
הָיָה	3548/28	to be	I-12	II-6	III-6	IV-1	V-2	VII-1
לָקַח	966/19	to take	I-8	II-5	III-3	IV-1	V-1	VII-1
עָשָׂה	2627/34	to do	I-5	II-17	III-4	IV-2	V-2	VII-4
טוֹב	495/61	good	I-8	II-39	III-1	IV-2	V-9	VII-2

9. Exclusive Words in Collections I, II, III, and V (36)

(1) Verbs (16)

בָּגַד	49/9	to be unfaithful	I-1	II-6	III-1	V-1
בִּין	171/33	to understand	I-9	II-14	III-3	V-7
בִּקֵשׁ	225/14	to seek	I-1	II-9	III-1	V-3
דָּבַר	1151/9	to speak	I-2	II-2	III-4	V-1
זוּר	78/15	to be a stranger	I-7	II-5	III-1	V-2
מָשַׁל	81/11	to rule	I-1	II-5	III-1	V-4
נָפַל	434/15	to fall	I-2	II-7	III-2	V-4
נָצַר	61/18	to keep	I-10	II-5	III-1	V-2
עָרַב	22/9	to give in pledge	I-1	II-5	III-2	V-1
פָּתָה	28/5	to be simple	I-1	II-2	III-1	V-1
קָרָא	738/19	to call	I-12	II-5	III-1	V-1
שָׂמַח	154/16	to be glad	I-1	II-6	III-4	V-5
שָׁחַת	187/5	to be ruin	I-1	II-1	III-1	V-2
שָׁלֵם	117/10	to be sound	I-2	II-6	III-1	V-1
שָׁמַע	1159/30	to hear	I-12	II-11	III-3	V-4
שָׁמַר	411/31	to keep	I-15	II-12	III-1	V-3

(2) Adjectives/Nouns (20)

אֱוִיל	26/19	foolish	I-2	II-13	III-1	V-3
אִוֶּלֶת	25/23	folly	I-1	II-17	III-1	V-4
אֹזֶן	187/14	ear	I-4	II-4	III-3	V-3
אַחֲרִית	61/13	end	I-2	II-5	III-4	V-2
אֵיד	24/6	distress	I-3	II-1	III-1	V-1
אֱמֶת	127/12	faithfulness	I-2	II-6	III-3	V-1
חֶדֶר	38/6	chamber	I-1	II-3	III-1	V-1
חֵמָה	125/8	heat, rage	I-1	II-5	III-1	V-1
כְּסִיל	70/49	fool	I-4	II-30	III-1	V-14
מָדוֹן	23/19	contention	I-2	II-10	III-1	V-6
מָוֶת	161/19	death	I-4	II-13	III-1	V-1
נָכְרִי	45/9	foreign, alien	I-5	II-1	III-1	V-2
נַעַר	240/7	lad	I-2	II-3	III-1	V-1
עוֹלָם	437/6	long duration	I-1	II-2	III-2	V-1
צָרָה	72/8	distress	I-1	II-4	III-2	V-1
רֹאשׁ	600/10	head	I-6	II-2	III-1	V-1
רַע	142/21	evil	I-6	II-10	III-2	V-3
רָעָה	319/21	evil	I-4	II-12	III-2	V-3
תְּבוּנָה	42/19	understanding	I-8	II-9	III-1	V-1
תּוֹעֵבָה	117/21	abomination	I-3	II-13	III-1	V-4

10. Exclusive Words in Collections I, II, III, V, and VI (8)

אָב	1225/26	father	I-5	II-11	III-4	V-4	VI-2
אַיִן	789/38	not	I-9	II-13	III-2	V-13	VI-1
גֶּבֶר	66/9	man	I-1	II-1	III-1	V-3	VI-3
דַּעַת	91/41	knowledge	I-14	II-20	III-5	V-1	VI-1
הוֹן	26/18	wealth	I-4	II-8	III-1	V-3	VI-2
חכם	27/13	to be wise	I-5	II-4	III-2	V-1	VI-1
עַיִן	868/46	eye	I-11	II-16	III-7	V-9	VI-3
שְׁאוֹל	65/9	Sheol, grave	I-4	II-2	III-1	V-1	VI-1

11. Exclusive Words in Collections I, II, III, V, VI, and VII (13)

(1) Verbs (4)

אכל	807/14	to eat	I-1	II-3	III-3	V-4	VI-2	VII-1
ידע	940/35	to know	I-10	II-8	III-7	V-6	VI-3	VII-1

| נָתַן | 2011/33 | to give | I-12 | II-8 | III-2 | V-5 | VI-1 | VII-5 |
| קוּם | 629/10 | to rise | I-1 | II-2 | III-2 | V-2 | VI-1 | VII-2 |

(2) Adjectives/Nouns (9)

אֵם	220/14	mother	I-3	II-4	III-2	V-2	VI-2	VII-1
בַּיִת	2036/37	house	I-15	II-12	III-2	V-3	VI-1	VII-4
בֵּן	4891/59	son	I-26	II-21	III-4	V-3	VI-2	VII-3
דֶּרֶךְ	706/75	way	I-29	II-33	III-2	V-5	VI-5	VII-1
חָכְמָה	153/42	wisdom	I-19	II-14	III-4	V-3	VI-1	VII-1
יהוה	6828/87	Lord	I-19	II-55	III-5	V-6	VI-1	VII-1
לֶחֶם	297/23	bread	I-5	II-5	III-2	V-6	VI-3	VII-2
מֶלֶךְ	2518/32	king	I-2	II-14	III-2	V-7	VI-3	VII-4
פֶּה	502/55	mouth	I-13	II-30	III-1	V-6	VI-2	VII-3

12. Exclusive Words in Collections 1, II, III, V, and VII (7)

בַּעַל	84/14	master	I-3	II-4	III-3	V-1	VII-3
יוֹם	2291/33	day	I-13	II-7	III-3	V-8	VII-2
יָשַׁב	815/8	to sit	I-2	II-3	III-1	V-1	VII-1
מָצָא	455/27	to find	I-14	II-9	III-1	V-2	VII-1
נֶפֶשׁ	753/56	soul, life	I-10	II-29	III-6	V-10	VII-1
רַע	203/31	evil	I-9	II-17	III-1	V-3	VII-1
שָׁלַח	860/11	to send	I-3	II-2	III-1	V-3	VII-2

13. Exclusive Words in Collections I, II, III, and VI (6)

בוז	14/8	to despise	I-2	II-3	III-2	VI-1
בִּינָה	37/14	discernment	I-10	II-1	III-2	VI-1
יָסַף	212/14	to add	I-4	II-7	III-2	VI-1
כָּזָב	31/9	falsehood	I-1	II-6	III-1	VI-1
מוּת	780/8	to die	I-1	II-5	III-1	VI-1
מָנַע	29/5	to withhold	I-2	II-1	III-1	VI-1

14. Exclusive Words in Collections I, II, III, and VII (5)

יַיִן	141/10	wine	I-3	II-2	III-3	VII-2
יָרֵא	336/8	to fear	I-2	II-3	III-1	VII-2
כַּף	193/9	palm	I-2	II-2	III-1	VII-4

נֵר	44/6	lamp	I-1	II-3	III-1	VII-1	
שַׁעַר	375/7	gate	I-2	II-1	III-2	VII-2	

15. Exclusive Words in Collections I, II, and IV (3)

חוּץ	164/6	the outside	I-4	II-1	IV-1
מְעַט	101/10	fewness	I-4	II-3	IV-3
שֵׁנָה	23/7	sleep	I-5	II-1	IV-1

16. Exclusive Words in Collections I, II, IV, and V (8)

חָסֵר	15/13	needy	I-4	II-7	IV-1	V-1
מַחְסוֹר	13/8	poverty	I-1	II-5	IV-1	V-1
מִשְׁפָּט	424/20	judgment	I-4	II-12	IV-1	V-3
עבר	547/12	to pass over	I-5	II-3	IV-1	V-3
עֵד	69/11	witness	I-1	II-8	IV-1	V-1
עָצֵל	14/14	lazy	I-2	II-7	IV-1	V-4
פָּנִים	2040/18	face	I-3	II-6	IV-2	V-7
רֵעַ	187/32	neighbor	I-6	II-14	IV-1	V-11

17. An Exclusive Word in Collections I, II, IV, V, and VI (1)

יכח	59/10	to rebuke	I-4	II-2	IV-1	V-2	VI-1

18. Exclusive Words in Collections I, II, IV, V, VI, and VII (2)

יָד	1617/31	hand	I-8	II-14	IV-1	V-3	VI-2	VII-3
רֵישׁ	7/7	poverty	I-1	II-2	IV-1	V-1	VI-1	VII-1

19. Exclusive Words in Collections 1, II, and V (50)

(1) Verbs (14)

אהב	208/25	to love	I-8	II-15	V-2
חפשׂ	23/3	to search	I-1	II-1	V-1
כבד	113/7	to be heavy	I-3	II-3	V-1
נחל	59/6	to possess	I-2	II-3	V-1
נקה	44/7	to be clean	I-1	II-5	V-1
סור	300/17	to turn aside	I-6	II-9	V-2

עָזַב	208/11	to forsake	I-6	II-2	V-3
עָנָה	316/7	to answer	I-1	II-3	V-3
פּוּחַ	15/7	to breathe	I-1	II-5	V-1
פָּרַע	16/6	to let go	I-3	II-2	V-1
צָפַן	32/9	to hide	I-5	II-2	V-2
קָשַׁב	46/8	to incline	I-6	II-1	V-1
רָבָה	176/11	to be much	I-3	II-2	V-6
שָׁגָה	21/6	to go astray	I-3	II-2	V-1

(2) Adjectives/Nouns (36)

אָח	629/8	brother	I-1	II-6	V-1
אֶשֶׁר	45/8	blessedness	I-3	II-3	V-2
בֶּגֶד	215/4	garment	I-1	II-1	V-2
בַּעַד	105/4	separation	I-2	II-1	V-1
בֶּצַע	23/3	gain	I-1	II-1	V-1
חָמָס	60/7	violence	I-2	II-4	V-1
חֵן	69/13	favor	I-6	II-5	V-2
יָשָׁר	118/25	upright	I-4	II-18	V-3
כָּבוֹד	199/15	glory	I-3	II-6	V-6
כִּסֵּא	135/6	chair	I-1	II-3	V-2
כֶּסֶף	403/13	silver	I-5	II-4	V-4
מָקוֹר	18/7	spring	I-1	II-5	V-1
מַרְפֵּא	16/8	healing	I-2	II-5	V-1
מָשָׁל	39/6	proverb	I-2	II-1	V-3
נָדִיב	26/5	noble	I-1	II-3	V-1
סוֹד	21/5	counsel	I-1	II-3	V-1
סֵתֶר	35/3	covering	I-1	II-1	V-1
עִיר	1042/4	city	I-1	II-2	V-1
עֵץ	329/6	tree	I-1	II-3	V-2
עֵצָה	88/10	counsel	I-3	II-6	V-1
עִקֵּשׁ	11/7	twisted	I-2	II-4	V-1
פִּנָּה	30/4	corner	I-2	II-1	V-1
פֶּתִי	19/15	simple	I-9	II-5	V-1
קָהָל	122/3	congregation	I-1	II-1	V-1
קִנְאָה	43/3	jealousy	I-1	II-1	V-1
קָצִיר	54/5	harvest	I-1	II-2	V-2
רֶגֶל	243/15	foot	I-11	II-1	V-3
רְחוֹב	43/5	open place	I-3	II-1	V-1
רַךְ	16/3	tender	I-1	II-1	V-1

שַׂר	421/3	chief	I-1	II-1	V-1		
שֶׁמֶן	193/5	oil	I-1	II-2	V-2		
תּוֹכַחַת	24/16	rebuke	I-6	II-7	V-3		
תֹּם	23/7	integrity	I-1	II-5	V-1		
תָּמִיד	103/4	continuity	I-2	II-1	V-1		
תָּמִים	91/6	perfect	I-2	II-2	V-2		
תִּפְאָרָה	51/6	beauty	I-1	II-4	V-1		

20. Exclusive Words in Collections I, II, V, and VI (11)

אֵשׁ	379/5	fire	I-1	II-1	V-2	VI-1	
בֹּרֵךְ	256/6	to kneel	I-2	II-2	V-1	VI-1	
דָּם	360/8	blood	I-4	II-1	V-2	VI-1	
חֶרֶב	411/4	sword	I-1	II-1	V-1	VI-1	
יצא	1067/11	to go out	I-1	II-3	V-3	VI-4	
ירד	379/7	to go down	I-3	II-2	V-1	VI-1	
מַיִם	580/14	water	I-5	II-4	V-3	VI-2	
קַיִץ	20/4	summer	I-1	II-1	V-1	VI-1	
רוּחַ	389/21	spirit	I-1	II-13	V-6	VI-1	
שׂבע	97/19	to be sated	I-3	II-6	V-6	VI-4	
שׂנא	112/26	to hate	I-7	II-10	V-8	VI-1	

21. Exclusive Words in Collections I, II, V, VI, and VII (2)

| אֶרֶץ | 2504/21 | earth | I-7 | II-4 | V-4 | VI-5 | VII-1 |
| אִשָּׁה | 782/23 | woman | I-8 | II-9 | V-2 | VI-1 | VII-3 |

22. Exclusive Words in Collections I, II, V, and VII (12)

אבד	184/10	to perish	I-1	II-6	V-2	VII-1
בטח	120/10	to trust	I-1	II-4	V-4	VII-1
חַיִּים	150/33	life	I-12	II-19	V-1	VII-1
יסר	42/5	to discipline	I-1	II-1	V-2	VII-1
לָשׁוֹן	109/19	tongue	I-2	II-12	V-4	VII-1
פְּרִי	118/10	fruit	I-2	II-5	V-1	VII-2
צֶדֶק	119/9	righteousness	I-5	II-2	V-1	VII-1
רַב	485/25	many	I-1	II-15	V-8	VII-1
רָחוֹק	85/4	far, distant	I-1	II-1	V-1	VII-1
שֶׁקֶר	113/20	falsehood	I-2	II-13	V-4	VII-1
תּוֹרָה	220/13	instruction	I-6	II-1	V-5	VII-1
תמך	21/9	to grasp	I-4	II-2	V-2	VII-1

23. Exclusive Words in Collections I, II, and VI (8)

אָוֶן	77/9	trouble	I-2	II-6	VI-1
לָעַג	18/3	to mock	I-1	II-1	VI-1
נשׂא	650/9	to carry	I-2	II-4	VI-3
עָצוּם	31/3	mighty	I-1	II-1	VI-1
עֹשֶׁר	37/9	wealth	I-2	II-6	VI-1
צַעַד	14/4	step	I-2	II-1	VI-1
רוּם	166/6	to be high	I-2	II-3	VI-1
רחק	57/6	to be far	I-2	II-3	VI-1

24. Exclusive Words in Collections I, II, and VII (5)

גמל	37/3	to deal fully	I-1	II-1	VII-1
חֶסֶד	246/10	love, mercy	I-1	II-8	VII-1
נֶדֶר	60/3	vow	I-1	II-1	VII-1
פְּנִינִים	6/4	coral, rubies	I-2	II-1	VII-1
שָׁלָל	75/3	spoil	I-1	II-1	VII-1

25. Exclusive Words in Collections I and III (13)

בְּאֵר	38/2	well, pit	I-1	III-1
גיל	45/5	to rejoice	I-1	III-4
חֵךְ	18/3	palate	I-2	III-1
כָּנָף	109/2	wing	I-1	III-1
כשׁל	62/5	to stumble	I-3	III-2
כתב	223/3	to write	I-2	III-1
לחם	6/4	to eat	I-2	III-2
מוֹעֵצָה	7/2	counsel, plan	I-1	III-1
מֵישָׁר	19/5	uprightness	I-3	III-2
מִשְׁכָּב	46/2	bed	I-1	III-1
פִּתְאֹם	25/4	suddenness	I-2	III-2
קיץ	22/2	to awake	I-1	III-1
קנא	34/4	to be jealous	I-1	III-3

26. An Exclusive Word in Collections I, III, and IV

שׁכב	212/8	to lie down	I-5	III-2	IV-1

27. An Exclusive Word in Collections I, III, IV, and V

חִנָּם	32/6	for nothing	I-3	III-1	IV-1	V-1

28. Exclusive Words in Collections I, III, and V (5)

גזל	30/3	to tear away	I-1	III-1	V-1
זנה	94/4	to fornicate	I-2	III-1	V-1
נֹפֶת	5/3	honey	I-1	III-1	V-1
רִיב	68/5	to strive	I-1	III-2	V-2
שֶׁבַע	164/3	seven	I-1	III-1	V-1

29. An Exclusive Word in Collections I, III, V, and VI

שָׁמַיִם	421/6	heaven	I-2	III-1	V-1	VI-2

30. An Exclusive Word in Collections I, III, V, and VII

שׁתה	217/8	to drink	I-3	III-1	V-1	VII-3

31. Exclusive Words in Collections I, III, and VI (2)

יָם	392/3	sea	I-1	III-1	VI-1
שׂים	586/3	to put, place	I-1	III-1	VI-1

32. Exclusive Words in Collections I, III, and VII (2)

אמץ	41/3	to be strong	I-1	III-1	VII-1
אשׁר	16/5	to go straight	I-3	III-1	VII-1

33. Exclusive Words in Collections I and IV (5)

חֹבֵק	2/2	folding	I-1	IV-1
נֹכַח	4/2	straightness	I-1	IV-1
נעם	8/3	to be pleasant	I-2	IV-1
נשׁק	32/2	to kiss	I-1	IV-1
תְּנוּמָה	5/3	slumber	I-2	IV-1

34. An Exclusive Word in Collections I, IV, and VI

| מָגֵן | 63/4 | shield | I-2 | IV-1 | VI-1 |

35. Exclusive Words in Collections I and V (38)

(1) Verbs (13)

אוּר	43/2	to be light	I-1	V-1
חוּל	40/4	to whirl	I-2	V-2
חָזַק	293/4	to be strong	I-3	V-1
חָלַק	9/4	to be smooth	I-2	V-2
חָתָה	4/2	to snatch up	I-1	V-1
יָרָה	79/4	to throw	I-3	V-1
נהם	5/2	to growl	I-1	V-1
פָּחַד	25/2	to dread	I-1	V-1
פָּרַץ	49/2	to break out	I-1	V-1
רָנַן	54/3	to cry aloud	I-2	V-1
רפס	5/2	to tread	I-1	V-1
שָׁבַר	148/3	to break	I-1	V-2
שָׁוָה	21/4	to resemble	I-2	V-2

(2) Adjectives/Nouns (25)

אֶחָד	970/2	one	I-1	V-1
אַחֵר	166/2	another	I-1	V-1
אֹרֶךְ	96/3	length	I-2	V-1
בּוֹר	64/3	pit	I-2	V-1
בֹּקֶר	214/2	morning	I-1	V-1
גַּחֶלֶת	18/3	coal	I-1	V-2
גַּנָּב	17/2	thief	I-1	V-1
דֶּלֶת	87/2	door	I-1	V-1
הַר	547/2	mountain	I-1	V-1
חָלָק	12/2	smooth	I-1	V-1
חֵץ	53/3	arrow	I-1	V-2
יָמִין	139/3	right hand	I-2	V-1
לָצוֹן	3/2	scorning	I-1	V-1
מָחָר	52/2	tomorrow	I-1	V-1
מַעְיָן	23/3	spring	I-2	V-1
מְאֵרָה	5/2	curse	I-1	V-1
נָגִיד	44/2	leader	I-1	V-1

עֹמֶק	2/2	depth	I-1	V-1	
פַּעַם	115/3	beat, time	I-2	V-1	
פֶּתַע	7/2	suddenness	I-1	V-1	
צִפּוֹר	40/4	bird	I-2	V-2	
קוֹל	505/7	voice	I-5	V-2	
קָצִין	12/2	chief, ruler	I-1	V-1	
רֶשֶׁת	22/2	net	I-1	V-1	
שִׁבְעָה	227/2	seven	I-1	V-1	

36. Exclusive Words in Collections I, V, and VI (2)

אֱלֹהִים	2603/5	God	I-3	V-1	VI-1
צרר	36/3	to bind up	I-1	V-1	VI-1

37. Exclusive Words in Collections I, V, and VII (4)

מַר	38/3	bitter	I-1	V-1	VII-1
נַעֲרָה	63/3	girl	I-1	V-1	VII-1
שׂחק	35/6	to laugh	I-3	V-2	VII-1
שׁפט	142/4	to judge	I-1	V-2	VII-1

38. Exclusive Words in Collections I and VI (8)

גנב	40/3	to steal	I-2	VI-1
חקק	19/4	to decree	I-3	VI-1
למד	86/2	to learn	I-1	VI-1
מלך	347/2	to be king	I-1	VI-1
נאף	31/2	to do adultery	I-1	VI-1
נְמָלָה	2/2	ant	I-1	VI-1
עַפְעַף	10/4	eyelid	I-3	VI-1
קָדוֹשׁ	116/2	holy	I-1	VI-1

39. Exclusive Words in Collections I, VI, and VII (2)

חֹק	129/3	decree	I-1	VI-1	VII-1
מחה	35/3	to wipe out	I-1	VI-1	VII-1

40. Exclusive Words in Collections I and VII (7)

חֵפֶץ	40/3	delight	I-2	VII-1
יֳפִי	19/2	beauty	I-1	VII-1
לַיְלָה	227/3	night	I-1	VII-2
מַרְבַד	2/2	coverlet	I-1	VII-1
סַחַר	7/3	traffic, gain	I-2	VII-1
רזן	6/2	to be weighty	I-1	VII-1
שׁכח	102/5	to forget	I-3	VII-2

41. Exclusive Words in Collection II (242)

(1) Verbs (89)

אבס	2/1	to feed	אזל	4/1	to go away
אזן	42/1	to listen	אטם	8/2	to shut up
אכף	1/1	to press, urge	אנה	6/1	to encounter
באשׁ	18/1	to stink	בזה	43/3	to despise
בחל	1/1	to gain by greed	בחן	28/1	to examine
בטה	4/1	to speak rashly	בקר	7/1	to inquire
ברח	65/1	to flee	גבה	34/2	to be high
גלע	3/3	to expose	גרר	5/1	to drag away
גרשׁ	47/1	to drive out	דחה	8/1	to push
הדף	11/1	to thrust, push	הפך	94/2	to overturn
זכה	8/1	to be clean	זעף	4/1	to be enraged
זרע	56/2	to sow	חלץ	27/2	to rescue
חנך	5/1	to train up	חפץ	86/2	to delight in
חפר	17/2	to search for	חרך	1/1	to set in motion
חרשׁ	47/2	to be silent	טול	13/1	to hurl, cast
טהר	93/1	to be clean	יבשׁ	61/1	to be dry
יעל	23/2	to profit	ירא	4/1	to pour
כאב	8/1	to be in pain	כול	38/1	to sustain
כפה	1/1	to subdue	כפר	101/2	to cover
כתר	6/1	to surround	לבט	3/2	to thrust down
לוה	14/3	to borrow	לון	71/2	to lodge, abide
לעע	3/1	to talk wildly	מושׁ	20/1	to depart
מעל	35/1	to act unfaithfully	מעט	22/1	to be small
מרק	4/1	to scour, polish	משׁך	36/1	to draw, drag
נדף	9/1	to drive	נוב	4/1	to bear fruit
נחת	10/1	to go down	סלף	7/4	to twist, pervert
סעד	12/1	to support	ספה	21/1	to sweep

עָוָה	17/1	to bend, twist	עוּר	80/1	to awake
עָבַר	14/4	to stir up	עָמָל	11/1	to labor
עָצָה	1/1	to shut	עָרַם	5/2	to be shrewd
פָּזַר	10/1	to scatter	פָּטַר	5/1	to separate
פָּנָה	135/1	to turn	פָּקַד	223/1	to visit, muster
פָּקַח	20/1	to open eyes	פָּרַד	26/5	to divide
פָּרַח	25/2	to bud	פָּרַר	50/1	to break
פָּשַׂק	2/1	to open wide	צָדַק	41/1	to be just
קָבַל	13/1	to receive	קָוָה	47/1	to wait for
קָלָה	7/1	to be dishonored	קָצַר	34/1	to reap
קָצַר	15/1	to be short	רָגַע	6/1	to disturb
רָדַם	7/1	to be in sleep	רָחַב	25/1	to be wide
רָצַח	16/1	to murder	רָקַב	2/1	to rot
רָשַׁע	35/2	to be wicked	שָׁבַר	21/1	to buy grain
שָׁבַת	71/2	to cease	שָׁחָה	172/1	to bow down
שָׁחַח	22/1	to bow	שָׁלֵם	15/1	to make peace
שָׁמַד	90/1	to be destroyed	שָׁקַט	41/1	to be quiet
תּוּר	25/1	to seek out			

(2) Adjectives/Nouns (153)

אֵבוּס	3/1	crib	אֹהֶל	345/1	tent
אוֹן	13/1	vigor, strength	אוֹפַן	35/1	wheel
אֵימָה	17/1	terror, dread	אֵיפָה	40/2	ephah
אֵיתָן	14/1	perennial	אֹכֶל	44/1	food
אַלְמָנָה	56/1	widow	אֶלֶף	8/1	cattle
אֹמֶן	8/3	faithfulness	אֲרֻחָה	6/1	meal
אַרְמוֹן	32/1	citadel	אָשׁוּר	7/1	step, going
אָשָׁם	46/1	guilt	בּוּז	11/2	contempt
בָּחוּר	44/1	young man	בַּר	13/1	grain
בַּר	7/1	pure	בְּרִיחַ	40/1	bar
גֵּאֶה	9/2	proud	גָּבֹהַּ	40/1	high
גֹּבַהּ	17/1	haughtiness	גֵּהָה	1/1	healing
גּוֹי	556/1	nation	גְּמוּל	19/2	dealing
גְּעָרָה	15/3	rebuke	דְּאָגָה	6/1	anxiety
דָּבֵק	3/1	clinging	הֲדָרָה	5/1	adornment, glory
הַוָּה	16/4	destruction	הֲפַכְפַּךְ	1/1	crooked
וָזָר	1/1	guilty	זֵד	13/1	arrogant
זָדוֹן	11/3	insolence	זַךְ	11/3	pure, clean
זֵכֶר	23/1	remembrance	זַעַף	7/1	raging, rage

Hebrew	Ref	Meaning	Hebrew	Ref	Meaning
זְעָקָה	18/1	cry	זֶרַע	229/1	sowing, seed
חַבּוּרָה	7/1	stripe, blow	חֵדֶק	2/1	brier
חֲזִיר	7/1	swine	חֹטֶר	2/1	branch, twig
חָנֵף	13/1	profane	חֵסֶד	2/1	shame
חָצָץ	2/1	gravel	חָרֵב	2/1	dry
חָרוּץ	5/5	sharp	חֹרֶף	7/1	harvest time
טוֹב	32/1	good things	טוֹבָה	62/1	welfare
יָהִיר	2/1	proud	יְסוֹד	20/1	foundation
יָפֶה	42/1	beautiful	יְקָר	17/1	preciousness
יָרָק	5/1	herbs	יֶתֶר	96/1	excess
כְּלִמָּה	30/1	reproach	כִּשָּׁלוֹן	1/1	a stumbling
מֵאָה	581/1	hundred	מָאוֹר	19/1	luminary
מֹאזְנַיִם	15/3	scales	מִגְדָּל	34/1	tower
מְגוֹרָה	3/1	fear	מִדְבָּר	271/1	wilderness
מִדְקָרָה	1/1	piercing	מְהוּמָה	12/1	confusion
מַהֲלֻמָה	2/2	blows	מוֹתָר	3/2	abundance
מַחֲלָה	2/1	sickness	מַחְסֶה	20/1	refuge
מְחִתָּה	11/7	terror, ruin	מַכָּה	44/1	blow
מָלֵא	63/1	full	מַלְאָךְ	212/3	messenger
מַלְקוֹשׁ	8/1	spring-rain	מֶמֶר	1/1	bitterness
מַס	23/1	laborer	מְסִלָּה	27/1	highway
מָעוֹז	33/1	refuge	מַעֲלָל	41/1	deed
מַעֲרָךְ	1/1	arrangement	מַצָּה	3/2	contention
מָצוֹד	4/1	net	מִצְעָד	3/1	step
מָרָה	1/1	bitterness	מְרִי	23/1	rebellion
מֵרֵעַ	8/2	friend	מְשׂוּכָה	1/1	hedge
מַשְׁחִית	11/1	ruin, destroyer	מִשְׁתֶּה	46/1	feast, drink
מַתָּן	5/3	gift	מַתָּנָה	17/1	gift
נַהַם	2/2	growling	נַחֲלָה	221/3	inheritance
נִיר	5/1	lamp	נִיר	3/1	fallow ground
נָכֵא	3/3	stricken	נֶצַח	45/1	perpetuity
נְשָׁמָה	24/1	breath	סֶלֶף	2/2	crookedness
עָב	31/1	dark cloud	עֶבְרָה	34/5	rage, fury
עַוְלָה	29/1	injustice	עָלֶה	19/1	leaf, leafage
עָמֵל	9/1	laborer	עֲנָוָה	7/3	humility
עֹנֶשׁ	2/1	fine, indemnity	עַצֶּבֶת	5/2	hurt, pain
עַצְלָה	1/1	sluggishness	עֵקֶב	15/1	reward, gain
עָרֵב	2/1	sweet	עֲרוּבָה	2/1	pledge
עָרִיץ	20/1	terrifying	עָשָׁן	25/1	smoke
פֶּלֶס	2/1	scale	פְּעֻלָּה	14/2	work

צוּף	2/1	honey-comb	צַיִד	19/1	hunting
צֵן	2/1	thorn?	צָנוּעַ	1/1	modest
צָרֶב	1/1	burning	קֹדֶשׁ	477/1	holiness
קֶסֶם	11/1	divination	קָצֶה	95/1	end
קָצֵר	5/2	short	רִאשׁוֹן	140/2	former, first
רָזוֹן	1/1	ruler	רַחֲמִים	39/1	compassion
רָכִיל	6/2	slanderer	רְמִיָּה	5/4	laxness
רִנָּה	33/1	cry, shout	רָקָב	5/2	rottenness
רִשְׁעָה	14/2	wickedness	שֹׂבַע	8/1	plenty
שְׂחוֹק	16/2	laughter	שֵׂיבָה	19/2	gray hair, old
שֶׂכֶר	2/1	hire, wages	שִׂמְחָה	94/8	joy
שֶׁבֶר	44/4	breaking	שֶׁבֶת	3/1	cessation
שַׁכּוּל	6/1	bereaved	שָׁלֵם	27/1	complete
שֶׁפֶט	16/1	judgment	שֹׁרֶשׁ	33/2	root
תַּאֲוָה	20/8	desire	תּוּגָה	4/3	grief
תּוֹחֶלֶת	6/3	hope	תַּחֲנוּן	18/1	supplication
תֹּמָּה	5/1	integrity	תַּעֲנוּג	5/1	luxury
תַּרְדֵּמָה	7/1	deep sleep			

42. Exclusive Words in Collections II and III (19)

(1) Verbs (12)

אוה	26/6	to desire	II-3	III-3
איב	281/2	to be hostile to	II-1	III-1
דעך	9/3	to be extinguished	II-2	III-1
זקן	18/2	to be old	II-1	III-1
חדל	59/3	to cease	II-2	III-1
חלה	75/3	to be weak	II-2	III-1
חשׂך	27/6	to withhold	II-5	III-1
יעץ	65/5	to advise	II-4	III-1
נכה	504/6	to smite	II-3	III-3
סוג	24/3	to move away	II-1	III-2
שׁדד	43/3	to ruin	II-2	III-1
תכן	18/3	to measure	II-2	III-1

(2) Adjectives/Nouns (7)

גְּבוּל	240/3	boundary	II-1	III-2
זִמָּה	29/3	evil device	II-2	III-1
מִלְחָמָה	316/3	war	II-2	III-1

עָמֹק	20/4	deep	II-3	III-1		
שֹׁד	25/2	violence	II-1	III-1		
שׁוּחָה	5/2	pit	II-1	III-1		
תְּשׁוּעָה	34/3	deliverance	II-2	III-1		

43. Exclusive Words in Collections II, III, and IV (2)

| מְלָאכָה | 166/3 | work, project | II-1 | III-1 | IV-1 |
| פֹּעַל | 38/5 | deed, work | II-3 | III-1 | IV-1 |

44. Exclusive Words in Collections II, III, and V (16)

(1) Verbs (6)

חקר	27/4	to search	II-1	III-1	V-2
חשׁב	123/5	to think	II-3	III-1	V-1
מוט	37/4	to totter	II-2	III-1	V-1
ילד	468/7	to bear, beget	II-3	III-3	V-1
עשׁר	17/6	to be rich	II-4	III-1	V-1
רעה	95/6	to associate	II-3	III-1	V-2

(2) Adjectives/Nouns (10)

דְּבַשׁ	54/4	honey	II-1	III-1	V-2
דַּל	47/15	needy, poor	II-7	III-2	V-6
מִבְטָח	15/4	confidence	II-2	III-1	V-1
מוֹקֵשׁ	27/8	snare	II-5	III-1	V-2
מָתוֹק	12/3	sweetness	II-1	III-1	V-1
פֶּצַע	8/3	bruise, wound	II-1	III-1	V-1
פַּת	14/3	fragment, bit	II-1	III-1	V-1
שֵׁבֶט	190/8	rod, staff	II-4	III-2	V-2
שְׁנַיִם	516/6	two	II-3	III-1	V-2
תִּקְוָה	32/8	hope	II-4	III-2	V-2

45. Exclusive Words in Collections II, III, V, and VI (2)

| אַף | 277/16 | nose, anger | II-8 | III-2 | V-4 | VI-2 |
| רִיב | 62/13 | strife, dispute | II-6 | III-2 | V-4 | VI-1 |

46. An Exclusive Word in Collections II, III, V, and VII (1)

| בֶּטֶן | 72/8 | belly, body | II-5 | III-1 | V-1 | VII-1 |

47. An Exclusive Word in Collections II, III, and VI (1)

| ירשׁ | 231/4 | to inherit | II-1 | III-1 | VI-2 |

48. An Exclusive Word in Collections II, III, VI, and VII (1)

| עָנִי | 75/5 | poor, afflicted | II-1 | III-1 | VI-1 | VII-2 |

49. An Exclusive Word in Collections II, III, and VII (1)

| עֹז | 93/9 | strength | II-6 | III-1 | VII-2 |

50. Exclusive Words in Collections II and IV (2)

| לְאֹם | 35/4 | people, nation | II-3 | IV-1 |
| קבב | 13/2 | to curse | II-1 | IV-1 |

51. Exclusive Words in Collections II, IV, and V (6)

אֶבֶן	269/11	stone	II-7	IV-1	V-3
בְּרָכָה	69/8	blessing	II-6	IV-1	V-1
הרס	43/4	to tear down	II-2	IV-1	V-1
זעם	12/3	to curse, scold	II-1	IV-1	V-1
כסה	156/11	to cover	II-8	IV-1	V-2
נכר	49/4	to recognize	II-1	IV-1	V-2

52. An Exclusive Word in Collections II, IV, V, and VI (1)

| עַם | 1850/9 | people | II-2 | IV-1 | V-4 | VI-2 |

53. An Exclusive Word in Collections II, IV, V, VI, and VII (1)

| עלה | 890/7 | to go up | II-2 | IV-1 | V-2 | VI-1 | VII-1 |

54. Exclusive Words in Collections II and V (90)

(1) Verbs (38)

אוץ	10/4	to hasten	II-2	V-2
אמן	100/5	to confirm	II-2	V-3
ארך	34/3	to be long	II-1	V-2
בוש	109/6	to be ashamed	II-5	V-1
גלה	113/7	to uncover	II-3	V-4
גלל	16/2	to roll	II-1	V-1
גרה	14/4	to stir up stripe	II-1	V-3
דלה	6/2	to draw	II-1	V-1
דשן	11/4	to be fat	II-3	V-1
חבל	23/3	to bind	II-2	V-1
חלק	56/3	to divide	II-2	V-1
חנן	78/6	to show favor	II-4	V-2
חרף	39/3	to reproach	II-2	V-1
טמן	31/2	to hide	II-1	V-1
טרד	2/2	to pursue	II-1	V-1
ישע	205/2	to deliver	II-1	V-1
כרה	15/2	to dig	II-1	V-1
להם	2/2	to swallow	II-1	V-1
מלט	95/3	to slip away	II-2	V-1
נגד	369/2	to tell	II-1	V-1
נוח	143/3	to rest	II-2	V-1
סתר	82/5	to hide	II-1	V-4
עבד	289/2	to work, serve	II-1	V-1
עבר	8/3	to be angry	II-2	V-1
עלץ	8/2	to rejoice	II-1	V-1
עמד	521/4	to stand	II-1	V-3
ענש	9/4	to fine, punish	II-3	V-1
עקש	5/2	to twist	II-1	V-1
עשק	37/4	to oppress	II-2	V-2
פגש	14/3	to meet	II-2	V-1
פשע	40/2	to transgress	II-1	V-1
קבץ	127/2	to gather	II-1	V-1
רגן	7/4	to murmur	II-2	V-2
רדף	144/8	to pursue	II-6	V-2
רוש	24/16	to be poor	II-12	V-4
רעע	8/2	to break	II-1	V-1
שגב	20/3	to be high	II-2	V-1
שנה	9/2	to repeat	II-1	V-1

(2) Adjectives/Nouns (52)

אֲבַדּוֹן	6/2	underworld	II-1	V-1
אֲדָמָה	225/2	ground	II-1	V-1
אֱמוּנָה	49/3	firmness	II-2	V-1
אֲרִי	35/3	lion	II-1	V-2
אָרֵךְ	17/4	long	II-3	V-1
גַּאֲוָה	19/2	pride	II-1	V-1
גַּג	30/2	roof	II-1	V-1
גַּו	6/3	back	II-2	V-1
גֶּרֶם	5/2	bone	II-1	V-1
דֹּב	12/2	bear	II-1	V-1
דִּבָּה	9/2	evil report	II-1	V-1
דֶּלֶף	2/2	dropping (rain)	II-1	V-1
זָהָב	387/7	gold	II-4	V-3
חֶבֶר	7/2	association	II-1	V-1
חוֹמָה	133/2	wall	II-1	V-1
חֹמֶץ	6/2	vinegar	II-1	V-1
חֹסֶן	5/2	wealth	II-1	V-1
טַעַם	13/2	taste, judgment	II-1	V-1
כּוּר	9/2	furnace	II-1	V-1
כְּלִי	324/2	utensil	II-1	V-1
כֵּן	22/3	right, honest	II-2	V-1
כַּעַס	21/4	vexation, anger	II-3	V-1
כְּפִיר	31/3	young lion	II-2	V-1
מְחִיר	15/2	price, hire	II-1	V-1
מַעֲנֶה	8/5	answer	II-4	V-1
מַצְרֵף	2/2	crucible	II-1	V-1
מָקוֹם	401/3	place	II-1	V-2
מִרְמָה	39/8	deceit	II-7	V-1
מַשְׂכִּית	6/2	imagination	II-1	V-1
מֶתֶק	2/2	sweetness	II-1	V-1
נָאוֶה	10/3	comely, fair	II-2	V-1
נֶזֶם	14/2	ring	II-1	V-1
סוּס	137/2	horse	II-1	V-1
עַד	47/2	perpetuity	II-1	V-1
עָרוּם	11/8	shrewd	II-7	V-1
עֵשֶׂב	33/2	herb	II-1	V-1
עָשִׁיר	23/9	rich	II-7	V-2
פֶּשַׁע	93/12	transgression	II-6	V-6

צִיר	6/2	messenger	II-1	V-1
צַלַּחַת	4/2	dish	II-1	V-1
קַר	3/2	cool	II-1	V-1
קֶרֶב	227/3	inward part	II-2	V-1
קָרוֹב	78/2	near	II-1	V-1
קִרְיָה	29/5	town, city	II-4	V-1
רוּם	6/2	haughtiness	II-1	V-1
רָחָב	20/2	wide	II-1	V-1
רֵיק	14/2	empty	II-1	V-1
שָׂבֵעַ	10/2	satisfied	II-1	V-1
שִׂנְאָה	17/4	hatred	II-3	V-1
שְׁמוּעָה	27/2	report	II-1	V-1
שָׁפָל	18/2	low	II-1	V-1
תְּפִלָּה	77/3	prayer	II-2	V-1

55. Exclusive Words in Collections II, V, and VI (3)

אֶפֶס	43/3	end	II-1	V-1	VI-1
עֶבֶד	799/10	servant	II-6	V-2	VI-2
שֵׁן	55/3	tooth	II-1	V-1	VI-1

56. Exclusive Words in Collections II, V, and VII (3)

דִּין	19/5	judgment	II-2	V-1	VII-2
הלל	150/9	to be boastful	II-2	V-4	VII-3
פרש	67/3	to spread out	II-1	V-1	VII-1

57. Exclusive Words in Collections II and VI (14)

בְּהֵמָה	190/2	cattle	II-1	VI-1
בַּעַר	5/2	brutishness	II-1	VI-1
גִּבּוֹר	159/3	strong	II-2	VI-1
חסה	37/2	to seek, refuge	II-1	VI-1
טָהוֹר	95/3	clean, pure	II-2	VI-1
יטב	101/5	to be good	II-3	VI-2
כזב	16/2	to lie	II-1	VI-1
נָבָל	18/3	foolish	II-2	VI-1
נַחַל	137/2	wadi, stream	II-1	VI-1
עַז	23/3	strong	II-2	VI-1
פעל	56/4	to do	II-3	VI-1

קָלַל	79/4	to be slight	II-2	VI-2	
שָׁאַל	172/2	to ask	II-1	VI-1	
שֵׁם	864/7	name	II-4	VI-3	

58. An Exclusive Word in Collections II, VI, and VII (1)

אֶבְיוֹן	61/4	needy, poor	II-1	VI-1	VII-2

59. Exclusive Words in Collections II and VII (9)

דָּרַשׁ	164/2	to seek	II-1	VII-1
הֶבֶל	73/3	vapor, breath	II-2	VII-1
הָדָר	30/2	splendor, honor	II-1	VII-1
זָקֵן	187/3	old	II-2	VII-1
חַיִל	244/5	strength	II-2	VII-3
חָסֵר	25/2	to lack	II-1	VII-1
מַעֲשֶׂה	234/3	deed, work	II-2	VII-1
צָפָה	36/2	to look out	II-1	VII-1
שֵׁכָר	23/3	strong drink	II-1	VII-2

60. Exclusive Words in Collection III (44)

(1) Verbs (15)

אָדַם	10/1	to be red		אָחַר	17/1	to be behind
אָלַף	5/1	to learn		גָּאַל	60/1	to redeem
דָּכָא	18/1	to crush		הָלַם	8/1	to smite
חָרָה	93/1	to be kindled		יָגַע	26/1	to toil
יָצַב	47/2	to take one's stand		נָשַׁךְ	16/1	to bite
סָבָא	6/2	to imbibe		עָלַז	16/1	to exult
פָּרַשׁ	1/1	to pierce		קָבַע	6/2	to rob
שָׁעַר	1/1	to calculate				

(2) Adjectives/Nouns (29)

אֲבוֹי	1/1	alas		גִּיל	9/1	rejoicing
הֶרֶג	5/1	slaughter		חֵבֶל	1/1	mast
חַכְלִילוּת	1/1	dullness (eye)		חָזָק	56/1	strong
חָשֹׁךְ	1/1	obscure, low		חֶתֶף	1/1	prey
יָתוֹם	42/1	orphan		כּוֹס	31/1	cup

כִּלְיָה	31/1	kidneys	לֹעַ	1/1	throat
מָהִיר	4/1	quick	מַטְעָם	8/2	tasty food
מִלָּה	38/1	word	מִמְסָךְ	2/1	mixed drink
מַשָּׁאָה	2/1	loan, pledge	נוּמָה	1/1	slumber
נָעִים	13/3	pleasant	פִּיד	4/1	ruin
צִפְעוֹנִי	4/1	serpent	צַר	41/1	narrow
קֶרַע	4/1	rag, torn piece	קֹשְׁט	1/1	truth
רָאמוֹת	3/1	corals	רֵבֶץ	4/1	dwelling place
שִׂיחַ	14/1	complaint	שַׂכִּין	1/1	knife
שִׁלְשׁוֹם	25/1	?(K)			

61. Exclusive Words in Collections III, IV, and V (2)

| חזה | 55/3 | to see | III-1 | IV-1 | V-1 |
| שׁית | 85/4 | to put, place | III-1 | IV-1 | V-2 |

62. An Exclusive Word in Collections III, IV, V, and VII (1)

| שָׂדֶה | 333/5 | field | III-1 | IV-2 | V-1 | VII-1 |

63. Exclusive Words in Collections III and V (3)

זלל	11/3	to be light	III-2	V-1
עוּף	26/3	to fly	III-2	V-1
קִיא	9/2	to vomit up	III-1	V-1

64. Exclusive Words in Collections III and VI (2)

| נָחָשׁ | 31/2 | serpent | III-1 | VI-1 |
| נֶשֶׁר | 26/3 | eagle | III-1 | VI-2 |

65. Exclusive Words in Collections III and VII (5)

לבשׁ	112/2	to put on	III-1	VII-1
מכר	80/2	to sell	III-1	VII-1
עָמָל	55/2	trouble, labor	III-1	VII-1
פתח	144/4	to open	III-1	VII-3
שׁנה	17/2	to change	III-1	VII-1

66. Exclusive Words in Collection IV (4)

גָּדֵר	14/1	wall	חָרוּל	3/1	kind of weed
עתד	2/1	to be ready	קִמָּשׂוֹן	1/1	thistles

67. Exclusive Words in Collection V (129)

(1) Verbs (42)

אנח	12/1	to sigh, groan	בהל	39/1	to be disturbed
בוס	12/1	to trample	דלק	9/1	to burn
הגה	4/2	to remove	הדר	6/1	to honor
חדה	2/2	to sharpen	חסד	1/1	to be ashamed
חרר	11/1	to be hot	ידה	117/1	to give thanks
יקר	11/1	to be precious	כלם	38/2	to be humiliated
כתשׁ	1/1	to pound	לאה	19/1	to be weary
להלה	1/1	to amaze	מעד	8/1	to slip, slide
נדד	27/1	to retreat, flee	נוד	26/1	to wander
נוס	157/2	to flee	סבב	162/1	to go around
סחף	2/1	to prostrate	עדה	9/1	to pass on
עלם	27/1	to conceal	עתק	9/1	to move
עתר	2/1	to be abundant	פנק	1/1	to indulge
צלח	55/1	to prosper	צפה	47/1	to lay over
קצה	5/1	to cut off	קשׁה	28/2	to be hard
רחם	47/1	to love	רמה	8/1	to deceive
שׂכר	20/2	to hire	שׁבח	3/1	to soothe
שׁיר	86/1	to sing	שׁכם	66/1	to start early
שׁנן	9/1	to sharpen	שׁפל	30/2	to be low
שׁקה	61/1	to cause to drink	שׁקק	3/1	to run
שׁרת	62/1	to serve	שׁתק	4/1	to be silent

(2) Adjectives/Nouns (87)

אָחוֹר	41/1	backwards	אַכְזְרִיּוּת	1/1	cruelty
אָלָה	37/1	oath	אֹפֶן	1/1	circumstance
בַּרְזֶל	76/2	iron	גֶּשֶׁם	35/2	rain
דַּי	39/2	sufficiency	דַּךְ	4/1	crushed
דְּרוֹר	2/1	swallow	זֵק	3/1	sparks, missile
דֶּשֶׁא	14/1	herb, grass	חָבֵר	12/1	companion
חוֹחַ	10/1	brier	חוֹל	23/1	sand
חָזוֹן	35/1	vision	חֲלִי	2/1	ornament

חֲמוֹר	96/1	donkey	חֶסֶר	2/1	poverty
חָצִיר	22/1	green grass	חֵקֶר	12/2	searching
חֲרָדָה	9/1	fear, anxiety	כָּבֵד	41/1	heavy
כֹּבֶד	4/1	heaviness	כֶּבֶשׂ	107/1	lamb
כֶּלֶב	32/2	dog	כֶּתֶם	9/1	gold
מִדְחֶה	1/1	stumbling	מַהֲלָל	1/1	praise
מִטָּה	29/1	bed	מָטָר	38/2	rain
מַכְתֵּשׁ	2/1	mortar	מָנוֹן	1/1	grief?
מַעֲדָן	3/1	delight	מַעְצָר	1/1	control
מַעֲשַׁקָּה	2/1	extortion	מֵפִיץ	1/1	disperser
מַפֶּלֶת	11/1	overthrow	מַרְגֵּמָה	1/1	sling
מַשָּׁאוֹן	1/1	guile	מֶתֶג	5/1	bridle
מַתָּת	6/1	gift	נֵזֶר	25/1	crown
נַחַת	5/1	rest	נֵטֶל	1/1	burden, weight
נֹעַר	4/1	youth	נְשִׂיא	4/1	vapor, mist
נְשִׁיקָה	2/1	kiss	נֶשֶׁךְ	12/1	interest
נֶתֶר	2/1	soda	סַגְרִיר	1/1	steady rain
סִיג	7/2	dross	עֵדֶר	38/1	flock, herd
עָוֶל	21/1	injustice	עֵז	74/1	goat
עָיֵף	17/1	faint, weary	עֱלִי	1/1	pestle
עֹרֶף	33/1	neck	עַתּוּד	29/1	goat
פֶּחָם	3/1	coal	פִּסֵּחַ	14/1	lame
צֹאן	273/1	flock	צִיר	1/1	hinge
צָמֵא	9/1	thirsty	צִנָּה	1/1	coolness
צָפוֹן	152/1	north	קָא	1/1	vomit
קְלָלָה	33/2	curse	קֵן	13/1	nest
קָרָה	5/1	cold	רַב	1/1	archer?
רִיפָה	2/1	grain? fruit?	רָעֵב	21/2	hungry
שׁוֹט	11/1	whip	שׁוֹק	19/1	leg
שְׁחוּת	1/1	pit	שַׁחַל	7/1	lion
שַׁחַת	23/1	pit	שֶׁטֶף	7/1	flood
שִׁיר	77/1	song	שִׁכּוֹר	13/1	drunken
שָׁכֵן	18/1	neighbor	תַּפּוּחַ	6/1	apple
תְּאֵנָה	39/1	fig-tree	תְּכָכִים	1/1	oppression
תָּם	15/1	complete	תַּרְבִּית	6/1	interest
תְּרוּמָה	76/1	contribution			

68. Exclusive Words in Collections V and VI (6)

אָדוֹן	334/3	lord	V-2	VI-1
אסף	200/2	to gather	V-1	VI-1
דּוֹר	167/6	generation	V-2	VI-4
חָלָב	44/2	milk	V-1	VI-1
צרף	22/2	to smelt, refine	V-1	VI-1
רגז	41/2	to be excited	V-1	VI-1

69. Exclusive Words in Collections V and VII (5)

כֶּרֶם	92/2	vineyard	V-1	VII-1
כבה	24/2	to be extinguished	V-1	VII-1
לְבוּשׁ	31/3	garment	V-1	VII-2
מֶרְחָק	17/2	distant place	V-1	VII-1
שֶׁלֶג	20/3	snow	V-2	VII-1

70. Exclusive Words in Collection VI (46)

(1) Verbs (13)

אשם	36/1	to be guilty		כחשׁ	22/1	to deceive
בעל	16/1	to marry		חצץ	3/1	to dive
טרף	25/1	to tear		יהב	33/2	to give
יכל	193/1	to be able to		לשׁן	2/1	to slander
נבל	25/1	to be foolish		נקר	6/1	to pick, bore
פלא	27/1	be wonderful		רחץ	72/1	to wash
תפשׂ	65/2	to grasp				

(2) Adjectives/Nouns (33)

אֱלוֹהַּ	57/1	God		אַלְקוּם	1/1	troop?
אִמְרָה	37/1	word, speech		אַרְבֶּה	24/1	locust
אַרְבַּע	154/5	four		גְּבֶרֶת	15/1	lady, queen
הֵיכָל	80/1	palace		זַרְזִיר	1/1	girded?
חֶמְאָה	11/1	curd		חֹפֶן	6/1	palm of hand
יִקְהָה	2/1	obedience		לַיִשׁ	3/1	lion
מַאֲכֶלֶת	4/1	knife		מִיץ	3/3	squeezing
מְתַלְּעוֹת	3/1	jawbone		נְאֻם	373/1	utterance
סֶלַע	56/1	crag, cliff		עֲלוּקָה	1/1	leech

עַלְמָה	7/1	young woman	עֹצֶר	3/1	restraint
עֹרֵב	10/1	raven	צֹאָה	5/1	filth
צוּר	74/1	rock	קָטֹן	101/1	small
רֶחֶם	32/1	womb	שִׂמְלָה	29/1	garment
שְׂמָמִית	1/1	lizard	שָׁוְא	53/1	emptiness
שָׁלֹשׁ	430/4	three	שִׁפְחָה	63/1	maid-servant
שָׁפָן	4/1	rock-badger	שְׁתַּיִם	252/2	two
תַּיִשׁ	4/1	goat			

71. Exclusive Words in collections VI and VII (5)

אֳנִיָּה	31/2	ship	VI-1	VII-1
בַּת	574/2	daughter	VI-1	VII-1
זמם	13/2	to consider	VI-1	VII-1
מַשָּׂא	66/2	utterance	VI-1	VII-1
מָתְנַיִם	47/2	loins	VI-1	VII-1

72. Exclusive Words in Collection VII (26)

(1) Verbs (6)

דין	25/1	to judge	זכר	222/1	to remember
חגר	43/1	to gird	טעם	11/1	to taste
נטע	58/1	to plant	סחר	20/1	to trade

(2) Adjectives/Nouns (20)

אַחֲרוֹן	51/1	coming after	אִלֵּם	6/1	dumb
אַרְגָּמָן	38/1	purple	בַּר	4/3	son
הֲלִיכָה	6/1	going, doing	זְרוֹעַ	91/1	arm
חֲגוֹר	3/1	belt, girdle	חֲלוֹף	1/1	vanishing
טֶרֶף	22/1	prey, food	כִּישׁוֹר	1/1	distaff
כְּנַעֲנִי	4/1	trader	מֶכֶר	3/1	value
סָדִין	4/1	linen wrapper	עֳנִי	36/1	affliction
עַצְלוּת	1/1	sluggishness	פֶּלֶךְ	2/1	spindle
פֵּשֶׁת	16/1	linen, flax	צֶמֶר	16/1	wool
שָׁנִי	42/1	scarlet	שֵׁשׁ	38/1	linen

Notes

Introduction

1. Gerhard von Rad, *Old Testament Theology* (vol. I; New York: Harper & Row, 1967), 418; R.N. Whybray, *The Intellectual Tradition in the Old Testament* (BZAW 135; Berlin: de Gruyter, 1974), 72f.; Walther Zimmerli, "The Place and Limit of the Wisdom in the Framework of the Old Testament Theology," *SJT* 17 (1964): 149; repr., in *Studies in Ancient Israelite Wisdom* (selected by J. L. Crenshaw; New York: Ktav, 1976), 314–26; James L. Crenshaw, "The Perils of Specializing in Wisdom: What I Have Learned from Thirty Years of Teaching," in *Urgent Advice and Probing Questions: Collected Writings on Old Testament Wisdom* (Macon, Ga.; Mercer University Press, 1995), 586.

2. Brian Brown, ed., *The Wisdom of the Orient* (Garden City, N.Y.: Garden City, 1941).

3. About Israelite wisdom and religion, Roland E. Murphy explains that "the separation of Yahwism from wisdom is an academic, theoretical separation," and continues to say that "wisdom and Yahwism are a blend, not two entities one imposed on the other." For this comment, see his, *Proverbs* (WBC 22; Nashville: Thomas Nelson, 1998), 106.

4. G. von Rad, *Wisdom in Israel* (trans. J.D. Martin; London: SCM Press, 1972), 61.

5. F. E. Greenspahn, "A Mesopotamian Proverb and Its Biblical Reverberations," *JAOS* 114 (1994): 33–38; R. C. Van Leeuwen, "The Background of Proverbs 30:4aα," in *Wisdom You Are My Sister: Studies in Honor of Roland E. Murphy, O. Carm., on the Occasion of His Eightieth Birthday* (CBQ Monograph Series 29; ed. M. L. Barré; Washington, D.C.: Catholic Biblical Association, 1997), 102–21. This type of proverbial question can be found in different cultures to express the notion of impossibility.

6. Edward Y. Kutscher, *A History of the Hebrew Language* (ed. R. Kutscher; Jerusalem: Magnes, 1984), 72.

1. The Relationship between Collection I and Other Collections

(1) Characteristic Exclusive Words in Collection I

1. In its 16 instances in the OT, *maʿgāl* occurs with *nĕtîbâ* in the same place only once in Isa 59:8, but even there *maʿgāl* is connected to *derek*, not to *nĕtîbâ*.

2. 2:9, 15, 18; 4:11, 26; 5:6, 21.

3. *HALOT*, 2:609, s. v. *maʿgāl*.

4. F. Delitzsch, *Biblical Commentary on the Proverbs of Solomon* (trans. M. G. Easton; 2 vols.; Grand Rapids: Eerdmans, 1950), 1:79; C. H. Toy, *A Critical and Exegetical Commentary on the Book of Proverbs* (ICC; Edinburgh: T. & T. Clark, 1899; 4th impression, 1948), 39; A. Meinhold, *Die Spüche* (ZBK; 2 vols.; Zürich: Theologischer, 1991), 1:66. M. V. Fox, quoting Malbim, a 19th century Jewish commentator, points out that *maʿgāl* is never used of a major highway. See his, *Proverbs 1–9* (AB 18A; New York: Doubleday, 2000), 115.

5. Meinhold, *Die Spüche*, 1:66.

6. R. N. Whybray, "City Life in Proverbs 1–9," in *"Jedes Ding hat seine Zeit . . . ":* *Studien zur israelitischen und altorientalischen Weisheit, Diethelm Michel zum 65. Geburtstag* BZAW 241 (ed. A. A. Diesel et al.; Berlin and New York: de Gruyter, 1996), 243–50; C. R. Yoder, *Wisdom as a Woman of Substance* (BZAW 304; Berlin: de Gruyter, 2001), 94.

7. *HALOT*, 4:1449, s. v. *šûq*.

8. B. K. Waltke points out three notions conveyed by *derek* and its synonyms: "course of life," "conduct of life," and "consequences of that conduct." See his, *The Book of Proverbs: Chapters 1–15* (NICOT; Grand Rapids: Eerdmans, 2004), 194.

9. N. C. Habel, "The Symbolism of Wisdom in Proverbs 1–9," *Int* 26 (1972): 131–57.

10. R. C. Van Leeuwen, "Liminality and Worldview in Proverbs 1–9," *Semeia* 50 (1990): 111–12.

11. M. V. Fox, *Proverbs 1–9*, 128–31.

12. N. Shupak, *Where Can Wisdom Be Found?: the Sage's Language in the Bible and in Ancient Egyptian Literature* (OBO 130; Göttingen: Vandenhoeck & Ruprecht, 1993), 277.

13. Two other major collections, II and V, contain 26 and 22 terms, respectively.

14. For the distribution of the words for anger in Proverbs, see Table 2.4.

15. Marcus Jastrow, *A Dictionary of the Targumim, the Talmud Babli and Yerushalmi, and the Midrashic Literature* (2 vols.; Brooklyn: Shalom; repr., 1967), 1:687.

16. The preference of *lēbāb* over *lēb* is also noted in 1 and 2 Kings (31 times to 19 times) and 1 and 2 Chronicles (40 times to 24 times).

17. Of the meaning of *'iššâ zārâ* "strange woman," P. Humbert's interpretation, "the wife of another man," seems gaining acceptance among recent commentators. For example, R. N. Whybray, *Proverbs* (NCBC; Grand Rapids: Eerdmans and Marshall Pickering, 1994), 55; Fox, *Proverbs 1–9*, 139.

18. M. Weinfeld, *Deuteronomy and the Deuteronomic School* (Oxford: Clarendon, 1972), 260–97.

19. 1:9; 3:3, 22; 6:21.

20. *HALOT*, 1:201–2, s. v. *gargārôt*.

21. For example, Otto Plöger, *Sprüche Salomos (Proverbia)* BKAT 17 (Neukirchen-Vluyn: Neukirchener, 1984), 53.

22. Fox, *Proverbs*, 203.

23. Plöger, *Sprüche Salomos*, 32; Meinhold, *Die Sprüche*, 1:76; Delitzsch, *Proverbs*, 1:88; Waltke, *Proverbs 1–15*, 246.

24. Toy, *Proverbs*, 61; Fox, *Proverbs 1–9*, 151.

25. *HALOT*, 4:1650–51, s. v. *šōr*.

26. Fox, *Proverbs 1–9*, 221.

27. R. E. Murphy, *Proverbs* (WBC 22; Nashville: Thomas Nelson, 1998), 40.

28. Fox, *Proverbs 1–9*, 240.

29. Weinfeld, *Deuteronomy and the Deuteronomic School*, 299–300.

30. Jastrow, *Dictionary*, 1:607; R. P. Smith, *A Compendious Syriac Dictionary* (ed. J. P. Smith; Oxford: Clarendon, 1903; repr., 1976), 203.

31. Although J. L. Crenshaw pointed out more than three decades ago that understanding wisdom as secular and non-historical is "too narrow and false," this understanding of Wisdom books still remains strong. See his, "Method in Determining Wisdom Influence upon 'Historical' Literature," *JBL* 88 (1969): 131; repr. in *Urgent Advice*

and Probing Questions: Collected Writings on Old Testament Wisdom (Macon, Ga.: Mercer University Press, 1995), 312–25.

32. An often cited scholar who has applied this view to the interpretation of Proverbs is W. McKane. He argues that the class C material (religious) belongs to a later stage in the wisdom tradition in the OT. For example, see his, *Proverbs: A New Approach*, (London: SCM, 1970), 11.

33. The first occurrence of *tôrâ* in reference to the mother in 1:8 would be a good example.

34. W. Zimmerli, "The Place and Limit of the Wisdom in the Framework of the Old Testament Theology," *SJT* 17 (1964): 147; repr. in *Studies in Ancient Israelite Wisdom* (ed. J. L. Crenshaw; New York: Ktav, 1976), 315.

35. Despite the common imagery in Mesopotamia and Egypt that the royal throne is founded on truth and justice, we suggest that Davidic kingship is present in Prov 20:28. Compare Prov 20:28 (*ḥesed we ʾĕmet yiṣṣĕrû melek*"Loyalty and faithfulness will guard a king") with Ps 61:8 (*ḥesed we ʾĕmet man yinṣĕruhû*"Appoint loyalty and faithfulness that will guard him [the king]!"

36. Zimmerli, "The Place and the Limit of the Wisdom," 318.

37. M. V. Fox, "Aspects of the Religion of the Book of Proverbs," *HUCA* 39 (1968): 55–69. He further explains, "Perhaps the early wise-men used 'Yahweh' in order to appear 'Yahwistic' and thus more Israelite, without changing the God-concept they inherited from Egyptian wisdom." (p. 64).

38. For the analysis of 1 Sam 16:7 as a proverb, see C. R. Fontaine, *Traditional Sayings in the Old Testament: A Contextual Study* (BLS 5; Sheffield: Almond, 1982), 95–108.

39. In 1979 Whybray himself expressed that drawing conclusions from his investigation of God-sayings would be premature. See his, "Yahweh-sayings and Their Contexts in Proverbs 10:1–22:16," in *La Sagesse de l'Ancien Testament* (BETL 51; ed. M. Gilbert; Gembloux, Belgique: Duculot, 1979), 37.

40. R. N. Whybray, *The Composition of the Book of Proverbs* (JSOTSup 168; Sheffield: Sheffield Academic, 1994), 76–78, 86–89.

41. The examples have been taken from Joseph Blenkinsopp, *Wisdom and Law in the Old Testament: The Ordering of Life in Israel and Early Judaism* (Oxford Bible Series; New York: Oxford University Press, 1983), 18.

42. L. Boström, *The God the Sages: the Portrayal of God in the Book of Proverbs* (Stockholm: Almqvist & Wiksell, 1990), 36.

43. The examples have been taken from Blenkinsopp, *Wisdom and Law in the Old Testament*, 18.

44. G. von Rad, *Wisdom in Israel* (trans. J. D. Martin; London: SCM, 1972), 61; also see, P. Skehan, "A Single Editor for the Whole Book of Proverbs," in *Studies in Israelite Poetry and Wisdom* (CBQMS 1; Washington, D.C.: The Catholic Biblical Association of America, 1971), 23.

45. We agree with R. E. Clements' view that what is reflected in biblical wisdom is a less-sacramental understanding of Israelite religion. See his, "Wisdom and Old Testament Theology," in *Wisdom in Ancient Israel: Essays in Honour of J. A. Emerton* (ed. J. Day, R. P. Gordon, and H. G. M. Williamson; Cambridge: Cambridge University Press, 1995), 274.

46. M. Lichtenstein, "Chiasm and Symmetry in Proverbs 31," *CBQ* 44 (1982): 202–11; V. A. Hurowitz, "The Seventh Pillar: Reconsidering the Literary Structure and Unity of Proverbs 31," *ZAW* 113 (2001): 209–18.

47. R. E. Murphy, *Proverbs*, 240.

48. We can add other foreign figures (kings and women) to this list. For the discussion of the integration of foreign wise men into biblical wisdom, see J. Day, "Foreign Semitic Influence on the Wisdom of Israel and Its Appropriation in the Book of Proverbs," in *Wisdom in Ancient Israel: Essays in Honour of J. A. Emerton*, 55–70.

49. Agreeing with Tur-Sinai's view, E. Y. Kutscher says that *bar* in 31:2 is an example for Aramaic coloring in the Wisdom books. See his, *A History of the Hebrew Language* (ed. R. Kutscher; Jerusalem: Magnes, 1984), 72.

50. Fox, *Proverbs 1–9*, 120.

51. It is because the parents and their son are Israelites in the context and because the "strange woman" means "another man's wife."

52. Meinhold, *Die Sprüche*, 1:69.

53. Fox, *Proverbs 1–9*, 120.

54. Murphy, *Proverbs*, 30.

55. For example, Toy, *Proverbs*, 110; McKane, *Proverbs*, 317; Fox, *Proverbs 1–9*, 198–99.

56. A. Hurvitz, *A Linguistic Study of the Relationship between the Priestly Source and the Book of Ezekiel: A New Approach to an Old Problem* (CahRB 20; Paris: Gabalda, 1982), 65.

57. Hurvitz, *A Linguistic Study*, 66–7.

58. Of the strange woman in Proverbs, three things are certain: she is a married woman, she is an Israelite, and her God is YHWH. For her identity, see Fox, *Proverbs 1–9*, 120, 134–41.

59. R. N. Whybray, *Wisdom in Proverbs: The Concept of Wisdom in Proverbs 1–9* (London: SCM, 1965), 48.

60. M. V. Fox, pointing out that the view is mainly supported by G. Boström, says that such interpretation is unwarranted here (*Proverbs 1–9*, 246).

61. M. Weinfeld, *Deuteronomy and the Deuteronomic School*, 212.

62. *HALOT*, 1:337, s. v. *ḥāsîd*.

63. M. V. Fox makes an excellent comment on the metaphor of the way in 2:8: "Once they (his faithful ones) step onto the right path, God helps them remain on it" (*Proverbs 1–9*, 115).

64. R. N. Whybray, *The Composition of the Book of Proverbs*, 59.

65. S. R. Driver, *An Introduction to the Literature of the Old Testament* (Meridian Books, 1956; repr., Gloucester: World Publishing, 1972), 536. For the use of *malkût* to explain the historical development, see Kutscher, *A History of the Hebrew Language*, §§ 65, 121, and 123; R. Polzin, *Late Biblical Hebrew toward an Historical Typology of Biblical Hebrew Prose* (HSM 12; Missoula: Scholars, 1976), 142.

66. P. Joüon and T. Muraoka, *A Grammar of Biblical Hebrew* (ed. and trans. T. Muraoka; Rome: Editrice Pontificio Istituto Biblico, 1991), §88Mj.

67. GKC (§86, n. 1) points out that a complete list of the feminine abstract noun with the *-ût* ending is available in E. König, *Historisch-kritisches Lehrgebäude des Hebräischen* (3 vols.; Leipzig, 1900), 2:205f.

68. Polzin, *Typology*, 11.

69. Polzin, *Typology*, 10.

70. Polzin, *Typology*, 11.

71. H. C. Washington, *Wealth and Poverty in the Instruction of Amenemope and the Hebrew Proverbs* (SBLDS 142; Atlanta: Scholars, 1994), 118.

72. The root of *ḥaklîl* is not certain. *HALOT* (1:313, s. v. *ḥaklîl*) suggests *kḥl* as the

root, but the cognates in other Semitic languages, Akkadian *ekēlu* and Arabic *ḥakala*, indicate that *ḥkl* could be the root.

73. For the three words as belonging to the wisdom vocabulary, see N. Shupak, *Where Can Wisdom Be Found?*, 193, 201–4, and 200–1.

74. For example, Washington, *Wealth and Poverty in the Instruction of Amenemope and the Hebrew Prophets*, 116–122; Yoder, *Wisdom as a Woman of Substance*, 15–38.

75. For example, E. Y. Kutscher points out the presence of the Aramaic roots, *mḥq* and *tny*, in the Song of Deborah (Judg 5), one of the earliest Hebrew poems in the OT (*A History of the Hebrew Language*, 73).

(2) The Relationship between Collections I and II

76. (I) 2:7; 3:21; 8:14; (II) 18:1.

77. R. N. Whybray, *The Intellectual Tradition in the Old Testament* (BZAW 135; Berlin: de Gruyter, 1974), 148–49.

78. BDB, on the basis of the Arabic cognate, lists it under the root *yšh* whose meaning is probably "assist," or "support" (444). *HALOT* suggests *yēš* "what exists" as its possible root, from which the meaning "strength" or "ability" is deduced (4:1713).

79. *HALOT*, 4:1713–15, s.v. *tûšiyyâ*; N. Shupak, *Where can Wisdom be Found?*, 251–52; M. V. Fox explains the meaning as an "inner power" and translates it as "resourcefulness" (*Proverbs 1–9*, 38 and 114).

80. Fox, *Proverbs 1–9*, 114.

81. (I) 1:15; 3:17; 7:25; 8:2, 20; (II) 12:28.

82. Delitzsch, *Proverbs*, 1:269. However, *ʾorḥôt* in Job 6:18 is now read by many as "caravans."

83. Prov 12:28b has several difficulties for translation: the relationship of the collocated "way" and "path," the unusual phrase *ʾal māwet* "not death," and the relationship between 12:28a and 28b. We take the relationship between the two cola as synonymous and *ʾal māwet* as Hebrew equivalent to Ugaritic *bl mwt* "immortality." See Waltke, *Proverbs 1–15*, 518, n. 38.

84. (I) 3:35; 6:33; 9:7; (II) 11:2; 12:16; 13:18; 18:3; 22:10.

85. (I) 5:11; (II) 11:17.

86. Hurvitz, *A Linguistic Study of the Relationship between the Priestly Source and the Book of Ezekiel*, 71, n. 51.

87. Hurvitz, *A Linguistic Study*, 72.

88. (I) 2:1; 3:1; 4:4; 6:20, 23; 7:1, 2; (II) 10:8; 13:13; 19:16.

89. In interpreting Prov 19:16 and 13:13, some commentators choose only the secular meaning, but A. Meinhold acknowledges that a religious understanding of the texts is possible (*Die Sprüche*, 2:320 and 1:223).

90. J. L. Crenshaw, *Old Testament Wisdom: An Introduction* (Atlanta: John Knox, 1981), 92.

91. (I) 8:18, 20; (II) 10:2; 11:4, 5, 6, 18, 19; 12:28; 13:6; 14:34; 15:9; 16:8, 12, 31; 21:3, 21, 21.

92. For example, R. J. Clifford, *Proverbs* (Louisville: Westminster John Knox, 1999), 122; Murphy, *Proverbs*, 81. However, Murphy says that it implicitly refers to God's judgment day.

93. For example, B. Gemser, *Sprüche Salomos* (2nd ed.; HAT 16; Tübingen: Mohr/Siebeck, 1963), 54; Meinhold, *Die Sprüche*, 1:187; McKane, *Proverbs*, 436.

94. R. B. Y. Scott, "Wise and Foolish, Righteous and Wicked," in *VTSup* 23 (1972), 160–61.

95. (I) 3:14; 8:10, 19; (II) 16:16.

96. The same phenomenon applies to "silver" which is found 13 times only in the three same collections (I, II, and V). However, *pĕnînîm* "pearls" occurs in collections I, II, and VII (31:10), and *rā'mōt* "corals" occurs only in collection III (24:7).

97. *Ketem* in Dan 10:5, the only occurrence of those words in prose, also occur in a vision, not in a real world.

98. *HALOT*, 1:352, s. v. *ḥārûṣ* I and 1:265, s. v. *zāhāb*.

99. (I) 8:35; (II) 10:32; 11:1, 20, 27; 12:2, 22; 14:9, 35; 15:8; 16:13, 15; 18:22; 19:12.

100. (I) 1:5; 4:2; 7:21; 9:9; (II) 16:21, 23.

101. (I) 2:15; 3:21, 32; 4:21; (II) 14:2.

102. (I) 6:13; (II) 10:10; 16:30.

103. (I) 2:22; (II) 15:25.

104. M. Weinfeld, *Deuteronomy and the Deuteronomic School*, 309 and 316.

105. R. N. Whybray, *Proverbs*, 57.

106. (I) 3:29; 6:14, 18; (II) 12:20; 14:22 (twice); 20:4.

(3) The Relationship between Collections I, II, and III

107. Since 1924, collection III has been at the center of scholarly debates as to its Egyptian connection. Recently, J. A. Emerton confirms the widely accepted view that, despite the differences between collection III and the Egyptian wisdom literature, *The Teaching of Amenemope*, Egyptian influence on Proverbs is probable, and that there are either 29 or 30 sayings in collection III which encourage to read the problematic word in 22:20 as "thirty" (*šĕlōšîm*). See his, "The Teaching of Amenemope and Proverbs 22:17–24:22: Further Reflections on a Long-Standing Problem," *VT* 51 (2001): 431–65.

108. (I) 2:12, 14; 6:14; 8:13; (II) 10:31, 32; 16:28, 30; (III) 23:33.

109. J. R. Boston, "The Wisdom Influence upon the Song of Moses," *JBL* 87 (1968): 198–202.

110. *Tahpûkôt* is one of those plurals that are found almost exclusively in poetry to convey the idea of intensity. For other examples, see GKC, §124e.

111. (I) 1:5; (II) 11:14; 12:5; 20:18; (III) 24:6.

112. *HALOT*, 4:1716, s. v. *tahbulôt*.

113. W. Zimmerli, "The Place and Limit of the Wisdom in the Framework of the Old Testament Theology," 149.

114. McKane, *Proverbs*, 17 and 450.

115. F. M. Wilson, "Sacred and Profane? The Yahwistic Redaction of Proverbs Reconsidered," in *The Listening Heart: Essays in Wisdom and the Psalms in Honor of Roland E. Murphy, O. Carm.* (JSOTSup 58; ed. K. G. Hoglund et al.; Sheffield: JSOT, 1987) 318–27, especially 321–22.

116. (I) 1:4; 2:11; 3:21; 5:2; 8:12; (II) 12:2; 14:17; (III) 24:8.

117. McKane, *Proverbs*, 347 and 448.

118. (I) 1:7, 29; 2:5; 8:13; 9:10; (II) 10:27; 14:26, 27; 15:16, 33; 16:6; 19:23; 22:4; (III) 23:17.

119. For example, *VOT* takes only eight occurrences of *yir'â* in the OT as nouns, and according to it, the noun form is not found at all in Proverbs.

120. J. Becker, *Gottesfurcht im Alten Testament* (Rome: Pontifical Biblical Institute, 1965), 214–22.

121. Fox, *Proverbs 1–9*, 308.

122. Becker, *Gottesfurcht im Alten Textament*, 226.

123. McKane, *Proverbs*, 486–87.

124. Fox, *Proverbs 1–9*, 67–68.

125. Fox, *Proverbs 1–9*, 68. Von Rad, referring to Joseph's fear of the Lord, also says in a similar way that the foundation (godly fear) is "the most important factor in the whole educational program." See, his "The Joseph Narrative and Ancient Wisdom" in *Studies in Ancient Israelite Wisdom* (ed. J. L. Crenshaw; New York: Ktav, 1976), 442; repr. from *The Problem of the Hexateuch and other Essays* (Edinburgh, 1965), 292–300.

126. (I) 1:11, 18; 7:12; (II) 12:6; (III) 23:28; 24:15.

127. In 1:18, "ambush" and "blood" are used ironically. The ambush of the sinners will ultimately cause them to shed their own blood.

128. (I) 1:22; 3:34 (2x); 9:7, 8, 12; (II) 13:1; 14:6, 9; 15:12; 19:25, 28, 29; 20:1; 21:11, 24; 22:10; (III) 24:9.

129. N. Shupak, *Where can Wisdom be Found?*, 205.

130. Fox, *Proverbs 1–9*, 42.

131. Shupak, *Where can Wisdom be Found?*, 206.

132. (I) 6:1; (II) 11:15; 17:18; (III) 22:26.

133. (I) 1:19; 2:8, 13, 15, 19, 20; 3:6; 4:14, 18; 5:6; 8:20; 9:15; (II) 10:17; 12:28; 15:10, 19, 24; 17:23; (III) 22:25.

134. *ʾōraḥ* and *derek* in 2:8, 13, 20; 3:6; 4:14; 9:15; 12:28; 15:19, *ʾōraḥ* and *maʿgāl* in 2:15; 5:6, and *ʾōraḥ* and *nĕtîbâ* in 8:20; 12:28.

135. Interestingly, Fox explains *ʾorhôt hayyîm* in 2:19 as "many paths leading to life," but he is silent on *ʾōraḥ ḥayyîm* in 5:6 (*Proverbs 1–9*, 122).

136. Fox, *Proverbs 1–9*, 129.

(4) The Relationship between Collections I, II, III, and IV

137. (I) 1:2, 3, 7, 8; 3:11; 4:1, 13; 5:12, 23; 6:23; 7:22; 8:10, 33; (II) 10:17; 12:1; 13:1, 18, 24; 15:5, 10, 32, 33; 16:22; 19:20, 27; 22:15; (III) 23:12, 13, 23; (IV) 24:32.

138. Shupak, *Where Can Wisdom Be Found?*, 33.

139. *Mûsār* occurs in the first colon in the following verses: 1:8; 3:11; 4:1, 13; 5:12; 8:10; 10:17; 12:1; 13:1, 18; 15:5, 10, 32; 19:27; 23:12.

(5) The Relationship between Collections I, II, III, IV, and V

140. *Ṣaddîq* (66 times): (I) 2:20; 3:33; 4:18; 9:9; (II) 10:3, 6, 7, 11, 16, 20, 21, 24, 25, 28, 30, 31, 32; 11:8, 9, 10, 21, 23, 28, 30, 31; 12:3, 5, 7, 10, 12, 13, 21, 26; 13:5, 9, 21, 22, 25; 14:19, 32; 15:6, 28, 29; 17:15, 26; 18:5, 10, 17; 20:7; 21:12, 15, 18, 26; (III) 23:24; 24:15, 16; (IV) 24:24; (V) 25:26; 28:1, 12, 28: 29:2, 6, 7, 16, 27.

141. *Rāšāʿ* (78 times): (I) 2:22; 3:25, 33; 4:14, 19; 5:22; 9:7; (II) 10:3, 6, 7, 11, 16, 20, 24, 25, 27, 28, 30, 32; 11:5, 7, 8, 10, 11, 18, 23, 31; 12:5, 6, 7, 10, 12, 21, 26; 13:5, 9, 17, 25; 14:11, 19, 32; 15:6, 8, 9, 28, 29; 16:4; 17:15, 23; 18:3, 5; 19:28; 20:26; 21:4, 7, 10, 12, 12, 18, 27, 29; (III) 24:15, 16, 19, 20; (IV) 24:24; (V) 25:5, 26; 28:1, 4, 12, 15, 28; 29:2, 7, 12, 16, 27.

142. For a history of research on the contrasting terms, see Shupak, *Where Can Wisdom Be Found?*, 258–67.

143. In 17:1–22:16 (four times), 17:15; 18:15; 21:12, 18; and in chapters 10–15 (30

times), 10:3, 6, 7, 11, 16, 20, 24, 25, 28, 30, 32; 11:8, 10, 23, 31; 12:3, 5, 7, 10, 12, 21, 26; 13:5, 9, 25; 14:19, 32; 15:6, 28, 29.

144. In chapters 25–27, 25:26; and in chapters 28–29, 28:1, 12, 28: 29:2, 7, 16, 27.

145. McKane, Proverbs, 420–21; R. B. Y. Scott, "Wise and Foolish, Righteous and Wicked," 160–61.

146. The agents of the verb are a thief (6:31), the adulterous woman (7:14), goodness (13:21), the Lord (19:17), an offended person (20:22), a guarantor (22:27), the Lord (25:22). The agent is not mentioned in 13:13, but God is the possible subject of the verb.

147. This is also Murphy's understanding. He calls the sentence an "a fortiori statement" to affirm the judgment on the wicked, presumably from God (*Proverbs*, 85).

(6) The Relationship between Collections I, II, III, IV, V, and VI

148. (I) 1:5, 6; 3:7, 35; 9:8, 9; (II) 10:1, 8, 14; 11:29, 30; 12:15, 18; 13:1, 14, 20; 14:1, 3, 16, 24; 15:2, 7, 12, 20, 31; 16:14, 21, 23; 17:28; 18:15; 20:26; 21:11, 20, 22; (III) 22:17; 23:24; 24:5; (IV) 24:23; (V) 25:12; 26:5, 12, 16; 28:11; 29:8, 9, 11; (VI) 30:24.

149. Whybray says that the purpose of chapters 25–29 is "similar to that which characterizes the instructions in chs. 1–9" (*The Composition of the Book of Proverbs*, 129).

150. R. C. Van Leeuwen, *Context and Meaning in Proverbs 25–27* (SBLDS 96; Atlanta: Scholars, 1988), 146–7.

151. Whybray, *Composition of the Book of Proverbs*, 126–9.

152. Fox, *Proverbs 1–9*, 40–41.

153. Shupak, *Where Can Wisdom Be Found?*, 206.

154. Van Leeuwen, *Context and Meaning*, 105.

155. Murphy, *Proverbs*, 21.

(7) Words Occurring in All the Collections

156. (I) 2:2, 10; 3:1, 3, 5; 4:4, 21, 23; 5:12; 6:14, 18, 21, 25, 32; 7:3, 7, 10, 25; 8:5; 9:4, 16; (II) 10:8, 13, 20, 21; 11:12, 20, 29; 12:8, 11, 20, 23, 25; 13:12; 14:10, 13, 14, 30, 33; 15:7, 11, 13, 13, 14, 15, 21, 28, 30, 32; 16:1, 5, 9, 21, 23; 17:3, 16, 18, 20, 22; 18:2, 12, 15; 19:3, 8, 21; 20:5, 9; 21:1, 2, 4; 22:11, 15; (III) 22:17; 23:7, 12, 15, 15, 17, 19, 26, 33, 34; 24:2, 12, 17; (IV) 24:30, 32; (V) 25:3, 20; 26:23, 25; 27:9, 11, 19; 27:23; 28:14, 26; (VI) 30:19; (VII) 31:11.

157. For the view that religious aspect is inherent in wisdom, see von Rad, *Wisdom in Israel*, 61; P. Skehan, "A Single Editor for the Whole Book of Proverbs," 23.

158. The notion that the human heart is originally sinful is probably universal. McKane mentions a Sumerian proverb ("Never has a sinless child been born to its mother") quoted in Gemser's commentary (p. 79), and says that some understand the meaning of the verse as moral impotence and bondage to sin (*Proverbs*, 548).

159. For the contrasting relationship between joy and sorrow in Proverbs, see C. Westermann, *Roots of Wisdom: The Oldest Proverbs of Israel and Other Peoples* (trans. J. D. Charles; Louisville: Westminster John Knox, 1995), 11–14.

160. Although there are two grammatical difficulties in 12:25a, the meaning is clear.

161. 6:32; 7:7; 9:4, 16; 10:13, 21; 11:12; 12:11; 15:21; 17:18; 24:30.

162. The association of *ḥāsēr* with an intellectual faculty is restricted to Proverbs. In Prov 28:16 *ḥāsēr* is connected to *tĕbûnâ* "understanding," implying the possibility that *ḥāsēr* could be connected to other intellectual terms to denote the state of foolishness.

163. Shupak, *Where Can Wisdom Be Found?*, 199–200. Fox appears to agree with her when he suggests that the phrase is likely an Egyptianism, and that it is nearly identical to *petî* (*Proverbs*, 39–40).

164. (I) 1:6, 23; 4:4, 20; (II) 10:19; 11:13; 12:6, 25; 13:5, 13; 14:15, 23; 15:1, 23; 16:20; 17:9; 18:4, 8, 13; 22:12; (III) 22:17; 23:8; (IV) 24:26; (V) 25:2, 2, 11; 26:6, 22; 27:11; 29:12, 19, 20; (VI) 30:1, 6, 8; (VII) 31:1.

165. The six instances of *ʾōmer* are included in the total number of the occurrence of *ʾēmer*.

166. Waltke, *Proverbs 1–15*, 57.

(8) The Relationship between Collections I, II, III, and V

167. (I) 5:23; (II) 12:23; 13:16; 14:1, 8, 17, 18, 24, 24, 29; 15:2, 14, 21; 16:22; 17:12; 18:13; 19:3; 22:15; (III) 24:9; (V) 26:4, 5, 11; 27:22.

168. The two terms are treated together by Shupak (*Where Can Wisdom be Found?*, 204) and Fox (*Proverbs 1–9*, 40).

169. For a brief history of the interpretation of the verses, see Murphy, *Proverbs*, 203.

170. Five different forms of the word are listed together: (I) 6:14, 19; (II) 10:12; 15:18; 16:28; 17:14; 18:18, 19; 19:13; 21:9, 19; 22:10; (III) 23:29; (V) 25:24; 26:20, 21; 27:15; 28:25; 29:22.

171. J. Barr, "A New Look at Kethibh-Qere," *OtSt* 21 (1981): 25.

172. Barr, "A New Look at Kethibh-Qere," 27.

173. Barr points out this phenomenon in the beginning of his study ("A New Look at Kethibh-Qere," 19).

174. Toy, *Proverbs*, 132.

175. Delitzsch, *Proverbs*, 1:145.

176. (I) 1:22, 32; 3:35; 8:5; (II) 10:1, 18, 23; 12:23; 13:16, 19, 20; 14:7, 8, 16, 24, 33; 15:2, 7, 14, 20; 17:10, 12, 16, 21, 24, 25; 18:2, 6, 7; 19:1, 10, 13, 29; 21:10; (III) 23:9; (V) 26:1, 3, 4, 5, 6, 7, 8, 9, 11, 12, 20; 28:26; 29:11, 20.

177. Whybray also points out that *kĕsîl* is a favorite term in Proverbs and Ecclesiastes (*The Intellectual Tradition in the Old Testament*, 146).

178. With the *petî* in 1:22, 32; 8:5; and with the *lēs* in 1:22; 19:29. For Shupak's gradation and description of the *kĕsîl*, see *Where Can Wisdom Be Found?*, 201–2 and 214.

179. (I) 3:32; 6:16; 8:7; (II) 11:1, 20; 12:22; 13:19; 15:8, 9, 26; 16:5, 12; 17:15; 20:10, 23; 21:27; (III) 24:9; (V) 26:25; 28:9; 29:27, 27.

180. Weinfeld, *Deuteronomy and the Deuteronomic School*, 267–271.

181. In addition to 28:9, Murphy says that it is possible to understand *tôrâ* in 28:4 as referring to God's law (*Proverbs*, 214).

182. R. E. Clements, "The Concept of Abomination in the Book of Proverbs," in *Texts, Temples, and Traditions: A Tribute to Menahem Haran* (ed. M. V. Fox et al.; Winona Lake: Eisenbrauns, 1996), 211–25.

183. Clements, "The Concept of Abomination," 224.

184. As quoted by Clements, "The Concept of Abomination," 224.

185. Clements, "The Concept of Abomination," 224–25.

186. L. Boström, *The God of the Sages*, 134–40.

(9) The Relationship between Collections I, II, III, V, and VI

187. (I) 1:13; 3:9; 6:31; 8:18; (II) 10:15; 11:4; 12:27; 13:7, 11; 18:11; 19:4, 14; (III) 24:4; (V) 28:8, 22; 29:3; (VI) 30:15, 16.

188. Fox, *Proverbs*, 151.

189. For the synonyms of da ʿat in Proverbs, see Table 10: Words for Wisdom. (I) 1:4, 7, 22, 29; 2:5, 6, 10; 3:20; 5:2; 8:9, 10, 12; 9:10; (II) 10:14; 11:9; 12:1, 23; 13:16; 14:6, 7, 18; 15:2, 7, 14; 17:27; 18:15, 15; 19:2, 25, 27; 20:15; 21:11; 22:12; (III) 22:17, 20; 23:12; 24:4, 5; (V) 29:7; (VI) 30:3.

190. Whybray, *The Intellectual Tradition*, 127.

191. Shupak, *Where Can Wisdon Be Found?*, 233.

192. Fox, *Proverbs 1–9*, 31–32.

193. Fox, *Proverbs 1–9*, 112.

194. The plural form of qādôš in 30:3 denotes divine honor or excellence. See Murphy, *Proverbs*, 226. For the same expression in 9:10, see Fox, *Proverbs 1–9*, 308, and B. K. Waltke, *Proverbs Chapters 1–15*, 428.

195. (I) 6:6; 8:33; 9:9, 12, 12; (II) 13:20; 19:20; 20:1; 21:11; (III) 23:15, 19; (V) 27:11; (VI) 30:24.

196. For detailed descriptions of ancient teaching and learning, see Shupak, *Where Can Wisdom Be Found?*, 46–77; Fox, *Proverbs 1–9*, 131–4.

197. (I) 1:8; 3:12; 4:1, 3; 6:20; (II) 10:1; 13:1; 15:5, 20; 17:6, 21, 25; 19:13, 14, 26; 20:20; (III) 22:28; 23:22, 24, 25; (V) 27:10; 28:7, 24; 29:3; (VI) 30:11, 17.

198. In 1962, using both literary-critical and form-critical methods, R. N. Whybray became the first scholar to identify the ten "discourses" in Proverbs 1–9; see his, *The Book of Proverbs: A Survey of Modern Study* (Leiden: E. J. Brill, 1995), 63–4, and, *Wisdom in Proverbs: The Concept of Wisdom in Proverbs 1–9* (SBT 45; London: SCM Press, 1965), 33–52.

199. For recent discussion of the father's identity, see M. V. Fox, *Proverbs 1–9*, 80–83, 173 and his article, "The Social Location of Proverbs," in *Texts, Temples, and Traditions: A Tribute to Menahem Haran* (ed. M. V. Fox et al.; Winona Lake: Eisenbrauns, 1996), 231.

200. Whichever interpretation is taken in regard to the identity of the father, the father's image as one who gives instruction is confirmed at least by môray "my teachers" in 5:13.

(10) The Relationship between Collections I, II, III, V, VI, and VII

201. (I) 1:7, 29; 2:5, 6; 3:5, 7, 9, 11, 12, 19, 26, 32, 33; 5:21; 6:16; 8:13, 22, 35; 9:10; (II) 10:3, 22, 27, 29; 11:1, 20; 12:2, 22; 14:2, 26, 27; 15:3, 8, 9, 11, 16, 25, 26, 29, 33; 16:1, 2, 3, 4, 5, 6, 7, 9, 11, 20, 33; 17:3, 15; 18:10, 22; 19:3, 14, 17, 21, 23; 20:10, 12, 22, 23, 24, 27; 21:1, 2, 3, 30, 31; 22:2, 4, 12, 14; (III) 22:19, 23; 23:17; 24:18, 21; (V) 25:22; 28:5, 25; 29:13, 25, 26; (VI) 30:9; (VII) 31:30.

202. Von Rad, *Wisdom in Israel*, 67.

203. L. Boström appears to agree with Delekat who suggests, on the basis of the ancient versions, that ʾĕlōhîm was replaced with YHWH by a late redactor (*The God of the Sages*, 35–36).

204. Since 16:1–3 are missing and 16:2 and 9 in the LXX appear to be double translations of Hebrew 16:4, the exact number cannot be known.

205. Yirʾat YHWH (1:7, 29; 2:5; 8:13; 9:10; 10:27; 14:26, 27; 15:16, 33; 16:6;

19:23; 22:4; 23:17) and the verb *yr'* with the Lord (3:7; 14:2; 24:21; 31:30).

206. Toy (*Proverbs*, 322) and McKane (*Proverbs*, 498) understand 16:6b as "by fearing Yahweh one will not suffer from misfortune (or harm)." But this understanding is incoherent with other parallel sayings, such as 3:7 and 8:13.

207. (I) 3:32; 6:16; (II) 11:1, 20; 12:22; 15:8, 9, 26; 16:5; 17:15; 20:10, 23.

208. R. E. Clements, "The Concept of Abomination in the Book of Proverbs," 214; M. Weinfeld, *Deuteronomy and the Deuteronomic School*, 268.

209. Clements understands "the abomination to the Lord" as the strongest condemnation of negative human conducts ("The Concept of Abomination," 224).

210. Clements, "The Concept of Abomination," 220.

211. Weinfeld, *Deuteronomy and the Deuteronomic school*, 268.

212. Clements, "The Concept of Abomination," 217.

213. For the subject, see L. Boströme, *The God of the Sages*, 90–140.

214. For the limitations of wisdom, see von Rad, *Wisdom in Israel*, 97–110.

215. C. Westermann, *Roots of Wisdom*, 123–24.

216. For this reason, McKane interprets 3:19f. as "another demonstration of the integration of wisdom with Yahwism" (*Proverbs*, 296–7).

217. This understanding follows Murphy's interpretation (*Proverbs*, 120). McKane interprets God's creation as the self-regulating order (*Proverbs*, 497).

218. J. L. Crenshaw, "The Perils of Specializing in Wisdom: What I Have Learned from Thirty Years of Teaching," in *Urgent Advice and Probing Questions* (Macon, Ga.: Mercer University Press, 1995), 586 (originally a paper presented as the plenary address at the Southwestern meeting of AAR/SBL/ASSR/ASOR in Dallas, on March 10, 1995).

219. Fox, *Proverbs 1–9*, 115.

220. Von Rad, *Wisdom in Israel*, 101.

221. J. L. Crenshaw, "The Concept of God in Old Testament Wisdom, in *Urgent Advice and Probing Questions*, 196; repr. from *In Search of Wisdom* (ed. L. G. Perdue et al.; Louisville: Westminster/John Knox, 1993), 1–18.

222. S. Harris, *Proverbs 1–9: A Study of Inner-Biblical Interpretation* (SBLDS 150; Atlanta: Scholars, 1995), 93–95.

223. Weinfeld points out that the expression *běkol lēb* "with all the heart" is not restricted to the Deuteronomic literature but also found in Jer 3:10; Joel 2:12; Ps 119:10, 34, 69 (*Deuteronomy and the Deuteronomic School*, 334).

224. (I) 1:2, 7, 20; 2:2, 6, 10; 3:13, 19; 4:5, 7, 7, 11; 5:1; 7:4; 8:1, 11, 12; 9:1, 10; (II) 10:13, 23, 31; 11:2; 13:10; 14:6, 8, 33; 15:33; 16:16; 17:16, 24; 18:4; 21:30; (III) 23:23; 24:3, 7, 14; (V) 28:26; 29:3, 15; (VI) 30:3; (VII) 31:26.

225. For a detailed study of *ḥokmâ* and *ḥākām* in the OT, see Whybray, *The Intellectual Tradition in the Old Testament*, 6–54.

226. For the examples that describe the limits of wisdom in Proverbs, see 16:2; 20:24; 16:1, 9; 19:14, 21; 21:30; 26:12; 27:1; 3:5, 7. These verses are quoted from von Rad, *Wisdom in Israel*, 99–102.

227. Shupak, *Where Can Wisdom Be Found?*, 206.

228. Whybray, *The Intellectual Tradition in the Old Testament*, 33–43.

229. Fox explains that a *nābôn* is the possessor of either *bînâ* or *těbûnâ* (*Proverbs 1–9*, 30).

230. (I) 1:1; 8:15; (II) 14:28, 35; 16:10, 12, 13, 14, 15; 19:12; 20:2, 8, 26, 28; 21:1; 22:11; (III) 22:29; 24:21; (V) 25:1, 2, 3, 5, 6; 29:4, 14; (VI) 30:27, 28, 31; (VII) 31:1, 3, 4.

231. For example, Clifford, *Proverbs*, 186; Murphy, *Proverbs*, 154.

232. W. Zimmerli, "The Place and Limit of the Wisdom in the Framework of the Old Testament Theology," 315.

233. For the thematic and literary affinities between Prov 1:20–33 and Jeremiah, see S. Harris, *Proverbs 1–9: A Study of Inner-Biblical Interpretation*, 93–95.

234. Whybray says that it is the view of a number of scholars (*The Intellectual Tradition*, 2).

235. C. Westermann, *Roots of Wisdom*, 4; F. W. Golka, *The Leopard's Spots: Biblical and African Wisdom in Proverbs* (Edinburgh: T. & T. Clark, 1993), 28–35.

236. For God's eternal throne, see Pss 9:8 (Eng. 7); 45:7 (Eng. 6).

(11) The Relationship between Collections I, II, III, and VI

237. (I) 1:2; 2:3; 3:5; 4:1, 5, 7; 7:4; 8:14; 9:6, 10; (II) 16:16; (III) 23:4, 23; (VI) 30:2.

238. Whybray, *The Intellectual Tradition*, 143.

239. Whybray, *The Intellectual Tradition*, 145.

240. (I) 6:19; (II) 14:5, 25; 19:5, 9, 22; 21:28; (III) 23:3; (VI) 30:8.

241. Shupak, *Where Can Wisdom Be Found?*, 97.

242. Delitzsch, *Proverbs*, 1:147.

243. Ezek 13:6, 7, 8, 9, 19; 21:34; 22:28.

244. For example, Ezk 13:7; Zech 3:13; Pss 5:7; 58:4; Dan 11:27; Judg 16:10, 13; Hos 7:13.

245. Although it is not completely certain, the form *yāpîaḥ*, especially in the fixed expression *yāpîaḥ kĕzābîm* (6:19; 14:25; 19:5, 9), can be taken as either a verb from *pwḥ* or a noun "witness" as attested in Ugaritic (cf. *HALOT*, 3:917, *pwḥ*).

(12) The Relationship between I, II, IV, and V

246. (I) 6:6, 9; (II) 10:26; 13:4; 15:19; 19:24; 20:4; 21:25; 22:13; (IV) 24:30; (V) 26:13, 14, 15, 16.

247. Whybray, *The Intellectual Tradition*, 124.

248. (I) 6:32; 7:7; 9:4, 16; (II) 10:13, 21; 11:12; 12:9, 11; 15:21; 17:18; (IV) 24:30; (V) 28:16.

249. *Ḥăsar lēb*, (I) 6:32; 7:7; 9:4, 16; (II) 10:13, 21; 11:12; 12:11; 15:21; 17:18; (IV) 24:30.

250. Shupak, *Where Can Wisdom Be Found?*, 214. She arranges the fools in the order from a positive fool (corrigible) to a negative fool (incorrigible): (1) *ḥăsar lēb* and *petî*, (2) *kĕsîl*, (3) *'ĕwîl*, (4) *lēṣ*, (5) *nābāl*.

251. (I) 1:3; 2:8, 9; 8:20; (II) 12:5; 13:23; 16:8, 10, 11, 33; 17:23; 18:5; 19:28: 21:3, 7, 15; (IV) 24:23; (V) 28:5; 29:4, 26.

252. Fox, *Proverbs 1–9*, 115. Waltke's comment is similar (*Proverbs 1–15*, 226).

(13) The Relationship between Collections I, II, IV, V, and VI

253. (I) 3:12; 9:7, 8, 8; (II) 15:12; 19:25; (IV) 24:25; (V) 25:12; 28:23; (VI) 30:6.

254. According to Shupak, the seven verbs are: *ysr, ykh, yrh, lmd, byn, śkl,* and *'lp* (*Where Can Wisdom Be Found?*, 46–51 and 344).

(14) The Relationship between Collections I, II, IV, V, VI, and VII

255. (I) 6:11; (II) 10:15; 13:18; (IV) 24:34; (V) 28:19; (VI) 30:8; (VII) 31:7.

(15) The Relationship between Collections I, II, and V

256. (I) 1:23, 25, 30; 3:11; 5:12; 6:23; (II) 10:17; 12:1; 13:18; 15:5, 10, 31, 32; (V) 27:5; 29:1, 15.

257. For her discussion of *tôkaḥat* in comparison with the Egyptian equivalent, see, *Where Can Wisdom Be Found?*, 34–39.

258. Fox, *Proverbs 1–9*, 99.

259. For the lexical definition of *ykḥ* and *tôkaḥat*, see *HALOT*, 2:410 and 4:1698–9 respectively. Unlike Shupak and Fox, Waltke says that the term belongs to the sphere of judicial proceedings (*Proverbs 1–15*, 203–4).

260. For other instances of "hardening the neck," see Deut 10:16; 2 Kgs 17:14; 2 Chr 30:8; 36:13; Jer 7:26; 17:23; 19:15; Neh 9:16, 17, 29.

261. 10:17; 12:1; 13:18; 15:5, 10; 15:31; 15:32 (*ʾōzen šōma ʿat* in 15:31 is taken in the same way).

262. (I) 1:4, 22, 22, 32; 7:7; 8:5; 9:4, 6, 16; (II) 14:15, 18; 19:25; 21:11; 22:3; (V) 27:12.

263. Whybray, *The Intellectual Tradition*, 137.

264. It may be possible that the form with *ʾālep* is later in time than the form without the letter because the function of *ʾālep* is to soften *yôd* (GKC, §93x).

265. Shupak, *Where Can Wisdom Be Found?*, 200–201; Fox, *Proverbs 1–9*, 42–43.

266. (I) 4:22; 6:15; (II) 12:18; 13:17; 14:30; 15:4; 16:24; (V) 29:1.

267. (I) 5:18; (II) 10:11; 13:14; 14:27; 16:22; 18:4; (V) 25:26.

268. (I) 1:25, 30; 8:14; (II) 12:15; 19:20, 21; 20:5, 18; 21:30; (V) 27:9.

269. W. McKane, *Prophets and Wise Men* (SBT 44; London: SCM Press, 1965), 55–62.

270. Whybray, *The Intellectual Tradition in the Old Testament*, 132–33.

271. Whybray, *The Intellectual Tradition in the Old Testament*, 133.

272. Clifford explains the "deep water" in 20:5 as a concealed plan (*Proverbs*, 182), but Mckane argues that the expression means "profundity of thought" (*Proverbs*, 536). McKane's interpretation is taken in our discussion.

(16) The Relationship between Collections I, II, V, and VI

273. (I) 1:23; (II) 11:13, 29; 14:29; 15:4, 13; 16:2, 18, 19, 32; 17:22, 27; 18:14, 14; (V) 25:14, 23, 28; 27:16; 29:11, 23; (VI) 30:4.

274. *HALOT*, 3:1197–1201, s. v. *rûaḥ*.

(17) The Relationship between Collections I, II, V, and VII

275. (I) 2:19; 3:2, 18, 22; 4:10, 13, 22, 23; 5:6; 6:23; 8:35; 9:11; (II) 10:11, 16, 17; 11:19, 30; 12:28; 13:12, 14; 14:27, 30; 15:4, 24, 31; 16:15, 22; 18:21; 19:23; 21:21; 22:4; (V) 27:27; (VII) 31:12.

276. GKC, §124d.

277. McKane (*Proverbs*, 419) and Murphy (*Proverbs*, 74) expound that in 10:17 the person who keeps instruction is a way to life for others, not for himself. However, it

would be more natural to understand that the meaning of the sentence includes "himself and others," as Waltke explains (*Proverbs 1–15*, 465).

278. McKane, *Proverbs*, 296.

279. Murphy, *Proverbs*, 106.

280. (I) 6:17, 19; (II) 10:18; 11:18; 12:17, 19, 22; 13:5; 14:5; 17:4, 7; 19:5, 9; 20:17; 21:6; (V) 25:14, 18; 26:28; 29:12; (VII) 31:30.

(18) The Relationship between Collections I, II, and VI

281. (I) 6:12, 18; (II) 10:29; 12:21; 17:4; 19:28; 21:15; 22:8; (VII) 30:20. ʾônîm in 11:7 is not included here although it is included in *VOT* and Whybray's *The Intellectual Tradition*.

282. Whybray, *The Intellectual Tradition*, 125.

283. *HALOT*, 1:22, s. v. ʾāwen; BDB, 19–20, s. v. ʾāwen.

284. McKane, *Proverbs*, 529.

285. (I) 3:16; 8:18; (II) 11:16, 28; 13:8; 14:24; 22:1, 4; (VI) 30:8.

286. Although the translation of 22:4 is not easy, commentators understand that wealth, honor, and life are rewards. See, Murphy, *Proverbs*, 164, Clifford, *Proverbs*, 196, and McKane, *Proverbs*, 570.

(19) The Relationship between Collections I, II, and VII

287. (I) 3:15; 8:11; (II) 20:15; (VII) 31:10.

288. Delitzsch, *Proverbs*, 1:92; BDB, 819, s. v. pĕnînîm.

289. For example, T. P. McCreesh, "Wisdom as Wife: Proverbs 31:10–31," *RB* 92 (1985): 41. For a survey of the studies on the relationship between chapters 1–9 and 31:10–31, see Murphy, *Proverbs*, 245–6.

(20) The Relationship between Collections I and III

290. (I) 4:17; 9:5; (III) 23:1, 6.

291. Toy, *Proverbs*, 93.

292. Fox, *Proverbs 1–9*, 305–6.

293. (I) 1:31; (III) 22:20.

294. S. L. Harris, *Proverbs 1–9: A Study of Inner-Biblical Interpretation*, 93–95.

295. (I) 1:3; 2:9; 8:6; (III) 23:16, 31.

296. GKC, §124e.

297. (I) 3:31; (III) 23:17; 24:1, 19.

(21) The Relationship between Collections I and IV

298. *Ḥibbuq* (I) 6:10; (IV) 24:33. *Tĕnûmâ* (I) 6:4, 10; (IV) 24:33.

299. In the 13 instances *ḥbq* always denotes embracing someone, except in Eccl 4:5 where it means folding the hands to sleep as in Proverbs.

300. James G. S. S. Thomson, "Sleep: An Aspect of Jewish Anthropology," *VT* 5 (1955): 421.

301. Thomson explains that from *tĕnûmâ* a sleeper slips into the next level of sleep *šēnâ* and, on occasion, into *tardēmâ* ("Sleep," 421); Fox, *Proverbs 1–9*, 214; Waltke, *Proverbs 1–15*, 334.

302. Daniel, C. Snell, *Twice-Told Proverbs and the Composition of the Book of*

Proverbs (Winona Lake, Ind.: Eisenbrauns, 1993), 81.

303. Delitzsch, *Proverbs*, 1:142.

304. Toy, *Proverbs*, 122.

(22) The Relationship between Collections I, IV, and VI

305. (I) 2:7; 6:11; (IV) 24:34; (VI) 30:5.

(23) The Relationship between Collections I and V

306. Snell, *Twice-Told Proverbs*, 83.

307. *Peta*ʿ (I) 6:15; (V) 29:1. *Šbr* (I) 6:15; (V) 25:15; 29:1.

308. Snell, *Twice-Told Proverbs*, 64–69.

309. (I) 1:12; 5:15; (V) 28:17.

310. The expression occurs 14 times in the OT: Isa 38:18; Ezek 26:20, 20; 31:14, 16; 32:18, 24, 25, 29, 30; Pss 28:1; 88:5; 143:7; Prov 1:12.

311. *Hālāq* (I) 5:3; (V) 26:28. *Ḥlq* (I) 2:16; 7:5; (V) 28:23; 29:5.

312. (I) 6:27; (V) 25:22.

313. Stanislav Segert offers an excellent survey of different interpretations of the expression "heaping coals on one's head." See his article, "Live Coals Heaped on the Head," in *Love & Death in the Ancient Near East: Essays in Honor of Marvin H. Pope* (ed. J. H. Marks and R. M. Good; Guilfor, Conn.: Four Quarters, 1987), 159–64.

(24) The Relationship between Collections I, V, and VI

314. (I) 2:5, 17; 3:4; (V) 25:2; (VI) 30:9.

315. McKane explains the collocation of the different divine names and *YHWH* in 30:1–14 as the transformation of the international tradition to Yahwism in the late pre-exilic period (*Proverbs*, 648, and *PWM*, 102f.).

316. For example, both Fox (*Proverbs 1–9*, 120–1) and Waltke (*Proverbs 1–15*, 123–24) hold the view, agreeing with G. P, Hugenberger's conclusions based on his thorough study on marriage (*Marriage as a Covenant*, VTSup 52; Leiden: Brill, 1993).

(25) The Relationship between Collections I and VI

317. (I) 6:6; (VI) 30:25.

318. W. F. Albright, "Some Canaanite-Phoenician Sources of Hebrew Wisdom" in *Wisdom in Israel and in the Ancient Near East* (ed. M. Noth and D. W. Thomas; VTSup 3; Leiden: Brill, 1955), 7.

319. J. Cook, *The Septuagint of Proverbs: Jewish and/or Hellenistic Proverbs?* (VTSup 69; Leiden: Brill, 1997), 166.

320. (I) 4:25; 6:4, 25; (VI) 30:13.

321. M. Dahood, "Hebrew–Ugaritic Lexicography VII," *Biblica* 50 (1969): 351–52.

322. (I) 6:32; (VI) 30:20.

323. J. J. Stamm with M. E. Andrew, *The Ten Commandments in Recent Research* (SBT 2.2; London: SCM, 1967), 100.

324. One may think that the son is also married because of the allegorical instruction in 5:15–20. However, Murphy comments that it is a lesson "for anyone to learn, married or not" (*Proverbs*, 32).

325. McKane, *Proverbs*, 658.

326. D. N. Freedman and B. E. Willoughby, *TDOT*, 9:113–18, s. v. *nā'ap*.

(26) The Relationship between Collections I and VII

327. (I) 3:14, 14; (VII) 31:18.

328. E. A. Speiser, "The Verb *SHR* in Genesis and Early Hebrew Movements," *BASOR* 164 (1961): 27.

329. T. P. McCreesh, "Wisdom as Wife: Proverbs 31:10–31," *RB* 92 (1985): 41–46.

330. (I) 8:15; (VII) 31:4.

331. *Marbad*: (I) 7:16; (VII) 31:22 and *layĕlâ*: (I) 7:9; (VII) 31:15, 18.

332. For example, R. C. Van Leeuwen, *The Book of Proverbs* (NIB V; Nashville: Abingdon, 1997), 85.

333. Fox comments on the items mentioned in 7:17 as follows: "Myrrh, aloes, and cinnamon were imported from Arabia and the Far East and were very expensive" (*Proverbs 1–9*, 247).

334. McCreesh in fact suggests that there is a link between 12:4 and 31:10–31: "the saying (12:4) seems to give hint of what is to come in chapter 31 and provides, in advance, an apt image with which to characterize the portrait drawn here" ("Wisdom as Wife," 40).

335. C. Yoder, on the basis of the occurrence of the word outside the Bible, explains that *marbaddîm* are bed coverings of royalty (*Wisdom and Woman of Substance*, 85).

336. In 7:16 the three words, *marbaddîm*, *hatubôt*, and *'ēṭûn*, are practically *hapax legomena*, and *šēš* and *'argāmān* in 31:22 are peculiar in the sense that they predominantly occur in Exodus. *Šēš* occurs 38 times in the OT, 33 of which are in Exodus to denote the fine linen to make the curtains of the tabernacle (25:4; 35:6, 23, 25, 35) and the priest's clothes (28:5;, 39; 38:28–29). *'argāmān* also occurs 38 times in the OT, 26 of which are in Exodus in reference to the same cultic items mentioned above.

337. GKC (§75v) lists the following examples: *hōmiyyâ* (Isa 22:2; Prov 1:21; 7:11; 9:13), *ṣôpiyyâ* (Prov 31:27), *bôkiyyâ* "weeping" (Lam 1:16), *pōriyyâ* "fruitful" (Isa 17:6; 32:12; Ezek 19:10; Ps 128:3), and *'ōtiyyôt* "things to come" (Isa 41:23; 44:7; 45:11).

338. A. Wolters, "*Ṣôpiyyâ* (Prov 31:27) as Hymnic Participle and Play on *Sophia*," *JBL* 104 (1985): 577–87.

339. GKC, §75v.

340. Wolters, "*Ṣôpiyyâ* (Prov 31:27), 580.

341. A. Wolters, "Proverbs 31:10–31 as Heroic Hymn: A Form-critical Analysis," *VT* 38 (1988): 446–57. Considering what is described in Prov 31:10–31 cannot be taken literally as achievements of a real woman, the category of hymn is too broad and inappropriate for the acrostic poem. Rather, more specific understandings, such as an instruction for young women (or young men) or a symbol of Wisdom, seem to be more reasonable.

342. In Wisdom books it is only in Job 28:28 where wisdom is directly equated with the fear of the Lord: "The fear of the Lord *is* wisdom." It is also said in Deut 4:6 that Israel's wisdom *is* keeping and doing God's commandments.

343. For example, C. Gottlieb, "The Words of the Exceedingly Wise: Proverbs 30–31," in *The Biblical Canon in Comparative Perspective* (ANETS 11; ed. K. L. Younger, Jr. et al.; Lewiston, N.Y.: Mellen, 1991), 290; Fox, *Proverbs 1–9*, 49; C. R. Yoder, *Wisdom as a Woman of Substance*, 33.

2. The Relationship between Collection II and Other Collections

(1) Characteristic Exclusive Words in Collection II

1. 15:25; 16:19.
2. H.-P. Stähli, *TLOT* 1:28587, s. v. *g ʾh.*
3. D. Kellermann, *TDOT* 2:346, s. v. *gāʾâ.*
4. *Gbh*, 17:19; 18:12. *Gābōah*, 16:5. *Gōbah*, 16:18.
5. R. Hentschke, *TDOT*, 2:356, s. v. *gābah.*
6. Hentschke, *TDOT*, 2:357.
7. *Zēd*, 21:24. *Zādôn*, 11:2; 13:10; 21:24.
8. On the basis of Arabic evidence, J. Scharbert suggests that *zwd* and *zyd* should be distinguished. The former means "to provide food for oneself" and the latter "to increase, surpass." He explains that Hebrew *zēd* and *zādôn* belong to *zyd* with the meaning of acting presumptuously (*TDOT*, 4:47, s. v. **zûd*).
9. L. J. Wood, *TWOT*, 1:239, s. v. *zîd.*
10. 20:22.
11. C. Westermann, *TLOT*, 3:1126, s. v. *qwh.*
12. Westermann, *TLOT*, 3:1127.
13. 10:3; 11:6; 17:4; 19:13.
14. *HALOT* (1:242, s. v. *hawwâ*) assigns the meaning "capriciousness, desire" to the three instances of *hawwâ* (Mic 7:3; Prov 11:6; 10:3) and "destruction, threats" to the rest of the instances.
15. S. Erlandsson, *TDOT*, 3:356, s.v. *hawwâ.*
16. Erlandsson, *TDOT*, 3:358.
17. 10:24; 11:23; 13:12, 19; 18:1; 19:22; 21:25, 26.
18. 10:28; 11:7; 13:12.
19. 12:7: 17:20.
20. K. Seybold, *TDOT*, 3:423, s. v. *hāpak.*
21. Waltke, *Proverbs 1–15*, 523. On the use of the infinitive absolute, see B. K. Waltke and M. O'Connor, *An Introduction to Biblical Hebrew Syntax* (Winona Lake, Ind.: Eisenbrauns, 1990), 593, P 35.5.1a.
22. 21:8.
23. K. Seybold, *TDOT*, 3:423, s. v. *hāpak.*
24. The meaning of *wāzār* is uncertain, see *HALOT*, 1:259, s. v. *wāzār.*
25. 13:6; 19:3; 21:12; 22:12.
26. 11:3; 15:4.
27. 12:8.
28. *HALOT*, 2:796–7, s. v. *ʿwh.*
29. 19:3.
30. H. Ringgren, *TDOT*, 4:111, s. v. *zāʿap*; *HALOT*, 1:277, s. v. *zʿp* II.
31. 19:12.
32. 11:4, 23; 14:35; 21:24; 22:8.
33. Murphy, *Proverbs*, 81; Waltke, *Proverbs 1–15*; Whybray, *Proverbs,* 177.
34. 20:10, 10.
35. 11:1; 16:11; 20:23.
36. 16:11.

37. God is implicitly understood as the subject in 24:12 ("Does not he who weighs the hearts know it?").

(2) The Relationship between Collections II and III

38. (II) 22:14; (III) 23:27.
39. Van Leeuwen, *Proverbs*, 207.
40. (II) 13:9; 20:20; (III) 24:20.
41. (II) 13:4; 21:10, 26; (III) 23:3, 6; 24:1.
42. W. C. Williams, *NIDOTE*, 1:304–5, s. v. ʾwh.
43. (II) 10:23; 21:27; (III) 24:9.
44. S. Steingrimsson, *TDOT*, 4:89–90, s. v. zmm.
45. Murphy, *Proverbs*, 181.
46. (II) 16:2; 21:2; (III) 24:12.
47. *HALOT*, 4:1733, s. v. tkn.

(3) The Relationship between Collections II, III, and V

48. (II) 20:30; (III) 23:29; (V) 27:6.
49. (II) 10:15; 14:31; 19:4, 17; 21:13; 22:9, 16; (III) 22:22, 22; (V) 28:3, 8, 11, 15; 29:7, 14.
50. R. N. Whybray, *Wealth and Poverty in the Book of Proverbs*, 60.
51. H.-J. Fabry, *TDOT*, 3:208–230, s. v. dal; Whybray, *Wealth and Poverty in the Book of Proverbs*, 14–23.
52. (II) 10:28; 11:7, 23; 19:18; (III) 23:18; 24:14; (V) 26:12; 29:20.
53. G. Waschke, *TDOT*, 12:566, s. v. qwh.
54. Waschke, *TDOT*, 12:569.
55. (II) 10:4, 22; 13:7; 21:17; (III) 23:4; (V) 28:20.
56. This statement is based on the translation of Prov 10:22b "and toil does not add to it."
57. G. F. Hasel, *TDOT*, 5:388, s. v. ygʿ.
58. Murphy, *Proverbs*, 175.
59. (II) 12:13; 13:14; 14:27; 18:7; 20:25; (III) 22:25; (V) 29:6, 25.
60. H. Ringgren, *TDOT*, 6:288, s. v. yāqaš.
61. (II) 10:13; 13:24; 22:8, 15; (III) 23:13, 14; (V) 26:3; 29:15.
62. *VOT*, 240, 429.
63. H.-J. Zobel, *TDOT*, 14:308–9, s. v. šēbeṭ.

(4) The Relationship between Collections II, III, VI, and VII

64. (II) 15:15; (III) 22:22; (VI) 30:14; (VII) 31:9, 20.
65. Most commentators interpret the antithetic parallelism between 15:15a and 15b as a contrast between the inner and outer circumstances of a poor person, not a contrast between poverty and wealth (e.g., Waltke, *Proverbs 1–15*, 625).

(5) The Relationship between Collections II and IV

66. (II) 11:26; 14:28, 34; (IV) 24:24.
67. H. D. Preuss, *TDOT*, 7:397–98, s. v. lěʾōm.

68. Van Leeuwen interprets that the people's curse and blessing are in effect prayers to God (*Proverbs*, 120).

(6) The Relationship between Collections II and V

69. *Maṣrēp*: (II) 17:3; (V) 27:21. *Kûr*: (II) 17:3; (V) 27:21.
70. *Delep*: (II) 19:13; (V) 27:15. *Ṭrd*: (II) 19:13; (V) 27:15.
71. *HALOT*, 1:223, s. v. *dlp*.
72. G. Dalman, in his description of the rainy days in Palestine which he had experienced during February and March in 1900, points out that a continuous dripping (*delep*) on the floor is not only annoying but damaging to the flour and grains in storage: see his, *Arbeit und Sitte in Palästina* (Hildesheim: Georg Olms, 1964), I/1:189.
73. J. C. Greenfield, "Lexicographical Notes," *HUCA* 29 (1958): 210–211. In view of the two passages quoted by Geenfield from the Mishanh, it is difficult to accept R. S. Hess's statement that the occurrences of *ṭrd* in connection with *delep* in the OT is accidental (*NIDOTE*, 384, s.v. *ṭrd*).
74. Greenfield, "Lexicographical Notes," 212.
75. Greenfield, "Lexicographical Notes," 212, n. 12.
76. *Rgn*: (II) 16:28; 18:8; (V) 26:20, 22. *Lhm*: (II) 18:8; (V) 26:22.
77. Van Leeuwen, *Proverbs*, 173.
78. Murphy comments that "friend" (*ʾallûp*) in the singular in 16:28 is to be understood as a collective (*Proverbs*, 124).
79. *HALOT*, 2:521, s. v. *lhm*.
80. *ʿārûm*: (II) 12:16, 23; 13:16; 14:8, 15, 18; 22:3; (V) 27:12. *ʿnš*: (II) 17:26; 21:11; 22:3; (V) 27:12.
81. H. Niehr, *TDOT*, 11:361, s. v. *ʿāram*.
82. (II) 19:24; (V) 26:15.
83. J. L. Kelso, *The Ceramic Vocabulary of the Old Testament*, BASORSup 5/6 (1948), 29–30.
84. (II) 10:4; 13:7, 8, 23; 14:20; 17:5; 18:23; 19:1, 7, 22; 22:2, 7; (V) 28:3, 6, 27; 29:13.
85. Murphy explains that "hate" in 14:20 and 19:7 do not have emotional overtones but it simply means choosing others against the poor (*Proverbs*, 143).
86. (II) 10:13; 19:29; (V) 26:3.
87. F. M. Cross, Jr., and T. O. Lambdin, "A Ugaritic Abecedary and the Origins of the Proto-Canaanite Alphabet," *BASOR* 160 (1960): 24, n. 21.
88. Murphy, *Proverbs*, 74.
89. (II) 17:22; (V) 25:15.
90. S. I. Feigin, "*Ḥamôr gārîm*, 'Castrated Ass'," *JNES* 5 (1946): 230–33.
91. J. Gray, *I & II Kings*, (OTL; London: SCM Press, 1964, 2nd ed., 1970), 543.
92. (II) 13:17; (V) 25:13.
93. (II) 10:12, 19; 12:13; 17:9, 19; 19:11; (V) 28:2, 13, 24; 29:6, 16, 22.
94. R. Knierim, *TLOT*, 2:1033–37, s. v. *pešaʿ*; *The Task of Old Testament Theology: Substance, Method, and Cases* (Grand Rapids, Mich.: Eerdmans, 1995), 425.
95. (II) 17:7; 19:10; (V) 26:1.
96. K.-M. Beyse, *TDOT*, 9:108, s. v. *nʾh*.
97. *Ḥeber*: (II) 21:9; (V) 25:24. *Gāg*: (II) 21:9; (V) 25:24.
98. H. Cazelles, *TDOT*, 4:193–94, s. v. *ḥābar*.
99. J. J. Finkelstein, "Hebrew *ḥbr* and Semitic **ḫbr*," *JBL* 75 (1956): 331.

100. McKane, *Proverbs*, 553–55.

101. *ʾărî:* (II) 22:13; (V) 26:13; 28:15. *Kĕpîr:* (II) 19:12; 20:2; (V) 28:1. *Dôb:* (II) 17:12; (V) 28:15.

(7) The Peculiar Relationship between Collections II and V

102. D. C. Snell, *Twice-Told Proverbs*, 35–41 and Chart 1 (64–65).

103. The table has been made in comparison with Snell's lists.

104. For example, G. Fohrer, *Introduction to the Old Testament* (tr. D. E. Green; Nashville and New York: Abingdon, 1968), 322.

105. Snell, *Twice-Told Proverbs*, 77.

106. In fact, Whybray prefers the Kethib over the suggested Qere in 20:16 (*Proverbs*, 296).

107. Murphy, *Proverbs*, 152.

108. GKC, §120h.

109. GKC, §93x.

110. R. N. Whybray, *Proverbs*, 193–94.

111. The first half of 12:13 can be translated in three different ways. See Whybray, *Proverbs*, 194–95.

112. Whybray, *Proverbs*, 194–95.

113. Whybray, *Proverbs*, 390–91.

114. O. Eissfeldt's view summarized by C. R. Fontaine in her, *Traditional Sayings in the Old Testament: A Contextual Study* (BLS 5; Sheffield: Almond, 1982), 7.

115. See the discussion of 22:2 and 29:13 below, where his theory cannot be accepted.

116. Snell, *Twice-Told Proverbs*, 41.

(8) The Relationship between Collections II, V, and VI

117. (II) 11:29; 12:9; 14:35; 17:2; 19:10; 22:7; (V) 29:19, 21; (VI) 30:10, 22.

118. W. M. W. Roth, *Numerical Sayings in the Old Testament: A Form Critical Study*, VTSup 13 (1965), 35.

119. R. C. Van Leeuwen, "Proverbs 30:21–23 and the Biblical World Upside Down," *JBL* 105 (1986): 599–610.

120. H. Ringgren, *TDOT*, 10:389, s. v. *ʿābad.*

121. Although the context of 11:29 is not clear, Whybray interprets that the fool also, after troubling his house, ends up being a slave of a more prudent creditor because of his unpaid debts (*Proverbs*, 188).

(9) The Relationship between Collections II, V, and VII

122. (II) 12:8; 20:14; (V) 25:14; 27:1, 2; 28:4; (VII) 31:28, 30, 31.

123. According to H. Ringgren, the verb is used only nine times in the *piʿel* to praise persons or things (*TDOT*, 3:405, s. v. *hll*).

124. For example, the buyer in 20:14 congratulates himself (*yithallal*) for purchasing goods at a low price after a supposed long bargain. In the light of the three instances (1 Kgs 20:11; Ps 64:11; Prov 20:14) the passive meaning of *tithallal* in 21:30 is questionable.

125. Delitzsch, *Proverbs*, 2:160–61.

126. McKane, *Proverbs*, 251 and 586.

127. M. A. Klopfenstein, *TLOT*, 3:1400, s. v. *šqr*.

128. Klopfenstein, *TLOT*, 3:1404.

129. McKane, *Proverbs*, 539; Whybray, *Proverbs*, 296.

(10) The Relationship between Collections II and VI

130. (II) 12:1; (VI) 30:2.

131. *HALOT*, 1:146, s. v. *ba ʿar*.

132. H. Ringgren, *TDOT*, 2:204, s. v. *b ʿr*.

133. (II) 17:7, 21; (VI) 30:22.

134. W. M. W. Roth, "NBL," *JBL* 10 (1960): 402–3.

135. Whybray, *Proverbs*, 417.

136. Roth, "NBL," 408.

(11) The Relationship between Collections II, VI, and VII

137. (II) 14:31; (VI) 30:14; (VII) 31:9, 20.

(12) The Relationship between Collections II and VII

138. (II) 20:1; (VII) 31:4, 6.

139. A. Hurvitz, *A Linguistic Study of the Relationship between the Priestly Source and the Book of Ezekiel*, 116–119.

140. (II) 15:3; (VII) 31:27.

141. For the discussion of *sph* in connection with Wolters' argument for the pun between *ṣôpiyyâ* and *sophia*, see "Exclusive Words in Collections I and VII."

142. Whybray, *Proverbs*, 430.

143. A. Wolters, "*Ṣôpirrâ* (Prov 31:27) as Hymnic Participle and Play on *Sophia*," 577–87.

144. (II) 12:4; 13:22; (VII) 31:3, 10, 29.

145. A. S. van der Woude, *TLOT*, 2:611, s. v. *kōaḥ*; *HALOT*, 1:311, s. v. *ḥayil*.

146. H. Eising, *TDOT*, 4:355, s. v. *ḥayil*.

147. For example, on the basis of the occurrences of *ʾēšet ḥayil* in 12:4 and 31:10, T. P. McCreesh suggests a link between 12:4 and 31:10–31. See his article, "Wisdom as Wife: Proverbs 31:10–31," *RB* 92 (1985): 40. For the literary unity of chapter 31, see M. H. Lichtenstein, "Chiasm and Symmetry in Proverbs 31," *CBQ* 44 (1982): 202–11; V. A. Hurowitz, "The Seventh Pillar_Reconsidering the Literary Structure and Unity of Proverbs 31," *ZAW* 113 (2001): 209–18.

3. The Relationship between Collection III and Other Collections

(1) Characteristic Exclusive Words in Collection III

1. According to our count, the number of *hapax legomena* in Proverbs is 74, and the following discussion is based on this number. However, F. E. Greenspahn's list shows that there are 70 absolute and non-absolute *hapax legomena* in Proverbs. According to his

"D" (deviation) index, the 70 *hapax legomena* in Proverbs is the sixth highest rate (after Isaiah, Job, Song of Songs, Lamentations, Psalms) in the Old Testament. See his, *Hapax Legomena in Biblical Hebrew: A Study of the Phenomenon and Its Treatment Since Antiquity with Special Reference to Verbal Forms* (Chico, Calif.: Scholars, 1984), 187–98. Several errors are noted in Greenspahn's absolute and non-absolute lists: *ʾōpen* (25:11, not 25:4), *gēʾâ* (8:13, not 7:13), *ktm* (31:19, this must be an error of *tmk*).

2. The nine words are *ʾăbôy* "oh!" (23:29), *pāraš* "pierce" (23:32), *šāʿar* "calculate" (23:7), *ḥibbēl* "mast" (23:34), *ḥaklīlût* "dullness" (23:29), *ḥetep* "prey" (23:28), *lōaʿ* "throat" (23:2), *nûmâ* "slumber" (23:21), and *śakkîn* "knife" (23:2).

3. *Prš* which occurs in the text describing intoxication (23:32) is not included in Greenspahn's list (*Hapax Legomena in Biblical Hebrew*, 187–198), but BDB (p. 831, s. v. *pāraš* II) and R. Hess (*NIDOTE*, 701, s. v. *prš*) suggest that it be separated from *prš* I.

4. Whybray points out that the passage is "built round the admonition in v. 31" (*Proverbs*, 340).

5. 23:20, 21.

6. M. Weinfeld, *Deuteronomy and the Deuteronomic School*, 303.

7. J. Schüpphaus, *TDOT*, 6:439, s. v. *yāšēn*.

8. J. G. S. S. Thomson, "Sleep: An Aspect of Jewish Anthropology," *VT* 5 (1955): 421.

9. For another example, compare *nwm* + *šēnâ* (Ps 76:6) with *yšn* + *šēnâ* (Jer 51:39, 57).

10. J. Hausmann, *TDOT*, 14:86, s. v. *śyḥ*.

11. Hausmann, *TDOT*, 14:86–88. It appears that Hausemann's view is an elaboration of the analysis of the term provided in *HALOT*, which had been formulated on the basis of Müller's study.

12. For the problem in translating *śîaḥ* in 1 Kgs 18:27, see *TDOT*, 14:87–88 and G. A. Rendsburg, "The Mock of Baal in 1 Kings 18:27," *CBQ* 50 (1988): 414–17.

13. At least in this sense, there may be difference between *śîaḥ* (masc.) and *śîḥâ* (fem.) because *śîḥâ* is used absolutely. It is also pointed out in *HALOT* (3:1321, s. v. *śîaḥ* II) that the relationship between the two words "still remains unclear."

14. N. C. Habel, *The Book of Job* (OTL; Philadelphia: Westminster, 1985), 197.

15. Two other words that occur synonymously with *śîaḥ* are *kaʿas* "vexation" (1 Sam 1:16) and *ṣārâ* "distress" (Ps 142:3).

16. BDB, 17, s. v. *ʾôy*. V. G. Wanke differentiates *ʾôy* from *hôy* in the following way: "*ʾôy* is to be understood as a cry of dread and lamentation, and derived from it as an expression of peril. On the other hand, *hôy* stems from a lamentation for the dead, and is used for the strengthening of prophetic invectives" ("*ʾôy* and *hôy*," *ZAW* 78 [1966]: 218).

17. C. H. Gordon, "The Wine-Dark Sea," *JNES* 37 (1978): 52; A. Brenner points out that Jewish commentators also understood *ḥaklîlî* as a color term. See her, *Colour Terms in the Old Testament* (JSOTSup 21; Sheffield: JSOT Press, 1982), 86.

18. *HALOT*, 3:469 (both *haklîl* and *ḥaklîlût* are listed as derivatives of *kḥl*).

19. With regard to the language of drinking, another resemblance between Proverbs and Isaiah is noted in the use of the *piʿel* participle of *ʾḥr* "to tarry" in connection with wine (Prov 23:30; Isa 5:11).

20. M. Dahood, "Hebrew-Ugaritic Lexicography V," *Bib* 48 (1967): 428–29. He argues that the meaning of the verb *msk* is "to pour" not "to mix"; J. L. Koole, *Isaiah III: Chapters 56–66* (HCOT; trans. A. P. Runia; Leuven: Peeters, 2001), 435.

21. A. S. Kapelrud, *TDOT*, 10:62, s. v. *nāšak*.

22. K. R. Joines, *Serpent Symbolism in the Old Testament: A Linguistic, Archaeological, and Literary Study* (Haddonfield, NJ: Haddonfield, 1974), 1–4; H. Wildberger calls *ṣipʿōnî* "young viper," a diminutive of *ṣepaʿ*, see his, *Isaiah 13–27* (CC; trans. T. H. Trapp; Minneapolis: Fortress, 1997), 96.

23. For the wisdom element in Ps 141, see L. C. Allen, *Psalms 101–150* (WBC 21; Waco, Tex.: Word, 1983), 272; H.-J. Kraus, *Psalms 60–150* (trans. H. C. Oswald; Minneapolis: Augsburg, 1989), 527.

24. E. A. Speiser, "I Know Not the Day of My Death," *JBL* 74 (1955): 252–56.

25. For a possible Aramaic connection of *matʿām*, see M. Wagner, *Die lexikalischen und grammaticalischen Aramaismen im alttestamentlichen Hebräisch* (BZAW 96; Berlin: Töpelmann, 1966), 61, no. 117 (*taʿam*).

26. For example, Whybray, *Proverbs*, 331–32; M. Wagner mentions only *śakkîn* in his study, *Die lexicalischen und grammatikkalischen Aramaismen*, 109.

(2) The Relationship between Collections III, IV, and V

27. (III) 22:29; (IV) 24:32; (V) 29:20.

28. Wagner, *Die lexicalischen und grammatikkalischen Aramaismen*, nos. 93–98; *HALOT*, 1:301, s. v. *ḥzh*.

29. A. Jepsen, *TDOT*, 4:280–90, s. v. *ḥāzâ*.

(3) The Relationship between Collections III and V

30. (III) 23:20, 21; (V) 28:7.

31. M. Weinfeld points out that *zll* and *sbʾ* occur in the same context of obedience to parents in Deut 21:20 and Prov 23:20–21 (*Deuteronomy and the Deuteronomic School*, 303).

32. (III) 23:8; (V) 25:16.

(4) The Relationship between Collections III and VI

33. *Nāḥāš*: (III) 23:32; (VI) 30:19. *Nešer*: (III) 23:5; (VI) 30:17, 19.

4. Exclusive Words in Collection IV

1. Whybray, citing three passages as examples (Ps 37:25, 35–36; Prov 7:6–8), says that recounting one's observation and drawing a lesson from it are common in them. The common words found in the examples are *rʾh*, *ʿbr*, and *hinnê* (*Proverbs*, 356).

2. *HALOT*, 1:181, s. v. *gādēr*.

3. M. Haran takes Prov 24:30 as an example to explain the case that, when a word pair is broken up, the meaning is restricted to the second component. According to him, the focus of the wise man in Prov 24:30 is on the vineyard (B), while the field (A) is mentioned only for the sake of parallelism. See his, "The Graded Numerical Sequence and the Phenomenon of 'Automatism' in Biblical Poetry," *VTSup* 22 (1972): 243–44.

5. Exclusive Words in Collection V

1. Whybray, *Proverbs*, 372.

2. The eight terms are: *šôr*, *ʾelep*, *běhēmâ*, *ʿēder*, *ṣōʾn*, *kebeś*, *ʿēz*, and *ʿattûd*.

3. Murphy mentions the creative interpretation of Prov 27:23–27 offered by Van Leeuwen who interprets the shepherd as king and the flock as his people. However, we agree with Murphy who considers that the literal sense is better (*Proverbs*, 210–11).

4. For a discussion about soil erosion and deforestation in ancient Israel which affected the landscape and animal life, see F. S. Bodenheimer, *Animal and Man in Bible Lands* (Leiden: Brill, 1960), 172–73.

5. Whybray, *The Composition of the Book of Proverbs*, 129.

6. For the domestic animals, see Table 33. The terms for grass and temperature which are found only in collection V are: *dešeʾ* "herb, grass" (27:25), *ḥāṣîr* "green grass" (27:25), *ṣinnâ* "coolness" (25:13), and *qārâ* "cold" (25:20).

7. Delitzsch, *Proverbs*, 2:210.

8. Dalman, *Arbeit und Sitte in Palästina*, I/1:189.

9. R. B. Y. Scott, "Meteorological Phenomena and Terminology in the Old Testament," *ZAW* 64 (1952): 23.

10. Scott, "Meteorological Phenomena and Terminology in the Old Testament," 19.

6. The Exclusive Words and Unity of Collection VI

1. Whybray, *The Composition of the Book of Proverbs*, 149.

2. R.J. Clifford, *Proverbs*, 256–58. For a coherent reading of at least 30:1–9 or 30:1–10, see P. Franklyn, "The Sayings of Agur in Proverbs 30: Piety or Scepticism?," *ZAW* 95 (1983): 238–52; J. L. Crenshaw, "Clanging Symbols," in *Justice and the Holy* (ed. D. A. Knight and P. J. Paris; Atlanta: Scholars, 1989), 51–64.

3. This is Toy's view (*Proverbs*, xxxiii). J. Cook, however, offers a view which is quite different from the widely accepted one. He thinks that the translator of the LXX reordered the material to make a contrast (between 29:27 and 31:10) or to conjoin collections with the same theme ("the king" in 31:1–9 and chs. 25–29). See his, *The Septuagint of Proverbs: Jewish and/or Hellenistic Proverbs? Concerning the Hellenistic Colouring of LXX Proverbs* (VTSup 59; Leiden: Brill, 1997), 312–15.

4. Some suggest the possibility that *bin yāqê* in 30:1 could mean "a pious man" or "an obedient man." Such a reading of *yāqê* can provide an implication that *yěqāhâ* "obedience" in 30:17 is an echo of *yāqê*. For example, Franklyn, "The Sayings of Agur in Proverbs 30," 239, and Crenshaw, "Clanging Symbols," 53.

5. The numeral "two" actually occurs eight times in Proverbs, but the two instances in 30:7 and 15 are considered unique for two reasons: first, they are the only feminine forms while the other six are masculine, and secondly, in the six instances (17:15; 20:10, 12; 24:22; 27:3; 29:13) "two" always occurs in the expression *šěnêhem* "two of them." It is further noted that the expression "two of them" may be a fixed idiom used for both genders of nouns. For example, in 20:12 it refers to the ear and eye which are both feminine (see also 20:10 where it refers to two feminine nouns, *ʾeben* and *ʾêpâ*).

6. There are other words in 30:1–14, which strengthen the unity of the unit. For example, Whybray (*Composition*, 149) points out that there are signs of the use of catchwords from v. 6, and mentions that the following words may function to link verses: "curse" (vv. 9 and 10) and "falsehood" (vv. 6 and 8). Crenshaw ("Clanging Symbols," 63) suggests that *mēʾādām* in v.14 alludes to *mēʾîš* in v. 2.

7. Those passages are commonly found in commentaries. The following passages

can be added to the list for their similarities to Prov 30:7–33: Deut 6:11–12; 8:12–14 (cf. Prov 30:9a); Ex 21:17; Lev 29:8; Deut 27:16 (cf. Prov 30:11); Isa 4:4 (cf. Prov 30:12); Joel 1:6 (cf. Prov 30:14a); Hab 2:2:5 (cf. Prov 30:16a); Joel 2:10; Amos 8:8 (cf. Prov 30:21a); Gen 36:7 (cf. Prov 30:21b); Isa 24:2 (cf. Prov 30:22a); Isa 24:2; Gen 16:4 (cf. Prov 30:23b); Isa 7:22 (cf. Prov 30:33a).

8. Clifford also notes that vv. 6 and 10 share the same syntax, and explains that v. 6 is the conclusion of vv. 1–5 and v. 10 is the conclusion of vv. 7–9, but he does not explain who the servant in v. 10 is (*Proverbs*, 257 and 263).

9. Crenshaw, "Clanging Symbols," 58–62.

10. As Flanklyn points out, the similarities (*nĕ ʾum haggeber* and *bĕ ʿōr/ba ʿar*) between Balaam's prophecy (Num 24:15) and Prov 30:1–2 is striking ("The Sayings of Agur," 240–41).

11. As commonly pointed out, it is probable that "two" in v. 7 and the repetition of *dôr* "generation" in vv. 11–14 could be the forerunners of the numerical sayings in the second half of the chapter.

12. P. W. Skehan and A. A. Di Lella, *The Wisdom of Ben Sira* (AB 39; New York: Doubleday, 1987), 152.

13. P. D. Miller, "The Place of the Decalogue in the Old Testament and Its Law," *Interpretation* 43 (1989): 229–42.

14. S. A. Kaufman explains that adding to God's law is tantamount to apostasy, and connects Deut 13:1 and 4:2 to the Third Commandment. See his, "The Structure of the Deuteronomic Law," *Maarav* 1/2 (1978–79): 126–27.

15. Kaufman connects Deut 19:14 (prohibition of moving the boundary stone) to the Sixth Commandment, saying that it was a frequent cause of disputes between individuals and nations, resulting in war and murder ("The Structure of the Deuteronomic Law, 137). Similarly, it is reasoned that the oppression of the poor in Prov 30:14 involved murder.

7. Exclusive Words in Collection VII
and the Relationship between VI and VII

1. On the differences in sequence between the MT and LXX, E. Tov says, " . . . even paraphrastic translators such as those of Isaiah, Daniel, and Esther did not change the sequence of the text." See his, "Some Sequence Differences between the MT and LXX and Their Ramifications for the Literary Criticism of the Bible," *JNSL* 13 (1987): 151.

2. Tov suggests that some significant discrepancies between the MT and LXX point to the fact that the translator used a Hebrew text of Proverbs different from the MT. His suggestion is based on the following three factors: (1) additions that cannot be ascribed to the translator, (2) transpositions of verses, particularly at the end of chapter 15 and beginning of chapter 16, and the different sequence of the collections, and (3) in some instances the text of the LXX is shorter than that of the MT. See his, "Recensional Differences between the Masoretic Text and the Septuagint of Proverbs," in *Of Scribes and Scrolls: Studies on the Hebrew Bible Intertestamental Judaism, and Christian Origins, Presented to J. Strugnell* (ed. H. W. Attridge et al.; Lanham, Md.: University Press of America, 1990), 43–56.

3. M. H. Lichtenstein, "Chiasm and Symmetry in Proverbs 31," *CBQ* 44 (1982): 202–11; Thomas. P. McCreesh, "Wisdom as Wife: Proverbs 31:10–31," *RB* 92 (1985): 25–46.

4. Victor A. Hurowitz, "The Seventh Pillar—Reconsidering the Literary Structure and Unity of Proverbs 31," *ZAW* 113 (2001): 211.

5. Crenshaw, "Clanging Symbols," 52–53.

Bibliography

Albright, William F. "Some Canaanite-Phoenician Sources of Hebrew Wisdom." Pages 1–15 in *Wisdom in Israel and in the Ancient Near East.* Edited by M. Noth and D. W. Thomas. VTSup 3. Leiden: Brill, 1955.

Allen, L. C. *Psalms 101–150.* WBC 21. Waco: Word, 1983.

Andersen, Francis I., and A. Dean Forbes. *The Vocabulary of the Old Testament.* Rome: Pontifical Biblical Institute, 1989.

Barr, James. "A New Look at Kethibh-Qere." *OtSt* 21 (1981): 19–37.

Becker, Joachim. *Gottesfurcht im Alten Testament.* Rome: Pontifical Biblical Institute, 1965.

Blenkinsopp, Joseph. *Wisdom and Law in the Old Testament: The Ordering of Life in Israel and Early Judaism.* Oxford Bible Series. New York: Oxford University Press, 1983.

Bodenheimer, F. S. *Animal and Man in Bible Lands.* Leiden: Brill, 1960.

Boston, J. R. "The Wisdom Influence upon the Song of Moses." *JBL* 87 (1968): 198-202.

Boström, Lennart. *The God the Sages: the Portrayal of God in the Book of Proverbs.* ConBOT 29. Stockholm: Almqvist & Wiksell, 1990.

Botterweck, G., and H. Ringgren, eds. *Theological Dictionary of the Old Testament.* Vols. 1–14. Grand Rapids: Eerdmans, 1974–2004.

Brenner, Athaliah. *Colour Terms in the Old Testament.* JSOTSup 21. Sheffield: JSOT Press, 1982.

Brown, Brian, ed. *The Wisdom of the Orient.* 2 vols. in 1. Garden City, N.Y.: Garden City, 1941.

Brown, Francis, Samuel R. Driver, and Charles A. Briggs. *Hebrew and English Lexicon of the Old Testament.* Repr., Oxford: Clarendon, 1959.

Childs, Brevard S. *The Book of Exodus: A Critical, Theological Commentary.* OTL. Philadelphia: Westminster, 1974.

Clements, Ronald E. "Wisdom and Old Testament Theology." Pages 269–86 in *Wisdom in Ancient Israel: Essays in Honour of J. A. Emerton.* Edited by J. Day, R. P. Gordon, and H. G. M. Williamson. Cambridge: Cambridge University Press, 1995.

———. "The Concept of Abomination in the Book of Proverbs." Pages 211–25 in *Texts, Temples, and Traditions: A Tribute to Menahem Haran.* Edited by M. V. Fox et al. Winona Lake: Eisenbrauns, 1996.

Clifford, Richard J. *Proverbs.* OTL. Louisville: Westminster John Knox, 1999.

Cook, Johann. *The Septuagint of Proverbs: Jewish and/or Hellenistic Proverbs? Concerning the Hellenistic Colouring of LXX Proverbs.* VTSup 69. Leiden: Brill, 1997.

Crenshaw, James L. "Method in Determining Wisdom Influence upon 'Historical'

Literature." *JBL* 88 (1969): 129–42.

———. *Old Testament Wisdom: An Introduction.* Atlanta: John Knox, 1981.

———. "Clanging Symbols." Pages 51–64 in *Justice and the Holy: Essays in Honor of Walter Harrelson.* Edited by D. A. Knight and P. J. Paris. Atlanta: Scholars, 1989).

———. "The Concept of God in Old Testament Wisdom." Pages 1–18 in *In Search of Wisdom.* Edited by L. G. Perdue et al. Louisville: Westminster/John Knox, 1993).

———. "The Perils of Specializing in Wisdom: What I Have Learned from Thirty Years of Teaching." Pages 586–96 in *Urgent Advice and Probing Questions: Collected Writings of Old Testament Wisdom.* Macon: Mercer University Press, 1995 (originally a paper presented as the plenary address at the Southwestern meeting of AAR/SBL/ASSR/ASOR in Dallas, on March 10, 1995).

Cross, Frank M., and T. O. Lambdin, "A Ugaritic Abecedary and the Origins of the Proto-Canaanite Alphabet." *BASOR* 160 (1960): 24

Dahood, Mitchell. "Hebrew–Ugaritic Lexicography V." *Biblica* 48 (1967): 421–38.

———. "Hebrew-Ugaritic Lexicography VII." *Biblica* 50 (1969): 337–56.

Dalman, G. *Arbeit und Sitte in Palästina.* 7 vols. Hildesheim: Georg Olms, 1964.

Day, John. "Foreign Semitic Influence on the Wisdom of Israel and Its Appropriation in the Book of Proverbs." Pages 55–70 in *Wisdom in Ancient Israel: Essays in Honour of J. A. Emerton.* Edited by J. Day, R. P. Gordon, and H. G. M. Williamson. Cambridge: Cambridge University Press, 1995.

Delitzsch, Franz. *Biblical Commentary on the Proverbs of Solomon.* Translated by M. G. Easton. 2 vols. Grand Rapids: Eerdmans, 1950.

Driver, S. R. *An Introduction to the Literature of the Old Testament.* Meridian Books, 1956. Repr., Gloucester: World, 1972.

Emerton, John A. "The Teaching of Amenemope and Proverbs 22:17–24:22: Further Reflections on a Long-Standing Problem." *VT* 51 (2001): 431–65.

Even-Shoshan, Abraham, ed. *A New Concordance of the Bible: Thesaurus of the Lanugage of the Bible Hebrew and Aramaic Roots, Words, Proper Names, Phrases and Synonyms.* Jerusalem: Kiryat Sefer, 1985.

Feigin, S. I. "*Ḥamôr gārîm,* 'Castrated Ass'." *JNES* 5 (1946): 230–33.

Finkelstein, J. J. "Hebrew *ḥbr* and Semitic **ḥbr.*" *JBL* 75 (1956): 328–31.

Fohrer, Georg. *Introduction to the Old Testament.* Translated by D. E. Green. Nashville: Abingdon, 1968.

Fontaine, Carole R. *Traditional Sayings in the Old Testament: A Contextual Study.* BLS 5. Sheffield: Almond, 1982.

Fox, Michael V. *Proverbs 1–9.* AB 18A. New York: Doubleday, 2000.

———. "Aspects of the Religion of the Book of Proverbs." *HUCA* 39 (1968): 55–69.

Franklyn, Paul. "The Sayings of Agur in Proverbs 30: Piety or Scepticism?" *ZAW* 95 (1983): 238–51.

Gemser, Berend. *Sprüche Salomos.* 2nd ed. HAT 16. Tübingen: Mohr/Siebeck, 1963.

Golka, Friedemann W. *The Leopard's Spots: Biblical and African Wisdom in Proverbs.* Edinburgh: T. & T. Clark, 1993.

Gordon, Cyrus, H. "The Wine-Dark Sea." *JNES* 37 (1978): 51–2.

Gottlieb, Claire. "The Words of the Exceedingly Wise: Proverbs 30–31." Pages 277–98 in *The Biblical Canon in Comparative Perspective.* ANETS 11. Edited by K. L. Younger et al. Lewiston, N.Y.: Mellen, 1991.

Gray, John. *I & II Kings.* 2nd ed. OTL. London: SCM, 1970.

Greenfield, Jonas C. "Lexicographical Notes." *HUCA* 29 (1958): 203–28.
Greenspahn, Frederick E. *Hapax Legomena in Biblical Hebrew: A Study of the Phenomenon and Its Treatment Since Antiquity with Special Reference to Verbal Forms.* SBLDS 74. Chico, Calif.: Scholars, 1984.
———. "A Mesopotamian Proverb and Its Biblical Reverberations." *JAOS* 114 (1994): 33–38.
Habel, Norman C. "The Symbolism of Wisdom in Proverbs 1–9." *Int* 26 (1972): 131–57.
———. *The Book of Job.* OTL. Philadelphia: Westminster Press, 1985.
Haran, Menachem. "The Graded Numerical Sequence and the Phenomenon of 'Automatism' in Biblical Poetry." *VTSup* 22 (1972): 238–67.
Harris, R. Laird et al., eds., *Theological Wordsbook of the Old Testament.* 2 vols. Chicago: Moody Press, 1980.
Harris, Scott L. *Proverbs 1–9: A Study of Inner-Biblical Interpretation.* SBLDS 150. Atlanta: Scholars, 1995.
Hurowitz, Victor A. "The Seventh Pillar: Reconsidering the Literary Structure and Unity of Proverbs 31." *ZAW* 113 (2001): 209–18.
Hurvitz, Avi. *A Linguistic Study of the Relationship between the Priestly Source and the Book of Ezekiel: A New Approach to an Old Problem.* CahRB 20. Paris: Gabalda, 1982.
Jastrow, Marcus. *A Dictionary of the Targumim, the Talmud Babli and Yerushalmi, and the Midrashic Literature.* 2 vols. Brooklyn: Shalom, repr., 1967.
Jenni, Ernst, and Claus Westermann, eds. *Theological Lexcon of the Old Testament.* 3 vols. Translated by M. E. Biddle. Peabody, Mass.: Hendrickson, 1977.
Joines, K. R. *Serpent Symbolism in the Old Testament: A Linguistic, Archaeological, and Literary Study.* Haddonfield: Haddonfield, 1974.
Joüon, Paul, and Takamitsu Muraoka. *A Grammar of Biblical Hebrew.* 2 vols. Edited and translated by T. Muraoka. Rome: Pontifical Biblical Institute, 1991.
Kaufman, Stephen A. "The Structure of the Deuteronomic Law." *Maarav* 1/2 (1978–79): 105–58.
Kelso, James L. *The Ceramic Vocabulary of the Old Testament.* BASORSup 5/6 (1948)
Knierim, Rolf. *The Task of Old Testament Theology: Substance, Method, and Cases.* Grand Rapids: Eerdmans, 1995.
Koehler, L., W. Baumgartner, et al., *The Hebrew and Aramaic Lexicon of the Old Testament.* 5 vols. Translated by M. E. J. Richardson et al. Leiden: Brill, 1994–2000.
Koole, J. L. *Isaiah III: Chapters 56–66.* HCOT. Translated by A. P. Runia. Leuven: Peeters, 2001.
Kraus, H.-J. *Psalms 60–150.* Translated by H. C. Oswald. Minneapolis: Augsburg, 1989.
Kutscher, Edward Y. *A History of the Hebrew Language.* Edited by R. Kutscher. Jerusalem: Magnes, 1984.
Lichtenstein, Murray H. "Chiasm and Symmetry in Proverbs 31." *CBQ* 44 (1982): 202–11.
McCreesh, Thomas P. "Wisdom as Wife: Proverbs 31:10–31." *RB* 92 (1985): 25–46.
McKane, William. *Prophets and Wise Men.* SBT 44. London: SCM, 1965.
———. *Proverbs: A New Approach.* London: SCM, 1970.
Meinhold, Arndt. *Die Spüche.* 2 vols. ZBK. Zürich: Theologischer, 1991.
Miller, Patrick D. "The Place of the Decalogue in the Old Testament and Its Law." *Interpretation* 43 (1989): 229–42.
Murphy, Roland E. *Proverbs.* WBC 22. Nashville: Nelson, 1998.

Plöger, Otto. *Sprüche Salomos. Proverbia.* BKAT 17. Neukirchen-Vluyn: Neukirchener, 1984.

Polzin, R. *Late Biblical Hebrew toward an Historical Typology of Biblical Hebrew Prose.* HSM 12. Missoula: Scholars Press, 1976.

Rendsburg, Gary A. "The Mock of Baal in 1 Kings 18:27." *CBQ* 50 (1988): 414–17.

Smith, R. P. *A Compendious Syriac Dictionary.* Edited by J. P. Smith; Oxford: Clarendon, 1903. Repr., 1976.

Shupak, Nili. *Where Can Wisdom Be Found?: The Sage's Language in the Bible and in Ancient Egyptian Literature.* OBO 130. Göttingen: Vandenhoeck & Ruprecht, 1993.

Rad, Gerhard von. *Old Testament Theology.* Translated by D. M. G. Stalker. 2 vols. New York: Harper & Row, 1962–65.

———. *Wisdom in Israel.* Translated by J. D. Martin. London: SCM Press, 1972.

———. "The Joseph Narrative and Ancient Wisdom." Pages 292–300 in *The Problem of the Hexateuch and other Essays.* Edinburgh/London, 1965. Reprinted in *Studies in Ancient Israelite Wisdom.* Edited by J. L. Crenshaw. New York: Ktav, 1976.

Roth, Wolfgang M. W. "NBL." *VT* 10 (1960): 394–409.

———. "The Numerical Sequence x/x+1 in the Old Testament." *VT* 12 (1962): 300–11.

———. *Numerical Sayings in the Old Testament: A Form Critical Study.* VTSup 13. Leiden: Brill, 1965.

Scott, R. B. Y. "Meteorological Phenomena and Terminology in the Old Testament." *ZAW* 64 (1952): 11–25.

———. "Wise and Foolish, Righteous and Wicked" (Prv 10–29). *VTSup* 23 (1972): 146–65.

Segert, Stanislav. "Live Coals Heaped on the Head." Pages 159–64 in *Love & Death in the Ancient Near East: Essays in Honor of Marvin H. Pope.* Edited by J. H. Marks and R. M. Good. Guilford: Four Quarters, 1987.

Skehan, Patrick W. "A Single Editor for the Whole Book of Proverbs." *CBQ* 10 (1947): 115–30.

———. *Studies in Israelite Poetry and Wisdom.* CBQMS 1; Washington, D.C.: Catholic Biblical Association of America, 1971.

Skehan, Patrick W., and A. A. Di Lella. *The Wisdom of Ben Sira.* AB 39. New York: Doubleday, 1987.

Snell, Daniel C. *Twice-Told Proverbs and the Composition of the Book of Proverbs.* Winona Lake, Ind.: Eisenbrauns, 1993.

Speiser, E. A. "I Know Not the Day of My Death." *JBL* 74 (1955): 252–56.

———. "The Verb SHR in Genesis and Early Hebrew Movements." *BASOR* 164 (1961): 23–28.

Stamm, J. J., and M. E. Andrew. *The Ten Commandments in Recent Research.* SBT 2.2. London: SCM, 1967.

Thomson, James G. S. S. "Sleep: An Aspect of Jewish Anthropology." *VT* 5 (1955): 421–33.

Tov, Emanuel. "Some Sequence Differences between the MT and LXX and Their Ramifications for the Literary Criticism of the Bible." *JNSL* 13 (1987): 151–60.

———. "Recensional Differences between the Masoretic Text and the Septuagint of Proverbs." Pages 43–56 in *Of Scribes and Scrolls: Studies on the Hebrew Bible Intertestamental Judaism, and Christian Origins, Presented to J. Strugnell.* Edited by H. W. Attridge et al. Lanham, Md.: University Press of America, 1990.

Toy, C. H. *A Critical and Exegetical Commentary on the Book of Proverbs.* ICC. Edinburgh: T. & T. Clark, 1899. 4th impression, 1948.

Van Gemeren, Willem A. et al., eds., *New International Dictionary of Old Testament Theology and Exegesis.* 5 vols. Grand Rapids: Zondervan, 1997.

Van Leeuwen, Raymond C. "Proverbs 30:21–23 and the Biblical World Upside Down." *JBL* 105 (1986): 599–610.

———. *Context and Meaning in Proverbs 25–27.* SBLDS 96. Atlanta: Scholars, 1988.

———. "Liminality and Worldview in Proverbs 1–9." *Semeia* 50 (1990): 111–44.

———. *The Book of Proverbs.* Pages 19–264 in NIB 5. Nashville: Abingdon, 1997.

———. "The Background of Proverbs 30:4aα." Pages 102–21 in *Wisdom You Are My Sister: Studies in Honor of Roland E. Murphy, O. Carm., on the Occasion of His Eightieth Birthday.* CBQ Monograph Series 29. Edited by M. L. Barré. Washington, D.C.: Catholic Biblical Association, 1997.

Wagner, Max. *Die lexikalischen und grammaticalischen Aramaismen im alttestamentlichen Hebräisch.* BZAW 96. Berlin: Alfred Töpelmann, 1966.

Waltke, Bruce K., and M. O'Connor. *An Introduction to Biblical Hebrew Syntax.* Winona Lake, Ind.: Eisenbrauns, 1990.

Waltke, Bruse K. *The Book of Proverbs: Chapters 1–15.* NICOT. Grand Rapids: Eerdmans, 2004.

Wanke, V. G. " 'ôy and hôy." *ZAW* 78 (1966): 215–22.

Washington, Harold C. *Wealth and Poverty in the Instruction of Amenemope and the Hebrew Proverbs.* SBLDS 142. Atlanta: Scholars, 1994.

Weinfeld, Moshe. *Deuteronomy and the Deuteronomic School.* Oxford: Clarendon, 1972.

Westermann, Clause. *Roots of Wisdom: The Oldest Proverbs of Israel and Other Peoples.* Translated by J. D. Charles. Louisville: Westminster John Knox, 1995.

Whybray, R. N. *Wisdom in Proverbs: The Concept of Wisdom in Proverbs 1–9.* London: SCM, 1965.

———. *The Intellectual Tradition in the Old Testament.* BZAW 135. Berlin: de Gruyter, 1974.

———. "Yahweh-sayings and Their Contexts in Proverbs 10:1–22:16." Pages 153–65 in *La Sagesse de l'Ancien Testament.* BETL 51. Edited by M. Gilbert. Gembloux, Belgique: Duculot, 1979.

———. *Wealth and Poverty in the Book of Proverbs.* JSOTSup 99. Sheffield: JSOT Press, 1990.

———. *Proverbs.* NCBC. Grand Rapids: Eerdmans, 1994.

———. *The Composition of the Book of Proverbs.* JSOTSup 168. Sheffield: JSOT Press, 1994.

———. *The Book of Proverbs: A Survey of Modern Study.* Leiden: Brill, 1995.

———. "City Life in Proverbs 1–9." Pages 243–50 in *"Jedes Ding hat seine Zeit . . . ": Studien zur israelitischen und altorientalischen Weisheit, Diethelm Michel zum 65. Geburtstag.* Edited by A. A. Diesel et al. BZAW 241. Berlin: de Gruyter, 1996.

Wildberger, H. *Isaiah 13–27.* CC. Translated by T. H. Trapp. Minneapolis: Fortress, 1997.

Wilson, Fredereck M. "Sacred and Profane? The Yahwistic Redaction of Proverbs Reconsidered." Pages 318–27 in *The Listening Heart: Essays in Wisdom and the Psalms in Honor of Roland E. Murphy, O. Carm.* JSOTSup 58. Edited by K. G. Hoglund et al. Sheffield: JSOT Press, 1987.

Wolters, Al. "*Ṣôpiyyâ* (Prov 31:27) as Hymnic Participle and Play on *Sophia.*" *JBL* 104 (1985): 577–587.

Yoder, Christine R. *Wisdom as a Woman of Substance.* BZAW 304. Berlin: de Gruyter, 2001.

Zimmerli, W. "The Place and Limit of the Wisdom in the Framework of the Old Testament Theology." *SJT* 17 (1964): 146–52. Reprinted in *Studies in Ancient Israelite Wisdom.* Edited by J. L. Crenshaw. New York: Ktav, 1976. Pages 314–26.

Index of Hebrew Words

a. Verbs

אדם	to be red, 187
אוה	to desire, 143
ארב	to lie in wait, 45
בחן	to examine, 81
בין	to discern, 83
גבה	to be high, 132–33
גרה	to stir up, 64
דעך	to be extinguished, 142
הלל	to be boastful, 175–76
המה	to murmur, 125
הפך	to overturn, 137
זלל	to be light, 191
זעף	to be enraged, 139
חבל	to bind, 41
חזה	to see, 190
חכם	to be wise, 72–73
חלק	to be smooth, 116
חרש	to devise evil, 39
חתה	to snatch up, 117
טרד	to pursue, 155–56
יכח	to rebuke, 91–2
יסף	to add, 37, 214
ירא	to fear, 32, 72
כון	to be firm, 85
להם	to swallow, 156–57
לוז	to turn aside, 38
לחם	to eat, 108–9
ליץ	to mock, 46
נאף	to commit adultery, 120–21
נסח	to pull away, 38–39
נצר	to keep, 33
נשך	to bite, 187
סבא	to imbibe, 184

סלף	to twist, 137
עוה	to bend, 138
עור	to awake, 64
ענש	to fine, 157
עשר	to be rich, 147–48
פוח	to breathe, 87
צפה	to look out, 125, 126, 180
צפן	to store, 33
קוה	to wait for, 135
קיא	to vomit up, 191
קנא	to be jealous, 110–11
קנה	to acquire, 87
קרץ	to nip, 38, 214
רגן	to murmur, 156–57
רוש	to be poor. 158–59
רזן	to be weighty, 122
שבר	to break, 115
שלח	to send, 13, 64
שמר	to keep, 33
תכן	to measure, 79, 143–44
תקע	to clap, 47

b. Adjectives/nouns

אב	father, 73–74
אביון	needy, 178–79, 212
אבן	stone, 140
אויל	foolish, 56
אור	light, 32
אולת	folly, 62, 66
און	sin, 105–106
איפה	ephah, 140
אכזריות	cruelty, 24

289